ARTIFACTS AND

ILLUMINATIONS

Artifacts &

Illuminations

CRITICAL ESSAYS ON

LOREN EISELEY

Edited and with an introduction by

TOM LYNCH AND SUSAN N. MAHER

University of Nebraska Press | Lincoln and London

The authors would like to thank
Dr. Vince Manguson, the vice chancellor
of academic administration at the
University of Minnesota, Duluth, for
professional development funds that
supported the final indexing of the book.

Library of Congress
Cataloging-in-Publication Data
Artifacts and illuminations:
critical essays on Loren Eiseley / edited
and with an introduction by
Tom Lynch and Susan N. Maher.
p. cm.   Includes bibliographical
references and index.
ISBN 978-0-8032-3403-1 (pbk.: alk. paper)
1. Eiseley, Loren C., 1907–1977 —
Criticism and interpretation. 2. Ecocriticism.
I. Lynch, Tom, 1955–
II. Maher, Susan Naramore.
PS3555.I78Z55 2012
818'.5409 — dc23   2011039565

Set in Arno by Bob Reitz.
Designed by Nathan Putens.

Contents

Acknowledgments

A project such as *Artifacts and Illuminations* comes to fruition because of the support and collaboration of many people, not just those who edit and contribute to the book. We would like to thank Bridget Barry and the staff at the University of Nebraska Press for their unwavering support and professional assistance, from our initial proposal to the book's completion. We are also grateful to the two anonymous readers, who gave careful readings of the draft manuscript and provided us and the contributors with important and detailed revision suggestions. The finished book is a stronger publication as a result.

A professional development leave from the University of Nebraska system allowed Sue Maher to work on her contributions to the book, and a generous invitation from Diane and Bruce Quantic to use Cabin Q outside Bailey, Colorado, allowed her to write without interruption through a number of snowy May days. The University of Minnesota, Duluth, extended research support to Sue as well, and she is grateful for her institution's belief that deans can be scholars, too.

Tom Lynch would like to thank the students in his Honors Seminar on Loren Eiseley at the University of Nebraska, Lincoln, for their insightful discussions of Eiseley and for their patience as he worked through some of his own interpretations of Eiseley, live and impromptu, during class.

We both thank our colleagues on the Loren Eiseley Society Board for their enthusiastic endorsement of this critical anthology. Board president Bing Chen is an inspiration and an indefatigable advocate for all things Eiseley. Finally, we thank our families for accepting the kinds of hours that academics keep. Al Kammerer kept the home fires burning for Sue, which was particularly important in the mountains of Colorado. Tom's spouse, Margaret Jacobs, continues to be a model for how to gracefully combine the life of a scholar, a parent, and a partner.

ARTIFACTS AND

———————

ILLUMINATIONS

Introduction

TOM LYNCH AND SUSAN N. MAHER

Acknowledged as one of the most important twentieth-century American nature writers, Loren Eiseley was a widely admired practitioner of creative nonfiction, a genre that, in part due to his example, has flourished in recent decades. Contemporary nature writers regularly cite Eiseley as an inspiration and model. General readers, as well, appreciate Eiseley's eloquent, complex, and informative essays; devoted readers have helped keep Eiseley continuously in print since his books first began appearing more than a half century ago. Clearly, Eiseley is a writer who matters.

As many observers lament, current environmental and other problems require a public and media that are conversant with both scientific and humanistic knowledge and values; however, we live in an age when such synthesis is hard to find, and our institutions of learning tend to discourage such synthesis. Fortunately, there are renewed efforts to transcend these artificial boundaries of knowledge. Recent articles in the *Chronicle of Higher Education* and other publications dedicated to trends in academe, for example, have called for new emphases on interdisciplinary research and pedagogy. E. O. Wilson's *Consilience: The Unity of Knowledge* is only the most notable of many recent books attempting to reconcile the split. As a writer who bridged the sciences and the humanities perhaps as well as any modern figure, Eiseley clearly has an important role to play in this trend.

In the past, however, Eiseley has proven a challenge for literary scholars often locked in those very disciplinary boundaries he sought to erase and so many lament. Indeed Eiseley is often cited as a figure whose creative importance is not matched by an equivalent body of scholarly analyses of his work. Anthony Lioi (featured in this collection) has argued that "only a few scholars have paid sustained attention to him." Lioi notes this irony: "[Eiseley] is, perhaps, the victim of the very split between science and humanism that he sought to mend, a situation which indicates again the need for his peculiar skills" ("Coasts" 42). While the journal *ISLE: Interdisciplinary Studies in Literature and Environment* has featured scholarly articles on Eiseley with some frequency, the overall publication rate of Eiseley-centered essays is unexpectedly thin for a writer of Eiseley's stature and influence. We believe this situation is unwarranted, and this collection is a small effort to rectify it.

In lamenting the dearth of previous Eiseley scholarship, we do not mean to imply that no such scholarship exists. Indeed many of the essays in this collection are indebted to these earlier efforts and, in some cases, are in fact written by scholars who have contributed to that earlier body of work.

Eiseley scholarship in peer-reviewed journals tends to fall into discrete schools of thought: a focus on time and space (Robert G. Franke; and Dimitri N. Breschinsky, "Reaching Beyond"); a focus on rhetoric (Joseph J. Comprone); a focus on myth and symbolism (David E. Gamble, Lawrence I. Berkove, and Kathleen Woodward, among others); and a dominant focus on biography (Joseph J. Wydeven; Jack Bushnell; Gale H. Carrithers, "Loren"; and Hilda Raz, among others). Extending and complicating this tradition, William H. Wisner's analysis of Eiseley and the genre of autobiography demonstrates Eiseley's vexed stance toward self-disclosure in *All the Strange Hours*. Wisner's careful reading of this late work provides an equally interesting discussion of nonfiction life writing, as his title articulates: "The Perilous Self: Loren Eiseley and the Reticence of Autobiography." Recently, scholars such as Lioi and Michael A. Bryson (also featured in this collection) have examined the philosophical and ethical dimensions of Eiseley's writing, with a particular interest in Eiseley's environmental philosophy. Moreover, Jeffrey Wagner, using economic theory, compares the writings of Eiseley, Henry David Thoreau, and Václav Havel and suggests their contributions to a new economic model that proposes global commons and allows for a "public sanction of free-riding" (103).

While journals as varied as *ISLE*, *Technical Communication Quarterly*, and *Sewanee Review* have been expanding Eiseley studies in rich, suggestive ways, book-length studies of Eiseley have been more rare. Several monographs and general overviews of Eiseley have been written, but most have been out of print for many years. The majority of them focus on Eiseley's biography. As Lioi argues in this collection, "The strength of Eiseley's self-conception has almost guaranteed that several generations of critics would feel obliged to approach his work primarily through the charism of autobiography." In 1983 three books were published on Eiseley: Andrew J. Angyal's *Loren Eiseley*; Leslie E. Gerber and Margaret McFadden's *Loren Eiseley*; and E. Fred Carlisle's *Loren Eiseley: The Development of a Writer*. The books by Angyal and by Gerber and McFadden, with identical titles, are similar in their chronological overviews and summaries of Eiseley's work, with an emphasis on biography and with minimal literary analysis. Carlisle's book is likewise an overview of Eiseley's oeuvre, but it differs in being a psychological biography, paying special attention to Eiseley's early life and writings. These biographical approaches to Eiseley culminated in the 1990 publication of Gale E. Christianson's *Fox at the Wood's Edge*, which provides the definitive biographical context for Eiseley's writing. But Christianson's book is not a literary study (he is a historian) and does not attempt a critical examination of Eiseley's writing. In 1991 Peter Heidtmann published *Loren Eiseley: A Modern Ishmael*. Heidtmann approaches Eiseley as a memoirist, an approach that again foregrounds biography. Most recently, in 1995 Mary Ellen Pitts published *Toward a Dialogue of Understandings: Loren Eiseley and the Critique of Science*. This book breaks away from the emphasis on biography so well demonstrated in the previous books and is essentially an examination of Eiseley's efforts to reconcile scientific and humanistic epistemologies. It begins to inform Eiseley scholarship with more recent critical approaches (see Pitts's new essay in this collection). Of these monographs, only two remain in print: Christianson's biography and Pitts's study.

Now that more scholars are seriously exploring knowledge at the intersections of disciplines, Eiseley studies, as we trust this collection demonstrates, are positioned to flourish in a way that they have not up to now. The past few decades have witnessed a burgeoning of scholarly interest in a variety of fields especially amenable to the interpretation of Eiseley, including both the serious consideration of creative nonfiction as an important genre of American literature, as well as the related scholarly analysis of science and nature writing. The study and teaching of writers such as Eiseley is a growing trend in academic institutions in the United States and around the world.

The fourteen essays in this collection represent a balance of established Eiseley scholars, such as Breschinsky, Bryson, Lioi, and Pitts, and a number of scholarly voices new to Eiseley studies. While some of these essays expand on familiar ground, many take Eiseley studies in fresh directions, particularly in the areas of place-conscious and ecocritical interpretations.

As arranged here, the essays spiral out through ever-wider contexts: biographical analysis leads to place studies, which turn toward more theoretical approaches, especially ecocriticism and rhetorical analysis. Finally, literary contexts and comparisons reveal some surprising historical and global significance. However, the essays do not create a strict linear progression. Certain themes recur, though altered by changing context, as they cycle outward.

In the first essay, "'The Bay of Broken Things': The Experience of Loss in the Work of Loren Eiseley," Susan Hanson focuses on the plethora of loss in Eiseley's life and reveals the spiritual dimensions to be found in his work. From his childhood on, Eiseley faced trauma and isolation, a sense of fragmentation across scales of existence, from the most personal to the global. Hanson, interested in Eiseley's spiritual responses to this landscape of loss, sees a parallel between the writer and apophatic mystics, witnesses to "the transience of things." While the mystics find God in their travails, Hanson argues that Eiseley "finds repose." Both are seeking "what Thomas Merton calls 'a hidden wholeness.'" Hanson connects Eiseley to a lineage of spiritual writing, including the theologian Martin Buber. In facing transience and brokenness, Eiseley learns to tap into the permutations of loss, to achieve, in the mystic's language, the "purgative way." His literary journeys into the dark, empty, lonely reaches of existence, in Hanson's assessment, serve to create "both psychological and spiritual catharsis." Bridging biography and literary analysis, Hanson reveals the influential spiritual leanings of Eiseley the author, a theme developed later in the collection as well.

M. Catherine Downs's lively, historical framing of Eiseley and hoboing, in "'Never Going to Cease My Wandering': Loren Eiseley and the American Hobo," demonstrates the inspiration that more profane experiences gave to Eiseley. Throughout his writing career, Eiseley regularly alludes to his formative wandering years, hopping freight trains to seek escape and illumination. The California freights allowed men (almost never women) a cheap way to travel — and for a curious and restless working-class young man like Eiseley, the lure was irresistible. "In his later years," Downs tells us, as Eiseley "ceased riding trains illicitly, and the experiences receded from his immediate life, they were turned to myth in the lines of essays and autobiographical writings." Digging deeply into hobo history and lore, Downs explores new connections for Eiseley readers. Her thorough examination of class and race prejudice, the hard-knocks world of riding the rails, also limns the mythic outlines of vagrancy. Homeless men, placeless characters, abound in Eiseley's writings, and his experience among them surely affected his sense of compassion. As Downs writes, "Eiseley is concerned with civilization's refuse, its neglected and overlooked. His tone of quiet despair is the burden carried by those who are free from surveillance, cherishing that freedom while hating how some use it." Movement and itinerancy, the motion of rail travel, helped shape one of Eiseley's prominent structures, the journey, and one of his most prominent archetypes for the human condition, the hobo.

From these explorations of Eiseley's life, the collection moves to an analysis of Eiseley's complex connections to both natural and urban places. In "'The Places Below': Mapping the Invisible Universe in Loren Eiseley's Plains Essays," Susan N. Maher places the environmental writer at the forefront of what William Least Heat-Moon has called deep-map writing. The horizontality of the Great Plains encouraged Eiseley, in his essays, to seek vertical knowledge, to delve deeply into the history, indeed the prehistory, of the places he studies. Examining essays from the beginning of his career (*The Immense Journey*) to the end (*The Night Country*), Maher explores the lure of what Eiseley calls in one signature essay "The Places Below." Such places are never wholly comprehensible: something enigmatic always remains, grounding Eiseley's literary cartography in unstable terrain.

In contrast, Bryson, while acknowledging the importance of the Great Plains to Eiseley's oeuvre, explores that other terrain that captures Eiseley's imagination: urban spaces. Eiseley is a formative urban environmental writer, Bryson notes in "Unearthing Urban Nature: Loren Eiseley's Explorations of City and Suburb," predating the current interest in urban nature by decades. Eiseley's "everyday encounters with natural entities — birds, mammals, insects, even wind-borne seeds" establish a rich, biological matrix within the city. Though Eiseley can also depict the "dark, fearful wasteland" of the city, his encounters with the natural within the built environment "validat[e] the ecological worth of the urban landscape and the organisms therein." This recognition is essential in the modern, increasingly urban world; as Bryson argues, "Cities and suburbs are all part of a complex urban ecosystem, a dynamic mosaic in which imperiled nature interacts with humans and their built environment." Whether walking to a commuter station, musing in an apartment building, or peering from a hotel window, Eiseley, the "literary naturalist," seeks illumination from the ancient ways of nature. The city, then, becomes a place of "environmental critique" in Eiseley's essays. The cityscape becomes a "vehicle for articulating an environmental ethic."

These place-conscious readings are followed by two ecocritical analyses by Kathleen Boardman and by Tom Lynch. In "Anthropomorphizing the Essay: Loren Eiseley's Representations of Animals," Boardman takes on those critics who have accused Eiseley of anthropomorphizing in his writings, for presenting what are alleged to be sentimental and unscientific representations of animal life. In Boardman's opinion, Eiseley "took seriously his identity as a scientist, historian, and critic of science: while his essays were not scientific writing, he *was* a scientist writing." Recent studies by primatologists and cognitive ethologists provide empirical data that support appropriate anthropomorphic strategies, and Boardman summarizes Eiseley's argument for "human-animal contact and openness to the possibility of shared characteristics." Moreover, the human body is not severed from the animal world; DNA analyses repeatedly demonstrate the genetic closeness of humans and many mammals. Boardman reads Eiseley's retort to his critics "as a defiant manifesto." Interpreting Eiseley's anthropomorphizing "in the context of scientific attitudes of his time and in terms of more recent controversies," Boardman provides a cogent, persuasive analysis of Eiseley's animal portraits, demonstrating that he was well ahead of his time in recognizing the limitations and dangers of objectifying animals.

Few scholars have explored Eiseley's poetic output. Indeed, some have called his poetry deplorable.[1] Lynch, in "'The Borders between Us': Loren Eiseley's Ecopoetics," believes that Eiseley's poetic reputation suffered because at the time he was publishing "neither the lingering New Criticism nor the emerging postmodern hermeneutics of skepticism had much sympathy for Eiseley's earnest engagement with serious questions regarding a world that lay very much outside the text." The emergence of ecocriticism, and by extension ecopoetics, has given new impetus to studying Eiseley's poetry. Summarizing recent definitions, Lynch sees in Eiseley "an early practitioner of what we now call ecopoetry." Eiseley's poetry brings scientific language and concepts into lyric form, presents what Boardman would call an appropriate anthropomorphizing, attempts to connect readers to the natural world, encourages a compassion for "and identity with a natural order that fewer and fewer readers have any direct contact with," and attempts to depict deep time and space "in the limited medium of language." Lynch underscores the importance of evolutionary theory: "an appreciation for the evolutionary matrix of all living things" is fundamental for Eiseley, in all his poems and essays. Importantly, Eiseley does not separate the human realm from this matrix; for this reason, his poems emphasize a biocentric, not an "anthropocentric," worldview. For Eiseley, this recognition of an evolutionary process is not simply an intellectual gambit. Lynch argues that Eiseley grasped this reality somatically, as "tactile sensation." Carefully reading a number of Eiseley's most noteworthy poems from his late volumes of poetry, Lynch opens up a productive dialogue on Eiseley as poet, claiming neither an elevated position of genius for these poems nor dismissing them outright as earlier critics have. Folding Eiseley into the pantheon of ecopoets, Lynch reclaims the artistry and substance of these lyrics.

As much as intellectual opinion makers argue that interdisciplinary study must restructure the academy, university life remains stubbornly discipline focused. C. P. Snow's description of two cultures remains an unresolved dichotomy in many university communities. Pamela Gossin has found that teaching Eiseley at the University of Texas at Dallas, an institution founded primarily as a science and technology campus, presents opportunities for challenging the two-cultures paradigm. Gossin intentionally tries to collapse the two-cultures training in her classroom, which she calls "an interdisciplinary field laboratory of sorts." Her "Lessons of an Interdisciplinary Life: Loren Eiseley's Rhetoric of Profundity in Popular Science Writing and 'Two Cultures' Pedagogy" first establishes a concept of a "rhetoric of profundity" and then focuses on her attempts to introduce this concept to a classroom that mingles students of science, technology, and the humanities. She has developed a classroom practice to undermine two-cultures bifurcated thinking, which places Eiseley's essay "The Judgment of the Birds" at the beginning of her course on "Reading and Writing Texts." Seeking a transformative experience for her students, Gossin believes that Eiseley promotes and explores layers of profundity, forcing his readers to ask, "What can I learn about the meaning of life from this?" Such shared exploration provokes interdisciplinary thinking. Gossin argues that "Eiseley's interdisciplinary life and work successfully model his synthesis of the humanities and sciences and provide students with a personal exemplum."

In her essay "Artifact and Idea: Loren Eiseley's Poetic Undermining of C. P. Snow," Pitts both continues the reexamination of Eiseley's poetry exemplified in Lynch's essay, while further exploring the two-cultures problem examined by Gossin. Starting with Snow's argument that science and the humanities have become "two cultures," Pitts revisits Eiseley's response in "The Illusion of Two Cultures" and connects this essay's argument to his later volumes of poetry. In arguing against a division "between utility and beauty, between *techne* and *poiesis*," Eiseley holds up an exemplary artifact: a well-wrought arrowhead. Clearly, he argues, this artifact displays both utility and aesthetics. Pitts calls this essay "a *tour de force* for Eiseley, urging reexamination of both science and art as 'constructs' of human beings, subject 'to human pressures and inescapable distortions.'" Then, selecting four poems from *Notes of an Alchemist*, Pitts posits that Eiseley is arguing against Snow's position, using "Snow's own exemplar, the Second Law of Thermodynamics" (which Snow had claimed most humanists could not identify) as a significant trope in his poetic volume. Pitts proposes that the poems "Notes of an Alchemist," "The Striders," "The Beaver," and "Arrowhead" demonstrate "Eiseley's master stroke" in the "undermining of C. P. Snow."

In an astute display of interdisciplinary analysis, Jacqueline Cason's "The Spirit of Synecdoche: Order and Chaos Contend in the Metaphors of Loren Eiseley" argues that Eiseley intuitively recognized the perpetual reiteration of order and chaos in the drama of evolution. Drawing on Kenneth Burke's "The Four Master Tropes" and Hayden White's *Metahistory*, Cason presents a tropological analysis of Eiseley's nature essays and history of science texts. Eiseley, she claims, prefigures the world of nature and human experience through the figure known as synecdoche, that figure of speech that recognizes a metaphysical connection between microcosm and macrocosm. "The synecdochic mode," Cason argues, "by prefiguring an inherent universalism, enables Eiseley to dramatize the individual as a microcosm who shares the spirit of the whole without sacrificing individual identity." His essay, "The Last Neanderthal," she suggests, with the imagery of blue plums and smoke, serves as an emblematic representation of the interplay between organization and entropy and the capacity for human memory to store, transmit, and preserve energy as complex wholes, in spite of individual mortality and inevitable dissolution. She further examines how synecdoche informs Eiseley's writing not only thematically but also structurally. The "concealed essay" enables Eiseley to explore nonlinear relationships among several events in time by juxtaposing analogical memories and embedding them within explanations of sequential and causally related events. The essay genre thereby functions as a form of ironic synecdoche that retains the humility of partial vision alongside the enlarged spirit of the whole.

Though Eiseley insisted strongly on his distinctive originality, scholars have long noted his habit of reading widely, eclectically, and comprehensively. Eiseley himself highlighted a number of these authors in his writings, for allusiveness is part of his characteristic style. Moreover, he had a particular pantheon of writers and thinkers that included Francis Bacon, Henry David Thoreau, and Charles Darwin. The next few essays explore new literary contexts for Eiseley's oeuvre.

Lioi makes an intriguing connection between Dante Alighieri and Eiseley, in "In a Dark Wood: Dante, Eiseley, and the Ecology of Redemption," noting that each "transgressed against the cabal of criticism by defining his own lineage and specifying the principles for the interpretation of his work." Significantly, in marking European influences on Eiseley, and by insisting on "a transatlantic conversation about science, literature, and myth," Lioi places Eiseley in a more "cosmopolitan," worldly, and "intergenerational" lineage than has been the case in American-centric Eiseley scholarship. Citing W. H. Auden, one of Eiseley's transatlantic connections and friends, Lioi returns to Dante's *Comedy* as a foundational text for Eiseley. In a reading of "The Star Thrower," arguably Eiseley's greatest essay, Lioi delimits its structure and purpose, proposing a medieval model that adapts "Dantean patterns of redemption." Eiseley revises this pattern to address "our own environmental crisis," Lioi proposes, "renewing the medieval sense that the whole world, not just the individual, is in danger." Eiseley's recovery and appropriation of Dante's comedic organization in "The Star Thrower" extends redemption to all living things. As such, Eiseley offers an "ecology of redemption" to his readers, weaving together the "scientific . . . existential and theological meanings of ecology." Finding joy, ultimately, in a bleak setting, Eiseley, like Dante, embraces love, compassion, and connection.

Eiseley's admiration of Henry David Thoreau has long been recognized in Eiseley scholarship. Eiseley's interest in this transcendentalist is obvious in his own writing, including an essay specifically on Thoreau, "Walden: Thoreau's Unfinished Business." Still, Jonathan Weidenbaum, in "Emerson and Eiseley: Two Religious Visions," highlights the older transcendentalist's significance to Eiseley's development as an essayist. Like Hanson earlier, Weidenbaum emphasizes Eiseley's spiritual interests, stating that "when placed next to Emerson . . . the uniqueness of Eiseley's religious thought is most vividly apparent." Indeed, Weidenbaum plainly attests, "If there is any larger purpose of this essay, it is to highlight Eiseley's genuine contribution to an authentically American spirituality." Like Emerson, Eiseley rejected organized religion. Emerson claimed in his journals, "I need hardly say to any one acquainted with my thoughts that I have no System" (*Selected* 87). In Emerson, the empirical knowledge of science blends with the spiritual knowledge of poetry, disconnecting his unsystematic belief process from his era's contemporary orthodoxy. Eiseley, Weidenbaum asserts, also "defies easy categorization." In his assessment, "Eiseley has contributed some of the most compelling and readable science writing in contemporary literature." At the same time, Eiseley, as "the author of *Darwin's Century* and a book on Francis Bacon[,] can state 'that the venture into space is meaningless unless it coincides with a certain interior expansion, an ever-growing universe within'" (*Star* 298). Together, Emerson and Eiseley help define what Sydney Ahlstrom and Harold Bloom have called the "American Religion," which Weidenbaum describes as "a creed of interiority, one centered within the deep recesses of the psyche."

In his comparison of Eiseley to a different author, the American naturalist and writer John Burroughs, Stephen Mercier places Eiseley in a different context, the tradition of the natural history essay, in particular the tradition of writing about evolution for a public audience. In his essay "Epic Narratives of Evolution: John Burroughs and Loren Eiseley" Mercier examines some of the astonishing similarities between Eiseley's *The Immense Journey* from 1957 and Burroughs's "The Long Road," published in *Time and Change* in 1912. Both writers employ similar rhetorical techniques, tropes, and imaginative prose to aid readers' understanding of evolution. They rely on the metaphor of the journey or road. Furthermore, both literary naturalists consider the processes of evolution as ongoing and creative. Similarly, Eiseley and Burroughs conceive of evolution in the first person, imagining their own bodies undergoing huge physiological transformations over aeons of geologic time. In these intimate portrayals, human beings are inextricably fused to their environments in essential ways. In the hands of Burroughs and Eiseley, Mercier argues, literary natural history stimulates wider conceptions of evolution and leads to a broader understanding of humans' place in the cosmos. These accounts, Mercier concludes, are inspiring and crafted to invoke wonder and awe. In the end, both writers ultimately insist on mystery.

In attempting to understand the evolution and mystery of the human psyche, Eiseley found himself, later in life, interested in the writings of Carl Jung. John Nizalowski, in "Eiseley and Jung: Structuralism's Invisible Pyramid," explores Eiseley's introduction to and absorption of Jungian archetypes and theories, most prominently that of the collective unconscious. Before he had read Jung carefully, Eiseley was internalizing Jung's ideas in his readings of other scientists and social scientists, such as Emile Durkheim, Lucien Lévy-Bruhl, and Claude Lévi-Strauss. Nizalowski argues that "whether Eiseley gained his Jungian ideas directly or indirectly through his readings of Lévi-Strauss and other structural thinkers, Jungian systems of thought consciously shape his essays." They were in the ether. Jung presents his key theory in an essay titled "The Concept of the Collective Unconscious," in which he distinguishes the collective unconscious from individual consciousness. The collective unconscious "is the realm of the archetypes," a matrix of knowledge that "owe[s] [its] existence exclusively to heredity." Eiseley, in numerous essays and poems, articulates patterns and archetypes that allow him to discern older, more ancient instincts, behaviors, and cognitive responses in living beings. "The Last Neanderthal" is a case in point. Moreover, Eiseley explores ideas of sacred time, "which rises above and beyond the historical and parallels Jung's ideas of timelessness in the collective unconscious." Moments of ordinary experience can suddenly open up, fall into, this timeless, expansive dimension beyond the normative boundaries of time and space. In this expansive mode, Nizalowski argues, humans can suddenly find themselves connecting deeply to the animal kingdom, as happens in Eiseley's short story "The Dance of the Frogs." Totem animals, a recurrence in Eiseley's essays, serve as spirit guides, expressions of a deeper connective reality not yet evident in the conscious mind. Dreams and visions, too, "are a major source of creative and scientific inspiration" in Eiseley. Taken together, these expressions of a unifying, communal unconsciousness demonstrate the significance of Jung's theories in Eiseley's writings.

In "From the American Great Plains to the Steppes of Russia: Loren Eiseley

Transplanted," Breschinsky provides a notably different context for Eiseley. A prolific and poetic translator of Eiseley's work into Russian, Breschinsky has spent more than two decades trying to "transplant" Eiseley's writings into modern Russian culture. His engaging discussion of this ongoing project, producing a "representative collection of Eiseley's essays and short stories," explains many of the challenges of a translator's job, including dealing with increasingly expensive copyright negotiations and with publishers who do not honor agreements. Publishing translations in Russian literary journals and in book form, Breschinsky works exactingly "to make the work sound as though Eiseley's native tongue were Russian." Word-to-word translation is only one concern; Breschinsky also hopes to capture "the sound of the words, the cadence of the lines, the particular associations that are peculiarly Russian." Translation becomes transmutation, transplantation: "Slowly, painfully, joyously Eiseley, who was born in Nebraska of pioneer German stock, *becomes* Russian." Breschinsky's project, which is gaining readers for Eiseley both in his printed versions and in copied, digitized (and often pirated) online versions of his translations, may help promote nature writing in Russia. Noting many of the formative Russian authors, such as Sergey Aksakov, Ivan Turgenev, Mikhail Prishvin, and Konstantin Paustovsky, who "reveal a deep appreciation of the natural world," Breschinsky ponders the dearth of nonfiction nature writing in the Russian tradition. "Nature writing as practiced in the United States," he explains, "never materialized in Russia." Without an established tradition, promoting Eiseley's writings has been challenging. Moreover, Breschinsky argues, Russians have never embraced Darwin's "unrelenting positivism and materialism." Marxist materialists had little patience with Darwin as well. Today, "creationism has captured the popular imagination" — not an encouraging development for Eiseley. Undeterred, Breschinsky sees his translation project as a developing bridge: "one of many," he concludes, "that will be needed if Russia is ever to fully embrace the best of Western civilization."

Whether approaching the essays in *Artifacts and Illuminations* selectively or collectively, readers will discover new interpretive avenues for their understanding of Loren Eiseley's endlessly rewarding body of work. As such, the chapters seek both to introduce his brilliant, memorable writings to a new generation who has yet to encounter them and to reintroduce him to those who feel they have known him perhaps all too well. As this overview has sought to make plain, this book displays a range of mostly new approaches to the study of Eiseley's writing. But it is by no means exhaustive. We are acutely aware that this collection does not cover all profitable approaches (surely, for example, a gendered reading of Eiseley is long overdue). It is meant to suggest rather than to delimit the possibilities. In that spirit, we present these essays not so much as artifacts of what has been accomplished but as illuminations of what is yet to be done.

NOTES

1. See, for instance, William H. Wisner's comment that Eiseley wrote "several extremely bad books of poetry (including *Notes of an Alchemist*, 1972, and *The Innocent Assassins*, 1973)" (88).

1

"The Bay of Broken Things"

The Experience of Loss in the
Work of Loren Eiseley

SUSAN HANSON

When he was a boy, Loren Eiseley recalls in *All the Strange Hours*, he for a time had the habit of whittling small crosses out of wood, decorating them with liquid gilt, and then erecting them atop the graves of birds he'd buried in the lot behind his house. He even went so far as to inter the printed obituaries of people who had died in heroic or tragic circumstances. These graves, too, were marked with a golden cross. "One day," he writes, "a mower in the empty lot beyond our backyard found the little cemetery and carried off all of my carefully carved crosses. I cried but I never told anyone. How could I? I had sought in my own small way to preserve the memory of what always in the end perishes: life and great deeds." The person to whom Eiseley revealed this secret shame — and he always associated loss with shame — was his friend W. H. Auden, who responded, "Yes, it was a child's effort against time. . . . And perhaps the archaeologist is just that child grown up" (*All* 27). The comparison is apt.

A man to whom solitude, darkness, and the absence of sound were simply givens, Loren Eiseley could not escape the reality of loss. He was, he knew, the product of an unhappy marriage, the son of a deaf, mentally unbalanced mother and a loving but often absent father. Like other children in such circumstances, he grew up fast. He also developed a need to confront the dissolution he saw as part of life — the "elemental night of chaos" represented by the erosion of the earth, the breakup of families, the slow but certain unraveling of his own mortal flesh — and a hunger to redeem it. Hearing the surf crash into the cliff below his window one night, he despairs of what he calls "the bay of broken things" that it leaves behind (*Night* 172). He responds to this chaos by imagining the waves to be the faces of the dead he once knew. Later, after dressing in the dark, Eiseley leaves his room and walks down to the rocky beach. There he confronts both an injured sea gull, which darts away from him, and a duck with a shattered wing, languishing on the sand. Unable to run away as the gull had, the duck "waddles painfully from its brief refuge into the water." Acting on instinct, the bird dives, then heads to sea. It is a gesture of futility: "A long green roller, far taller than my head, rises and crashes forward. The black head of the waterlogged duck disappears. This is the way wild things die, without question, without knowledge of mercy in the universe, knowing only themselves and their own pathway to the end. I wonder, walking farther up the beach, if the man who shot that bird will die as well" (173). He will, of course, as Eiseley knows, and so will the homeless old men of whom he later writes, and the pigeons pecking dumbly at their feet.

While a melancholy, even depressive undercurrent flows through his writing, Loren Eiseley somehow makes peace with the darkness in his life. In this regard he is reminiscent of the apophatic mystics who, like himself, suffer from an unnaturally strong awareness of the transience of things. In their "dark night," they find God; Eiseley, in contrast, finds repose. For these individuals, human limitations — imposed by time, by intellectual failure, by the inability of words to communicate the numinous — are not to be reviled but, rather, understood as a place of sacred demarcation. They signify the precipice from which the mystic — or the poet — falls. "Beyond," Eiseley writes in "The Hidden Teacher," "lies the great darkness of the ultimate Dreamer, who dreamed the light and the galaxies. Before act was, or substance existed, imagination grew in the dark" (*Unexpected* 55).

Just as the mystic must endure periods of spiritual dryness before finding consolation, so did Loren Eiseley have to navigate a series of losses on his way to finding solace in the natural world. This is not to say that he had no *appreciation* of nature as a child or young adult; indeed, just the opposite is true. What is also true, however, is that in spite of the losses in his life, Loren Eiseley was able to see beyond abandonment and death and, in the very expression of those losses, discover what Thomas Merton calls "a hidden wholeness" (*Collected Poems* 363).[1]

Writing in "Mystical Union and Grief," David Aberbach observes that grief — the normal response to loss — can foster a desire for the numinous: "a remarkable correspondence exists between the process leading to mystical union and the process of grief following a bereavement" (310). As an example, he cites a passage from Martin Buber's *Daniel*: "On a gloomy morning, I walked upon the highway, saw a piece of mica lying, picked it up and looked at it for a long time; the day was no longer gloomy, so much light was caught in the stone. And suddenly as I raised my eyes from it, I realized that while I had looked I had not been conscious of 'object' and 'subject'; in my looking the mica and I had been one; in my looking I had tasted unity" (140).

On several levels, Eiseley's experience is psychologically analogous to Buber's. According to Buber's biographer, Maurice Friedman, when Buber was three, his mother "literally disappeared without leaving a trace, and the home of his childhood was broken up. This had a depressing effect on all the family," Friedman continues, "and particularly on the young Martin, who, though he never spoke of it, bore signs of mourning and bereavement all his youth." With no explanation given for his mother's disappearance — he would later learn that she had gone to Russia and remarried — young Buber was sent to live with his paternal grandparents, whose emotional distance would only "intensify his sense of isolation and abandonment." Fully expecting his mother to return one day, three-year-old Martin learned otherwise not from his grandparents, but from a neighbor child. "No, she will never come back," Buber later recalled the older girl telling him matter-of-factly. "This was the decisive experience of Martin Buber's life," Friedman argues, "the one without which neither his early seeking for unity nor his later focus on dialogue and on the meeting with the 'Eternal Thou' is understandable" (4).

For Loren Eiseley, too, loss in its many permutations — death, loneliness, rejection, professional disappointment — was both a subject of and a force behind his work. Put another way, it was the "dark night" through which he passed en route to a deeper, more visceral perception — and expression — of his place in the natural world. In creating his "literature of loss," Loren Eiseley effectively achieved both psychological and spiritual catharsis, what for the mystic would be called the "purgative way."

His predilection for the dark, which runs through all of his work, is nothing Eiseley had to cultivate or coax; it was as much a given as his lineage, his ties to the mysterious "mad Shepards" of his mother's line. Early on, Eiseley writes, he had the sense that he was "different" in some way: "It begins in the echoing loneliness of a house with no other children; in the silence of a deafened mother; in the child head growing strangely aware of itself as it prattled over immense and solitary games. The child learned that there were shadows in the closets and a green darkness behind the close-drawn curtains of the parlor; he was aware of a cool twilight in the basement. He was afraid only of noise" (*Night* 4). Nowhere does Loren Eiseley offer a traditional, linear account of his life, but by reading his most clearly autobiographical works — *All the Strange Hours, The Night Country*, and the snippets of writing collected in *The Lost Notebooks of Loren Eiseley* — one can build at least a partial narrative of his childhood. "A creature molded of plains dust and the seed of those who came west with the wagons" (*All* 23), Eiseley writes, "I was born seven years after the start of the century in the wrong time, the wrong place, and into the wrong family. I am not insensible of the paradox: It is this which made me" (*Lost* 117). This awareness of being *mis*placed, with only tenuous ties to home and family, is a wound, a loss he carried all his life.

An experience that illustrates this consciousness occurred when Eiseley was a very young child, "shivering in the cold bed" and trying to make sense of his parents' continual fighting. He writes, "I remember the pacing, the endless pacing of my parents after midnight. . . . Once, a small toddler, I climbed from bed and seized their hands, pleading wordlessly for sleep, for peace, peace. And surprisingly, they relented, even my unfortunate mother. Terror, anxiety, ostracism, shame; I did not understand the words. I learned only the feelings they represent" (*All* 24). As Eiseley points out in *The Night Country*, his family was indeed ostracized, "shunned as unimportant and odd," primarily due to his mother Daisy Eiseley's unpredictable behavior (197). Deaf since childhood, she was a talented, but unsuccessful prairie artist whose only means of communicating with her son were "hand signals, stampings on the floor to create vibrations, [and] exaggerated lip movements" (198). Though he was a far more stable figure in his son's life, Clyde Eiseley was away and therefore unavailable much of the time. A struggling hardware salesman, he worked long hours and traveled often between the small Nebraska towns around Lincoln. Clyde's efforts notwithstanding, the Eiseley family remained poor, living "in a series of small frame houses on the southern outskirts of Lincoln and [keeping] to themselves" (Angyal, *Loren* 4). All his life, Eiseley remained baffled by his parents' strange, not to mention *strained*, relationship; what possibly could have attracted them to one another? Granted, his mother had been a beauty once, but even in his youth she appeared "savage," often "behaving in the manner of a witch" (*All* 32). His father, on the other hand, was a "mild-mannered man with a deep faith in the essential goodness of the working class" (9). An itinerant actor as a young man, Clyde Eiseley "read with great grace and beauty," causing his son to "shiver when he read from Shakespeare" (16, 178). Fittingly, Clyde Eiseley's main legacy to his son was his well-used copy of Shakespeare, a book the writer would keep for the remainder of his life.

Though he believed that he and his parents somehow "loved each other fiercely" (25), Loren Eiseley was "a haunted man who grew up in a haunted house" (Finch). This is nowhere clearer than in an incident that occurred during his father's final days. Summoned home from California by letter, the younger Eiseley had returned to Lincoln to find a defeated and broken man, an "aging, unaggressive salesman," who had spent too many "solitary nights among the artificial palms of small-town hotels." Clyde Eiseley was clearly dying. "He came home yellow and cadaverous," Eiseley writes. "Already, though he did not speak of it, he must have known the truth: cancer." Eiseley would care for his father at home for as long as possible, but in time, the elder Eiseley was "removed to the hospital by a callous ex-Army surgeon who infrequently visited his bedside. There," the writer says, "he died by inches" (*All* 15). On what would be their father's final day, Eiseley's half-brother, Leo, appeared. Fourteen years Loren's senior, Leo had been born to Clyde and his first wife, Anna. When the older brother arrived, in response to a cable that Loren had sent, a nurse attempted to awaken the unconscious father: "She shouted in his ear, 'Your son Leo is here. Leo has come. Leo. Leo is here.'" What followed astonished them all: "Slowly, to my boundless surprise, the dying man's eyes, indifferent to me for many hours, opened. There was an instant of recognition between the two of them, from which I was excluded. My father had come back an infinite distance for that meeting. It was wordless" (13).

It was also a grim epiphany for Eiseley. "My brother who had been summoned was the one true son, not I," he writes. "For him my father had come the long way back, if only for a moment." Would his father have done the same for him, had the nurse been asked to rouse him once again? Eiseley considered the question but dismissed it almost outright. He was a "changeling," he realized, the product of a loveless marriage, born late in his father's life. Leo, on the other hand, "was the son of [his] father's youth, of a first love who had perished in her springtime and of whom [his] father could never bring himself to speak" (13). Beyond the worn edition of Shakespeare, Eiseley's only inheritance would be a small sum of money and a collection of letters written by his father. Even before he could read them, however, the aunt with whom he was staying burned the letters out of her "morbid dread of disease." "As I stood beside her," Eiseley recalls, "a charred sheet turned over. Written across it in the fine bold penmanship of my father was a sentence rapidly being obliterated in the flames." That sentence: "Remember the boy is a genius, but moody." Though he considered himself no genius, Eiseley says that he found his father's words "proudly comforting. My father had recognized me after all" (14).

Eiseley's mother, Daisy, would live another thirty-one years, but the two would never be reconciled; the hurt that Eiseley experienced at her hand had simply been too deep. "Her whole paranoid existence from the time of my childhood had been spent in the deliberate distortion and exploitation of the world about her. Across my brain," Eiseley writes, "were scars which had left me walking under the street lamps of unnumbered nights. I had heard her speak words to my father on his deathbed that had left me circling the peripheries of a continent to escape her always constant presence. Because of her, in ways impossible to retrace, I would die childless" (223).

Having spent much of his early adulthood on the move — traveling to the Rockies and the California desert to recover from a severe pulmonary infection, then riding the rails as a drifter for months at a time — Eiseley was physically and emotionally rootless. As biographer Gale E. Christianson notes, he made an "obligatory pilgrimage" to Lincoln each summer to see his mother and aunt, who had been living together since his father's death. After their marriage in 1938, it would be Eiseley's wife, Mabel, who tended to most of the women's needs, as well as those of her own aging parents, who also lived in Lincoln (*Fox* 320). When Daisy died at the age of eighty-four, Loren and Mabel made the trip to Lincoln yet again, but at the funeral, Eiseley at first refused to view his mother's body. "Power to destroy me you always had," he writes, reflecting on his thoughts at the time. "I have survived the indignities and the words that left me homeless" (*All* 224). Years later, Eiseley would write about the life cycle of the giant Sphexes, the digger wasp that spends its winter pupating underground. When its "molecular alarm" sounds, the wasp erupts from its case and struggles toward the surface. Here one must ponder the significance of this process for Eiseley. He writes, "On that brief journey the wasp may well trip over the body of its own true mother — if this was her last burrow — a tomb for life and a tomb for death. . . . The dead past, its husks, its withered wings are cast aside, scrambled over, in the frantic moment of resurrection" (243). In losing his last physical connection to "home," Eiseley experiences no definable "moment of resurrection," no emergence into a future free of shadows. He does, however, recognize something important about his *present* life. "I took my wife's hand and walked away from the gravediggers," Eiseley writes. "'You have come the whole way,' I said, a little brokenly — 'the only one who knew everything, accepted everything.' I lifted my hands and let them fall." What Eiseley has realized is that the relationship between himself and Mabel is nothing like that between Clyde and Daisy, or between himself and his oppressive mother. "It was different with us," he tells Mabel (225–26). And it is that difference that allows him to find within a toxic family narrative a measure of personal peace.

Like many only children, especially those from unhappy homes, young Loren Eiseley found companionship in both the natural world and books.

The library was his childhood refuge, but so was the nearby countryside, where he studied ants and collected fish and plants for his homemade aquarium. At the age of fourteen, he announced what he wanted to do with his life; "I want to be a nature writer," he wrote as part of a class assignment. This short but prophetic essay reveals that, in spite of his youth, Eiseley already knew something of the paradoxes of nature: "As in human life, there are tragedy, and humor, and pathos; in the life of the wild, there are facts of tremendous interest, real lives, and real happenings, to be written about, and there is little necessity for drawing on the imagination" (*Lost* 14). Given his love for the subject, as well as the encouragement he received from his teachers and from the publication of his work in *Prairie Schooner*, English seemed the logical major for Eiseley. But as biographer Christianson notes, he had seen the hardships faced by friends who tried to write for a living, and "he wished for no part in the classroom beyond the role of student; the stultifying task of reading freshman themes had convinced him of that" (*Fox* 91). His declared major had been science when he entered the University of Nebraska in 1925, but by 1930, when he returned from his last railroad adventure, he had still taken no classes in physics, chemistry, or mathematics. Searching for a new direction, he enrolled in two anthropology courses that fall and did well in both. His participation in a research expedition the following spring sealed the decision: his major would be anthropology. Eiseley would go on to receive his AB in anthropology and English from the University of Nebraska, and his MA and PhD from the University of Pennsylvania. He would publish the requisite scholarly articles and do significant and valued fieldwork as an archaeologist. He would be sought after as a curator and administrator. Then, in his midforties, Eiseley's career would take a significant turn; he "started to use scientific material in a different way, trying to arouse the interest of the general reader in subjects that fascinated him" (*Lost* 19). Ironically, the very popularity of this lyrical and accessible form would be the source of much professional difficulty for Eiseley.

A particularly scathing review of *The Firmament of Time* illustrates this point well. A member of Yale's Department of Anthropology at the time, John Buettner-Janusch called Eiseley's writing "sentimental and trite," adding that prior reviews praising the work as an "iridescent study" were grossly misleading.[2] "Chapter five — How Human is Man? — is a series of moral parables on a somewhat higher level than those found in the repertory of a fundamentalist preacher," Buettner-Janusch observed. Deeming the book "a work of obscurantism," the reviewer went on to argue that because science is exciting in itself, "we need not inject mystery, fevered prose, overblown metaphors, and sentimental twaddle into our subject" (693–94). Random House editor Robert Linscott had issued a similar opinion earlier in Eiseley's career. Of one essay in *The Immense Journey*, he stated, "The last two paragraphs are an example of how the author succumbs to the temptation of going anthropomorphic. It's cute but is it science?" (qtd. in Christianson, *Fox* 292). Eiseley's response: "There is a sense in which when we cease to anthropomorphize, we cease to be men, for when we cease to have human contact with animals and deny them all relation to ourselves, we tend in the end to cease to anthropomorphize ourselves — to deny our humanity" (*Lost* 200).

Though he was speaking of himself as a student, Eiseley's observation in *All the Strange Hours* is pertinent to his later life as well: "For a thin-skinned young man, still emerging from long isolation, encounters with the realities of the academic world were not always pleasant" (76). A letter from his friend Lewis Mumford years later would suggest just how much the disdain of his critics hurt Eiseley: "I wanted to tell you how fully I understand the wounds and scars left by the casual reviewers of this world. All I can say — and I know too well it does not compensate for the hurt — is that you have received distinguished recognition. As an academic professional I frequently find myself bitterly castigated by those in my own field who resent any attempt to venture into the domain of literature. There were years when I preferred silence. There were years when I wrote only professional papers" (*Lost* 217).

Early in Eiseley's lackluster tenure as provost at the University of Pennsylvania, he happened to run into a former colleague who had taken an administrative post in Washington. After the two had exchanged comments about their work, the friend offered an insightful analysis of Eiseley's future in academia: "You . . . are a freak, you know. A God-damned freak, and life is never going to be easy for you. You like scholarship, but the scholars, some of them, anyhow, are not going to like you because you don't stay in the hole where God supposedly put you. You keep sticking your head out and looking around. In a university, that's inadvisable" (*All* 201). Eiseley would remain at the University of Pennsylvania until his death in 1977, but his friend's prediction was borne out when a colleague at the University of Nebraska attempted to nominate Eiseley for an honorary doctorate, with the Department of Anthropology serving as his sponsor. As Christianson notes, "Its faculty balked on the ground that the nominee had not sufficiently distinguished himself in the discipline to warrant such an accolade." The degree would be awarded, but in humane letters and not in science (*Fox* 327).

Eiseley was not unaware of his odd position, straddling the worlds of science and literature. "I guess I'm not a very good scientist," he writes, recalling a conversation with his mentor, Frank Speck. "I'm not sufficiently proud, nor confident of my powers, nor of any human powers" (*All* 90). Later Eiseley calls to mind a telling experience that occurred during the war years when he was teaching briefly in the University of Kansas's pre-medical program. Christianson calls the account of the event "largely fictional" (*Fox* 207), but Eiseley says that it "affected [him] more than the turmoil that swept around [him]" (*All* 143).

As Eiseley goes on to explain, he was at the time assisting a senior faculty member in dissecting a cadaver. "He was a kind and able teacher," Eiseley explains, "but a researcher hardened to the bitter necessities of his profession." One of these "necessities" was experimentation with live animals — specifically, dogs. Entering the "animal house" with his colleague, Eiseley is distressed by what he sees, a pen full of dogs that appear to him "like men in a concentration camp" (*All* 143). The researcher singles out one and injects it with something that renders him unconscious. As the anatomy professor does his work, demonstrating venous flow in the abdomen, only a few of the students gather around to watch. Even these, Eiseley believes, will not remember what they have seen. Eiseley, in contrast, *will* remember, but what he recalls will be the empathy he felt for a fellow creature. "I still stood by the window trying to see the last sun for him," he writes. "I had been commanded" (144).

Eiseley knows that he is not responsible for what just happened, that it would have occurred had he been there or not. But he nonetheless feels remorse for the dog's death. As Eiseley explains, "He had looked at me with that unutterable expression. 'I do not know why I am here. Save me. I have seen other dogs fall and be carried away. Why do you do this? Why?'" Years later, Eiseley related this experience to a physician he knew. "I was a scientist," he writes. "I was groping for some way to explain." Though he was a "good man," the friend clearly missed the point. Instead, he argued that such experimentation was "necessary" and that the dog couldn't possibly have had the reaction Eiseley described. Eiseley would have none of it. Had the experiment not been conducted, he writes, "the dog might have had just one more day, one more day, even in the animal house. One more day of life, of sentience" (144–45).

"I was a scientist" — while this was certainly true, Eiseley was also increasingly conscious of what he was giving up to pursue his work as a writer. He states this most plainly in "The Star Thrower," when he finds himself looking through an old satchel full of pictures and other items that once belonged to his mother. In recalling how "all her life she had walked the precipice of mental breakdown," he senses that he is being confronted by a presence in the room. Will he love the universe, or reject it as "the long crucifixion" his mother had endured? His answer: "'I *do* love the world. . . . I love its small ones, the things beaten in the strangling surf, the bird, singing, which flies and falls and is not seen again. . . . I love the lost ones, the failures of the world.' It was like the renunciation of my scientific heritage" (*Unexpected* 86). Throughout his work, Eiseley's preference for "the small ones," "the failures of the world," comes through clearly. The stray mongrel he adopts while living as a drifter; a fellow passenger he befriends on the train, the man with the "tiger claw" hands; the waste places of the world where pack rats collect all manner of refuse for their nests — these are the subjects of his concern (*All* 58, 117, 250).

What ultimately separates Eiseley from the scientific community is his contention that "in the world there is nothing to explain the world." He may believe in evolution, but he nonetheless can find "nothing to explain the necessity of life, nothing to explain the hunger of the elements to become life, nothing to explain why the stolid realm of rock and soil and mineral should diversify itself into beauty, terror, and uncertainty. To bring organic novelty into existence, to create pain, injustice, joy, demands more than we can discern in the nature that we analyze so completely" (242). Having lost not just the rootedness of family and home but also the prospect of academic esteem, Loren Eiseley is now moving into the territory of the mystics: he is acknowledging the loss of certainty, the inability of the human mind to grasp the Ultimate Mystery. As an archae-ologist, peering at the ruins of former civilizations, Eiseley gained more than historical knowledge; he also gained the mystic's perspective. "The modern world was small, I thought, tiny, constricted beyond belief," he writes. "A little lost century, a toy, I saw suddenly, looking upon our truck and pretentious archeological gear" (104). Though not religious in the conventional sense — his family belonged to no church and he had no religious training — Eiseley is nonetheless intensely aware of a dimension beyond the world he sees; he was, says Richard E. Wentz, "a contemplative who gazed into and *through* the otherness of reality" ("American" 432). As Eiseley explains,

> I am treading deeper and deeper into leaves and silence. I see more faces watching, non-human faces. Ironically, I who profess no religion find the whole of my life a religious pilgrimage. The origins of this hunger are as mysterious as the reasons why we, who are last year's dust and rain, have risen from that dust to look about with the devised crystal of a raindrop before we subside once more into snow and whirling vapor. But, however that one autumn may still color my memory, life is com-plex; it changes, and my world was destined to change with it. (*All* 140)

To refer to Eiseley as a mystic is, without doubt, to invite controversy. More than a few critics — Arizona State professor Gene Glass, chief among — have flatly refused to attribute any mystic sensibility to Eise-ley's work. "To regard Eiseley as a mystic does him no particular honor," Glass has argued. "The tag hangs awkwardly on a man who labored as a paleontologist during the most rigid and positivist half century of the science" (2). To support his position, Glass refers to the preface to *The*

Innocent Assassins, where Eiseley writes, "Some have called me Gothic in my tastes. Others have chosen to regard me as a Platonist, a mystic, a concealed Christian, a midnight optimist. Like most poets I am probably all these things by turns, or such speculations are read into me by those who are pursuing some night path of their own" (11). In further developing his argument, Glass reveals a considerable misunderstanding of the mystical experience: "No matter how much one might see in Eiseley's work, in the end to call it 'mystical' is faint-hearted, a withholding of comprehension, perhaps even a staunching of an emotional response. One wishes to bar from conscious experience the unwelcome thoughts of death and love that Eiseley evokes with tangible objects and common actions. Mysticism is that which cannot be rationally grasped; a work deemed mystical need not be fully apprehended and may be forgotten more easily." Yes, the mystical is "that which can not be grasped," but this in no way negates the possibility of finding the numinous in "tangible objects and common actions." In fact, just the reverse is true. "For many of us the Biblical bush still burns," Eiseley writes, "and there is a deep mystery in the heart of a simple seed" (*Firmament* 8). Elsewhere he states, "The green world is [humanity's] sacred center" (*Invisible* 1). Eiseley may have been uncomfortable with the label "mystic," but the characterization fits nonetheless.

What constitutes a mystical experience is, fundamentally, an encounter with Otherness. This Other, which Eiseley variously refers to as the "Player," the "Synthesizer," or the "ultimate Dreamer," is, in reality, unknowable (Wentz, "Loren" 583). As the author of *The Cloud of Unknowing*, puts it, "Thought cannot comprehend God. . . . Though we cannot know him we can love him. By love he may be touched and embraced, never by thought" (Johnston 54). The mystic, in short, must be satisfied with the sheer *longing* for God. Writing "In the Red Sunset on Another Hill," Eiseley describes the experience of unearthing an encampment where a shaman had once practiced the seer's craft. Though much has certainly changed, Eiseley asserts that such men can still be found today. "Some" he writes, who "practice science, like me, are not scientists" (*Innocent* 33). Rather, appearing as scientists, they simply "wear a disguise best fitted for the times" because, after all, "the peaked cap with the stars [is] no longer suitable" (lines 34, 36). Today, these seeming scientists might "sit / before a microscope, or watch the Pleiades" (36–37), nevertheless they really "belong to an old craft" and are "wizards who loved / the living world, loved mystery" (38–39). It is true they may have "never solved a thing," but in fact they do not want solutions (40). Instead, they are among those who have "preferred mystery" (43). In the old times, this "ancient brotherhood," Eiseley continues, remained secret because its members might otherwise be "stoned / or burned, or hanged" (83, 84–85). Today, the consequence is not so dire, yet even so those who love mystery more than certainty can expect to "suffer the ostracism of the seeming learned" (86). As a member of this ancient brotherhood, Eiseley is resigned to accept the loss of honor among "the seeming learned." As Richard Wentz puts it, "Whether or not we like the terms 'religion' or 'religious,' Loren Eiseley insists that we become cultural heretics who move beyond certitude to a sense of the holy" ("Loren" 583).

Tied to this loss of certainty is an acute awareness of human finitude and the limitations imposed by time and change. Writing in what is likely his most anthologized essay, "The Brown Wasps," Eiseley recalls several commonplace experiences that reinforced his sense of mortality. In the first, he was walking home through a field he had passed through many times. A new suburban department store would be built there soon, he realized; the field, so like that field of golden crosses in his youth, was about to be leveled, scraped clean of every living thing. "Thousands of obscure lives were about to perish," he writes, "the spores of puffballs would go smoking off to new fields, and the bodies of little white-footed mice would be crunched under the inexorable wheels of the bulldozers. Life disappears or modifies its appearances so fast that everything takes on an aspect of illusion" (*Night* 230).

In another instance, Eiseley had returned to his childhood home, expecting, as people are wont to do, that everything would be the same as he remembered it. "I have spent a large portion of my life in the shade of a nonexistent tree," he admits. "It was planted sixty years ago by a boy with a bucket and a toy spade in a little Nebraska town. That boy was myself." Unlikely as it was, Eiseley had expected that cottonwood sapling to still be there, to have grown to a height sufficient to shade his family's little house. "I came close to the white picket fence and reluctantly, with great effort, looked down the long vista of the yard," Eiseley writes. "There was nothing there to see." Why had that memory played such an important role in his life? "It was part of my orientation in the universe and I could not survive without it," he explains. "There was more than an animal's attachment to a place. There was something else, the attachment of the spirit to a grouping of events in time; it was part of our mortality" (*Night* 234, 235). And it was gone.

The writer's awareness of the contingency of life is even more pronounced in the final chapter of *All the Strange Hours*. "This is the story of a dream," writes Eiseley, the dream that is his life. As the dream begins, Eiseley says, he is feeling slightly feverish, teetering between "the reality we know" and the one that is "no longer causal or successive in character." He is back in the freight car of his youth, a drifter once again; he is himself as the young man he once was, and himself as the old man that he is. The third rider, who does not speak at first, is the Other Player (259).

When the old man awakes from his dream within a dream, he finds the Player still with him. He wants the Player to tell him what has become of the people he knew in his youth. "Do you think it wise to ask?" the Player cautions. The old man who is Eiseley does not respond.

"Can you not be content?" asks the Player. "You are an old man, a scholar now. You have come a long way through time. You have written books. You can name men since history began. You have stood in the places of the dead, handled their skulls."

The Player asks if Eiseley remembers the ruined house he came upon as a child, and the game of dice he played there on the floor. Eiseley replies that he does, and the Player continues,

> "You played against all your possible futures. You played in the dim room at sunset. Remember?"
> "I remember."
> "You lost the unborn, remember?"
> "I remember."
> "You lost fame."

"I remember."

"And fortune."

"I remember." (260–61)

Eiseley's life *could* have been different, he realizes, but he has thrown the dice; as the Player has told him, "There is only the one game. . . . You play but once. That is why the days are counted. Lie back, you have already played" (262). Not wanting to accept this fact, Eiseley the dreamer travels back in time yet again. He is in Mexico, thirty years before. He is in the Caribbean, sleeping in the sun. He is the escaped convict Tom Murry on a snowy western hilltop, running for his life but finding death at the hands of a posse. Finally, he is back with the shepherd dog he knew as Wolf, out in the drifting snow. "We were merely creatures who hunted and shared together," he says of the two of them. "I did not care for taxonomic definitions, that was the truth of it. I did not care to be a man, only a being." In the end, Eiseley notes, he and Wolf would "no longer be man and dog, but creatures, creatures with no knowledge of contingency or games. . . . We would vanish together as an anonymous grey blur" (265–66).

Ultimately, Eiseley claims no human privilege for himself. He is content to be the creature of flesh and blood that he is, taking his chances with a shape-shifting universe. "It hides its work," Eiseley writes. "Look close and it dissolves in aimless atomies. Look again and it is slyly engaged in performing miracles in a web of its own light." As a result of a fall down the stairway of his college rooming house, he says he realized he was "a genuine stranger in the cosmos." "No blood cell, no single neuron would ever inform me how the light of consciousness had been relit," Eiseley states, noting that he was *their* creature and not the reverse. In making this admission, he says, he is being neither self-pitying nor mawkish. "Scarcely that," he maintains. "I am merely recognizing the existence of mystery, of the unknown" (*All* 78). For Loren Eiseley, the ensuing darkness is familiar territory indeed.

NOTES

1. "There is in all visible things an invisible fecundity, a dimmed light, a meek name-lessness, and a hidden wholeness. This mysterious Unity and Integrity is Wisdom, the Mother of all, *Natura naturans*" (Merton, *Collected Poems* 363).

2. After a distinguished career, Buettner-Janusch was convicted in 1980 of using his lab assistants to make LSD and quaaludes for sale. Paroled in 1983, he was charged in 1987 with sending poisoned Valentine's candy to the judge in his first case. Convicted, he died in prison in 1992 (Lambert).

2

"Never Going to Cease My Wandering"

Loren Eiseley and the American Hobo

M. CATHERINE DOWNS

In the summer of 1926 or thereabouts, young Loren Eiseley and his friends from high school hopped a freight in California (Christianson, *Fox* 50–54).[1] One of their number was, in the slang of Eiseley-the-boy's favorite author Jack London, a *profesh*, a boy who had jumped trains in previous acts of derring-do. Perhaps in earlier years he had enticed Eiseley on short runs from the freight yards of Lincoln, Nebraska, where they were living, to the next town, but this California trip was a real adventure. Their trip had the hallmarks of boys' rough play and concomitant bad planning. The Model T ("Old Purgatory") into which they had been pouring oil had finally broken down. One of the boys had wired home for money, since their funds were running short. It became obvious that a boy with a physical disability, as one of their number had, would not square with their train-jumping ambitions. Eventually, however, most of the group rode California freights as nonpaying passengers before finding their way home by more conventional means. The young Loren Eiseley who hopped the California freights lived in relative poverty in Lincoln, Nebraska, it is true, but it would be close to three years before he would lose his father to cancer; it was before his own brush with tuberculosis as well. He was no down-and-out man, beating his way across America in a kind of desperation because there was nothing else for him to do. Although in 1926 Eiseley and his friends would return safe and sound to their homes in Lincoln, they were of the hobo-kind.

Vagrants in America have long borne either social scorn or adulation, and sometimes both at once. In Eiseley's time, the railroad was simply the only means of timely long-distance travel, and migrant workers, almost exclusively men, followed the road seeking work. For some individual wanderers, a temperament that grew restive when too closely restrained by whatever went by the name of civilization at the moment sought freedom from social encumbrances; a number of men newly mustered out of the armed services, unable to call anywhere "home," found companions on the road who could not be found in more stable populations. Some vagrants honorably supported families by working the harvests; some were thieves who used the rails to make an escape. Those who scorned hobos and those who admired their seeming freedom could each find in vagrant men objects for their feelings. As a boy, Eiseley encountered vagrancy both as fact and myth. In his later years, as he ceased riding trains illicitly, and the experiences receded from his immediate life, they were turned to myth in the lines of essays and autobiographical writings. The present essay begins with the facts of train travel in the early years of the twentieth century, examining, at the last, the mythic journey that Eiseley saw repeated in every wanderer.

Loren was born to wander; his family fortunes were tied to the railroad. His father's father, Charles Frederick Eisele, fled Stuttgart to avoid conscription in 1838, crossed the ocean to the United States, and took the Oregon Trail to build a farm north of Omaha, Nebraska, on loess soil (Christianson, *Fox* 3). The name of the soil and the pioneer bent of the grandfather were recapitulated in Charles's grandson, Loren. "Loess" is the geologic term for soil that is deposited by wind during the era of glaciation; the term, from Norwegian, means "loose" or "free." Charles Frederick, like his grandson, moved like windblown soil across the western landscape, seeking freedom from the social and cultural constraints that had burdened him. The grandson would come to study the Ice Age and Ice Age hunters. Charles Frederick, despite his canny and energetic nature, became impoverished when the railroad bypassed the town where he kept a hardware store. The grandson was enriched by spending much of his childhood and young manhood in Lincoln, a rail division with an extensive train yard. The grandfather and grandson participated in the movement westward of great numbers of Americans across the face of the continent, and their gains and losses were connected with the rails.

Charles Frederick's grandson came of age during a golden age of drifting, bumming, and hoboing. Times were especially propitious for disaffected young men to leave circumstances they found uncongenial or to seek work in other states via the rail lines that crossed and recrossed the American West. The development of rail in the Deep South had been hampered by state's rights advocates and by legislation that could not ease the joining of rail lines between states (Gordon 151). The East was so densely settled that jumping a train to travel at high speed (as youths enjoyed doing) between destinations was hampered by frequent passage through towns and cities (DePastino xxii). It was in the West that one could sight down the rails and follow them until they converged on the horizon at the vanishing point, for which, among some groups of men, plunging toward that point at sixty miles per hour and more was a goal. The automobile, traveling mostly on dirt roads, could not come close to matching the speed of rail travel. Heavier-than-air travel was practiced by barn stormers and flying aces, not by ordinary paying passengers. As historian Roger Bruns notes, young boys began hopping trains to travel a mile to school, or ten miles to the next town (33). Families walked to the depot to watch trains come in because one could not know just who might step down from the Pullman sleepers and day coaches. To migrant job seekers, families seeking entertainment, disaffected young men, boys on a lark, or criminals on the lam, the trains covering the vast expanses of the West beckoned.

During the time when Eiseley began drifting, conflicting ideals concerning the value of work became entangled with America's views of the rail industry. Not so far in the past was the Pullman Strike of 1894 in Chicago, in which 125,000 workers had walked out on the job. The strike disrupted transport and resulted in thirteen deaths and the involvement of twelve thousand U.S. troops (Arvich 34). In the next twenty years, the Industrial Workers of the World, or Wobblies, aggressively recruited hobos, thus drawing, in the public eye at least, a connection between bumming and organized labor. Vagrants found themselves forced by overzealous recruiters to buy the IWW "red card." Many hobos displayed red cards simply to avoid rough hazing from labor organizations (Bruns 156–57).

If, however, migrant laborers chose to exercise their right to work and followed recruiters to the vineyards and fruit orchards of Oregon and California, they may have found themselves sleeping in the weather under crowded, louse-infested conditions; forced to buy rancid meat or infested flour from a company store; paid less than they had been promised because there were more workers than work; and obliged to visit latrines overflowing with ordure in labor camps where bathing was not available (139–40). As a result, hoboing, like striking or scabbing a place of work, entered a deeply divided American conversation about values, capital, and labor. Those who carried the red card would find themselves associated with socialist leader Big Bill Haywood, tried in 1907 for murder (acquitted) and in 1919 for sedition (fled to Russia); or with the Marxists in Russia, who had succeeded in overthrowing the monarchy during the October Revolution in 1917. Those migrant laborers who sought work at subsistence wages might find themselves storied in one of several works in the new discipline of sociology, which placed vagrancy as a social ill that needed to be documented. E. Fred Carlisle mentions estimates of the numbers of vagrants at 13,745 in 1929 and 186,000 in 1931 (*Loren* 34–35). This nexus — either one works and participates in the creation and spending of capital or one is a problem — sets up dualistic thinking for which becoming a knight of the road was and is an escape.

One late twentieth-century hobo set for himself a third possibility: a hobo's life partook of joy because he awoke each day and did not know what would happen or where he would be. He would not be entering an office at the same time every morning, or leaving the same time each afternoon to make money. Instead, the day opened to him and offered possibilities (Maharidge and Williamson 18). The words of Montana Blackie and other oral histories of hobos consulted for this essay make note of subjects that came to occupy Loren Eiseley's thought: time counted in seasons or geologic eras, not in minutes and hours on a clock; experience measured by the degree to which it enlarges human ideas and ideals, not by dollars and cents; work that somehow escapes the production and marketing targets required by Big Business; freedom from being counted, listed, or timed.

But trains also attracted lawlessness in the early twentieth century. Wealthy paying passengers used private Pullmans and exclusive lounge cars to enjoy drinking, gambling, and prostitution that was relatively unregulated because the train, passing through states on rails that belonged to the rail industry, were not governed by any particular state laws (Gordon 190). Excluded by their socioeconomic status, train jumpers performed acts of trespassing on railroad property by joining the train as nonpaying passengers. In this act, the drifter was already outside the law. As Todd DePastino notes in his introduction to *The Road*, Jack London's 1907 account of hobo life, being criminal and then escaping danger was, for some vagrants, part of the attraction of the road. Some hobos shared a culture of scoring, besting, and publicly jumping trains and eluding authorities; theirs was a constant performance of (dominant, white) manhood (xviii).

Contrary to the public behavior of white men on freights, African Americans and Latin Americans on the road who did not keep a low profile might be met with hazing or worse. Persons of color became targets for sadistic brakemen, who are reputed to have "greased the rails" with their corpses (Bruns 42). Brakemen, or brakies, were ubiquitous on trains before 1900. During Eiseley's youth, brakes had to be set on each train car; thus a certain number of brakies were required as part of a full crew. Modern air brakes, which can be set from one location for the whole train, slowly replaced the older technology, and thus few brakies are required today (Gordon 184–85). Assuming power above the law, brakies in Eiseley's day were paid to scour every train car for nonpaying riders and earned everlasting enmity among hobos for siding with the captains of industry instead of the knights of the road.

Another tale repeated in the literature about hobos concerns the brakie who put off people of color in the middle of the Mojave Desert with no water (Schmidt 85). The Scottsboro Boys frame-up and trial is also from the period under study here: in 1931 nine black workers who had hopped a train to a job in Alabama were accused of rape and jailed — some for decades — on trumped up charges ("Scottsboro Boys"). Some white male hobos seem to have expropriated railroad property for their own ends and to have flaunted their temporary "ownership" of it. To perform their theater of exclusion, such hobos had to be deliberately public, on a train, in motion, or else the performance had no veracity. To draw a great deal of attention, they had to be public and *bad*. On this moral continuum — captains of industry, bad brakies, bad hobos, courteous knights of the road — Eiseley would later range his writer's persona squarely against the brakies and captains of industry, and squarely of the company of hobos, thus embracing, in his mind, a society that was welcoming and inclusive.

The decades during which Eiseley grew up and came of age saw an upwelling of mythmaking and media coverage surrounding the idea of vagrancy, whether pursued on foot or by rail. Eiseley-the-boy was devoted to a pulp magazine called *Railroad Stories* (Christianson, *Fox* 89). Through his visits to the Lincoln city library, and later the grown young man's English classes and visits to the University of Nebraska library, Eiseley could have discovered Walt Whitman's "Song of the Open Road" ("Allons! The road is before us!" [line 220]); Robert Service's "The Tramps" ("When time was yet our vassal and life's jest was still unstale" [line 5]); Bliss Carman's "The Vagabonds" ("We are the vagabonds of time / And roam the yellow autumn days / When all the roads are gray with rime / And all the valleys blue with haze" [lines 1–4]); or Vachel Lindsay's "On the Road to Nowhere" ("Were you thief or were you fool / or most nobly free?" [lines 7–8]). Carl Sandburg's *American Songbag,* a collection of folk songs gathered while Sandburg was on the bum, appeared in 1927. Jack London, one of Eiseley's (and America's) favorite authors, jumped trains in 1896. Later, in need of cash, he published nine essays on his experiences in *Cosmopolitan* in 1907, collecting these in a separate volume, *The Road.* As Eiseley developed interest in a literary career and became a writer and editor for the newly formed little magazine *Prairie Schooner,* he was already embedded in a written conversation about tramping. In addition, an affair of the heart connected him with the road. One of his teachers during his senior year in high school would later become Mabel Eiseley, his wife. During the years he began train jumping, Mabel's father worked as a brakie (Christianson, *Fox* 61).

The new medium of film added to popular mythology concerning bums: the humorous, slightly naughty, yet piquant figure of the Little Tramp. Charlie Chaplin (1889–1977) pulled himself up by his bootstraps from virtual homelessness in London to wide acclaim in America. Chaplin created his film *The Tramp* in 1915. As Kenneth Lynn reminds modern readers, at that moment, the daily newspapers were filled with stories about how often tramps flouted the law (150). However, increasingly, the public turned from the scare stories of the daily news and evinced a growing sympathy for the down-and-out (151). Chaplin's film *City Lights* followed *The Tramp* in 1931, and *Modern Times* appeared in 1936; his films kept Chaplin's attractive and entertaining myth of the tramp alive through all the years that Eiseley was tramping. Perhaps the Little Tramp myth arose because an enormous wave of young men were looking for work and using the rails as fast transport, or perhaps the Little Tramp myth calmed public worry enough so that the number of tramps *could* increase without arousing public invective. Hobos and hoboing had leaked into public regard so that Eiseley, and any young man in any western town, would be aware of hobos' existence and mythology as reality, ideal, language, entertainment, escape, and adventure.

Eiseley's adventures on trains coincided with a deepening interest among modernist poets and artists in the era of the troubadour poets, the "tramps" of Occitan. From 1890–1914, the growing movement called modernism toyed with the troubadours as models of what artists should be to their culture. The troubadours may not have had much in common with American hobos, but mythically, in the eyes of the "lost generation," they joined migration, art, and work. Poet Ezra Pound, who valorized the troubadours, could have connected Eiseley to these new modernist notions, because at the height of Pound's powers, he maintained the position of European editor of Harriet Monroe's *Poetry*, the same little magazine in which Eiseley sought and obtained publication in 1927.

The troubadours were at least enough on modernists' minds that in America itinerant poet Vachel Lindsay (1879–1931) walked from city to city, declaiming poetry such as "The Congo" and "General William Booth Enters into Heaven" on street corners for food. Proclaiming his poetic message, Lindsay wandered hundreds of miles in 1906 and 1912, some of them on trains; in 1928–29 *Poetry* granted Lindsay a lifetime achievement award. "Poetry must be recited — the troubadour must be revived," Conrad Aiken quotes Lindsay as saying in a short essay about Lindsay's achievement (3). The idea was, the troubadour came with an ethic derived from an occupation: wandering and dispersing art that was not mass produced. In the troubadour, modernists saw the possibility of rekindling an ethic that subverted a growing — and ultimately deadly — nationalism. But an anarchist who committed murder in Serbia led to the erasure of the modernists' hopes. It was in the aftermath of World War I that Eiseley came to hop freights, coedit the newly formed *Prairie Schooner*, and write poetry. Like a modern troubadour, he was joining vagrancy with beauty and offering his work to readers. Later, his writing about these years of wandering became enfolded in the artistry of his mature prose.

During Eiseley's early twenties, the *Prairie Schooner* gave him a publishing outlet at the University of Nebraska, where he was a student, and his early prose and some of his poetry were about hoboing. His sketches about the road, "Riding the Peddlers" and "The Mop to K. C.," appeared in 1933 and 1935 in the *Prairie Schooner*. An unpublished poem, "A Road Night, '23," includes the particularly realistic detail of cinders flying into the mouths of hobos who are riding the decks, or tops, of the boxcars (*Lost* 31–32, 47–49). Like his idol Jack London, he called the railroad in the poem by the familiar slang, *The Road*. He was only in his midtwenties when his two works of rail fiction were published; still, Eiseley's mature themes can be glimpsed in miniature in these early works.

In the short story "Riding the Peddlers," the first-person narrator, unable to hop the high-speed "manifest" freight, resigns himself to riding the "peddler," a train that stops at all small towns along a journey.[2] Because of the many stops, the peddler's timetable is irregular, for which the young writer notes "we had slipped tunnel-like through time" (*Lost* 38). The ride on the peddler becomes a train journey into a kind of Eden. The train ride *takes* time, but it is not *measured* strictly against any timetable exterior to the moving train. The train jumpers and the train are enfolded in their own universe that creates its own chronology.

To underscore the idea of the peddler as a special train, Eiseley has the brakemen kindly show the vagrant men the most comfortable cars for their passage. The rogue brakie was Eiseley's special bête noire, because he lacked the human sympathy that could help cement the primitive society of humans on the move. Says Eiseley of the peddler, "It wasn't long before we realized that we had slipped, momentarily at least, out of a world of hatred and class struggle" (35). The hobos do not know hunger because the slow train allows them to jump on and off as they pass apple orchards, where they pluck heavy fruit off fecund trees; one hobo sings a verse of "The Big Rock Candy Mountain" (38). The act of wandering as a way of knowing, timelessness, the oneness of the human family—these ideas that would come to occupy Eiseley as a mature writer — are crystallized in this early short fiction.

Eiseley's other early piece of rail fiction, "The Mop to K. C.," concerns the relation of power that governs the meetings of men on the road. In the story, a lonesome and insecure boy and an older first-person male narrator find themselves in the same boxcar on a Missouri-Pacific train ("Mop") bound for Kansas City ("K. C."). The boy approaches the older man coyly, which reveals that the boy has probably been kept at one time as a sexual object. The child, evincing a helplessness that leaves him open to abuse, snuggles against the older man and falls asleep, but not before reiterating that he is headed home. The older man, disgusted by the probable abuse of the child, by the child's own weakness, and by a world that condones the use of the weak by the strong, stays awake and muses that the boy is really headed to no destination and has no home. His meeting with the boy reminds him that there are men who are Other, that there is trouble he cannot begin to repair. As with some later works, Eiseley is concerned with civilization's refuse, its neglected and overlooked. His tone of quiet despair is the burden carried by those who are free from surveillance, cherishing that freedom while hating how some use it. The tone is one that Eiseley sounds in many of his mature essays.

Eiseley could have based his two early rail fictions on actual train jumping pursued in the late 1920s and early 1930s, or his ideas could have come from visiting the hobo camps in far western Nebraska, where the South Party of the Morrill Expedition, which Eiseley had joined, was digging fossils during the years when he was a young writer (Angyal, *Loren* 13). Later, as a mature writer, Eiseley wrote essays that frequently travel westward and backward in time as well. He rarely wrote about vagrancy; however, snippets of what Eiseley learned on the road appear in his essays of the

1950s and 1960s. His tramping days play a central role only in some famous chapters in his 1975 autobiography, *All the Strange Hours.*

All the Strange Hours is a complex book, layering a history of Eiseley's life experiences, a history of primitive humankind's development, and a history of Eiseley's own changing thoughts about being human. Despite the oversimplification to which it may lead, I chose a bouquet of chapters from Eiseley's autobiography to discuss here in terms of what being a hobo may have taught him. In "The Rat That Danced" and "The Other Player," the first and last chapters in the book, appear the "villains" of the autobiography. The first is a brakie who tries to beat a young hobo — Eiseley — to force him to fall under the wheels of a speeding train and die (7). Eiseley is able to avoid death only by the train's approach to a town (during which the brakie has to attend to the duty of stopping the train). The badly beaten young hobo is taught a life lesson by an old hobo said to be an ex-con: "men beat men," he says, intimating that violence is to be expected among the range of human encounters. The villain of the last chapter is the "Other Player," a shadow figure against whom Eiseley has himself play a game of dice from time to time throughout the autobiography (259–63). The Other Player is a consummate villain, because he tricks the younger man into thinking that hope and chance can control time's corrosive wear on the fragile lives ensconced in it. Eiseley has his youthful self-image and believes he can win against the Other Player. The older Eiseley's final epiphany is that there is no control, and the Other Player always wins. Deliberate brutality in the brakie and false hope in the dice game of life are the great villains of *All the Strange Hours*; accepting the existence of the two villains is a final milestone in human knowing.

The cruelties of the brakeman lie in Eiseley's facility with naming. He, the brakie, is a Santa Fe or a Burlington and Northern employee; the hobo is jobless. The brakeman has a home in a city at a certain address; the hobo is homeless, placeless. The brakie is worth a certain amount per annum, funds he plans to save or spend at some named future date; the hobo has no funds and plans no future. The hobo's inability to name who he is by declaring his address and net worth, at some subliminal level, is what attracts the brakie's ire. Eiseley expands on his trouble with the human need to name in another of his essays, "The Cosmic Prison" (*Invisible*). In this work, Eiseley notes our determination to affix names to all things: "A word spoken creates a dog, a rabbit, a man. It fixes their nature before our eyes, henceforth their shapes are, in a sense, our own creation. They are no longer part of the unnamed, shifting architecture of the universe" (31).

The hobo code of ethics during Eiseley's traveling years prevented one from asking the given name of a fellow traveler or speaking too precisely of one's past or one's plans (*All* 62). Actual hobos created road names for themselves: "Fry-pan Jack," "Cardboard," and "Utah Phillips" hid the versions of themselves whose names were inscribed on birth certificates, who had relatives, a past, and a culture. Hobos shared a spoken cant with which they solidified their belonging to their outsider group, and which was so colorful that some of its terms, such as "riding the rods," "bum," "working stiff," "beat it," "gay cat," and "punk," entered the common vernacular. A hobo, in passing through a town, might write his or her handle, or a sign or message, on water towers next to rail lines, or on fences and lampposts. Stringing together the record of hobo handles and signs on property through which they had passed, one can construct a narrative. The narrative is covered over and erases the pentimenti of the hobos' "real" lives for created lives, imagined lives. While the mores of travelers did not afford drifters the luxury of speaking of their pasts in historical or emotional terms, great importance was placed on the telling of stories, of enfolding their actual lives in signs and myths (Bruns 83–84). Only humankind, Eiseley would note much later, can control time by recreating the events of their lives as fictions (*Invisible* 145). In a way, the villainous brakie, freighted with a name, title, uniform, and schedule, tries to obliterate the unnamed, because the unnamed is an honest and frightening representative of chaotic forces that can wipe out human lives. But the unnamed is also the vast creative force of evolution.

The Other Player represents villainy at a sneakier level than the class hatred of the brakie. The Other Player taunts each of us because we yearn to know the future. Eiseley handles villains who tell the future in yet another essay, "Instrument of Darkness," where the true evil of Shakespeare's weird sisters in *Macbeth* is that the futures that they predict are "inflexible" (*Night*

49). Once the weird sisters predict that Macbeth will be king and that he must beware Macduff, Macbeth's imagination of what he *could be* is shrunk so that his future as a murderer becomes set. Uncertainty and the unplanned, to Eiseley, beget the constant, nervous need to create futures for ourselves, escaping planned futures that require blood. Aimless drifting, notes Eiseley, renders the human being less firmly defined, as dust is, but free also, as dust is (*Lost* 236). Uncertainty, more than positivism, is perhaps the watchword of the twentieth century. For the hobo, indeterminacy and open-endedness are necessary baggage for the journey, both the train journey into the future and the evolutionary journey of human beings. A too-close attention to names, times, and places seems to determine a future, but the determination is a lie because, for Eiseley at the end of *All the Strange Hours*, naming the future is a futile exercise.

Eiseley's villains bookend the autobiography. About a third of the way through appears a band of men who act as Eiseley thinks they should act with respect to time and to each other, and so, while they are perhaps not heroes, they may be the most human of men. The chapter is "The Most Perfect Day in the World," and it is placed at the end of the section that handles Eiseley's youth and train-jumping days, "The Days of a Drifter."

In "The Most Perfect Day," Eiseley has a group of vagrant men enjoy a lazy afternoon despite speaking different languages and coming from different ethnic backgrounds. He says that he cannot name the date of the meeting: "We were out of time, secret, hidden" (*All* 62). His companions include "an Indian, with an utterly wild face," who appears to be from the Ice Age (63); a youth who had climbed in breakneck fashion over the decks of the fast express they had ridden the night before (62); and a man who looks like a "Homeric hero" (64). Eiseley does not ask their names, because naming would drive the wedge of class difference between the travelers (62). Their namelessness, their attempts to communicate, their acceptance of one another, and their existence outside the stream of time echo thoughts from "Riding the Peddlers," written decades before (*Lost*). Published two years before his death, "The Most Perfect Day" concerns, Eiseley claims, an afternoon from the 1930s, containing references to the Ice Age and Homeric times, as well as to the scientist he was in the 1960s.

Thus, the essay folds time back on itself so that human lives separated by thousands of years can touch in Eiseley's pages.

In "The Most Perfect Day," and in other essays as well, Eiseley writes of what was impossible to measure or observe: primitive humans' life of the mind. Having experienced vagrancy himself, he moved from being a vagrant to studying and writing about the first vagrants, human hunter-gatherers. In his experience, he replicated his subjects' activities: a search for food, a desire for companionship, a fear of death. In his writings, he asks his readers to perform, with him, a leap of imagination — based on the physical experience of hoboing — to understand the psychological origins of humankind. The first hominid, he says in "How Flowers Changed the World," was a "n'er-do-well, an in-betweener . . . an outcast," because the growing savannas in Africa left the erstwhile tree-dwelling apes no trees (*Immense* 75). In Eiseley's estimation, our first step on the way to becoming modern humans was made by adopting the gait of the tramp and the vagrant. Our status as outcasts exerted the evolutionary force necessary to create our humanity out of an essentially animal frame.

Skills of survival developed by vagrants were tokens, to Eiseley, of their oneness with early hominids (*Lost* 238). In addition, among the members of the primitive social group, the deep urge to join other humans forged a society prior to words or contracts. Hunger or thirst, while not absent, did not create division among primitive societies but were mitigated by the desire to share whatever one had with members of what amounted to one extended family (*All* 63). Having been at the mercy of time and the weather, hunger and thirst, made Eiseley a better scientist. One way toward knowing primitive human societies is to enter in sympathy, beyond race and language.

Hobo "Reefer Charlie," in Jacqueline Schmidt's oral history, notes that hobos are particularly "obsessed with a desire for personal freedom" (58). My final comments on "The Most Perfect Day" concern that urge. In her history of the rise and fall of the rail industry, Sarah Gordon notes that the trains were laws unto themselves, and when hobos hopped a freight, they gained not just the ordinary freedoms taken for granted by Americans today, but a freedom of a radical order because they were in motion on a train (190–91).

Before leaving Eiseley's autobiography, a detour in early to mid-twentieth-century science may shed light on Eiseley's — and science's — complex notions concerning freedom in the 1960s and early 1970s, when Eiseley was writing his essays. "Strangeness in the Proportion," an essay in *The Night Country*, concerns freedom as a physical and intellectual property, necessary for the creation of novelty. Eiseley would have read the terms "freedom" and "creation" not so much emotionally, but rather as properties necessary for natural selection to operate. Eiseley begins with an incident in which the great anatomist William Harvey disparaged the intellectual gifts of Francis Bacon. Harvey implied that Bacon's reasoning was imprecise, somehow unscientific. Of Harvey and his ideas, Eiseley notes, "Science creates uniformity from which the mind of the individual once more flees away" (141). He counters Harvey's ideas with one of Bacon's, from Bacon's never-finished novel, "The New Atlantis": "Liberty . . . is when the direction is not restrained to some definite means, but comprehendeth all the means and ways possible" (qtd. in *Night* 133). The language here echoes hobos' notions: "a hobo has broken the mold into which society would force him," notes "Snapshot" in Schmidt's oral history (32). Dale Maharidge comments in his essay about his friendship with hobo "Montana Blackie" in *The Last Great American Hobo*: citizens "look on freights, and the hobos who ride them as some do a ship on the ocean — a carrier of fantasies" (Maharidge and Williamson 1). A ride on the rails or at sea, a primitive human group on an evolutionary journey, "The New Atlantis," *The Night Country*: all are without exact location. The train, the ship, and humans are in motion; Bacon's book is a utopia; Eiseley's *Night Country* exists only in dreams. In these places that are not places, something is left undefined, and therefore the creation of a new species or a new idea can happen.

In "Strangeness in the Proportion," when Eiseley writes that a "principle of uncertainty" holds in particle physics and also in the way the human mind at liberty works, he is referring to Heisenberg's Uncertainty Principle. Werner Heisenberg, who conceived of the principle in 1926 and who lived in a Germany heading fast toward a deadly uniformity, loved to go hiking in remote areas, to be a vagrant undefined by human community (Cassidy 134). The Uncertainty Principle states that one cannot measure a particle's velocity and position, or its exact energy at a moment in time, with accuracy (228). Heisenberg's formulation has broad philosophical implications that Eiseley seems to be applying to human thought in his essay. It is precisely trying to observe something too exactly that creates, *causes*, the greater degree of uncertainty. The particle, it seems, becomes vagrant and escapes definition, and we are made of such particles and forces.

In the late 1950s, at the height of Eiseley's powers, Watson, Crick, and their associates revealed the structure of the gene. Although the unzipping of the double-helix DNA strands seems to the curious nonscientist a very exacting process in which certain molecules always combine with certain others, it is not the case. When the cell divides, genes do not always combine or break evenly; in genetic "mistakes," the proteins the genes code for become changed, new. This is evolution in action, which Eiseley calls "genetic indeterminacy" and celebrates as the great creative force in life (*Night* 141). What cells and dust do not do, human lives should not do, and the minds of scientists should not do either. His idea about indeterminacy and creation appears like a mantra: cultivate indeterminacy, become vagrant and, like a hobo, adopt a "handle" so that no one knows your name. In that mindset of not-knowing, there, in the place that is no place, creation and a deep understanding of life are paradoxically revealed.

"Perhaps there is no meaning in it [life] at all," Eiseley wrote in one of his volumes of essays, "save that of the journey itself" (*Immense* 6). It is the "journey itself" that forces travelers to encounter, first, the environment, but next, themselves. Eiseley's allusions to other writers in his essays reveal his deep identification with wanderers: he mentions Charles Darwin's *Voyage of the Beagle* and Herman Melville's "The Encantadas" and *Moby-Dick* in the introduction he wrote for a volume of Eliot Porter prints, published by the Sierra Club. Eiseley was an expert on Darwin (whose ideas crystallized as he, Darwin, wandered); a 1962 reprint of Jack London's *Before Adam* has an epilogue by Eiseley, attesting to London's continued place in Eiseley's thoughts as he came to pen the essays he is known for. Near the end of his life, he celebrated the importance of the journey in his autobiography, its focus on indeterminacy and freedom and its hatred of entrapment and narrowness.

Halley's comet, the wanderer that travels far and then returns, remained a touchstone for Eiseley's thinking as a grown man and seemed to pattern, in fact, his own life into one which flung thought far, then reeled it back to beginnings. Eiseley recalls in an essay a long-lost night in his boyhood when his father held him in his arms, pointing to Halley's comet near its perihelion in May 1910 (*Invisible* 7). Clyde set up his son to have a rendez-vous with the cosmos. Although Loren did not live long enough to see the returning comet in 1986, he did keep the meeting with the cosmos, thinking and writing about the human relation to space and time. Halley's comet, and Eiseley's essay on his relation to the comet, "The Star Dragon" in *The Immense Journey*, is a good place to end this exploration on wandering, for Eiseley begins the essay on the comet with an image of a train.

In the essay Eiseley imagines Halley's comet as the headlight of an oncoming freight (9). The man watching the comet could be a hobo of the twentieth century, who not only stands on a hobo planet that drifts on the elliptical rails of gravity laid down by the sun, but is also a wanderer who hops that comet, the fast freight to outer space, at least in the mind. Hobos are exposed to far more stars than city dwellers, both actual and metaphori-cal. They watch the stars from the doorways of propped-open boxcars as if the doorway were a screen and the night a cosmic film. In Eiseley's youth hobos rode trains called "The Comet," after Halley's comet, which hur-ried them far from home, then rocketed them back again (New Haven). Trains and stars, stars and trains. The word "comet," for Eiseley, writing in the last half of the twentieth century, linked him with his dead father, and thus the word transported him not spatially, but temporally. For Eiseley, a lost or absent father and the attendant poverty helped initiate rambling; the lost father bothered him enough that he mentions his fatherlessness in "The Most Perfect Day" (*All* 64). For Eiseley, jumping trains seemed to form some rite of passage into manhood that the absent father could have presided over, had he been present. The act of jumping a train left behind the father's poverty, the boy's lower-class status, his aloneness in the world, but affirmed the grown son's relation to his lost father. In remembering youthful hobo days through his autobiography, the hobo returns to the father, gone in fact on a voyage of no return, but ever returning in memory.

Hobos have invented two notions to describe death. When a hobo dies, he "catches the westbound," as they say in their cant, or slang. However, Schmidt has the hobo "Steam Train Maury" say that, when a hobo dies, his or her spirit rides the tail of Halley's comet to heaven (29). The conceit is that of a wanderer. As Eiseley points out in his essays and stories about vagrant men, even as they rocketed forward on trains bound to nowhere and everywhere, their minds cast back toward home. They knew they could never return, or if they did, they could never be the same people they were when they left. But still their lips formed the syllable "home," and thus in thought at least, the elliptic was described, a perihelion reached, the return begun. As the writer of the vagrant men's stories, Eiseley knew that the twentieth century had swept him along the decades. He could never quite escape the one set of rails across which his life hurried.

Eiseley's essays replay scenes of a very American ambiguity: that sometime in our lives, we want to be free of all social encumbrances, mount our stainless-steel stallions, and head west. The figure of the hobo still attracts today. In reality, there is the dirt, the poverty, the lice, the danger, the social ostracism. And yet there are always stars and comets passing in panoply just outside the boxcar door. Loren Eiseley's essays move toward explaining how people are torn between civilization and wandering, being freighted with household and societal positions or leaving them behind. The wanderer's desire is enfolded into our culture's crude signs and symbols, chalked on gateposts. Even now, you may be listening, waiting to hop that fast express whose whistle and bell are playing an old, old tune that you have known so long, it seems as if it were in your very genes.

NOTES

I would like to thank Dr. Dean Ferguson, Dr. Wayne Gunn, Dr. Russ Huebel, Dr. Michelle Johnson-Vela, Dr. Brenda Melendy, Dr. Susan Roberson, Dr. Roberto Vela, and graduate student Raymond Garcia for insights they shared with me on an early version of this essay. My thanks also go to Mr. Michael Hess, with whom I have had the happy fortune of sharing many acts of wandering, in fact and in mind.

    1. The title of this essay is taken from 1920s-era hobo song lyrics (Sandburg 189).

    2. The manifest would have been carrying expensive goods, and therefore, for higher

security, it did not stop often, except to take on fuel or water. The goods carried would have come with a manifest, or bill of lading. The terms "hot shot" and "fast freight" also appear in Eiseley's writings about catching fast trains. If speed were desired, Eiseley might have also caught a mail train, which might have been carrying cash and therefore would have traveled under high security with few stops, or the "limited" passenger, which made a limited number of stops as well (Gordon 185–56, 273). Considered high-quality rides for boys bent on "scoring," any of these fast trains might have quickly taken Eiseley "over the hump," or across the continental divide.

3

"The Places Below"

Mapping the Invisible Universe in
Loren Eiseley's Plains Essays

SUSAN N. MAHER

During the 1940s and 1950s, essayist Loren Eiseley was conscious that he was inventing a new form of nonfiction essay, one that could embrace the depths of time that geology, evolutionary biology, and astrophysics had revealed to the modern world. Trained in anthropology, with expertise in paleontology and archaeology, Eiseley often finds himself pondering the mysteries of time and space, the shifting landscapes of epic gestation, the "strange transmutation" of cartographic imagination, and "the inner forest" of the collective unconscious (*Night* 206, 207). Positioning himself within a literary line of descent that commences with Thoreau, Eiseley aligns himself to a "new geography" that "may take humanity a generation to absorb" (208). Keenly attentive to the smallest details of life lived in the present yet inextricably connected to the past, Eiseley absorbs this truth: "Life is never fixed and stable. It is always mercurial, rolling and splitting, disappearing and re-emerging in a most unpredictable fashion" (69). How then to map this mutable, illegible space, this variable life, when we "are in a creative universe" (70)? How does one enter a landscape that always keeps something from the truth seeker, "that glistens and invites [one] from below," that keeps one "on the edge of a country," that projects "distances . . . greater than they seem," he queries in his essay "The Places Below" (17). This desire to map life's transfigurations is one of the central impulses in Eiseley's writing and would reshape the contemporary nonfiction essay.

Biographer Gale E. Christianson notes that Eiseley's invention of the "concealed essay" guides him toward an assembled form that could expand through geologic time and evolutionary history or contract focus onto a minute, ephemeral artifact of the present. This adaptable structure allows Eiseley to integrate "fictional and autobiographical material . . . merged with scientific fact, literary allusion, and poignant quotations" (Introduction xi). He is able to negotiate multiple dimensions of time and space, to meditate over vexing philosophical and scientific questions, and to connect his teeming materials to one life, one mind — Eiseley himself — in transit. Eiseley, ever aware of human frailty, incompletion, and mortality, projects the creative imagination as his most forcible counterstroke against erasure. In his imagined worlds, as Dimitri N. Breschinsky explains, "the time frame can be considerably broader, extending back indefinitely into prehistoric times. Such an atavistic experience," Breschinsky concludes, "can be breathtaking, opening up new vistas of space and long-forgotten dimensions of being" ("Reaching" 78). At the same time, Robert G. Franke argues that Eiseley charts "mythic" dimensions, "which might also be termed *sacred, primordial, infinite, cosmic, cyclical, horizontal,* or as Mircea Eliade has it, 'Great Time.'" Franke notes Eiseley's "complex view of time," in which historical and ahistorical time frames are "deftly interwoven" (147).

From an early age, Eiseley was drawn to spaces and objects that elicited his sense of multiple dimensions. Indeed, I would argue that Eiseley's formative years on the Great Plains shaped his distinctive response to the world and his ability to map "new vistas." Eiseley himself has commented on the significant alignment of time and place in 1907, his birth year, explaining that "I was born in the first decade of this century, conceived in and part of the rolling yellow cloud that occasionally raises up a rainy silver eye to look upon itself before subsiding into dust again. That cloud has been blowing in my part of the Middle West since the Ice Age" (*Night* 197). Kathleen Boardman recalls the author's early years, when "he spent hours exploring the fields, hedgerows, and wooded creeks at the edge of town," bonding with place. Eiseley would remember these early years "vividly," Boardman continues, and the map of that formative, childhood geography underlies many of his most significant essays. "In later writings," she elucidates, "he referred to himself as a son of the middle border, descendant of pioneer immigrants" ("Loren Eiseley," *Dictionary* 130). As a teenager, Eiseley took to the rails, hoboing across the American West, expanding his map of place. At both the University of Nebraska and the University of Kansas, he joined field expeditions that took him from the Badlands of western Nebraska to Doniphan and Smith Counties in northeastern and north-central Kansas. In the late nineteenth and early twentieth centuries, the Great Plains had begun to reveal its ancient secrets to bone hunters, and by the 1930s and 1940s anthropologists were seeking knowledge of the earliest Plains tribes from the vestiges of old camp and burial sites. Eiseley entered this scientific query at its inception and heyday, and his encounters on the Plains landscape, particularly of western Nebraska, ignited his literary imagination. Indeed, the poems and prose writings of this period, as Christianson has documented, give a hint of the future writer and the "concealed essay" form (Introduction). In these early writings, grounded in his experience on the Great Plains, Eiseley explores the cartographic and cosmological entry points where the past, present, and future conflate.

Eiseley's distinctive approach set the stage for an innovative "map of the imagination," the nascent narrative design of what William Least Heat-Moon would eventually call the deep map. Randall Roorda, noting the emergence of deep-map writing, discerns that a "rift between subjective familiarity and objectified cartography has widened in modern times, and nonfiction writers on nature have sought to dramatize this antimony." The dynamic space between subjective and objective measures of landscape and other realities — what Roorda calls "this sedimentation of impressions" — underlies many of Eiseley's meditative essays. Roorda also notes the deep map's many foci; as genre, it "is marked by attention to the ways in which the smallest, most closely circumscribed locale eventuates from the deepest recesses of time and is subject to attention in the most diverse, disparate terms from the widest array of perspectives" (259). Many-faceted narrative marks Eiseley's experimentation in the concealed essay, an early expression of deep-map writing.

In the genesis of this environmental genre, Eiseley's somatic forays underground, on the water, on the rails, into homesteads, and through dark tunnels in search of the "invisible" universe loom large. Kent Ryden has argued that "an essay of place is a trial, an attempt — an attempt to lay bare the meaning of a place. It is a trying out of narratives, of possible interpretations; it is an earnest stab at the difficult work of making maps speak, of turning names into stories." To capture the essence of place, its many layerings and unseen landscapes, Ryden argues that the modern essayist is "at once a cartographer, a landscape painter, a photographer, an archivist, and a folklorist, as well as a storyteller" (251). He recognizes the significant accomplishment of Eiseley's translation of place:

> Place grows out of life and sustains life, as Eiseley comes to understand; it provides a stable imaginative refuge from change and flux. It pins down and organizes images and history, preventing memory from becoming random, identity from becoming episodic and fragmented. Time alters and transforms the world and the self; geography shifts and scrambles; landscapes scrape off old familiar surfaces and accrete new ones in a sort of fantastically accelerated man-made process of erosion and sedimentation.... Place anchors the filament of continuity which runs through our lives, providing a richly evocative connection to the pasts which create us. (266)

Formative experiences on the Great Plains helped Eiseley distill the essence of a new geography, a new literary cartography. Eiseley uses the Plains landscape as a platform on which to stage his deeper mapping of time, space, and mutability. At the same time, he elicits a unique telling of the Plains, one that counters openness and horizon, that privileges the vertical dimension over the horizontal. Eiseley's Plains sensibility is nuanced and downward glancing, the opposite of panoramic. A born digger, Eiseley explores the hidden pockets of the expansive grasslands, the cavernous spaces and inverted canyons, the sunken river beds and concave bone yards, where the past reveals itself. In plumbing rather than scanning, Eiseley challenges a vista-and-sky representation of the Plains surface and offers instead a complex reading of interiors, foldings, and chasms.

The deeper landscape of the Plains guided Eiseley throughout his literary explorations, which are at once intensely personal and subjective, despite their "raiment of science" (Christianson, Introduction xi). As Jack Fischer, Eiseley's editor, notes, the Eiseley essay "moves in the borderland between science, religion, philosophy, and poetry; this is terrain of the first importance, but it is difficult country and the reader needs to be led into it slowly and carefully" (qtd. in Christianson, *Fox* 282). Eiseley's deep mapping crosses genres, an unfamiliar nonfiction narrative concept in the 1940s and 1950s. Landscape that is itself a series of cultural, biological, and geologic cross-sections demands new treatment. A signature movement in Eiseley's essays is to begin at a moment of intimate encounter and to journey from there into an expansive meditation of scientific or meta-physical, cosmological significance. Perhaps a memory jars a connection or a physical, somatic experience releases the synthesizing imagination; sensuous engagement, often at the borders of culture and the wild, provides an initial measure of familiarity and assurance before Eiseley plumbs the deeper recesses of his story. As Boardman explains, his essays move "from the specific to the abstract, emphasizing vivid images rather than abstract theories. This technique allows an audience to join Eiseley vicariously on his journey of discovery" ("Loren Eiseley: *Immense*" 35). In moving through multiple dimensions, Eiseley charts his revelations and attempts a clearer map of meaning than "the maps we carry in our separate pockets," with their "contradictory . . . indecipherable" landscapes (*Night* 75).

In Eiseley's writings, one sees the genre of the deep map coalescing. His essays combine many of the features we now recognize in deep-map writing, particularly that from the Great Plains: personal, somatic experience guiding one into a landscape; multiple spatial and temporal measures in critical, creative dialogue; vertical exploration of a horizontal terrain illuminating cross-sections of natural, national, and personal history; a reflective tenor of loss that leads to the retrieval of lost worlds and honors vestiges of the past; and an ecocritical viewpoint that assesses humankind's impact on and place in the natural world. An essayist of unusual grace and powerful imagination, he reinvigorates, revisions, and remaps the Great Plains essay of place and, by extension, the American nature essay. He invents a methodology that would find later adherents in Wallace Stegner, William Least Heat-Moon, John Janovy Jr., and other deep mappers from the Plains and beyond.

Early essays such as "The Slit" and "The Flow of the River," published in *The Immense Journey* in 1957, establish Eiseley's modus operandi. Late in his career, Eiseley was still working to perfect his signature approach in arguably his greatest collection, *The Night Country*, from 1971. Among his most noteworthy Plains essays in this collection, "The Places Below" and "The Relic Men" provide a toehold into Eiseley's complex consciousness, the "two worlds" (among many) that existed from his boyhood to late manhood, forming his intellectual peregrinations, his walks "from one world to the other by day and by night" through "invisible boundaries" (196). Throughout a long, productive career, Eiseley returned to the rich soils of his youthful past, the material and cultural landscape of the Plains. The interface between the physical and the imagined, between sensuous stimuli and interior response, defines his preferred contact zone in which to generate ideas and connections.

"The Slit" begins with an appraisal of landscape, of a "flat and grass-covered," seemingly eternal sun-touched prairie as it abuts an outcrop-ping "of naked sandstone and clay" (*Immense* 3). Eiseley's senses are on heightened alert, seeking the dark recesses where time's artifacts reveal themselves to his creative imagination. In this border landscape, he dis-covers the slit, a point of entrance into deep time.

Eiseley sees the slit in Styx-like terms, a liminal passageway between the living and the dead, between the real and the dreamlike phantoms of lost worlds. Suddenly the sky itself morphs into a new timescape, and Eiseley becomes aware of "some future century I would never see" (4). Time becomes surreal for him; the borders between the past, present, and future dissolve in his descent. The slit of the present becomes a port key into a world tens of millions of years old. Here Eiseley discovers the skull of an early mammal, a "shabby little Paleocene rat," also a creature of grasslands (8). The oreodont skull belies its deadness, becoming for Eiseley all of those adapting and surviving species that culminate in his humanity and his moment on the Plains. In the nexus of place, Eiseley comments, "I had come a long way down since morning; I had projected myself across a dimension I was not fitted to traverse in the flesh" (11). The same can be said of the physical remainders of the "shabby pseudo-rat." Yet both signify life on the Plains, the life of "sunlight and . . . grass" that stretches across epochs (10).

In this Plains landscape, Eiseley also discovers the mappable nature of flesh and the body. Part of the landscape through time is embedded in the

DNA of flora and fauna. As the basic component of life, in contact with the physical challenges of emplacement, of living in place, DNA charts a succession of evolutionary history. Evolutionary biology finds that early grassland mammals and modern humans share a cellular deep map. As Eiseley elucidates, "Though he was not a man, nor a direct human ancestor, there was yet about him, even in the bone, some trace of that low, snuffling world out of which our forebears had so recently emerged. The skull lay tilted in such a manner that it stared, sightless, up at me as though I, too, were already caught a few feet above him in the strata and, in my turn, were staring upward at that strip of sky which the ages were carrying farther away from me beneath the tumbling debris of falling mountains" (5). Stirred by this revelation, Eiseley acknowledges "that we are all potential fossils still carrying within our bodies the crudities of former existences, the marks of a world in which living creatures flow with little more consistency than clouds from age to age" (6). Despite their ephemerality, though, living bodies preserve a history of adaptation to place and even reflect the chemical components of place. The prairie-dog towns of the modern grasslands continue this mammalian journey. So, too, do the towns and highways of modern humans. Where these modern species will end up is a mystery, but both carry the map of the future in their bones. Rodents and primates took different evolutionary paths on the grasslands, but in the slit Eiseley holds them up together, signifiers of chance and connection.

The slit contains the passing show of grassland life, the deep map of many worlds, distant and near, bound together yet separate and distinct. The slit also embodies the starker truth of history. Thinking of the oreodont, Eiseley remarks, "Like the wisteria on the garden wall he is rooted in his particular century. Out of it — forward or backward — he cannot run" (11). Eiseley is similarly circumscribed. What releases him — and by extension the oreodont — from time's arrow is the synthesizing mind capable of producing a multifaceted, multilayered narrative, inspired by Eiseley's vertical descent. From a "remote age near the beginning of the reign of mammals," Eiseley charts an "immense, at times impossible," journey (11, 12). Eiseley tells the reader that this particular record is one of many "prowlings of one mind which has sought to explore, to understand, and to enjoy the miracles of this world" (12). It is also a journey that demonstrates humanity's integral connection to the natural world, a connection that allows each person to "possess" a "wilderness" from which to observe "marvels" (13). Ultimately, though, the new map he conjures up must remain incomplete; our ability to see into the mystery of all things is limited. As Eiseley discerns our voyage, we "have joined the caravan, you might say, at a certain point; we will travel as far as we can, but we cannot see all that we would like to see or learn all that we hunger to know" (12). The places below, like the slit, can give us only a starting point into unknown country, a commencement point into an ever-vanishing and changing landscape.

Peter Heidtmann, in his study *Loren Eiseley: A Modern Ishmael*, emphasizes Eiseley's intimate exploration of landscapes, real and imagined. As a "literary naturalist," Eiseley had a long apprenticeship. As a boy in Nebraska, he forayed "into geographical wilderness areas." However, his "most significant wilderness" as an adult "was the realm where the individual soul encounters the world" (50). As "The Slit" and "The Flow of the River" demonstrate, Eiseley's sense of the world is complex, multidimensional, and abetted by physical immersion in the dynamic edge of place. While the Mauvaise Terres — the Badlands — receive much attention in *The Immense Journey*, "The Flow of the River" reminds us that Eiseley's landscapes range from the cavernous abysses of sewers and underground cavities to the riverine and grasslands ecosystems of past and present. His essays map the diverse landscapes of his Plains years in Nebraska and Kansas, connecting the Paleozoic depths to the quaternary years of modern humans. In the Platte River, Eiseley touches all of this deep history.

Ephemerality and mutability are writ large on the surface of moving water. Whether a rain puddle or the deepest ocean, water in Eiseley's appraisal is "magic," a medium on which life itself is in translation (*Immense* 15). Eiseley presents a naturalist's baptism in "The Flow of the River," his recollection of a High Plains day in the Platte River. He frames his experience as extraordinary, "once in a lifetime," when "whole eons . . . might pass in a single afternoon without discomfort." Water's atomic structure "reaches everywhere," Eiseley muses. "It touches the past and prepares the future." Like the earth medium of "The Slit," the Platte River enfolds temporal and spatial dimensions and transports the author's imagination across an entire continent. In this particular cartographical essay, Eiseley first maps the contours of the Platte and "the extension of shape by osmosis" (16). Then, in a colder season on the Platte watershed, he collects a river dweller, an old catfish, and removes it to a tank in his city basement. The fish, embodying a cellular deep map, surprises Eiseley with unexpected knowledge of place.

Before Eiseley's appropriation of this fish, however, he must become the fish in his imagination, indeed become all of the fauna and the very earth that supports life. Usually fearful of the water, Eiseley uncharacteristically trusts his body to the water's energy and experiences "the meandering roots of a whole watershed," his fingers "touching, by some kind of clairvoyant extension, the brooks of snow-line glaciers at the same time that you were flowing toward the Gulf over the eroded debris of worn-down mountains" (16). At this moment, Eiseley slips into "a philosophical category of daydream" that Gaston Bachelard calls "intimate immensity" (183). In a sense, he has entered in Bachelardian terms the vast "non-I" of the river and the life it supports in his somatic encounter (188).

The Platte River, its north and south branches originating in the Rockies, cuts into the foundations of three major mountain-building orogenies spanning hundreds of millions of years. The "vast tilted face of the continent" that Eiseley rides carries the vestiges of former worlds (19). The "grain by grain, mountain by mountain" texture of river and bank, urged eastward and then southward to the Gulf of Mexico, provides an expansive view of the watershed. Spatially, Eiseley imaginatively merges into North America; temporally he is "streaming over ancient sea beds thrust aloft where giant reptiles had sported." He is "wearing down the face of time and trundling cloud-wreathed ranges into oblivion." Amid detritus of modern and old — "the broken axles of prairie schooners and the mired bones of mammoth" — he becomes the element. In one of Eiseley's most recognizable moments, he declares "I *was* water and the unspeakable alchemies that gestate and take shape in water" (19). As in "The Slit," Eiseley's humanity becomes decentered, and he imagines the evolutionary and geologic processes that produce and destroy life, the forces of adaptation that connect humankind to various life forms and that presage *Homo sapiens'* demise: "I, too, was a microcosm of pouring rivulets and floating driftwood gnawed by the mysterious animalcules of my own creation. I was three fourths water, rising and subsiding according to the hollow knocking in my veins: a minute pulse like the eternal pulse that lifts Himalayas and which, in the following systole, will carry them away" (20). Eiseley acutely understands the passage of life on these Plains, which is paradoxically both ephemeral and connected to the deep past, bridging all time.

In another season, Eiseley journeys to one of the Platte's tributaries. The landscape, frozen, "stark and ice-locked," is disorienting; "the willow thickets made such an array of vertical lines against the snow," he explains, "that tramping through them produces strange optical illusions and dizziness" (21). Strangeness frequently projects Eiseley into unexpected insight or connection. Caught in a block of "wind-ruffled" ice lies a huge catfish such as accompanied Eiseley the day he flowed with the river. Trapped or bedazzled into its predicament, the catfish suggests a sudden intimacy between the human and the piscine worlds, between "bleak, whiskered face" and clean-shaven scientist, both mortal and stuck in time. "Struck by a sudden impulse," Eiseley removes the fish to his car and brings him home "to test the survival qualities of high-plains fishes" (22). This impulse foretells a new immense journey, one that makes science the essence of artful imagination.

Back in the city, the catfish surprises Eiseley. As the ice melts, the catfish awakens from hibernation, "the selective product of the high continent and the waters that pour across it." Unlike introduced cattle that die "standing upright in the drifts" of "prairie blizzards," the catfish is the progeny of species adaptation through deep time in a particular place. For the winter, housed in a tank and placed in a basement, the catfish accepts with docility its existence. Come spring, however, the fish surprises again. Pushed by "a migratory impulse or perhaps sheer boredom," the catfish leaps from its tank and dies on the floor. Animated with Eros and instinct, it "gambles" in a dramatic leap and loses all (23). Its symbolic movement — a leap of faith — invokes Eiseley's penchant for telescoping temporal and spatial dimensions: "A million ancestral years had gone into that jump . . . a million years of climbing through prairie sunflowers and twining in and out through the pillared legs of drinking mammoth" (24). The leap, like his day of floating on the river, opens up landscapes for Eiseley, brings past, present, and future into "the momentary shape I inhabit," he muses. Once again, he sees "fin and reptile foot" etched in his hand. Fish body, scientist's body: they are overlays of a deeper, longer landscape and contain the imprint of a "mysterious principle known as 'organization'" (26).

Across his career, Eiseley returned obsessively to questions of life's origins, to life's patterns and illegible plans, to explorations of deep time and space. As he writes in "The Creature from the Marsh," "my sense of time is so heightened that I can feel the frost at work in stones, the first creeping advance of grass in a deserted street" (*Night* 158). Confronted with "carved sarcophagi" and other vestiges of older human life, he can "hurl the mind still backward into the wilderness where man coughs bestially and vanishes into the shape of beasts" (158–59). *The Night Country* presents his lifelong journey as a "student of artifact" — the telling, illuminating object in context — that brings "melancholy," paradoxical secrets, and knowledge of life's ephemerality and deep time's passage (80–81). This collection retrieves vivid memories — if doctored and artfully heightened — of Eiseley's early years on the Plains. Once again, he returns to childhood haunts and to the semiarid stretches of western Nebraska.

Night Country itself takes many forms — a storm sewer's enclosure, the dark recesses of a childhood home, a grandmother's kitchen, the canyoned spaces of skyscrapered cities, the Guadalupe country of New Mexico — and Eiseley's mature essays range over varied intertextual materials, from Francis Bacon to Charles Darwin and from Robert Louis Stevenson to Walter de la Mare. An entire lifetime's experience crams into this collection, but that singular existence becomes Eiseley's jumping-off point into terra incognita, into "that vast sprawling emergent, the universe, and its even more fantastic shadow, life" (202). The borderland between common day and Night Country — what Christianson calls "a dialogue at two levels of consciousness" — provides Eiseley with an interface of rich portent (*Fox* 412).

"The Places Below," the second essay in Eiseley's last collection, begins
with this admonition: "If you cannot bear the silence and the darkness, do
not go there; if you dislike black night and yawning chasms, never make
them your profession." The darkness and its attendant sounds, smells, and
visual shadows hide knowledge and desire, however, and for this reason
the curious, the voyagers of Night Country, will "be drawn to it by cords
of fear and longing" (15). Eiseley cannot ignore the call of the dark; it is
a siren song he has acknowledged since childhood.

Cellars and sewers are this essay's portals into temporal depth. Eiseley remembers "an old, warm farmhouse" on the edge of the Plains, at
the interface between civility and the wild. The normalcy of the farmhouse — "where people rock on the porch in the starry evening" — belies
its terrifying cellar (16). This dark space "seems ordinary at first glance,"
he explains, but descending the stairs one becomes aware of "damp" air,
"a faint sulphur smell," even the "living rock" out of which the stairs are
cut. The cellar is "a little deeper than some," and this depth gives one the
impression of a mythical entrance to some monster's den or perhaps to
Hell itself. "You go zigzagging and sliding," Eiseley remarks, "through some
accidental tremendous fissure torn in the bowels of the earth." Instead, the
cellar passage ends at the aquifer, a lovely "vast, blue chamber that glistens
and invites you from below" (17). The water seems to hide an elusive Blue
Room, a space that obsesses the owner, who has "been watchin' my whole
life an' I'm never going to see it all" (18).

To the owner, the "cold blue" is a living essence, a fluid monster that rises
and falls in mysterious cycles, always threatening his home and existence.
But apocalypse never comes. Instead, an unfathomable equilibrium, a
perplexing treaty exists between home and the watery tunnel, between
Plains land and the aquifer below, between light and dark. Eiseley perceives
another dimension: "It is part of the places below. And whether the places
below lie in the dark of an old cellar or in the crypts and recesses of the
mind, or whether they are a glimmering reflection of both together," is
veiled and uncharted. The scientific mind notes as well the evolutionary
adaptations to such spaces: "There are blind fish that have chosen this
world and prefer to live there. There are crickets as white as the fungi under

rotting boards. There are bats that turn their little goblin faces uneasily in the glow of your lamp and squeak down at you protestingly" (18). The cellar is an ecosystem with its own peculiar geography and natural history. But it is also Night Country for Eiseley, where time and space fold and expand in his imagination.

In the third section of "The Places Below," Eiseley shifts to his childhood and "the dripping labyrinth that underlies [city] streets." Above, the sun lights up the city landscape, the quotidian world of human activity; below Eiseley becomes a nocturnal creature attuned to aural and tactile clues in the darkened "hollow maze of tubes" (19). With his childhood friend, a boy called the Rat, Eiseley searches these chambers, "undertheground," with rodent-like energy and quickness (20). The Rat leads his pack, like a latter-day Tom Sawyer, into imaginative play. They are all cavemen or a rat pack or some other cast of characters in the Rat's mind. Charismatic and persuasive, he initiates the boy Eiseley into undertheground and pro-vokes his protégé's time-traveling imagination. The Rat, a creature of the moment, never learns Eiseley's trick of "tele[scoping] fifty thousand years" and returning to the early twentieth century or of projecting ahead to some postapocalyptic future, when "men may sometime live in the ruins of New York" (21). In his mind's eye, Eiseley connects undertheground to the Neanderthal past and to a sci-fi future; the sewer world gives pas-sage to all time.

The Neanderthals lost their cave-protected world, and Eiseley and the Rat would lose theirs too. The sewer world, like the cellar, has its dangers. Water, one of Eiseley's trickster elements, is among them. The antithesis of "The Flow of the River," this later essay posits another kind of water journey — into oblivion where time stops for the once living. Storm sewers are large enough to carry the flooding waters of rain bursts out of the city and back into the watershed. One day Eiseley and the Rat find themselves deep in the sewers when water begins to rise, "a little murmuring in the water, a little whisper, a little complaint" that foretells disaster. "We were only ten years old," Eiseley remembers, "and suddenly this place was very narrow and we were tired of playing like men" (22). The expansive land-scape of the imagination contracts, and all the two boys can think about is survival. Undertheground becomes potential burial ground. The boys find their way out, but before a month has passed, the Rat dies "of some casual childhood illness" (25). The irony of escaping watery death only to succumb to a disease is not lost on Eiseley.

Near the end of his life, Eiseley reexamines this childhood play and underscores its significance. The places below give space to Eiseley's desires. To enter them is to be "filled with . . . backward yearning" (26). Such cavernous retreats fill him with love and fear. What expands the imagination also threatens with destruction. Womb becomes grave. Eiseley balances in the dynamic edge between dimensions, because in the cusp he finds transmutation, imaginative passage across space and time. Yet his experience in "The Places Below" is vividly somatic, expressed through physical contact only the mortal body can provide.

The mortal world is not without its frustrations, as the opening of "The Relic Men" makes clear. Eiseley recreates an encounter between his professor persona and a flock of reporters seeking a story with "human interest." Science itself is not interesting enough, and they want none of "that Pleistocene business" (107). The professor and the reporters talk at cross-purposes. The reporters want a dramatic story, nature red in tooth and claw. Finally, they settle on a photograph. "It's about the only way to get any human interest into a science like this," a reporter explains. While waiting for the photographer, the professor/Eiseley relishes the quiet, "the High Plains silence that has swallowed a quarter of your lifetime," he muses to himself. In second-person voice, Eiseley continues, "You sigh, and your knees feel unaccountably weak. You sit on the edge of the trench and press your hands into the warm soil. The thing is out of your hands now" (108). In touching the Plains ground, Eiseley returns to memory grounded in wind, dust, and hardscrabble country "of topsy-turvy, where great dunes of sand blew over ranch houses and swallowed them, and where, after the sand had all blown away from under your feet, the beautiful arrowheads of ice-age hunters lay mingled with old whiskey bottles that the sun had worked upon" (109). Artifacts, vestiges of the near past and the far past, propel him into two stories that merge human time scales.

The second section of "The Relic Men" recalls a peculiar encounter with an aging pioneer in love with "an oddly shaped lump of mineral matter" that he calls a "petrified woman" (114). Eiseley and his colleague, Mack, learn about this petrified woman at a barbershop. Sitting in "an 1890 chair," Eiseley, his face covered with lather, overhears an odd conversation. Attuned to any talk that might reveal the presence of ancient bones or artifacts, Eiseley comments, "You can hear a lot of odd conversations in barbershops, particularly in the back country, and particularly if your trade makes you a listener, as mine does. But what caught my ear at first was something about stone. Stone and bone are pretty close in my language and I wasn't missing any bets." The field season for Eiseley's expedition has proven miserable: "The institution for which we worked had received a total of one Oligocene turtle and a bag of rhinoceros bones" (109). Pricked by a gambler's instinct, Eiseley determines to seek out the old codger hiding his petrified woman.

Throughout "The Relic Men," Eiseley resorts to images and language that connect to the pioneer West, the movement that brought his own people to the Plains. His prose, as well, echoes the tall tales, extended hyperbole, and cynicism of American humorists such as Mark Twain, Artemus Ward, and Ambrose Bierce. "The Relic Men" is funny in its poignancy, for the Old West is quickly dying, and the replacement culture, signified by the shallow journalists of the opening scene, is lacking depth. The human time frame promotes rapid change, which might explain old Buzby's fierce protection of his "beautiful" petrified woman (114).

As a relic man, Eiseley seeks knowledge of much older worlds. He knows from experience that chance encounters in the present can prove enormously illuminating of the deep past. "You can never tell what will turn up in the back country," he explains. "Once I had a mammoth vertebra handed to me with the explanation that it was a petrified griddle cake." Despite skepticism, Eiseley hopes that the petrified woman might turn into "a mastodon's femur." In a thin season of digging for ancient mammals and signs of prehistoric humans, Eiseley decides that the petrified woman is too tempting a story to ignore. The men in the barbershop insist that it was "a *whole* woman" somewhere out in the back country, so Eiseley drags a reluctant Mack to visit the old bachelor and seek "that shiny bony vision in my head" (110).

The tarpaper shack that is old Buzby's abode is an untouched, decaying relic of the brief pioneer years. Set against an ancient landscape, where "the wind had been blowing . . . since time began," it speaks to the ramshackle nature of dreams, the corrosive effects of neglect, madness, and empty westering myths: "There was a rusty pump in the yard and rusty wire and rusty machines nestled in the lee of a wind-carved butte. Everything was leaching and blowing by degrees, even the tarpaper on the roof." When the old pioneer emerges from his sad-sack home, Eiseley notes with discernment that Buzby is no run-of-the-mill homesteader, with "starved hounds" and eyes flaming with hope that his relic is special or his land aflood with oil. Buzby elicits dignity, shabby gentility. "He was small and neat," Eiseley remembers, "and wore — I swear it — pince-nez glasses. I could see at a glance," he concludes, "that he was a city man dropped, like a seed, by the wind" (111). Though the trajectory of the story leads to the relic men's disappointment — the petrified woman is only a concretion — Buzby, a relic of a nearer age, fascinates. Eiseley, alert to the poignant, telling details of Buzby's life, sees a "man clinging to order in a world where the wind changed the landscape before morning, and not even a dog could help you contain the loneliness of your days" (112). Within the human world, time rushes by and change takes place daily, and only civilization's order can slow the sense of loss.

As Eiseley and Mack extend their visit, they become aware of the man's tenuous hold on life. Following him outside to walk through canyon land to the petrified woman, Eiseley hears the wind again, "flaking and blasting at every loose stone or leaning pinnacle," steadily eroding the place and sculpturing "pipy concretions" that stand "teetering on wineglass stems" (113–14). Even the earth feels tenuous against this ancient wind. The petrified woman is a product of the wind, a facsimile of humanity, with "bumps in the right places, and a few marks that might be a face." From the beginning, Eiseley knew this quest was abortive. The petrified woman, as a relic of desire, goes up in smoke. To the isolated Buzby, however, she remains a glamorous object of desire. "She — she's beautiful, isn't she?" he blurts, and at this point Eiseley's pity and humanity take hold, and he lies: "'It's remarkable,' I said. 'Quite remarkable.'" His colleague, Mack, backs away from "such painful hope" (114).

Still, the two younger men take the petrified woman with them, at Buzby's insistence: "Only I don't want her in a glass case where people can stare at her." A few days later, they jettison the curvaceous concretion into "the canyon of the big Piney, a hundred miles away" (116). The intensely uncomfortable encounter with the crazed old man — an exaggeration of relic men and other doomed questers — is too much for the young scientists. As the petrified woman breaks to pieces in the canyon, Eiseley feels regret. Mack replies sensibly, "The old geezer won't know" (117). A hundred miles to Valentine, Nebraska, Eiseley takes over the wheel, and tries to put this story to bed. But he knows he has been complicit with the old man's dream, with the taste of desire, with the wind-induced madness of loneliness and imagination.

The third section of "The Relic Men" picks up on this note of extremism, though this time the focus is on religious fundamentalism. Relic men in the field have to deal with all kinds of people. Many of them detest bone hunters, scientists who discredit their idea of creation, their belief in the literal rather than poetic truth within the creation stories of Genesis. Connected with notions of "the missing link," bone hunters are "apt to appear triumphantly waving the thigh bone of some creature not mentioned in Holy Writ" (117). Again, Eiseley proceeds with humor, often self-deprecating, but with an edge. As in Buzby's story, the story of Mr. Mullens examines current life on the Plains and finds it distressing to one seeking greater knowledge of the world, past, present, and future. Eiseley suggests that often the only sane response to human ignorance is laughter, but laughter that often kicks back at himself.

The Mullens family lives in canyon country, too, amid the Wildcat Hills of western Nebraska. Eiseley and his field director approach Mr. Mullens after reading a newspaper account about "the only impressive bone in the whole county — a veritable giant of a bone." The catch: it "was owned by a devout member of a sect which lent no ear to modern geological heresies" (118). Eiseley's essay suggests that those who survive in such wind-blasted country often fix themselves tenaciously to extreme visions or beliefs, like prophets of old in the wilderness. Still, Mrs. Mullens's announcement to her husband that "Relic men" are at the door suggests the arrival of a different kind of prophet, aligned with modern science. Relics, in a religious sense, are believed to be sacred objects, even if that belief is sometimes misapprehended or foolish. Eiseley plays with this ambivalent casting of the word "relic" and gently mocks the notion that he is a "Relic" man. At the same time, the deep history of creation edges into sacred space and time, and Eiseley's essay examines deep-time artifacts as oracles of an unorthodox sort.

Mr. Mullens, like old Buzby, defies the stereotype of an extremist. Eiseley sees the "merry, wondering, wandering eye of the born naturalist." Despite his anti-Darwinian sect, Mr. Mullens cannot help but respond to "some wind out of the Pliocene." He is excited to show the director and Eiseley his fabulous bone: "He swept the parlor curtain aside. A great brown bone, seamed with the weather onslaughts of more than a million years, stood upright on a pedestal behind the curtain." The director and Eiseley perceive a significant find, the vestige "of vanished mammoth and mastodon" (119). Mr. Mullens proudly calls it his "elyphant," imagining instead the modern animal, killed when God flooded the earth and then saved only Noah and his ark. The juxtaposition of scientists and fundamentalist gives the story its comical edge, but not at the expense of either party. Surprisingly, these modern antagonists cooperate in this tale.

Found twenty years before, the bone is now separated from the quarry of origin. Mr. Mullens must retrace his steps to the excavation site, a prospect that dims the relic men's hopes. Would they be facing another petrified woman disappointment? What if Dad Mullens's yarn is just a tall tale within Eiseley's own version of a tall tale? The quest for the quarry site turns into a near Keystone-cops slapstick comedy, as the group "drove over sand banks and up dry arroyos." "We rose and fell over short grass prairie," Eiseley chronicles. "We lowered fence wire and intruded on the privacy of range cattle so remote from civilization that they never went to market. We came at last to a barrier of stony hills" (121). Their journey across rugged High Plains terrain has seemingly stopped. The hills ahead appear endless, and Eiseley's hopes dim on such a chimerical quest. At the point of greatest despair, however, Mullens shouts "Hallelujah!" In the transcendent glow of late afternoon sun, the director and Eiseley perceive "five million years of the planet's history lying there on that hillside with the yucca growing over it and the roots working through it, just the way the old man had remembered it from a day long ago in the sun." Strange bedfellows, the scientists and the fundamentalist rejoice in this conflation of past and present. Amazed at the profusion of ancient bones — tusked elephants, "bear-dog carnivores," "shovel-tusked amebelodont" — Eiseley proclaims, "I tell you I saw it with my own eyes and I knew, even as I looked at it, that I would never see anything like it again" (122). Resting on the surface, deep history lies exposed. The places below have revealed, at least partially, their secrets.

A contemporary of Eiseley's in the 1940s, John K. Wright of the American Geographical Society presented a ringing presidential address titled "*Terrae Incognitae*: The Place of the Imagination in Geography." Delivered in December 1946, Wright's address lauds practitioners of the imagination, for "the imagination not only projects itself into *terrae incognitae* and suggests routes for us to follow, but also plays upon those things that we discover and out of them makes imaginative conceptions which we seek to share with others" (4). Wright highlights cartography among the subdisciplines of geography and notes that "this is an almost completely virgin field for ingenious experimentation" (13). In the 1940s Eiseley began his own ingenious experimentation in deep-map writing. Inspired by the geographical particularities of a formative Plains landscape, Eiseley invented new narrative routes for his readers to follow. Late in his career, he continued to ponder the places below, the terrae incognitae of deeper history, both human and natural. Eiseley's narrative explorations of complicated passages, juxtaposed realities, and unsounded landscapes remain ambiguous to the end. Mysteries and darkness remain, terrae incognitae truncated and incompletely exposed and illuminated. At the end of "The Relic Men," Eiseley remarks on the encroaching darkness in the Wildcat Hills. Old Mullens, now dead, takes his "small, tight world of marvels," his set religious traditions, to the grave. Eiseley himself ponders the fate of modern relic men, bone hunters, who are at heart "lonely people." In mapping the cross-sections of histories, in delving deeply into time and space, relic men unseat themselves. Deep mapping, as a project, necessarily unsettles, sets one adrift in the world. In pursuing ingenious, imaginative narration, in creating a new literary cartography, a bone man like Eiseley paradoxically loses his bearings. "Perhaps, in the end," Eiseley offers, "we did not know where we belonged." The reporter and photographer return at essay's end to declaim, ironically, on human interest. Their narrow vision — *"Stand right there and point. It's the best sort of human interest, you and that bone. Just keep pointing"* — exists in stark contrast to the aims of a deep mapper, a surveyor of the invisible, enigmatic, and illegible places below (123).

4

Unearthing Urban Nature

Loren Eiseley's Explorations
of City and Suburb

MICHAEL A. BRYSON

Loren Eiseley used the compelling landscapes of his native Great Plains as well as the arid West as both setting and subject for his poetic yet scientifically rigorous explorations of evolution, natural history, and the human condition. But as a literary naturalist, Eiseley also mined the urban environment for inspiration and recognized the importance of analyzing nature close at hand in city and suburb in a rapidly urbanizing world, in which more than 50 percent of the world's population now lives in cities.

This essay explores how the physical environment and natural history of city and suburb serve multiple (and sometimes conflicting) functions in Eiseley's prose and poetry. At times Eiseley depicts the city as a dark, fearful wasteland, a place in which the contrast between a benign natural world and an oppressive built environment is rendered in stark terms. In other instances Eiseley finds insight into biological evolution and the human condition in everyday encounters with natural entities — birds, mammals, insects, even wind-borne seeds — during his urban travels by train or on foot. In this regard, contact with and awareness of nature in the city becomes an important means of establishing a sense of place and validating the ecological worth of the urban landscape and the organisms therein, however common or marginal the latter may be. Alternatively, Eiseley fashions the city into a powerful metaphor of humanity's global environmental impact — a potent symbol and unsettling literal expression of the human species' exponential growth and consumption of natural resources. Yet Eiseley's city landscape is also a setting haunted by visions of decay and decline, of a crumbling technological civilization succumbing to the inevitable forces of nature reclaiming dominion.

Eiseley's evocations of the urban environment thus reveal some of the contradictions and ambiguities our culture maintains about the character of cities. On one hand is the notion of the city as the antithesis of nature, a formulation that creates both an illusion of technology-mediated independence from the natural world and a profound yet often unfulfilled longing for contact with wildness within the environmentally impoverished cityscape. On the other hand is the ecological recognition that cities and suburbs are all part of a complex urban ecosystem, a dynamic mosaic in which imperiled nature interacts with humans and their built environment. Not only do Eiseley's representations of urban nature and the city landscape artfully express these tensions, they also help persuade us that urbanized areas are important sites of human contact with nature, as well as places in which habitat and biodiversity must be harbored and conserved.

THE CITY AS ENVIRONMENT

For those possessing the slightest familiarity with the life and writings of Loren Eiseley, the Great Plains of Nebraska and the Dakotas come quickly to mind as his crucial "landscape of both fact and feeling," to paraphrase a motif from twentieth-century urban literature articulated by critic Carlo Rotella (3). Besides setting many of his essays and poems within the geography of the American West (sometimes specifically, other times in a less concrete but still evocative way), Eiseley explicitly points to the landscape of the Plains as a defining influence on his poetic sensibilities and scientific perspective. As he notes in the preface to his 1973 poetry collection, *The Innocent Assassins*:

> I . . . was born on the Great Plains and was drawn almost mesmerically into its rougher margins, the Wild Cat Hills and the Badlands, where bone hunting was a way of life. . . . As a young man engaged in such work, my mind was imprinted by the visible evidence of time and change of enormous magnitude. To me time was never a textbook abstraction. Its remnants lay openly about me in arroyos, in the teetering, eroded pinnacles of Toadstool Park, or farther north in the dinosaur beds of Wyoming. Finally, through some strange mental osmosis these extinct, fragmented creatures merged with and became part of my own identity. (11–12)

This is not just a statement about how a sense of geologic and evolutionary time was developed within Eiseley's young scientific consciousness; it is also a romantic evocation of a particular place and an apt summary of how such landscapes serve as critical settings in so many of Eiseley's essays and poems.

Given the powerful appeal of the western landscapes for Eiseley and his readers, it is rather surprising at first in reviewing his writings to note how often he evokes a far different setting: that of the urban and suburban environment, particularly in Philadelphia, its suburbs, and New York City. Such evocations occur throughout nearly all his works, reflecting the many years that Eiseley lived in Wynnewood, Pennsylvania, taught at the University of Pennsylvania in Philadelphia, and made frequent trips to New York for professional engagements or to simply haunt the city's bookstores. Yet it is also important to note that Eiseley spent the majority of his youth and adolescence living in Lincoln, Nebraska — a burgeoning capital city of 43,973 in 1910 and 54,948 in 1920 and a vital educational and cultural center that has been characterized as an early twentieth-century "Athens of the Plains" (Luebke 218). Long before he rode the rails throughout the American West as a young man or, later on, conducted anthropological field expeditions to remote sites in the Plains and arid regions, Eiseley explored Lincoln's creeks, empty lots, sewers, and surrounding countryside (Christianson, *Fox* 26–28, 31–32). These experiences not only helped stoke his interest in the natural world but also, I would argue, suggested (if merely subconsciously) that the natural and built environments are inextricably intertwined. Later, as an established professor of anthropology, Eiseley settled into a highly urbanized environment in the eastern United States and shifted his research focus from empirical field studies to creative writing projects that fused science and literature (beginning with *The Immense Journey* in 1957), as well as scholarly projects in the history of science, particularly evolutionary thought (signaled by 1958's *Darwin's Century*).

This trajectory suggests that Eiseley, as a careful observer of nature and the biota within it (whether living or fossilized), would have left a detailed chronicle of his experiences exploring the urban environment — and such, in fact, is the case. The following section focuses on one facet of Eiseley's treatment of the city: as an unsettling place of fear and foreboding, a representation of nature that draws on the American antiurban tradition of seeing cities as unnatural and even dangerous (Short 45, 47).

That sense of fear, tempered by an innate and undeniable curiosity, is perhaps no better expressed than in the essay "The Unexpected Universe," the title piece of Eiseley's 1969 essay collection. It begins with a richly drawn scene within a shadowy urban wasteland and an archetypal Eiseley story of a train ride through an area of "silence and man-made desolation that might well take terrifying material forms." After all, "there is nothing like a stalled train in a marsh to promote such reflections — particularly if one has been transported just beyond the environs of a great city and set down in some nether world that seems to partake both of nature before man came and of the residue of what will exist after him" (26). Once the train stops, Eiseley's narrator decides to descend and explore this curious region: "It turned out to be a perpetually burning city dump, contributing its miasmas and choking vapors to the murky sky above the city. Amidst the tended flames of this inferno I approached one of the grimy attendants who was forking over the rubbish. In the background, other shadows, official and unofficial, were similarly engaged. For a moment I had the insubstantial feeling that must exist on the borders of hell, where everything, wavering among heat waves, is transported to another dimension. One could imagine ragged and distorted souls grubbed over by scavengers for what might usefully survive" (27).

This is a near-Gothic scene of swirling imagery ("miasmas and choking vapors"), straight out of nineteenth-century fiction, where the human presence is manifest as "shadows," liminal beings existing on the edge of life and the netherworld, outcasts from ordered society whom Eiseley portrays as "ragged and distorted souls" and "scavengers." In such a world, outside of but made possible by an unnamed city, Eiseley's narrator tries a jarringly misplaced bit of small talk to glean information beyond the obvious as well as to, perhaps, forge some kind of valid human connection in a place where such would seem impossible.

"I suppose you get everything here," I ventured to the grimy attendant.

He nodded indifferently and drew a heavy glove across his face. His eyes were red-rimmed from the fire. Perhaps they were red anyhow.

"Know what?" He swept a hand outward toward the flames.

"No," I confessed.

"Babies," he growled in my ear. "Even dead babies sometimes turn up. From there." He gestured contemptuously toward the city and hoisted an indistinguishable mass upon his fork. I stepped back from the flare of light, but it was only part of an old radio cabinet. (*Unexpected* 27–28)

That last gesture by the "grimy attendant" speaks volumes. The hellish evocation of the city as a source of dirt, waste, violence, loss, decay, and hideous pollution is capped by the horrific image of a dead infant thrown away in the trash, all of which can be laid at the feet not of an individual but of a place — the urban environment. Eiseley's narrator clearly does not subscribe to that cause-and-effect hypothesis implied by the worker; yet he recognizes the inevitable truth in the man's claim that "We get it all [at the dump]. . . . Just give it time to travel, we get it all." Consequently, as the essay moves on to consider how "the archaeologist is awake to memories of the dead cultures around us, to our destiny, and to the nature of the universe we profess to inhabit," Eiseley is careful to remind us that he must "speak of these things not as a wise man, with scientific certitude, but from a place outside, in the role, shall we say, of a city-dump philosopher" (28–29).

The city is also a place of sometimes disquieting and even disturbing encounters with urban wildlife, many examples of which are less than pleasant in Eiseley's world. Despite being a student of science and a fairly skilled naturalist, Eiseley was aware of the very human fear of the unknown, of the comings and goings of nocturnal creatures; as he puts it in *The Night Country*, "My confession is that of a man with night fear, and it is also the confession of a very large proportion of the human race" (32). Accordingly, he relates the story of "friend of mine [who] took a room in the heart of a great city," only to have a sizable animal plop onto "his feet as he lay stretched out in bed." Upon lighting a match to find out what kind of creature was paying him a visit, the man was horrified to find "a sewer rat as big as a house cat . . . [sit] up on its haunches and . . . [glare] into the match flame with pink demonic eyes. . . . That sort of thing, you know, is like getting a personal message from the dark. You are apt to remember it a lifetime" (33). We fear the tough city rodent not just because it inspires visceral loathing but also because it represents all the creatures and forces, real and imaginary, that populate the darkness of the night, out of our sight and cognizance, ever unknowable.

Last, an important consequence of modern urban life for Eiseley is the way in which it results in a profound disconnection and alienation from the natural world—a separation that is not merely an ethical problem, but one evident in how the human species adapts (or fails to adapt) to its physical surroundings. Placed within the broad anthropological context of human social evolution, today's "scientific [and, one might add, urban] civilization in the full sense is an anomaly in world history. . . . Never before have such large masses of people been so totally divorced from the land or the direct processing of their own foodstuffs." Such a situation is perfectly symbolized for Eiseley in the "tragedy of a single man in the New York blackout in 1965" (*Invisible* 82). Trapped in darkness within a skyscraper during the episode, the man lights a candle and attempts to find a stairway leading to an exit. Instead, he accidentally walks through an elevator service door and falls to his death at the bottom of the elevator shaft. Eiseley sees in the event not an instance of individual misfortune, however, but rather a consequence of our diminished observational powers brought on by gradual acculturation to an artificial city environment. The victim and "his inadequate candle had plunged recklessly forward and been swallowed up as neatly by a machine in its tunnel as by a leopard on a dark path" (83).

This view of the city as a site of danger and challenge to survival is not limited to the fate of humans but also applies to nonhuman life. Elsewhere in *The Invisible Pyramid*, Eiseley recounts, "One evening, in a drab and heartless area of the metropolis, a windborne milkweed seed circled my head. On impulse I seized the delicate aerial orphan which otherwise would have perished. Its long midwinter voyage seemed too favorable an augury to ignore. Placing the seed in my glove, I took it home into the suburbs and found a field in which to plant it. Of a million seeds blown on a vagrant wind into the city, it alone may survive" (55–56). On a literal level, the episode illustrates Eiseley's recognition of the harsh conditions presented to plant life within the concrete wilderness of the city and contrasts this vision with the more bucolic suburban regions, where open fields were still to be found in the 1960s. Yet perhaps most significant about the passage is how it represents a simple form of connection between humans and the urban biota, an indication that, as Eiseley reflects, "I am not yet totally a planet eater and wished that something green might survive" (56). Such a positive note, which represents a dramatic contrast to the previous examples cited earlier, aptly segues to Eiseley's capacity for finding and observing the biodiversity and ecological processes within the urban landscape.

WILDERNESS IN THE CITY

A contemporary of Eiseley's and one of his many admirers was the Chicago writer Leonard Dubkin, a journalist and self-taught naturalist who, until his death in 1972, explored everyday nature within parks and forest preserves, empty lots, the industrialized riverfront, patches of open land between housing developments, tenement slums, dank underground passages, railroad embankments, and sidewalk cracks. From his observations of these places, Dubkin created a fascinating discourse of urban nature that is singular in Chicago's literary history, as well as relevant to contemporary efforts in reimagining how nature functions (and might flourish) in the environment of cities. Dubkin produced a string of meditative and observation-rich books on urban nature, broadly defined, starting with *The Murmur of Wings* in 1944 and ending in 1972 with *My Secret Places*. He also maintained friendships and regular correspondence with important writers, naturalists, and scientists of his day, including Ben Hecht, Nelson Algren, Rachel Carson, and — last but hardly least — Loren Eiseley, who delivered the 1963 commencement address at Bryn Mawr for Dubkin's daughter's graduation, the occasion that marked the first time the two men met in person (Yearwood).

In fact, it is Eiseley who penned what might be the most eloquent tribute to Dubkin's skill and significance as a city-based naturalist writer.

In a 1972 letter to Dubkin, he included a carbon copy of a draft dust jacket blurb for Dubkin's final book, *My Secret Places*, a compact bit of praise that ironically was never published:

> Mr. Dubkin has no parallel as the naturalist of the city and its environs. An able and expert journalist, he has the heart and eye of a child. It is this which convinces those of us lost in adult affairs that there is still truly a hidden place between the last billboard and the viaduct, a place as worthy of preservation as a forest. In such spots a rare human gentleness can sometimes be nurtured. Leonard Dubkin is a graduate of that kind of innocent back lot school which Americans are close to losing forever. His work is not only readable, it is utterly sincere.

Eiseley recognized not just the singularity of Dubkin's unique perspective and literary ability but also the value of his lifelong efforts to bring the neglected yet fascinating manifestations of urban nature to light. Even more important, Eiseley ever so briefly yet explicitly acknowledges the importance of the remnant natural areas in the urban landscape, despite their dramatic contrast to the more charismatic images of mountains, canyons, or mature forests — places associated with the idea of wilderness rather than the city.[1]

In fact, this recognition figures significantly throughout Eiseley's work, and while not a relentlessly dominant focus as it was for Dubkin, the urban and suburban landscapes indeed provide Eiseley with plenty of rhetorical space in which to muse on the value of biodiversity, the wonder of individual species' adaptations to the built environment, and the complexity (and often mystery) of ecological processes. A simple yet beautiful example of this approach to urban natural history is an unpublished observation dated December 16, 1955, just two years before the appearance of his breakthrough book, *The Immense Journey*.[2] In this case, Eiseley's observations center on the specific behavioral adaptations of that ubiquitous and much maligned city bird, the pigeon, and its ascribed cleverness in exploiting the potential for food and shelter in the urban environment:

> Looking out of a sixteenth-floor window of the Barbizon-Plaza Hotel in New York, I saw several pigeons turning round and round, apparently

warming themselves in the warm air currents emanating from some chimneys or air vents in a roof immediately below me. Looking closer I discovered several such chimneys emerging from the wall on the side nearest to me. On each chimney sat a pigeon, his little bottom carefully tucked over the warmth. . . .

Later, descending to the street, I found clouds of pigeons in places where they were not to be found in rush hours. They were picking up bits of crust and other garbage in front of bars and grocery stores before the increasing traffic of the morning would force them aloft again. Obviously they have the ecology of the city well worked out.

There could be added here the brave way these small birds seek their living and survive. No mean feat. (*Lost* 95)

While many more examples could be cited of Eiseley's engagement with and exploration of various aspects of urban nature, one essay from *The Night Country* in particular seems to encapsulate multiple dimensions of his distinctive way of seeing and drawing insight from life within the city landscape. "The Brown Wasps" is the final essay in that volume and thus serves as both a coda to the book and a melancholy meditation on the capacity of memory to create a sense of place as well as a feeling of belonging — a capacity that Eiseley traces not just in humans, whether in himself or the huddled poor who inhabit the corners of railway-station waiting rooms, but also in animals. Yet it is the essay's repeated invocations of the ever-changing qualities of urban ecosystems and the effects they have on the organisms present within them that endow it with special significance in Eiseley's oeuvre and suggest that "It is the place that matters, the place at the heart of things. . . . We cling to a time and a place because without them man is lost, not only man but life" (229).

"The Brown Wasps" is composed of five parts (though they merge seamlessly, as Eiseley's essays tend to do), each with its own setting and protagonist: the first section describes "a certain element of the abandoned poor," who find temporary refuge "in the waiting room of one of the great Eastern stations" and who remind Eiseley of brown wasps that revisit an abandoned hive in winter, "the hum of the spring hive still resound[ing] faintly in their sodden tissues" (227). The second shifts the scene to a suburban field, a small open patch of ground near a shopping center that by the evidence of a developer's sign is also destined for the bulldozer, where Eiseley spies a mouse running through the grass. The third scene follows said mouse from field to Eiseley's own apartment, where (or so he imagines) it finds shelter not in the typical haunts of the seasoned house mouse but in the root system of a potted fern, within which it carves out a burrow. Eiseley next shifts his focus to the pigeon in the ecological context of the abandoned Philadelphia elevated-train system. Finally, he ends the essay by breaking with the urban setting and telling a story of a journey home to an unnamed Nebraska town (probably Lincoln) to find the tree he had planted as a youth with his father, one that had grown tall in his imagination over the last sixty years but had in fact been cut down long ago, after his departure.

Eiseley's explicit objective in "The Brown Wasps" is not to provide a systematic urban natural history; his point, as is often the case in his writings, is much more philosophical and conjectural, steeped though it is in concrete imagery and physical observations of the landscape and its biota. Yet it is fascinating how, much like Leonard Dubkin, Eiseley locates four out of the five sections of the essay in urban contexts, only one of which is an obviously "natural" ecosystem: the suburban field. The remainder of the settings — train-station waiting room, apartment interior, elevated-train station / streetscape — are not at all typical places for your garden-variety literary naturalist to seek inspiration. However, as Eiseley's backdrops they harbor inhabitants that reward careful observation, and they illustrate the functions of ecosystems with clarity and force, if not in minute detail. They also underscore the constant human presence and mark on the urban landscape — sometimes as something to be mourned, as with the impending devastation of an open field in Eiseley's suburb, other times as a way to merely place the human alongside the natural, with the implicit suggestion that we are not separate from the landscape we have reshaped and transformed but are an intimate, interdependent part of it.

In the fourth section of the essay, Eiseley describes how a new subway system's construction renders the old elevated commuter trains obsolete, but in the process of one transportation technology displacing another, an ecological community is affected — one that includes both humans and beasts alike: "This ancient El with its barnlike stations containing nut-vending machines and scattered food scraps has, for generations, been the favorite feeding ground of flocks of pigeons. . . . Hundreds of pigeons were dependent upon the system. . . . Probably very few among the waiting people who tossed a crumb to an eager pigeon realized that this El was like a food-bearing river, and that the life which haunted its banks was dependent upon the running of the trains with their human freight." The river metaphor is an important one to Eiseley, for it evokes the cycles of time and the close interdependency between species and a particular landscape, just as the rivers of the Great Plains (such as the Platte) sustain a wild profusion of life within their waters and along their margins. The river of the El, though, is made of train traffic and (more to the point) people: a flow of humans that arrives in fits and starts; dispenses nutrients to the expectant pigeons, whether in the form of gifts or waste; and stops with shocking abruptness, "like a great river subsiding suddenly into desert sands" (232).

Since Eiseley's theme is place memory, the innate longing of many creatures (including ourselves) "for a way of life or a locality that has long been cherished" (233), he recounts the return of the station's flock after the structure's abandonment; indeed, it is the activity of demolition that attracts them back to the station, presumably with hopes of getting food from a restored river of humanity. Only when the station is reduced to rubble do they leave the scene. But the acknowledgment of a highly artificial yet somehow functional urban ecosystem is the salient feature of this passage: no, this is no substitute for high-quality open space, or even for a low-quality parkland, yet it aptly demonstrates the cause-and-effect connection between human action and the status of urban wildlife and underscores the dramatic impacts that changes in the built environment have on the natural environment. Human decision making, "The Brown Wasps" suggests, cannot exist in splendid isolation within an urban context — one action affects (or causes) another, in what can be at times ever-increasing complexity.

To be sure, Eiseley's stories of urban wildlife and analyses of city ecosystems, large and small, are not devoted to the cataloguing of native species or the description of ecological restoration efforts — to name just two contemporary items within the broad agenda of urban ecology. Eiseley's project instead seems to be more humanistic than scientific, in the sense that his observations of commonplace species in everyday contexts highlight the process of adaptation (by which organisms find food and establish a niche in the built environment) and the amazing resilience with which a city's nonhuman denizens make their ecological living amid steel and concrete.

THE CITY AS PLACE OF ENVIRONMENTAL CRITIQUE

Today's urban ecologists point out what might be called the paradox of cities: from the standpoint of environmental sustainability, the earth's urban areas are responsible for the bulk of human consumption (of energy and resources) as well as waste production. Given the accelerating rate of urbanization begun in the twentieth century and expected to continue well into the twenty-first, this fact will likely become even more problematic (McNeill 269–95). Yet at the same time, cities — by virtue of their population density, vertical structure, public transportation networks, and creative human capital — are also at the vanguard of sustainability initiatives, such as energy conservation and greenhouse gas–emissions reduction, and thus have been identified as part of a potential solution as well as a persistent problem (Grimm et al. 756).

Loren Eiseley seems to have recognized this long before the term "sustainability" became commonplace, let alone identified with urban environments. In fact, the fundamental tenets of Eiseley's environmental ethic are most forcefully expressed in the essay collection in which he mentions cities most frequently, 1970's *The Invisible Pyramid* (M. Bryson 384–86). For Eiseley, urban areas are potent symbols and literal expressions of human consumption and the alteration of nature, but they are also places where the limits of technology and the impermanence of human society's constructions are visible. This long-range view of urbanization is enabled, one might suggest, by Eiseley's anthropological perspective, which views history along a temporal scale of thousands and millions of years, rather than years or decades.

Eiseley's critique of the urban impact on biodiversity and habitat occurs along a continuum of intensity, from rueful meditations on the harsh challenges cities pose for plants and animals (and the remarkable adaptations that sometimes result from this) to passionate denunciations of humanity's desecration of the landscape through pollution and urban development. An example of the former is this excerpt from the poem "Desperate I Walked" from *The Innocent Assassins*, in which the narrator observes a piece of "thistledown, / journeying the wrong way toward the city's heart" (lines 4–5). As the poem continues, the poet takes the seed "gently from the air" and walks the city streets, "seeking / a place where it could be for the winter and be given / a chance to grow" (10, 11–13). Finding only "car lots, highways" (16), "pruned hedges," and "formal gardens" (17), the poet realizes that if he "dropped the seed its life would perish" (18).

At first glance this scene strikes a familiar chord, given Eiseley's previous use of this image of a wayward seed (*Invisible* 55–56, discussed earlier). Here, though, the narrator is a rescuer of sorts, an empathetic naturalist helping a single seed avoid a fate of falling on infertile ground in the harsh environs of the city or the deceptively verdant yet still dangerous gardens and lawns of suburbia. Given the prolific seed production of plants using the mechanism of wind-borne dispersal, such a rescue is symbolic rather than necessary, as the vast majority of any plants fail to find purchase and take root under normal circumstances. Eiseley's point, however, is two-fold: the urban environment is a challenge for native species not just because of a lack of exposed habitat (here, decent soil and open space) but also because the human denizens of that environment strive to eliminate unplanned irruptions of life in their efforts to sculpt and maintain their variously contrived landscapes.

A much harder-hitting and more radical environmental critique, though, is offered in the essay "The World Eaters" from *The Invisible Pyramid*, in which the human species is characterized as a "planet virus," a metaphor that begins in the shadowy context of a dream state:

It came to me in the night, in the midst of a bad dream, that perhaps man, like the blight descending on a fruit, is by nature a parasite, a spore bearer, a world eater. The slime molds are the only creatures on the planet that share the ways of man from his individual pioneer phase to his final immersion in great cities. . . . This is because, when their microscopic frontier is gone, as it quickly is, the single amoeboid frontiersmen swarm into concentrated aggregations. At the last they thrust up overtoppling spore palaces, like city skyscrapers. The rupture of these vesicles may disseminate the living spores as far away proportionately as man's journey to the moon. (53)

On one level, the figurative language in this passage tests our ability to grant Eiseley's reasoning credibility. Unlike, say, the practice of studying primate behavior for clues about early human social interaction, the comparison of slime molds and humans is an imaginative stretch that crosses gaps of anatomical difference and of time itself: the amoeba-to-aggregate phase occurs in minutes and hours with the slime mold, while the "pioneer phase" of humanity Eiseley refers to is most likely the period of small, dispersed bands of early hunter-gatherers. Yet the metaphor is undeniably effective: the use of "pioneer" and "frontier," in an American context, simultaneously evokes the westward expansion across the continent — a process in which environmental resources were consumed rapidly and, for the most part, without check or balance. Most significant is the repeated evocation of cities in this passage. On one hand, Eiseley is taking a broad view by implicating technology — and by extension, science — in the rapid expansion of humanity on the globe through references to "great cities," "skyscrapers," and the recent "journey to the moon." On the other hand, cities are not just a convenient metaphor for human overpopulation and technological hubris; they are most certainly ecological problems of the first magnitude, for they are humankind's most dramatic and large-scale representation of the technological alteration of the natural environment and the excessive consumption of natural resources, both within the city proper and throughout its vast rural hinterlands.[3] As a later passage in *The Invisible Pyramid* makes clear, it is not just urbanization that is the problem — the underlying issue is even broader and more problematic: "In simple terms, the rise of a scientific society means a society of constant expectations directed toward the oncoming future. What we have is always second best, what we expect to have is 'progress.' . . . In the endless pursuit of the future we have ended by engaging to destroy the planet" (104–5).

As is often the case, Eiseley here moves quickly from the macro to the micro, and in the process makes a compelling argument about the ways in which cities do not just consume tabulated resources and produce pollution but transform land — acre by acre, empty lot by empty lot. In this instance Eiseley's storytelling is knife-edge sharp, and he looks no further than the landscape of his suburban home for inspiration. In the essay "Man in the Autumn Light," Eiseley recounts a winter nighttime walk he took through "a remaining fragment of woodland" near his suburban home. Preserved for many years by virtue of being part of a vast estate — one of the common mechanisms for the preservation of open space in urban areas in America — the woodland's continued presence pleases Eiseley and inspires him to ask whether "man still, after all his ravages, possess[es] some fear of the midnight forest or some unconscious reverence toward the source of his origins" (*Invisible* 128). But then, coming to a clearing in the woods and the sudden observation that the opening was not natural but "artificial, a swath slashed by instruments of war," the narrator realizes that his brief reflection on the possibility of human restraint and kinship with the natural world is an illusion: "I had taken the thin screen remaining from the original wood for reality. Only the snow, only the tiny footprints of the last surviving wood creatures, had led me to this unmasking. Behind the little stand of trees the world eaters had all the time been assiduously at work" (130).

This martial metaphor applied to the description of urban development and sprawl is a recurring feature of Eiseley's later prose; it crops up in *The Unexpected Universe* when he "peer[s] hopelessly upon the relentless advance of suburban housing" (196), and it takes on particular intensity in the essay "The Last Magician" from *The Invisible Pyramid*, in which Eiseley creates an indelible image of the urban organism seen from a God's-eye perspective:

Not long ago I chanced to fly over a forested section of country which, in my youth, was still an unfrequented wilderness. Across it now suburbia was spreading. Below, like the fungus upon a fruit, I could see the radiating lines of transport gouged through the naked earth. From far up in the wandering air one could see the lines stretching over the horizon. They led to cities clothed in an unmoving haze of smog. From my remote, abstract position in the clouds I could gaze upon all below and watch the incipient illness as it spread with all its slimy tendrils through the watershed. (151)

Multiple metaphors are at work here: overlaid on an evocation of nostalgia for the lost landscape of his youth are Eiseley's observations of the fungal advance of suburban development, which he characterizes not as a benign or neutral process but as an "illness," a disease that undercuts the integrity and health of both earth and water (both evoked in one fell swoop by the word "watershed"). One cannot escape the conclusion that Eiseley, an unabashed lover of the cultural vitality of cities, nonetheless sees them in an ecological context as a pathological blight.

And yet . . . while these horrifying realizations are sufficient to convince Eiseley that humanity "threatens to destroy the earth," his alarm is tempered by certainty that cities — and the science and technology of human culture that makes them possible — are but temporary constructions in the scope of geologic time. Eiseley does not harbor a positive vision of the concrete ways in which urban areas might be reenvisioned and reengineered to become more sustainable, a line of thinking that began to emerge in the mid-1990s, a generation after his death, and that characterizes one of the leading edges of the sustainability movement today in the early twenty-first century.[4] His ecological consciousness is more along the lines of Barry Commoner's and Paul Ehrlich's warnings in the 1960s about the danger of corrupting and damaging "spaceship earth" (albeit with less inflammatory rhetoric), tempered by an awareness traceable in many of his works that nature shall someday overtake and reclaim the handiworks of humankind. In *The Immense Journey*, for example, Eiseley imagines pigeons "taking over the spires of Manhattan" (167); in *The Night*

Country, he relates a mysterious anecdote about "walking in the ruins of the city," in which he visualizes the death of a city through an archaeologist's eye while, incongruously, shopping with his wife (153).

A powerful expression of this idea is projected by the imagery in "And As for Man," from *The Innocent Assassins.* On a train ride out of New York during which, after leaving the station and gazing at a retaining wall that runs along the tracks, the poem's narrator spots "a small ledge," where "ragweed, beggar's-tick, foxtail" cling to life in a place where man has determined that "nothing is ever intended to grow" (lines 13, 14, 16). Eiseley marvels that "incredibly they live, between the tunnel's darkness / and the sky" (20–21). Prolific in their production of seed, they are "waiting for the last train to enter the tunnel," waiting, that is, for the demise of humans, who, the poem notes, when they do go, "will not be coming back" (28, 32). Just as pioneer species of plants manage to find a foothold in the tightest sidewalk crack, so too does Eiseley tenaciously cling to the notion that for all our spires and spectacles nature itself shall reclaim its territory, even displace us, given time enough. But his articulation of this vision is less rueful than gently hopeful — for though the anthropologist in him knows that we are a young species and that with many uncertainties ahead no guarantee exists for our survival, there is some comfort to be had in the expectation that life, in all its other forms, will indeed prevail.

Today, urban nature in all its various forms — waterways, city parks, forest preserves, wetlands, green rooftops, community gardens, landscaped public spaces, city-based farms — is more important than ever before, as the world rapidly urbanizes and cities strive to make themselves more environmentally sustainable. The desire to regain meaningful contact with nature is transforming the cultural constructions of "wilderness" and "city." While scientists study the ecological processes of urban systems, artists and writers plumb the significance of nature in the city, from protected pockets of native habitat that have survived decades of development to the various manifestations of engineered nature and what those suggest about our relationship to the world around us.[5]

Like anything else, all this empirical and creative work has important antecedents, and the work of Loren Eiseley is a heretofore unrecognized yet significant source of observations on and meditations about the urban environment. Eiseley's literary-scientific engagement with the suburban and urban landscape from the 1950s through the early 1970s illustrates the fractured notion of cities as antithetical to the natural, yet dependent on and intimately bound up with ecological processes. While Eiseley at times bemoans the city as a place of environmental poverty and degradation, he also emphasizes and even celebrates the persistence and adaptability of life within the often harsh cityscape. Moreover, in his ruminations on the human condition and limits of science in an era when the modern American ecological conscience was beginning to take shape, Eiseley uses the city as a vehicle for articulating an environmental ethic — one that critiques the ways in which technological society expands, consumes, and pollutes, yet still acknowledges the impermanence of humanity's reshaping of the earth, as well as nature's power to reclaim, over time, the built environment.

NOTES

1. See the first section of William Cronon's essay, "The Trouble with Wilderness" (69–77).

2. This journal entry was later published posthumously in *The Lost Notebooks*.

3. The countryside is connected to urban economic and ecological processes in myriad ways, as Cronon has demonstrated in his study of Chicago, *Nature's Metropolis*. Such are the power of such connections, Cronon argues, that the separation between them is an artificial construct reflecting our *ideas* about the nature of city and country more than material reality. "Chicago had become 'urban,' spawning belching smokestacks and crowded streets, at the same time that the lands around it became 'rural,' yielding not grass and red-winged blackbirds but wheat, corn, and hogs. Chicago's merchants and workers had built their warehouses and factories in the same decades that farmers had plowed up the prairie sod and lumberjacks had cut the great pine trees of the north woods. City and country shared a common past, and had fundamentally reshaped each other. Neither was as 'natural' or 'unnatural' as it appeared" (7–8).

4. For a comprehensive and accessible introduction to the many dimensions of urban sustainability, consult *The Sustainable Urban Development Reader*, edited by Stephen Wheeler and Timothy Beatley.

5. A definitive example of a fully integrated, interdisciplinary study of a major urban area is the Baltimore Ecosystem Study, an initiative funded by the National Science

Foundation to study long-term ecological processes in a representative range of the earth's ecosystems. Recent explorations of the American urban landscape from the standpoint of the arts and humanities include Michael Bennett's essay "From Wide Open Spaces to Metropolitan Places" (cultural/literary criticism), H. Rutherford Platt's *The Humane Metropolis* (urban history and planning), Terrell Dixon's *City Wilds* (urban nature writing), Terry Evans's *Revealing Chicago* (photography), and John Tallmadge's *The Cincinnati Arch* (memoir/urban ecology).

5

Anthropomorphizing the Essay

Loren Eiseley's Representations of Animals

KATHLEEN BOARDMAN

"*Anthropomorphizing*: the charge of my critics." With these abrupt words, Loren Eiseley began a one-paragraph notebook entry defending his representations of animals and animal-human relationships from the attacks of real and imagined detractors. On the day of the entry—January 22, 1970—Eiseley was in the midst of a productive late-career period: *The Unexpected Universe* had recently been published, *The Invisible Pyramid* was about to appear, and no doubt Eiseley was in the process of assembling and revising the essays—most of them previously published—that would compose *The Night Country*. In addition, he was drafting chapters for *The Snow Wolf*, an unpublished novel written from the wolf's point of view, and working on a memoir that would become *All the Strange Hours*. According to Eiseley's editor, Kenneth Heuer, the publication of his books was always "a traumatic experience" for Eiseley, who was so "insecure" that in spite of many enthusiastic, even reverent responses to his work, he was "often hurt by indifferent reviewers" (Eiseley, *Lost* 161). In 1963 a scathing review by a fellow physical anthropologist had stung him badly, for it suggested that he had traded scientific rigor for "sentimental twaddle" (Buettner-Janusch).[1] In Eiseley's midcentury academic world, the term "anthropomorphizing" was entirely pejorative, connoting sloppiness, sentimentality, and lack of scientific rigor.[2] As Jack Bushnell points out, "All of Eiseley's popular essays are about how science becomes personal," so it is little wonder that he took the "anthropomorphizing" charge so personally (259).

Most readers of Eiseley's essays can vividly recall at least one or two stories in which the narrator's inferences about animals' thoughts, feelings, consciousness, or judgment play a key role. Two hawks wheel and scream with joy at their freedom; a young fox invites Eiseley to play; a field mouse tries to recreate its home in a flower pot; a rat arrives "like a messenger

from space, at an appropriate point in a very significant conversation";
a bowing cat craves applause; a laboratory dog pleads for its life; birds
deliver a judgment.[3] Like the vivid characters in beast fables, these animal
exemplars and messengers aid in a symbolic reading of the world: all life
is constantly changing, forms are not fixed, and compassion draws species
together. Eiseley's imaginative excursions into the consciousness of other
animals are powerful for readers who appreciate evocative uses of language;
insofar as they can be categorized as "allegorical and personification" and
thereby "restricted to nonscientific writing," they may be considered "not a
problem in science" (Rivas and Burghardt 9). However, a literary defense
of Eiseley's choices is not sufficient, for he also took seriously his identity
as a scientist, historian, and critic of science: while his essays were not
scientific writing, he *was* a scientist writing.[4]

James Serpell provides a brief definition of anthropomorphism that is
relevant to this study: anthropomorphism is "the attribution of human
mental states (thoughts, feelings, motivations, and beliefs) to animals"
(122). While humanists may connect anthropomorphism with myth, use
it creatively as metaphor, or study it as a trope or effect of language, scientists generally use the word pejoratively as a label for an embarrassing
and potentially dangerous error. In particular, scientists who study animal
behavior (behavioral psychologists, ethologists, sociobiologists) have been
warned repeatedly against anthropomorphism. Recently, however, these
purely negative connotations have been questioned: perhaps not all attribution to animals of "human" qualities is *mis*attribution. As primatologist
Frans B. M. de Waal asserts, "Of course, if anthropomorphism is defined
as the *misattribution* of human qualities to animals, no one wishes to be
associated with it. But much of the time, a broader definition is employed,
namely the description of animal behavior in human hence intentionalistic
terms . . . as a heuristic tool" (xv). That is, anthropomorphism, used with
care, may be a "legitimate and particularly creative way to do science if it
is used to develop hypotheses that can be tested in a rigorous manner"
(Rivas and Burghardt 10). In addition, as cognitive ethologists such as
Donald R. Griffin and Marc Bekoff have claimed, the boundaries between
human and nonhuman motivations and behaviors are not clear cut and

are still under study. To this way of thinking, because some attributions of emotions, consciousness, or even morality to animals may turn out to be correct and verifiable, it is unwise to assume a priori that a given motivation or characteristic or emotion is uniquely human. Thus, labeling a practice or description as inappropriately "anthropomorphic" could be a presumptuous error.

Eiseley's brief, sharp notebook response to the "anthropomorphizing" label is of course unrevised, but it deftly outlines the advantages of blurring animal-human boundaries. First he represents anthropomorphism as a humanizing influence: "My countercharge: . . . when we cease to anthropomorphize, we cease to be men, for when we cease to have human contact with animals and deny them all relation to ourselves, we tend in the end to cease to anthropomorphize ourselves — to deny our own humanity. We repeat the old, old human trick of freezing the living world and with it ourselves" (*Lost* 200–201).[5] Unlike writers who shrug off anthropomorphism by saying, "It's just a metaphor," Eiseley insists that it arises not only from humans' efforts to make sense of the world through symbols but also from natural, often empathetic, connections between human and other animals. Like the contemporary behavioral scientists mentioned earlier, Eiseley maintains that anthropomorphism is not a sloppy error but a strategic choice in the interpretation of the natural world: it entails animal-human contact and openness to the possibility of shared characteristics. We do not just impose human traits onto other animals; on the contrary, we may be able to see qualities in animals that we then recognize in ourselves. Part of being human is our connection to the natural world, he argues, and the basis of that connection is evolution. In the natural world an evolutionist sees constant change and interrelationships among species. It is a mistake to try to "freeze" the world and insist on the human being as a stable, separate final product.

Granting that his is a symbolic reading of the natural world, Eiseley's notebook paragraph goes on to argue that symbolic language is no mere decoration: "We do create our world by our ability to read it symbolically." Purely analytical, mechanistic perspectives on animal-human relationships are just as symbolic as so-called anthropomorphizing accounts, and perhaps no more scientific: "miming nature down to its ingredients, including ourselves. This [mechanistic view of animal behavior] is really only another symbolic reading, certainly no more 'real' than what I have been charged with" (201). Eiseley implies that those who reject the symbolic language that allows for animal-human analogy and connection turn inevitably to a mechanistic symbol system that perceives the whole as no more than the sum of its parts. Those who perceive other animals in this way eventually take the same view of humans.[6]

Eiseley's countercharge can be read as a defiant manifesto: he will continue to anthropomorphize as if the fate of humanity depended on it. But the defensive tone of the paragraph also suggests that some of Eiseley's negative feelings about anthropomorphism may come from within. Educated as a social scientist in the mid-twentieth century, Eiseley certainly internalized warnings against unscientific practices. Many of his animal anecdotes are suffused with a certain tension: how far should he go toward making connections with animals, how much "relation to ourselves" should he claim for animals? How much anthropomorphic language would be consistent with his identity as a scientist observing the natural world? Although Eiseley utilized anthropomorphism boldly in critiques of scientific orthodoxy, in other animal anecdotes he was cautious, even ambivalent. Although he claimed "never [to have] disturbed the journals in my field with my off-hour compositions," he still felt he was being held accountable by colleagues for what he called "the state of my interior heavens" (*Night* 214). Concern about his scientist identity, personal sense of alienation, perhaps doubt about how far language could take him may have inspired coyness in some descriptions of animal consciousness and empathy. Even while railing against the science of his day, Eiseley was certainly aware of serious consequences — for both animals and humans — of the careless, unobservant attribution of "human" motives to other animals. Not only is this bad science, but it is oppressive to animals, as Kimberly W. Benston points out: while humans hold power over other animals, anthropomorphism is a means of "making and enlarging 'humanity' by effacing (writing over ...) animality" (551).

This essay examines Eiseley's animal anecdotes in the context of scientific attitudes of his time and in terms of more recent controversies regarding anthropomorphism in humans' interpretations of animal behavior. The disciplines that Eiseley drew on for his work continue to discuss attitudes toward anthropomorphic language and its implications for animal welfare and environmental ethics movements. In their study of how the "irresistible taboo" of anthropomorphism works culturally — even in modern scientific cultures — Lorraine Daston and Gregg Mitman have noted that when we "think with animals," these animals "do not just stand for something . . . *they do something*." For one thing, "the heuristic utility of anthropomorphism in generating hypotheses to test in the study of animal behavior is beyond question" (9). But humans also practice what we might call "thinking *along with* animals" in an attempt to empathize or share their perspective. As Daston and Mitman put it, "Humans assume a community of thought and feeling between themselves and a surprisingly wide array of animals; they also recruit animals to symbolize, dramatize, and illuminate aspects of their own experience" (2). The following sections consider Eiseley's anecdotes in light of the continuing conversations among scientists and humanists about anthropomorphism. Eiseley's anthropomorphic writing can be read through several lenses: anthropomorphism as error (a label he played with in his resistance to scientific orthodoxy); as an effect of language; and as a way of "thinking *with* animals" that enables exploration of evolutionary continuity and empathetic connections. Eiseley's anthropomorphism, clearly a source of tension in his writing, may also be seen as a viable, ethical "in-between" position, given all that was and is still unknown about humans and other animals. In their own overview of anthropomorphism, Daston and Mitman emphasize that "what it means to think with animals varies with time, place, and medium" (9). Eiseley's animal anecdotes constitute, at least in part, an exploration of those varying contexts.

ANTHROPOMORPHISM AS ERROR AND RESISTANCE

In *The Unexpected Universe*, Eiseley narrates an encounter between himself and a conventional young social scientist who accuses him of anthropomorphism. At the conclusion of a lecture, Eiseley is "approached and chided by a young lady who informed me with severity that I was betraying evidence of a foolish anthropomorphism, which would certainly place me under disfavor and suspicion in the psychological circles she frequented" (150). Eiseley had told a story about a deer mouse that attended a famous historian's lecture on the Byzantine Empire; he described the mouse sitting on the edge of a seat, listening with rapt attention. Responding to the young woman's accusation of "foolish anthropomorphism," Eiseley declares that evolution is open-ended, continuous, and sometimes surprising and that some life forms (such as *Homo sapiens*) have made sudden leaps in development, as if they had come through a "chink in nature." He tells her, "I admit that the creatures do not always work out and that the chances seemed rather against this one but who is to say what may happen when a mouse gets a taste for Byzantium rather beyond that of the average graduate student?" (151). Although his tone is playful, even disingenuous, Eiseley's response has an edge: it is not only condescending to the "young lady" but also sharply defensive. Having chosen the anecdote of the mouse to make a serious point about evolution, Eiseley also chooses to embed this little narrative in an altercation over anthropomorphism. The young graduate student's view is the orthodox one: anthropomorphism is an error no behavioral scientist should ever make.

Encounters with skeptical, disapproving, and often unimaginative scientists are fairly common in Eiseley's essays. In this particular anecdote, it is significant that the accuser is a young psychologist and Eiseley the older, more experienced scientist-academic. As a historian of science and student of Darwin's work, Eiseley was well aware that scientists had not always been worried about avoiding anthropomorphism. Darwin himself was interested in exploring shared characteristics of human and nonhuman animals and in debunking claims of human exceptionalism. He drew no conclusions about benchmarks — like language and tool use — that set humans apart from other animals. In his thinking Darwin was inclined toward *evolutionary parsimony*: "if closely related species act the same, the underlying mental processes are probably the same, too. The alternative would be to assume the evolution of divergent processes for similar behavior; a wildly uneconomic assumption" (De Waal xiv). However, the rise of behavioral science in the early twentieth century entailed a preference for mechanistic interpretations of animal behavior and a reliance on *cognitive parsimony*, or Morgan's canon: if a behavior or other phenomenon can be explained by referencing lower mental capacities (e.g., instinct, reflex), one should not invoke higher ones (e.g., consciousness, reflection, problem solving). Pamela Asquith points out that by the middle of the twentieth century, "among behaviorists, any explanation of behavior that remotely suggested conscious activity was unacceptable. In psychology and biology there were few exceptions to this tradition and to the related stress on parsimonious explanations" (25).

Eiseley was more in sympathy with the older Darwinians and natural historians, although his education and career as an anthropologist spanned the mid-twentieth-century ascendancy of behavioral science — and a growing conflict over what counted as objective scientific description. In this period, while behavioral psychologists preferred laboratory studies, where variables could be more easily controlled, ethologists such as Niko Tinbergen and Konrad Lorenz went into the field to make close observations of animal behavior, and "naturalistic animal behavior studies were set against [the] objectivist trend" of the lab studies (26). Although they, too, aimed at objective language, the ethologists developed methods that would help them see the world from the animal's point of view: getting down on the ground, making certain sounds, doing some of the things the study animals did.

In 1976, a year before Eiseley's death, ethologist Donald R. Griffin proposed a new subfield: cognitive ethology, the study of mental experiences in animals. Although touchy about being labeled anthropomorphizers, cognitive ethologists are receptive to claims of animal consciousness and intentionality and skeptical of purely mechanistic explanations of animal behavior. They echo Eiseley's notebook entry in their claims that *mechanomorphism* is merely a point of view, like anthropomorphism, and certainly no more objective. Griffin charges that during most of the twentieth century, "curiosity about what life is like for members of other species" was "discouraged, even repressed, among scientists concerned with animal behavior," and that this "taboo . . . is seriously impeding investigation of important scientific problems" (x–xi). As primatologist Frans de Waal puts it, "Students of animal behavior are faced with a choice between classifying animals as automatons or granting them volition and information-processing capacities. Whereas one school warns against assuming things we cannot prove, another school warns against leaving out what may be there" (xv).

The conflict over the definition and appropriate uses of anthropomorphism continues today. While acknowledging that radical behaviorists were probably excessive in their mechanistic language and forays against anthropomorphic thinking, J. S. Kennedy warns against a "new anthropomorphism." Cognitive ethologists such as Marc Bekoff continue to include in their books for the general public a spirited defense against charges of anthropomorphism and occasionally with a countercharge of "anthropomorphobia" — "persistent vigilance against the charge of anthropomorphism" (Crist 36).

Although neither practicing nor proposing cognitive ethology, Eiseley was certainly participating in twentieth-century discussions about science's methods, limitations, and role in the culture — discussions he took personally, as we have seen. Occasionally he portrayed himself as a marginal individual, "one of those hang-dog characters who float about in the limbo between science and literature, sometimes pierced by the shafts of both establishments" (*Lost* 160), but elsewhere he fiercely insisted that there was no limbo, no gap, between these "two cultures": "in a sense, the 'two cultures' are an illusion . . . a product of unreasoning fear, professionalism, and misunderstanding." In the scientific disciplines as well, divisions are the product of small minds, he asserted, "with the institutionalization of method, with the appearance of dogma and mapped-out territories . . . an unpleasant suggestion of fenced preserves begins to dominate the university atmosphere" (*Star* 276). The anecdote of the lecture-going mouse and the stern young psychology student exemplifies Eiseley's resistance to this atmosphere.

As a physical anthropologist, Eiseley was a student of human cultures rather than animal behavior science, but he resisted any marginalization of his discipline from the study of evolutionary theory. In the conclusion of *Darwin's Century*, he insists on the importance of anthropology for the

directions of biological investigation: "In reality biological and anthropological thinking have influenced each other and have been part of the same
intellectual climate for a long period of time. It has been man's curiosity
about himself, extended to the origins of the world around him, that has
led to the discovery of the evolutionary process" (337). In this insistence
on the connections among scientific fields — and by extension on his role
as insider rather than marginal gadfly — Eiseley also reveals his personal
inclinations and disciplinary viewpoint: it is his curiosity about "Man"
that propels his investigations of the natural world and other animals.

Still, when writing about science, Eiseley often represents himself as
writing against the grain, and anthropomorphism is part of this process.
"The Bird and the Machine" exemplifies his resistance to mechanomorphism — viewed as the only alternative to anthropomorphism. Eiseley narrates an experience with two hawks that, he claims, permanently altered his
perspective on both animals and humans. A member of an archaeological
expedition, Eiseley was instructed to capture live birds and animals, for
"a zoo somewhere abroad [that] needed restocking. It was one of those
reciprocal matters in which science involves itself" (*Immense* 186). Eiseley
encounters a pair of sparrow hawks in an abandoned building and manages
to capture one. His description of the captive hawk includes language of
emotion and intentionality: "The little fellow had saved his mate by diverting
me, and that was that. He was born to it, and made no outcry now, resting
in my hand hopelessly, but peering toward me in the shadows behind the
lamp with a fierce, almost indifferent glance. He neither gave nor expected
mercy and something out of the high air passed from him to me, stirring
a faint embarrassment" (189). As a scientist, Eiseley is participating in an
endeavor that is problematic for two reasons: it promotes mechanistic
explanations of animal and human behavior, and it involves the abuse of
creatures that have feelings. "An assassin has to get used to these things,"
Eiseley writes sardonically. "I had a professional reputation to keep up"
(190). The essay's climax, however, is not the capture but the release of
the bird, the essay's argument less about the ethical treatment of animals
than about the shortcomings of mechanistic interpretations of life. Upon
releasing the bird, Eiseley realizes that its mate has for hours been circling

high above, waiting; he hears "a cry of . . . unutterable and ecstatic joy" as the mate sees the captive bird released (191).

Eiseley's prose is ecstatic — arguably unscientific — as he tells of the birds' reunion and evokes the impact that the experience has had in his memory. The essay closes, though, with an explicit contrast between the language of mechanomorphism and anthropomorphic language that allows for animal emotions. First, Eiseley quotes a newspaper article, "What Next in the Attributes of Machines": "It does not seem that there is anything in the construction, constituents, or behavior of the human being which it is essentially impossible for science to duplicate and synthesize. On the other hand . . ." (192). Taking the last phrase as a starting point, Eiseley launches a new perspective: "Ah, my mind takes up, on the other hand, the machine does not bleed, ache, hang for hours in the empty sky in a torment of hope to learn the fate of another machine, nor does it cry out with joy nor dance in the air with the fierce passion of a bird" (193). Accepting a rich emotional life for animals, Eiseley arms himself to resist mechanistic assumptions that threaten not only animals but human beings.

In a useful analysis of current scientific positions regarding anthropomorphism, Sandra D. Mitchell draws some conclusions that in part vindicate Eiseley's defense against blanket accusations:

> The global arguments against anthropomorphism cannot be maintained in a post-Darwinian scientific world. Given that humans are biologically related to other species, the ascription of concepts whose natural home is in describing human features and behaviors may very well apply to nonhumans. That being said, there is also no global support for the cavalier exportation of human descriptive concepts to nonhumans. . . . In short, anthropomorphic models are specific, scientifically accessible claims of similarity between humans and nonhumans. As such, they must be substantiated by evidence that there are similar causal mechanisms responsible for generating the apparently similar behaviors that are observed. (114)

However, although certainly more open-minded than Eiseley's anecdotal psychology student, Mitchell does require that statements that claim to be scientific must be scientifically accessible. Unsubstantiated by evidence of similar causal mechanisms, "The Bird and the Machine" may be read as literary sentimentalism or scientific error; however, it can also be viewed as a case of strategic — even seductive — resistance to professional habits of mind that, in Eiseley's eyes, need correction. Playing on humans' needs for empathy and connection with the natural world, Eiseley exploits the anthropomorphic tendencies of language to critique contemporary science, allowing space for neither substantiation nor counterargument. In cases like these, Eiseley has his countercharge ready before the charge can be made.

ANTHROPOMORPHISM AS AN EFFECT OF LANGUAGE

In an appreciation essay on the nineteenth-century naturalists, Eiseley makes a comment that might also be read as a defense of his own language choices: "No one need object to the elucidation of scientific principles in clear, unornamental prose. What concerns us is the fact that there exists a new class of highly skilled barbarians — not representing the very great in science — who would confine men entirely to this diet. . . . Even though they were not discoverers in the objective sense, one feels at times that the great nature essayists had more individual perception than their scientific contemporaries. Theirs was a different contribution . . . something that lies beyond the careful analyses of professional biology" (*Night* 142). In trying to see the world from a different perspective — to understand the world from the animal's point of view — Eiseley argues, the naturalists provided a "sensitivity" not found in workaday scientific writing. It is not necessarily a better perspective or a better language, just a different one. However, without such a perspective, humans are disadvantaged: "we will lack pity and tolerance, not through intent, but from blindness" (143). In such passages, Eiseley, often praised by nonscientists for his beautiful, evocative language, maintains that language like his has a place in science (though not in professional scientific journals).

As we have seen, one important reason for the fierceness of Eiseley's notebook countercharge is that anthropomorphism has functioned over the years more as a general pejorative than as a specifically defined or definable term. Asquith notes that "the appellation of anthropomorphism rests largely on cultural biases and certain linguistic properties of terms, rather than on correspondence to an agreed-upon standard terminology. . . . What we consider to be uniquely human is affected as much by culture and historical fashion as by our ignorance of the animals themselves" (23). Sociologist Eileen Crist agrees that "the reason that 'anthropomorphism' is not crisply definable or identifiable is that it is an effect of language, rather than a set of circumscribable features of its use" (32). That is, a "reader's understanding of the nature of animal life" is unavoidably shaped by the language that has been chosen to represent it. In sketching out diametrically opposed positions toward the study of animal behavior, De Waal, too, draws attention to the anthropomorphism that is embedded in language: "Inasmuch as descriptions . . . place animals closer to us than to machines, they adopt a language we customarily use for human action. Inevitably, these descriptions sound anthropomorphic" (xv). Likewise, Crist recognizes just two alternatives — everyday language and technical language. A behavior can be described as if the animal is a *subject*, acting purposefully and experiencing the world as meaningful, or as if the animal is an *object*: "In virtue of its affiliation with everyday reasoning about human action, the use of ordinary language of action reflects a regard for animals as acting subjects; the immanent, experiential perspective of animals is treated as real, recoverable, and invaluable in the understanding of their actions and lives. Technical language, on the other hand, paves the way toward conceptualizing animals as natural objects. . . . [This choice of language] is agnostic and often inimical toward the idea that animals have an experiential perspective" (2). That is, technical language represents animals as "blind to the upshot of their behaviors, and without command over their expression" (Crist 9). Crist characterizes this language, which maintains a distance between animal and human worlds, as "mechanomorphic."

Kennedy agrees that "our ordinary everyday speech is anthropomorphic" (26) but for this very reason does not see everyday language as a viable choice for the scientific description of animal behavior. Subjective, anthropomorphic language is seductive, and even neobehaviorists underestimate its influence, Kennedy warns (151). His prescription: "if we stop to think. . . . we can often pick more objective terms — with some loss of vividness perhaps, but not necessarily any loss of crispness" (161–62): "Pausing to translate one's racy anthropomorphic account of a behavioural sequence into a detailed description of what was actually observed can bring to light features that the racy account missed or glossed over. . . . We now have to look closely at the animal's actual movements, identify what kind they are and analyse their organization" (164). Kennedy argues that the alternative to anthropomorphic language is not mechanomorphism but rather careful observation. He warns that careless anthropomorphism can lead to "supernaturalism" or animism, though he does allow that "mock anthropomorphism" — a clearly labeled "metaphoric" use of anthropomorphic language, or "merely pretending for argument's sake that an animal can think or feel as we do" — can do little harm and may be valuable for hypothesis generating (9).

In "The Bird and the Machine," as we have seen, Eiseley argues that a mechanistic view of life is the alternative to a perspective that includes emotion, pain, attachment, intentionality — what Kennedy and Crist agree is inherently anthropomorphic everyday language. He then expands the scope of that everyday language to include both close observation and flights of language bordering on the miraculous. Expectably, it is the label "miracle" that is most controversial, and Eiseley, again, seems to be playing the gadfly when he uses it: "I know that the word 'miraculous' is regarded dubiously in scientific circles because of past quarrels with theologians. The word has been defined, however, as an event transcending the known laws of nature. Since, as we have seen, the laws of nature have a way of being altered from one generation of scientists to the next, a little taste for the miraculous in this broad sense will do us no harm" (Star 290–91). The occasional brief "miracle," still defined in terms of science, provides one temporary way out of the problem of language — language as anthropomorphic or mechanistic, animals as subjects or objects — in the search for a language that is beneficial both for animals and to nature.

ANTHROPOMORPHISM AS THINKING *WITH* ANIMALS

In "Paw Marks and Buried Towns," which he chose to include in *The Night Country*, Eiseley opens with an anecdote about a dog he had as a childhood pet:

> Mickey, I know, wanted very much to be a genuine human being. If permitted, he would sit up to the table and put his paws together before his plate, like the rest of the children. If anyone [pretended] to have paws and rest[ed] his chin on the table as Mickey had to do, Mickey would growl and lift his lip. He knew very well he was being mocked for not being human.... Though people refused to take Mickey's ambition seriously, the frustration never affected his temperament. Being of a philosophic cast of mind, he knew that children were less severe in their classifications.... Mickey tried hard to be a human being. (80)

The first part of the anecdote seems to come out of a children's story. It is naively and even presumptuously anthropomorphic: Mickey has goals (to be human), emotions (frustration), knowledge (that he is being mocked), and judgment (a philosophic cast of mind). He is a conscious subject reaching out for a connection with human beings. All this is inferred from the position of his paws on the table and a curl of his lip. With the assertion, "I know," Eiseley, too, appears to be reaching for a conscious connection between human and animal.

Yet the full story of Mickey — along with the analogy between paw prints and buried towns that Eiseley develops — emphasizes the distance between dog and man, between humans and all other species. Only children take Mickey's "ambition" — and his consciousness — seriously. From an adult point of view (behavioral scientist or not), the evidence of Mickey's consciousness is just too slender. Nevertheless, Eiseley insists, both Mickey and Man aim at transcendence: "Mickey tried hard to be a human being. ... It [has] struck me that every ruined civilization is, in a sense, the mark of men trying to be human, trying to transcend themselves" (80). In this anecdote, Eiseley equivocates on the meaning of "being human," and he makes assumptions about animal consciousness. But no matter: both attempts at transcendence (of species limitations) are failures. Both dog and human reach for continuity and connection — and do not succeed.

Recent discussions of anthropomorphism have centered on the issue of animal consciousness, and this, in turn, has implications for the possibilities of connection between humans and other animals. Crist asserts that *all* "representations of animal life, whether intentionally or not, are always addressing what is for Western thought a most engrossing mystery — the contentious topic of animal mind or animal consciousness" (1). To date, there are still no definitive, agreed-upon answers to questions like these: "Do animals plan, think, or feel?" or "What is it like to be a bat?" While skeptics such as Kennedy say such questions can never be answered "with the certainty that science can bring," cognitive ethologists argue that the existence of emotions in animals has already been established. While admitting, "We will never know *exactly* what it is like to be a wolf," Bekoff and Jessica Pierce assert that scientific evidence shows that animals consider the future and have a capacity for empathy — in their own terms, appropriate for their species (*Wild* 44). Bekoff continues, "Ethological studies and research in social neuroscience show that humans aren't the sole occupants of the emotional arena" (*Emotional* 15). Thus, any human who feels alienated in a world of un-conscious animals is not paying enough attention to animals or to scientific findings: "Data suggest that there is enough continuity in physiology and psychology to safely infer significant experiential common ground" (*Wild* 44).

Donna Haraway utilizes these physiological continuities in her reconsideration of what she calls the "Great Divides between what counts as . . . nonhuman and human" by retheorizing what happens "when species meet." She says, "I love the fact that human genomes can be found in only about 10 percent of all the cells that occupy the mundane space I call my body; the other 90 percent of the cells are filled with the genomes of bacteria, fungi, protists, and such. . . . I become an adult human being in company with these tiny messmates. To be *one* is always to *become with* many" (3–4). Her vision of the continuity and interdependence of life is reminiscent of Eiseley's account of a serious fall, when, bleeding and reeling from a head injury, he addresses his own "blood cells, phagocytes, platelets" by pleading, "Oh, don't go. I'm sorry, I've done for you" (*Unexpected* 177–78). Eiseley, however, distances himself somewhat from this curious vision of togetherness by providing a double perspective — his own, as the injured man, and that of the increasingly curious spectators who hear him babbling.

Psychologist Clive D. L. Wynne, who warns against anthropomorphic assumptions that animals are "like us" simply because we have all evolved (evolutionary continuity), reflects nevertheless on the profound implications of animal consciousness for humanity:

> Are we human beings . . . alone on this planet in our consciously thinking minds, or are we surrounded by knowers whose thoughts are just too alien for us to understand? To contemplate this question is to stand, not on the edge of an abyss, but on the cusp between two abysses. Either outcome would be astonishing. To know for sure that we had thinking companions on this planet would be an amazing discovery. . . . On the other hand, to know with the certainty that science can bring that we stand unique in our reflective, thoughtful intelligence — that would also give me to pause [*sic*]. (10)

Likewise, Eiseley's essays not only evoke the emotional and intellectual importance of such questions but also suggest that Eiseley, too, finds himself "on the cusp between two abysses." In *The Immense Journey*, as in his study of Darwin, he explains and exemplifies evolutionary continuity. However, he appears to be of two minds on the questions of animal consciousness, human uniqueness, and the possibilities for empathy between humans and other animals.

For one thing, in addition to biology, human beings are also shaped by culture, which they in turn shape through tools and language. "In man, by contrast with the animal," Eiseley writes, "two streams of evolution have met and merged: the biological and the cultural. The two streams are not always mutually compatible. . . . Man's predicament is augmented by the fact that he is alone in the universe. He is locked in a single peculiar body; he can compare observations with no other form of life" (*Night* 128–30). Thus, while *Homo sapiens* shares with other animals the biological fluidity and constant change represented by evolutionary forces, "man" is the sole beneficiary — and victim — of an evolutionary leap that set humans apart from other animals. In "The Long Loneliness," Eiseley writes,

> There is nothing more alone in the universe than man. He is alone because he has the intellectual capacity to know that he is separated by a vast gulf of social memory and experiment from the lives of his animal associates. He has entered into the strange world of history, of social and intellectual change, while his brothers of the field and forest remain subject to the invisible laws of biological evolution. Animals are molded by natural forces they do not comprehend. To their minds there is no past and no future. There is only the everlasting present of a single generation.
>
> Man, by contrast, is alone with the knowledge of his history until the day of his death. When we were children we wanted to talk to animals and struggled to understand why this was impossible. Slowly we gave up the attempt as we grew into the solitary world of human adulthood.... Only in acts of inarticulate compassion, in rare and hidden moments of communion with nature, does man briefly escape his solitary destiny. (*Star* 37)

Viewed through the lens of Crist's theory of language, this passage represents animals not as active subjects but as objects of other forces. Yet elsewhere in the same essay, Eiseley makes room for animals as subjects: "all animals which man has reason to believe are more than usually intelligent — our relatives the great apes, the elephant, the raccoon, the wolverine, among others — are problem solvers, and in at least a small way manipulators of their environment." Drawing on the scientific findings of his time, Eiseley argues that it is the inability of animals to communicate, "save for the instinctive calls of their species," that is responsible for the gulf between animal and human: "No matter how high the individual intelligence, its private world remains a private possession locked forever within a single, perishable brain. It is this fact that finally balks our hunger to communicate even with the sensitive dog who shares our fireside" (42).

But there is a way out of this impasse (albeit temporary), and in some of his most memorable anecdotes Eiseley takes it: he recounts the "rare and hidden moments of communion with nature" (37). In these essays Eiseley, as narrator, yearns for, speculates on, and occasionally finds short-lived empathetic connections between himself and another animal. In "The Innocent Fox," he is briefly successful; he claims to have seen a "miracle":

> I saw it because I was hunched at ground level smelling rank of fox, and no longer gazing with upright human arrogance upon the things of this world. . . . [A] small neat face looked shyly up at me. The ears moved at every sound. . . . They crinkled, I began to realize, only with curiosity; they had not learned to fear. . . . It was a small fox pup from a den under the timbers who looked up at me. . . . He innocently selected what I think was a chicken bone from an untidy pile of splintered rubbish and shook it at me invitingly. There was a vast and playful humor in his face. . . . Gravely I arranged my forepaws while the puppy whimpered with ill-concealed excitement. I drew the breath of a fox's den into my nostrils. On impulse, I picked up clumsily a whiter bone and shook it in teeth that had not entirely forgotten their original purpose. Round and round we tumbled for one ecstatic moment. (*Unexpected* 209–10)

In this episode, Eiseley uses a method favored by ethologists — doing what the animal does, seeing the world from its point of view — to make a brief and transformative animal-human connection. Abandoning his "human arrogance" and forgetting to be cautious with his conclusions, he infers the fox's shyness, innocence, playfulness, humor, and excitement. Having embarked on an amazing journey of possibility — communication and empathy between human and animal, unhampered by self-consciousness or fear — Eiseley comes firmly back to solid ground and everyday life. "For just a moment I had held the universe at bay," he declares and then continues with superlatives: "It is the gravest, most meaningful act I shall ever accomplish." But then comes the reality check: "there is no use reporting it to the Royal Society" (212). A "miracle" is by definition scientifically unverifiable. The representation of an anecdote as a miracle or visitation operates as an end run around scientific charges of anthropomorphism.

For Eiseley, in this anecdote as in others, the point is not really whether animals are conscious — whether the fox enjoys the romp with the man — but rather the nature of the consciousness that is *raised* in humans (and in Eiseley himself) by the presence and actions of animals. Examining the relationships between humans and domestic and companion animals, Serpell seems to concur with Eiseley when he says that anthropomorphism "appears to have its roots in the human capacity for so-called reflexive consciousness, that is, the ability to use . . . the knowledge of what it is like to be a person, to understand and anticipate the behavior of others" (123). He cites archaeologist Stephen Mithen's claim that "without anthropomorphic thinking neither pet keeping nor animal domestication would ever have been possible" (124) and adds that "anthropomorphism provides us with a unique opportunity to bridge the conceptual and moral gulf that separates humans from other animals. Indeed, it is questionable whether animal protection and conservation movements would even exist if not for the bond of sympathy engendered for nonhuman animals by anthropomorphic thinking" (132).

When anthropomorphism involves animal consciousness and animal-human connections, it entails questions about the ethical treatment of animals. In "A Small Death," a chapter in his autobiography, Eiseley sketches a painful and guilty memory: witnessing the killing of a laboratory dog for a demonstration before an "indifferent class that had gained little from the experiment." The dog, Eiseley recalls, "looked at me with that unutterable expression. 'I do not know why I am here. Save me. I have seen other dogs fall and be carried away. Why do you do this? Why?'" (*All* 144). Eiseley says he felt for the dog because he, too, "would have begged for one more hour of light" (145). Moving away from his empathetic response to the doomed dog, describing himself as "a scientist . . . groping for some way to explain," Eiseley sketches a conversation with a physician who tries to reassure him with a different viewpoint on animal emotions and cognizance — "My friend. . . . You are imagining things. Dogs don't think like that. You merely thought he was looking at you" (144) — and then moves on to the opinion of "a very great experimentalist, who has said that to extend ethics to animals is unutterable folly. Man cannot do this and learn" (145). Eiseley does not follow up with a discourse on the ethical treatment of animals but rather leaves readers to consider the starkly stated views of several men of science — including only one, himself, who is not content to accept the reassurance, "Dogs don't think like that."

Eiseley's brief anecdote of the laboratory dog certainly takes advantage of the opportunity that Serpell sees in anthropomorphism for bridging "the conceptual and moral gulf" between humans and other animals. Serpell, however, goes on to discuss certain caveats: "Sadly, however, instead of accepting and appreciating companion animals for what they are, we seem more inclined to abduct them across the animal-human divide [and] render them in our own 'image'" (132). Serpell's focus is on pets being dressed up or, more seriously, bred to look like cute humans. Could it be argued that in stories such as those of Mickey and of the innocent fox, Eiseley has conceptually abducted these creatures over the animal-human divide? In these anecdotes, I would argue, there is no abduction, and Eiseley maintains a respectful, even lonely, distance: Mickey remains a dog, and Eiseley quickly leaves the young fox's den when he knows the adult foxes will soon be returning. As we have seen, he terms it a "miracle" — an event contrary to science — that his brief romp with the fox has occurred at all. His descriptions of dying animals — an ailing gull, an injured duck on the beach — are not maudlin. He evokes sympathy for them while preserving their otherness.

Finally, in this example from "The Brown Wasps" in *The Night Country*, Eiseley brings a scientist's careful observation along with anthropomorphic language into a literary essay about what we might call the homing instinct — or, alternatively, the longing for remembered place:

> We cling to a time and a place because without them man is lost, not only man but life. . . . This feeling runs deep in life; it brings stray cats running over endless miles, and birds homing from the ends of the earth. It is as though all living creatures, and particularly the more intelligent, can survive only by fixing or transforming a bit of time into space or by securing a bit of space with its objects immortalized and made permanent in time. For example, I once saw, on a flower pot in my own living room, the efforts of a field mouse to build a remembered field. I have lived to see this episode repeated in a thousand guises, and since I have spent a large portion of my life in the shade of a nonexistent tree I think *I am entitled to speak for the field mouse*. (229; emphasis added)

Drawing on his own close observation as evidence for an assertion about human and animal longings, Eiseley implies that his observation of the mouse has been verified through many similar observed events. He claims that these observations *combined with* his own experience — his knowledge of his own emotions and motivations — entitle him to speak for the field mouse, that is, to speculate on one aspect of "what it is like to be a mouse."

A defiant practitioner of anthropomorphism when he is fighting against mechanistic interpretations of both human and animal life or criticizing those who feel no empathy for animals (or for scientist-essayists), Eiseley is ambivalent about questions of animal consciousness and animal-human communication and empathy. A hint or vision of what such a connection might be can be found in the "miracles" that he narrates — his own brief encounters with other animals — and then wistfully encapsulates as special cases. Finally, in spite of the memorable prose of his animal anecdotes and the issues they raise, Eiseley's primary interest is in what he calls "Man" — in human nature, human culture, and its (that is, our) relationship to the rest of the world. This is not necessarily an anthropocentric preoccupation — as it would be if Eiseley assumed *Homo sapiens* to be the center of the world and the culmination of evolution, as he certainly does not. Eiseley's concern with humans is an occupational inclination of the anthropologist. Ultimately, as Asquith suggests, anthropomorphism does have more to do with humans than with animals: "Insofar as we are incapable of providing evidence for the nature of animal cognition," she says, "our discussions about anthropomorphism in fact are discussions about our perceived place in nature" (34). With a passionate interest in humanity's place in nature and an equally strong concern with his own place in science and literature, Eiseley unapologetically put anthropomorphism to work in his essays into the natural world.

NOTES

1. Christianson (*Fox* 352–53) is one of several Eiseley scholars who reference this review and comment on Eiseley's strong reaction to it. In "The Illusion of the Two Cultures," Eiseley may be referring to himself when he states, "I know of at least one scholar who, venturing to develop some personal ideas in an essay for the layman, was characterized by a reviewer in a leading professional journal as a worthless writer, although, as it chanced, the work under discussion had received several awards in literature, one of them international in scope" (*Star* 268).

2. I have not located a published review that uses the word "anthropomorphizing." Eiseley may be referring to verbal attacks, such as the one he narrates in *The Unexpected Universe* (150); he may also have inferred this charge from other reviewers (such as Buettner-Janusch) who accused him of too much purple prose and not enough scientific rigor.

3. *Immense* 179–93; *Unexpected* 194–212; *Night* 227–36; *Night* 34; *All* 128–30; *All* 143–44; *Immense* 163–78.

4. Commentators on Eiseley appear to agree that Eiseley's essays cannot simply be categorized as "nonscientific writing" and evaluated as such. Mary Ellen Pitts develops Eiseley's "quest for a dialogue of understandings" between science and the humanities in his popular essays and notes that he "re-announc[es] his allegiance to his 'scientific heritage'" in his later works (304–5). Bushnell argues that "instead of 'expanding the personal essay for scientific purposes,'" Eiseley has "transmuted the scientific essay for personal purposes" (258).

5. Although unrevised, Eiseley's brief notebook entry on anthropomorphism was striking enough to be included in an excerpt that appeared (under the title "Reading Nature") in *Harper's* during the same month that *The Lost Notebooks of Loren Eiseley* was published.

6. Recently the editors of a special issue of *Social Cognition* took a similar view of the ethical implications of anthropomorphism in humans' treatment of other human beings: "The way we see other humans is inextricably intertwined with the way we see nonhumans. . . . Anthropomorphizing may be viewed as the reverse of dehumanizing. One over-includes and the other under-includes [usually vulnerable groups] . . . in the human category" (Kwan and Fiske 125–27).

6

"The Borders between Us"

Loren Eiseley's Ecopoetics

TOM LYNCH

for I
love forms beyond my own
and regret the borders between us.
LOREN EISELEY, "MAGIC"

Loren Eiseley's literary reputation today rests almost exclusively on the significance of his nonfiction nature essays, which deservedly stand as influential exemplars of creative nonfiction science and nature writing. However, in his early years as an undergraduate at the University of Nebraska, Eiseley had the reputation as an important and promising poet, and he published poetry in a range of literary journals. Most notably, his work appeared in the earliest editions of *Prairie Schooner*, whose editorial staff he joined in 1927, the year after it began publication. And, not limited to his own school's journal, he published in a variety of other venues, even in Harriet Monroe's prestigious *Poetry* magazine. As a young man, Eiseley was immersed in the lively poetry world of the 1920s and 1930s and poised to become an important voice in that world. In particular, he was an enthusiastic champion of Robinson Jeffer's controversial inhumanistic poetry. Eiseley admired Jeffers "above all modern writers because of their common heritage — 'the poet and the scientist in one'" (Christianson, *Fox* 191).

Eiseley's education exemplified this mix of poet and scientist; he received dual bachelor's degrees in English and anthropology. But for a variety of reasons, English lost out, and Eiseley chose to pursue graduate studies in anthropology. In spite of the promising start to his career as a poet, his poetic publications diminished precipitously after he took his first teaching job in 1937 at the University of Kansas. By 1945 he had ceased altogether to publish poetry. Alas, he would seem to have become that all too familiar, pitiful spectacle, the promising poet nipped in blossoming bud by the cold shears of economic necessity. It seems likely that to have continued to publish poetry while simultaneously pursuing a career in science would have been not only a distraction but likely a hindrance to professional advancement, for who would take him seriously as a scientist if he were also publishing, of all things, poetry. And later, at the University of Pennsylvania during the 1950s and 1960s, even as his reputation as a popular writer of science and nature essays grew, he nevertheless continued to refrain from poetry — from publishing it, that is, but not, it would seem, from writing it.

Ever the furtive fox, Eiseley had continued to scribble poems through these years among the data and scientific trivia accumulating in his notebooks, while outwardly conforming to the sober and responsible demeanor of a scientist, interchanging, as he says, "an artifact for a poem or a poem for an artifact" (*Notes* 11). In his later years, as his academic career drew to a close and being known as a publishing poet could no longer injure his professional reputation, Eiseley released in quick succession three volumes of poetry: *Notes of an Alchemist* in 1972, *The Innocent Assassins* in 1973, and *Another Kind of Autumn*, posthumously published in 1977.

In general, Eiseley scholars have tended to overlook his poetry. At best, they have seen his youthful poetry as a formative apprenticeship, laying the foundation for his real work, the crafting of his nonfiction prose essays. That his prose essays are so often praised for their poetic qualities has not seemed to suggest that his poetry itself might deserve a closer look. Poetry scholars have likewise overlooked Eiseley's poetry. At the time of the publication of his poetry books in the mid-1970s, poetry criticism was ill-suited to assessing and appreciating Eiseley's poetic output. Neither the lingering New Criticism nor the emerging postmodern hermeneutics of skepticism had much sympathy for Eiseley's earnest engagement with serious questions regarding a world that lay very much outside the text.

ECOPOETICS

In recent years, however, a new approach to the analysis of poetry has emerged, ecopoetics, which provides new opportunities for exploring and explicating poetry that exhibits the sorts of characteristics represented in Eiseley's work. So far, scholars applying ecopoetics have analyzed writers from a number of literary traditions. The English Romantics have been appropriately addressed. Jeffers has received long-overdue attention, and considerable work has been done on more recent American poets such as Wendell Berry, Gary Snyder, Mary Oliver, W. S. Merwin, Joy Harjo, and Linda Hogan. In spite of its obvious relevance to ecopoetics, however, I have been unable to find any reference to Eiseley's poetry anywhere in the growing body of ecopoetical studies. It is my contention that this neglect is a serious oversight and that Eiseley should be seen as an important figure in the development of the ecopoem.

I forthrightly acknowledge some of Eiseley's weaknesses as a poet, especially his professor's tendency to lecture, his propensity to allow images to serve as illustrations of ideas, and his sometimes too prosaic prosody. So I do not want to make the case that Eiseley is an overlooked poetic genius. But I do want to offer that he was an early practitioner of what we now call ecopoetry; he struggled with some of the same issues that bedevil ecopoets today and therefore deserves greater recognition for his accomplishments. These challenging issues include how to incorporate scientific ideas and vocabulary into poetry, how to express empathy for other animals without colonizing their subjectivity, how to evoke compassion for and identify with a natural order that fewer and fewer readers have any direct contact with, and how to generate a sense of cosmic, geologic, and evolutionary time and space in the limited medium of language.

Ecopoems are a type of poetry that, while clearly related to the long-standing tradition of nature poetry, engage with various new understandings of the character of the natural world and of the responsibility of poetry toward it. (An analogy might be made with feminist poetry: while many poems have women in them, only a small subset of those could be considered feminist poems. Similarly, while many poems have nature in them, only a few of those could be considered ecopoems.) In ecopoetry, nature is perceived not as a storehouse of images observed and ordered by the poet primarily as figurations of some other more primary concern, such as the poet's emotional state, but as a complex, evolving, simultaneously autonomous and yet reciprocal ecology in which the poet is a part but typically only a very small part. What precisely distinguishes ecopoetry from more traditional nature poetry is an area of some dispute. Undoubtedly there is more of a continuum than a fixed boundary, and so establishing a rigid dichotomy is misleading (as well as a violation of ecocriticism's oft-professed distrust of binary thinking). Nevertheless, some distinctive ecopoetical tendencies can be outlined. Terry Gifford, for example, proposes that ecopoems differ from traditional nature poems in their engagement "directly with environmental issues" (3). Leonard M. Scigaj has argued for what he calls a sustainable poetry "that treats nature as a separate and equal other and includes respect for nature conceived as a series of ecosystems — dynamic and potentially self-regulating cyclic feedback systems" (5). J. Scott Bryson states that ecopoems are distinguished by "an emphasis on maintaining an ecocentric perspective that recognizes the interdependent nature of the world," by "an imperative toward humility in relationships with both human and nonhuman nature," and by their display of "an intense skepticism concerning hyperrationality, a skepticism that usually leads to an indictment of an overtechnologized modern world and a warning concerning the very real potential for ecological catastrophe" (5–6). David W. Gilcrest suggests that "as a first principle . . . the ecological poem allies itself with ecological science's complaint against atomistic and mechanistic Newtonian science" (16). Perhaps most fundamental, as Scigaj proposes, ecopoets seek to alter our perceptions of nature to engender a more sustainable relationship with it. Ecopoems "provide models of altered perception that promote environmental awareness and active agency" (22). As I hope to show, all of these characteristics of the ecopoem are present in varying degrees in Eiseley's poetry.

Furthermore, Eiseley adds a key feature that is implied but unstated in some of these descriptions of ecopoems and that we ought to consider as an essential dimension to ecopoetry: an appreciation for the evolutionary matrix of all living things. Indeed, I would suggest that an evolutionary understanding is the foundation for a poem's ability to do many of the sorts of things that ecopoetics envisions; certainly, it is the crucial factor in providing us with a sense of nature as an ever-emergent process rather than as a finished and static product. Eiseley's evolutionary consciousness imbeds contemporary humans and our culture deeply into the processes that gave rise to all living things and provides us with an understanding of how an awareness of such processes helps us engage with and perhaps resolve a major anxiety-provoking issue in ecopoetics: our potential to empathize with, express solidarity for, and imaginatively represent the lives of other animals. For Eiseley this evolutionary matrix bonds us, in both affirming and sometimes ominous ways, to every other living thing. An evolutionary perspective is also key to shifting us from an anthropocentric to an ecocentric understanding of our place in the cosmos. A humbling awareness of the myriad permutations of living forms through cosmic and geologic time, and of the mind-boggling array of random chances that accumulated to bring about the emergence of Homo sapiens, can only serve to shift our locus of understanding from the anthro- toward the ecocentric, fundamentally altering our perceptions of what it means to be a human being on a planet we share with 30 million to 100 million other similarly evolved and enduring species. As Gilcrest argues, among the key factors that led to the emergence of ecopoetry was "the development of a geological and evolutionary sense of time that served to de-emphasize the importance of human experience and human history" (2). With Walt Whitman and Robinson Jeffers as notable antecedents, Eiseley was among the earliest to incorporate this profound sense of time into his poetry.

NATURE AT RISK

A key feature of ecopoetry is the poet's recognition that over the past few centuries nature has been increasingly injured by human activity and that it is no longer appropriate to portray nature exclusively as an idyllic escape from the human world. Eiseley was well aware of human abuse of nature, both of the natural world in general, and of animals in particular. Very few of his poems could be described as unreflective, innocent portrayals of an idyllic nature. Rather, they show both overtly and by implication the injury humans have caused. For example, in "No Place for Boy or Badger," from Another Kind of Autumn, he laments the destruction of the woods and fields on the outskirts of Lincoln that were his boyhood haunts and their replacement by suburban development. Returning to Lincoln many decades after he had moved away, he wanders his childhood neighborhood, displeased by what he finds. The "straight streets" and "endless suburbs" have obliterated the tangled mess of wild nature in which he once played and the neat lawns now provide "no place for boy or badger to hide in the hedgerows" (lines 4, 5, 9). The rich diversity of nature has been replaced by a stifling monocultural conformity that allows for "no milkweed pods in autumn, no tiger swallowtails floating" (12).

The loss of wild habitat is not just a loss for badgers and foxes, milkweeds and tiger swallowtails, but for children as well, who are deprived of the foundational experience of intimate contact with unruly nature. This loss of childhood time in nature is a concern recently expressed by many environmental educators (most notably Richard Louv), but Eiseley anticipated this current lament decades ago. And given Eiseley's bleak home life, the opportunity for escape presented by nearby wildlands would have been all the more cherished, and the implications of its loss all the more deeply felt.

Eiseley's poem "The Box Tortoise," published in *The Innocent Assassins*, focuses such concern on the plight of a single wild animal that finds itself surrounded by the multifarious dangers of the modern city. Just as human progress has left no place for boy or badger, so it has left no place for box turtles.[1] In the poem, the narrator rescues a box turtle he finds attempting to "crawl across the / Pike" (line 1). Knowing well that the "roaring speedway would kill anything," the narrator scoops up the turtle and carries him to safety (3). But, after having risked his own life to rescue the unappreciative turtle, the narrator then realizes that in this urban, ecophobic environment there is no safe place to which he can restore it. The surrounding environment is full of manicured garden apartments "notable in spring for chain saws, tree sprays," and whose inhabitants "dislike old reptile shapes that wander by" (7, 9). He further worries that the turtle, left alone, might "go right back to that concrete / roadway he had been rescued from" (11–12).

As in "No Place for Boy or Badger" the injury humans cause to nature in "The Box Tortoise" is not so much intentional and malicious as inadvertent, which makes it all the more sinister and difficult to redress. Nobody wants to kill the turtle, but we need our roads, don't we? And so the lives of creatures such as turtles are placed at risk. People who would be appalled at the idea of directly killing a turtle, or any other animal, nevertheless freely participate in a modern lifestyle that includes the destruction of habitat and the incursion of highways, phenomena that are every bit as deadly to animals as are hunting rifles or slaughterhouses.

In response to his question of, "What to do then?" (line 6) the poet seeks a refuge for the turtle. He finds an "unsold estate," whose lot is conveniently enclosed in an "old stone wall" and where neglect has allowed the leaf mould to build up thick and a "half-wild undergrowth" to persist (29, 28, 30). Hopping the wall, the poet leaves the turtle in this sanctuary of neglect, hoping the turtle will not find a way out but will "just settle in, sink down in leaves / to wait / an age or two" (33–35). The poet's answer to the question of "what to do" satisfies the immediate concern of how to save the turtle, but the larger question of what to do about the loss of habit is only deferred; in Eiseley's grim assessment one can only hunker down in the leaf mould and hope for the best, patience being a very turtle-like virtue.

NATURE AS CYCLICAL FEEDBACK SYSTEM

Another characteristic that distinguishes ecopoets is their perception of landscapes not as simple scenery but as complex and dynamic fields of energy transformations. In such transformational processes the poet is not simply a witness, but, whether willingly or not — indeed, whether consciously or not — also a participant. In many of his poems, perhaps most notably in "The Sunflower Song" from *The Innocent Assassins*, Eiseley celebrates just these sorts of cyclings and transformations that occur as soil grows a sunflower that produces a seed that feeds a cardinal who sings a song that gladdens the poet's generally rather somber heart, a song that he then vainly strives to imitate by consuming the same seeds the cardinal has eaten. The poet concludes that it is "the seeds that sing" because "without seeds, / the cardinal could not sing" (lines 26–27). And, indeed, it is the earth that sings because "the seeds are brought / up from the leaf mould" (27–28). Beginning rather conventionally, the poet asserts that "I think this bird a miracle / to so transform a seed" (34) but continues this line of thinking along its ecological course to muse that "I think the flower / also a miracle and so work down to earth, the one composer / no one has ever seen but all have heard" (35–37). Seeking to become a part of this creative cycle, and transfer its energy to his own struggling poetic efforts, the poet decides to "eat one of his sunflower seeds and try again" (39).

While poems reveling in the songs of various birds are legion, few consider the energy source of that song, or of its very literal connection to human acts of creativity. The power of soil to transform through various stages into song and poetry is at once scientifically explicable and yet at the same time remains "a miracle." In some very real sense this is a transformation that lies at the heart of ecopoetics, raising the fundamental question: how does poetry literally, not just figuratively, spring from the soil?

This cycling process, however, goes both ways. As soil becomes seed becomes bird, so bird becomes, alas, once again, soil. While Eiseley intellectually understands this inevitable downward side of the cycle, he expresses an honest sense of discomfort with the process in his poem "From Us without Singing," published in *Notes of an Alchemist*. Again, the focus of the poem is a bird, but this time the bird is not singing joyfully but is rather a discarded and decaying carcass he passes daily in his yard and on which "all the ugly innocent necessary work of nature / is carried on by beetles, ants, blowflies" (lines 3–4). Such a necessary, if unseemly, process, he realizes, will "ensure / the endless procession of pine needles, new eggs, / new birds," but also, he must conclude, "in their turn / new deaths" (6–9).

At this point, the poem is what we typically expect. Death is redeemed by the cycle of life. But the last line, isolated by the enjambment, introduces a troubling notion; the cycle does not conclude with the new life but returns again to death. While the molecules that make up our being persist through the various permutations of the cycle, our individual identity, our consciousness, is lost, which in this poem leads to confusion, dismay, and resentment: "I resent the slow / disarticulation of this summer bird" (25–26). And, as readers have probably inferred at this point, the poem is not just about the bird but the poet as well: "I am bound like this bird / to my own carcass, I / love this year's light, / the music in his, / my mind" (29–32).

In this remarkable poem we can see the poet struggling with the tension between his appreciation for the cycle of life and his emotional desire to resist the inevitable transposition of his own molecules and hence the extinction of his own identity and consciousness. At times the vast panoply of the cycle of life is consoling and even inspiring, but at other times, with but a slight shift of mood, we must admit, it is also terrifying. In this poem Eiseley seems concerned with how consciousness, how "mind," how, that is, individual identity and awareness, is implicated in this process. How is it that, bound to our own carcasses, we yet love the music of birdsong? And how is it that, though merely a physical form, a fortuitous concatenation of molecules, we nevertheless possess a mind that resists and resents its own dissolution back into molecules? Eiseley was never one to shrink from the terrors of life. In this poem Eiseley rejects the consolation of his own culture's religious tradition, that he, unlike the bird, has an immortal soul, a discrete consciousness that will transcend life's terrible cycles. He likewise avoids the easy consolation that being dissolved into something impersonal yet cosmically vast is any compensation for the loss of one's own loved and loving individual identity.

SKEPTICISM OF SCIENCE

Ecocriticism is engaged in a delicate dance with science, a dance Eiseley himself helped to choreograph. On the one hand, ecocritics and ecopoets are entirely beholden to science for the knowledge and insights that are signaled by the cherished and definitive "eco" prefix. To abandon the methods and findings of science is to abandon any justification for the use of that distinctive designation. To reject science is to turn an ecocritic into just a critic. Yet as history has too amply demonstrated, science is not an unmixed blessing and has at times served as both agent and tool of the degradation of nature and the abuse of animals that ecocriticism critiques. So the ecopoet and the ecocritic find themselves in a quandary.

For example, in Bryson's claim, previously cited, that ecopoets possess "an intense skepticism concerning hyperrationality, a skepticism that usually leads to an indictment of an overtechnologized modern world," he employs several qualifications that seek to dance around the difficulty (6). As he formulates it, ecopoets are not skeptical of "rationality," but only of "*hyper*rationality." Nor do they indict technology per se, but only the "*over*technologized." While one might praise the pirouettes of nuance here, one might also sense a deft evasion. Surely few are in favor of *hyper* or *over* anything; indeed, the formulation is a bit of a tautology. The rather significant question of when the rational becomes the *hyper*rational or the technological becomes the *over*technological is left unanswered. Gilcrest sees a way out of this dilemma in considering that the science of ecology, being holistic, is itself subversive in regard to mainstream science, which is, on the whole, reductive. In this case, the criticism is that atomistic and mechanistic science is too enamored of reductivism and not engaged enough with the sort of holistic perspective whose elucidation is the desire of ecology (26).

Eiseley was all too familiar with this debate. While grateful for the knowledge and insights of science, he felt that its unmistakable powers had too often resulted in a hubristic dismissal of other values. Although Eiseley was both a practicing scientist as well as a historian of science who championed such figures as Bacon and Darwin, this sort of critique of science's hyperationalism pervades his prose essays.

It also arises in his poetry. Indeed, one might well argue that Eiseley chose to write poetry specifically to have a forum in which to express this tension between science and something-more-than science. For example, in "Five Men from the Great Sciences" from *The Innocent Assassins*, the narrator describes five scientists whom he has overheard discussing how, thanks to the powers of science (and to the powers of men such as themselves), humans had at last succeeded in transcending nature. The skeptical poet, we are not surprised to read, is dubious, for he sees these men of science as trapped and limited rather than liberated by their increasing specialization and reliance on fancy tools. These men, he considers, "were caught inside . . . in a perpetually narrowing corner" (lines 6–7). What they are "really looking / for" he speculates, is "something beyond human cognizance" (8–9). However, he concludes, "We have not found it in the laboratory; / we have not found it in a billion light years; / we have not found it in the cyclotrons;" nor have we found it in any of the other sparkling apparatus of modern science (11–13). And yet the poet concludes, "It exists and lies truly outside or beyond nature, / conceived / in some intangible way by her (20–22).

What this "it" is, this "something beyond human cognizance," is, not surprisingly, left unclear. Some readers would be prompt to label it God, but the notion that this "it" is conceived by nature, rather than the other way around, might suggest a different sort of answer. Perhaps "it" is not something specific, but only the ever-mysterious unknown that lies just beyond the horizons of our knowing. Certainly, its evasiveness suggests that we adopt a more humble position in regard to nature, the sort of position advocated by ecopoetics but alien to the sorts of scientists Eiseley overhears.

SOLIDARITY WITH ANIMALS

One of Eiseley's main critiques of science (although clearly not original with him) is its willingness to "murder to dissect." Eiseley possessed a deep and lifelong sense of empathy for animals and was disturbed by their confinement or use in scientific experiments. In 1976 he received the Joseph Wood Krutch medal from the National Humane Society for a lifetime of service to the welfare of animals.

Eiseley was clearly a believer in some version of what has come to be called animal rights, and this ethic appears repeatedly in his poetry. For example, in the poem "The Changelings," he discusses his sorrow at the unwarranted confinement of animals: "My childhood was preoccupied with dreams / of how to free all animals immured / in shabby local zoos, / in boxes foul" (lines 67–70). In "The Last Days," he reflects on the widespread notion that humans are engaged in a war against nature, signaling his own mixed allegiance by punning on the ambiguity of the word "den": "My den is a command post, / a suburban fire center" (*Notes*, lines 17–18). He notes, however, the persistence of animals, a fox in a neighbor's garden, a tiger swallowtail "by god in spite of DDT" (21). If such a war is in fact in progress, Eiseley is unsure of his loyalties and considers the possibility of "defecting," because "animals are beginning to look better / than my own kind" (70, 75–76). "Sometimes," he admits, "I think they are talking. / My cat is talking / but I don't quite hear" (78–80).

In poems such as this Eiseley indicates that his allegiances are with the rest of nature and cannot be counted on by his own species. His inability to hear his cat talking, however, raises a potentially vexing limitation to the human capacity to sympathetically identify with other animals, the seemingly fundamental gap opened by our acquisition of language. A number of critics have proposed that the idea that humans can empathize with and "speak for" the interests of animals is, though well intended, nevertheless a colonizing gesture. For them the barriers between humans and other creatures are insurmountable and any attempt to speak for animals is redolent of sentimentalism, if not a whiff of imperialism. Gilcrest, for example, argues "that the attempt to represent nonhuman entities as speaking subjects, while serving to establish a less hierarchical relationship with the nonhuman by depriviieging human linguistic ability, is appropriately viewed as a colonizing move that remains susceptible to serious epistemological and ethical critique." He proffers a solution, arguing that "an environmental ethic does not necessitate the identification of the human and the nonhuman, whether in terms of linguistic competency or along any other dimension, and may in fact require the conservation of difference. . . . I argue . . . that by resisting identification with the nonhuman by embracing an antagonistic poetics, the contemporary nature poet cultivates an ethic of restraint consistent with ecocentric values" (6). While ethics of restraint are certainly laudable in our relations with animals, Eiseley offers a different solution, a solution based on human-animal similarity that is derived from our common evolutionary heritage.

ARCHEOPOEMS AND EVOLUTIONARY CONSCIOUSNESS

Eiseley's evolutionary consciousness can attenuate the seemingly insurmountable border that exists between humans and other animals. As E. Fred Carlisle has noted, Eiseley not only accepted evolution intellectually but "also interiorized the theory, so that it functioned as a major structure for perceiving and comprehending experience. He dwelt in it, so to speak, and through it he made contact with reality" ("Achievement" 42). By interiorizing an evolutionary perspective, Eiseley made a major contribution to the development of the ecopoem: the poem of evolutionary consciousness. This consciousness is most obvious in what I refer to as his archeopoetry. In such poetry Eiseley dramatizes the uncovering of an artifact in order to place humans within the vast context of geologic and evolutionary history, seeking to evince in the reader an appreciation for the long view of time and an understanding of humans as recently evolved animals whose distinctive features may make us feel superior but, in fact, in the context of evolution, are no different than the distinctive features of any other species.

Eiseley's signature archeopoem is "The Innocent Assassins," in which the recovered item is a sabertooth skull (*Innocent*). But similar poems include "The Little Treasures," in which the found object is a flint blade (*Another*); "Arrowhead," in which he finds a flint arrowhead (*Notes*); "The Beaver," in which he uncovers a beaver skull; "The High Plains," where he discovers a "pink catlinite bowl of an Indian pipe" (line 54); "The Hand Ax," where he stumbles across an incongruous stone ax; and "An Owl's Day," in which is found a bone needle, a flint knife, and the bones of an owl.

Poems of this sort seek to evoke both awe and humility, anxiety and hope, and work to internalize in the reader a subjective and visceral appreciation for the place of humans within the vast panoply of evolutionary time, while also revealing that the barrier we have erected between ourselves and other animals is the product of a self-important but deluded vanity. In such poems we often experience a sudden and perhaps disorienting enlargement of our psychic horizons. Initially, our attention is drawn downward to some small object immediately present on the ground. Excavating that object from the shadows, the poet illuminates its implications, and our perspective suddenly leaps to encompass vast dimensions of space and time. Sharing the archaeologist-poet's perspective, we glance up from the unearthed artifact to the landscape around us, and that landscape is forever altered. Through the intervention of the artifact, the familiar, drab ground on which we stand becomes numinous.

Many of these poems are based on Eiseley's experiences during his undergraduate years, when he spent parts of three summers as a sort of work-study research aid on paleontological digs in the panhandle of western Nebraska. These expeditions, known as the South Party and sponsored by the University of Nebraska's Morrill Hall Natural History Museum under the leadership of C. Bertrand Schultz, unearthed a wide variety of fossil remains, including oreodonts, mastadons, rhinos, camels, saber-toothed cats, and the tools of early humans. When these expeditions were conducted, the scientific consensus was that humans had inhabited North America for around two thousand years. The evidence collected on these expeditions helped to push that timeline back to about fifteen thousand years (Christianson, *Fox* 157).

Eiseley, the impressionistic and moody young poet, was transformed by his experience searching for and digging up fossil remains in the rugged reaches of the short-grass prairie, and his time on these expeditions in the Nebraska panhandle served as inspiration and material for much of the writing he was later to do. Forty years later, he dedicated his second book of poetry, *The Innocent Assassins,* to "the bone hunters of the old South Party, Morrill Expeditions 1931–33." In his autobiography he graciously thanks Schultz for enabling him to accompany these archaeological expeditions, an experience that "seared its way into my brain and into my writing" (*All* 83). Among the many things that seared into his brain was the recognition that evolution was not just a matter of intellectual thought, but of tactile sensation. Evolution was a phenomenon that could not only be imagined by the mind but felt by and within the body as well.

Eiseley was involved in three notable archaeological finds, all of which found their way not only into scholarly papers but also into poems. One was the early excavations at the Signal Butte bison quarry, west of Scottsbluff. Here, Folsom points were found in association with remains of the extinct *Bison antiquus,* evidence that pushed the dating of the first humans in the Americas back several thousand years. This discovery resulted in a joint publication with Schultz, "Paleontological Evidence for the Antiquity of the Scottsbluff Bison Quarry and Its Associated Artifacts."

However, skeptics could still suggest the remains had been tumbled together at this site, and so the find did not provide conclusive evidence of simultaneous human–*Bison antiquus* occupation. This archaeological work was followed by an excavation at Lindenmeier, north of Fort Collins, Colorado, in which Eiseley found the smoking gun, a Folsom point that was actually imbedded in the vertebra of a *Bison antiquus* (Christianson, *Fox* 161). This find was recounted in a poem published many years later in *Notes of an Alchemist*, titled "Flight 857." On an airplane approaching Denver, the poet looks down from "thirty thousand feet" at the Lindenmeier site, where he had dug trenches forty years earlier, and ponders "what the earth covers" there (line 2). Though he and his colleagues, he admits, never found the human remains for which they were searching, they did uncover remains of the "Ice Age long-horned bison, / the deadly point buried still / in the massive vertebra (16–18).

Though not as scientifically important as his finds at Scottsbluff and Lindenmeier, Eiseley's best-known discovery was what has come to be known as the "Innocent Assassins" skull, after his poem and book of that title. It is the skull of a saber-toothed cat, a 25 million-year-old smilodon, with its tooth piercing the humerus of another of its kind. The poem opens with an evocation of a landscape that resembles the Toadstool Park area of Nebraska: "Once in the sun-fierce badlands of the west / in that strange country of volcanic ash and cones, / runneled by rains, cut into purgatorial shapes, / where nothing grows" (lines 1–4). And, indeed, in his biography of Eiseley, Christianson identifies Toadstool Park as the location of the find (*Fox* 131). However, work by Bing Chen and others has concluded that the actual site of the find was in the Wildcat Hills near Chimney Rock.[2] This discrepancy suggests that Eiseley took liberties in his portrayal of the landscape where this artifact was uncovered. The poem describes a more barren and lifeless landscape than the one in which the skull was actually unearthed, evoking a sense of a surreal "purgatorial" desolation he felt more appropriate for the ominous character of the artifact and the mood he was seeking to evoke in the poem. And this is not the only change Eiseley made. He also altered the type of bone that was pierced by the tooth, referring to it as a "scapula," when in fact it is a humerus. The word "scapula" certainly sounds better in the phrase "fractured scapula" but is not factually correct (*Innocent,* line 16). Oddly, Christianson refers to the bone as a "tibia" (*Fox* 131).

In this scene Eiseley sees a striking tableau of a possible, and to him quite likely, human future. Like this sabertooth, we too can be destroyed by our own excessive weaponry. The Cold War's Mutually Assured Destruction scenario would seem to have been played out by these two sabertooths.

TRANSCENDING BORDERS

Evolution taught Eiseley that, despite what many of us would prefer to think, we humans were not so different from other animals. And while this thought had certain frightening implications, they were more than compensated for by the bonds it revealed. Put simply, the further back in time we look, the closer humans become to the other animals. During the Paleolithic period, for example, we lived in much greater intimacy with wild nature, and as Eiseley describes, the animals were our gods. Then, as we descend further back in time, we reach a point where "we" are no longer humans at all, where the borders between us and animals entirely dissolve as we, quite literally, become them. For Eiseley, unlike for most of us, these earlier periods are not remote. His professional career was about tracing them down and finding their artifacts. And they remain alive in us today as part of our evolved and not really so distant heritage, the artifacts of which, through acts of the imagination such as poetry, we can reach into ourselves and unearth.

In his poem "The Old Ones," Eiseley expresses a preference for the old animistic religions rather than the worship of humanlike deities, such as Zeus and his later monotheistic manifestations. This interesting poem, from *Notes of an Alchemist,* begins "The old gods are mosaics," by which he means that the gods humans originally worshipped often possessed combinations of human and animal features (line 1). As the poem proceeds, he berates the Greeks for having turned the gods into solely human figures. Rather, he finds the human-animal mosaic gods more appropriate because, as evolution teaches, and as DNA studies have since confirmed, we are in fact complex mosaics of all that has come before us. "I have found animals in me when I stroll in the forest" the poet writes. He notes that he will "step / like a cat in the night" and that he has "felt something / lift along my neck / when a wolf howls" (22, 23–26).

Such passages illustrate how our instincts tie us to our animal kin, revealing our mosaic status. And it further implies that many of the poetic metaphors we employ ("I step / like a cat in the night") are perhaps not just flights of fancy, but intimations of our evolutionary past that serve to write us back into the animal realm. The poem suggests that the traditional folk tales of oral cultures reveal a far greater, and for Eiseley a truer, degree of intimacy between humans and animals than modern monotheistic religions are willing to recognize. In tales of "how the beaver got his tail" or of how one might "marry the seal's daughter," we see our kinship with nature displayed (33, 35). Though the poet lives in "a very ordinary landscape," nevertheless, he reports, "I feel in my body / the lost mosaic" (36–37). Identifying with the figures of Native American mythology, he imagines, "I am Lone Man and Snow Rabbit: the earth pleases me. / The wind has stolen my coat away, / my thoughts are becoming animals" (38–40). And he concludes that "In this suddenly absurd landscape I find myself / laughing, laughing" (41–42).

The move toward what we call civilization, toward the wearing of coats as well as the worship of humanlike gods and the consequent drift to monotheisms, has been a move away from our animal kin. The old ones, that is, the shamans, were closer to animals, and their thoughts could, by shedding their human coats, as it were, become animals in an absurd trickster world that inspires a life-affirming laughter. To feel in one's body the lost mosaic is to reconnect with that heritage that is ever-present in us. In this sense, we are, as it were, always already animals, and our separation from them is an illusion, an illusion Eiseley's poetry seeks to correct.

In numerous poems Eiseley feels himself becoming those previous incarnations of what we once were, and in many ways still are, ever-so-much further back in time even than the Pleistocene. In "The Leaf Pile," for example, from *The Innocent Assassins*, he meditates on how the sense of smell, part of our reptile brain, can trigger deep responses when earlier parts of our being are activated by a particular scent, producing a nostalgic longing for the world of 10 million centuries ago. Having raked leaves in his yard, Eiseley inhales the scent and feels something stirring within, something that "has slept a long time" (line 24). This being who "breathes and snuffles," we are told, "has been a long time in the black dark, / scaled, snouted" (27, 28–29). Nevertheless, resurrected by the scent of autumn leaves, this creature begins to breathe the autumn air and is, the poet claims, "part of myself" (33). This being "has rooted his way up / through dynasties of neocortex" (36–37). Therefore, we are advised, "Let him breathe. / Let him savor the earth; / let him nuzzle the leaves" (38–40).

In evolutionary poems such as these, we see hints for an ecopoetical solution to the problem of human divorce from nature, as well as a suggestion of how, by tapping into the visceral dynasties lurking beneath our evolved neocortex, we can relearn to savor the earth. Surely this is a poetic affect worthy of consideration as an expression of ecopoetry.

NOTES

1. Typically, scientists distinguish between tortoises and turtles. Tortoises are strictly terrestrial, while turtles are usually aquatic. In this poem, Eiseley uses the terms "tortoise" and "turtle" interchangeably. It seems likely the creature referred to in the poem is an eastern box turtle (*Terrapene carolina*), a terrestrial turtle common throughout the eastern half of the United States, including the Philadelphia area, the likely setting for the poem. No tortoises live in this region.

2. According to a personal e-mail from Bing Chen, "As to the Innocent Assassins skull discovery location, the field notes from the South Party indicate that it was found in Black Hank Canyon which is approximately 3 miles to the south and 1 mile to the east of Chimney Rock. If nothing else, the appearance of the red fox during our search on June 25th, 2008 confirmed it for me. An earlier visit with Dr. Voorhees confirming the discovery site is another vote for Black Hank canyon."

7

Lessons of an Interdisciplinary Life

Loren Eiseley's Rhetoric of Profundity in Popular
Science Writing and "Two Cultures" Pedagogy

PAMELA GOSSIN

From an early age, Loren Eiseley lived his life betwixt and between various kinds of "two cultures" experiences: the two linguistic worlds of his parents' disparate communication styles; the distinct realms of private thought and public expression; the separate but concentric spheres of personal and professional discourses; and the two intellectual and academic domains traditionally described as "*the* two cultures" — the poetic, imaginative, and humanistic versus the technical, rational, and scientific.[1] Driven to explore both sides of such cultural differences, Eiseley observed, valued, and experimented with each approach separately. Over time, he developed vital skills of empathy and analysis and learned important lessons in interdisciplinary communication that enabled him to solve one term in relation to the other and effectively mediate between them. Eschewing to choose, he engaged multiple modes of expression and lived experience outside of zero-sum systems of polarity and hierarchy, embracing, struggling with, and practicing them all. By young adulthood, he emerged as *Prairie Schooner* poet *and* Badlands bone digger, and ever after refused to define himself — personally or professionally — along conventional fault lines of disciplinary fissure.

Extensive biographical and autobiographical evidence supports the view that Eiseley's experiences with miscommunication and misunderstanding deeply affected him emotionally and psychologically. Some of his most powerful childhood recollections concerned the deep fears and anxieties he developed in response to his parents' late-night arguments. Equally powerful was his memory that his innocent symbolic effort to make peace — to signal toward harmony by holding his parents' hands — worked.[2] The early connection forged between such emotional trauma, discursive discord, and gestures of reconciliation seems to have had a profound shaping effect on his identity and personality.[3] As Eiseley repeatedly experienced the similar pain of psychological confusion, interpersonal disputes, and aesthetic and academic contention within professional and discursive communities, he developed a rich repertoire of adaptive strategies of conflict avoidance and conflict resolution — "both/and" thinking, an appreciation for paradox, an acceptance of the ineffable and the insoluble, transcendent synthesis — that enabled him to cope with and survive difference. As a mature writer, he drew on the tension and forces at play in such moments to fashion a creative fusion of personal, aesthetic, and philosophical insights with his understanding of the natural world.

Through personal pain and professional practice, Eiseley perfected his rhetorical abilities as go-between, translator, and intermediary and deployed them on the larger social and political stage. In the immediate postatomic era, Eiseley joined C. P. Snow, Jacob Bronowski, and a select group of other public figures in fully embodying the unity of the sciences and the humanities in an attempt to articulate a viable worldview that might help fit humankind for survival in the Cold War and Space Race eras. Writing popular science texts — both poetry and prose — over the course of many years, Eiseley continued to learn from the critical responses of both admiring and resistant readers to refine his experiment with cross-disciplinary discourse, developing a unique "rhetoric of profundity" that effectively communicated his philosophy of life and of nature.

Eiseley's best popular science writing imaginatively combined biculturally sensitive literary strategies with an adept interdisciplinary voice that enabled him to rhetorically engage some of the most profound existential, epistemological, and phenomenological dilemmas that human individuals encounter as living beings, including (1) the essential tension between the individual and universal aspects of human nature; (2) the paradoxical relationship between nature and humankind; (3) the mystery and ineffability of the unknown and unknowable (especially the very real limits of human knowledge and ways of knowing); and (4) the complexity of our attempts to comprehend phenomena in nature and human nature that are rarely observed and even more rarely recorded, communicated, and understood. The philosophical and rhetorical strategies that Eiseley used to seek and create meaning out of the materials of his life experience in the natural world continue to offer readers and students compelling insights and useful models for their own meaningful experiments in interdisciplinary understanding and communication.

EARLY EXPERIMENTS WITH VISUAL AND VERBAL
SIGNS AND PRIVATE AND PUBLIC VOICES

From his first moments as a viable being on this planet, Eiseley experienced human communication as problematic. All but his loudest newborn cries were inaudible to his mother, Daisy, whose childhood hearing loss had significantly progressed by the time of his birth (Christianson, *Fox* 15). Growing up in what he later described as a primitive culture, a "silenced household of the stone age — a house of gesture," the young Loren was by turns afraid, confused, frustrated, embarrassed, and angered by his mother's attempts to make herself understood through an awkward repertoire of high-pitched and off-key vocalizations and incomprehensible and ungainly combinations of hand signals, arm waves, foot stamps, and exaggerated facial expressions (*All* 22). Equally bewildering and anxiety provoking to him as a child were the secretive whisperings of extended family members — his aunt, grandmother, and others — who kept their worried murmurings of inheritable insanity just below his mother's detection yet still accessible to his.

Within the close confines of his family, the emotionally sensitive young Eiseley experienced oral communication as a strange brew of cacophony and silence, a bitter mixture of misunderstandings wrought by the inability to express effectively and the purposeful stifling and muffling of what could have been uttered but would not be said. In striking contrast, his father's dramatic oratory and formal recitation of literary passages — performed from memory or read aloud from books — seemed to open up for him a whole new world of sound and sense. When Eiseley listened to his father, a former amateur thespian, recite Shakespeare, even when the words were "full of sound and fury, signifying nothing" they did successfully signify *something*. The richness of his father's deep, baritone voice was well matched by the richness of the vocabulary he read, and together they "produced" what Eiseley would later describe as "the miracle of words" (22). In a very real sense, the boy's world, both actual and imagined, expanded literally: through the grandiloquent diction, detailed verbal descriptions of nature, and vivid word-pictures of his favorite adventure stories. If between family members, face-to-face communication so often failed, the written word on the page seemed to offer a different potential for human expression, tangible evidence that, given certain conditions, words could work.

Through adolescence and early adulthood, Eiseley's appreciation for the power and value of effective oral and written expression was reinforced for him through significant educational and social experiences. As an initially uncertain high school student, his confidence in his own personality and writing skills grew hand in hand as he increasingly received approving feedback from peers and teachers alike. Although the quality of his writing so far surpassed that of other students his age that he at least twice attracted agonizing accusations of plagiarism, the temporary traumatic effects of such charges were effectively cancelled out by the intermittent positive reinforcement of insightful mentors such as Agnes Graham, Letta May Clark, and his later college English professors and editors. Through the persistent praise of such readers, Eiseley received an important message from the world-at-large: small transitory moments of private individual insight can take on greater meaning within public contexts, if expressed and described in accessible and captivating form.

Essential, too, to the development of Eiseley's writing skills were the social and conversational abilities he acquired through his long friendship with and eventual courtship of his former student-teacher, Mabel Langdon. Part soul sister, part surrogate mother, tutor, editor, life coach and literary agent, her nurturing yet astute critique earned Eiseley's trust. For over a decade before their marriage, they spent many long afternoons and evenings together, talking and reading aloud to each other, discussing the works of other writers and previewing new works of their own (Christianson, *Fox* 167). Their conversations seemed to work on Eiseley almost as an informal kind of talk therapy, enabling him to organize his thoughts and feelings and put words to his introspection.[4] Mabel provided Loren with a safe haven emotionally and intellectually, serving him as an almost ideal audience, listening, questioning, redirecting, and skillfully socializing his sometimes abrasive manner, moodiness, and tendency to make insensitive and off-putting remarks. Lessons learned in private dialogue were later practiced in public, as they both were frequent participants in the immensely active intellectual exchange among creative writers on campus at the University of Nebraska. Together they attended public literary readings and gave their own, worked for the Poetry Division of the Nebraska Writers' Guild, and contributed their editorial talents and original poetry and prose to the *Prairie Schooner*.

As Eiseley learned more formally about poetic conventions and writing techniques in his college literature classes and exchanges with other peers and editors, his concurrent conversations with Mabel encouraged him to think out loud, literally sound out and experiment with his own poetic style. In verses he wrote during this time, the tenor and tone of his emergent poetic voice seems to arise from an increasing awareness of his own stream of consciousness, the internal world of his mind where words first attach themselves to feelings and experiences. This voice — that of the self-conscious participant-observer, one living being among many within the natural world — will surface time and again in various guises and circumstances throughout Eiseley's writing career. Empathetically identifying with the plight of life caught within a common cosmic dilemma, the essential qualities of this persona already resonate through the narration of many of his earliest published poems (ca. 1928–33), such as "Spiders," "Our Small Minds Cry," "The Poet Surveys His Garden," "Coyote Country," "Song for the Wolf's Coat," and others.

Talking and writing together, the couple's relationship deepened as Eiseley's competence with language grew, enabling him to bridge the gap between the disparate communication styles that he had been exposed to in his parents' home — one predominately visual and gestural, the other highly verbal, both oral and aural. As he became increasingly adept at integrating the eye and ear, imagery and sound, the written text and speech, he also began to more effectively mediate between his own internal thinking/ writing voice and his more public speaking voice. For the rest of his life, however, he would always feel far more comfortable reading and writing texts than engaging in the disconcerting complexities and seemingly unpredictable confrontations he so often experienced in social and interpersonal verbal exchange. With Mabel's gentle guidance, he continued to refine his ability to synthesize image with word, thought with feeling, text with speech, as he experienced marked personal and professional transitions in his move from the relatively isolated and taciturn work environment of bone-digging expeditions through the high-profile social hobnobbing of the arts and literary scene in New Mexico and on to his first academic teaching job in anthropology.

CRAFTING AN INTERDISCIPLINARY VOICE
THROUGH ACADEMIC DISCOURSE AND THE
SYNTHESIS OF "TWO CULTURES"

Over the course of his long career as an academic and writer, Eiseley would repeatedly shuffle and reshuffle these basic patterns of positive and negative interaction with written and oral forms of communication. As an up-and-coming research professor at the University of Kansas, at Oberlin, and at the University of Pennsylvania, he experienced significant instances where direct interpersonal conversations with colleagues and administrative heads were awkward and messy, if not overtly antagonistic. At times, recollecting his thoughts and feelings in tranquillity, Eiseley would compose follow-up letters to clarify and reconcile situations with colleagues, administrators, or editors when spoken words had failed. At others, he simply avoided uncomfortable discussions at all costs, even when the management of such matters fell directly under his own administrative responsibility (e.g., as provost at the University of Pennsylvania; Christianson, *Fox* 322–26). In the classroom, Eiseley built a reputation as a fine and admired lecturer, a professor who had honed and polished the style and substance of his texts to a fine finish and gave formal presentations brilliantly, but he was not someone known for making off-the-cuff comments, inviting open discussion, or for venturing very far from his prepared materials or note cards (231). Socially and intellectually, he warmed up best to those he knew well, like-minded thinkers such as Frank Speck or Wright Morris, but he fared poorly at large parties and academic gatherings, often growing morose and silent and keeping to himself (194).

However painful his sensitivity to criticism and conflict-avoidance may have been to him, Eiseley nonetheless turned the lessons learned from such experiences to good professional use. In his earliest scientific writing, first in articles cowritten with more experienced colleagues, C. Bertrand Schultz and Speck, and then in those entirely his own, Eiseley's work demonstrated a keen awareness of and responsiveness to the professional expectations of his fellow specialist readers. Relatively sure of the anthropological identities of his audience members for articles he wrote in *American Anthropologist, American Antiquity, Transactions of the Kansas Academy of Science, Science Monthly,* and *Scientific American* from the midthirties to the midforties, he exhibited a clear understanding of his readers' needs and effectively worked within the formal conventions of the scientific article to meet them. Yet even in the process of producing these relatively early publications, he already sensed that the traditional requirements of the scientific paper limited him as an author, forcing him to omit and edit out important aspects of the process of scientific exploration and discovery. Indeed, the formal constraints of the genre itself essentially compelled him to falsify his full experience as a scientific observer and recorder of natural phenomena. As he much later reflected back on this realization: "A long dormant aspect of my mind began to stir again. . . . There flitted before me the episodes of earlier years — emotional reactions, stories, anecdotes of birds and animals — all those things that have been piling up in my memory." And all of those things, he knew, paraphrasing Thoreau, it was "no use reporting . . . to the Royal Society" (Christianson, *Fox* 233; *Star* 65).

In both his early poetry and early scientific writing, then, Eiseley successfully addressed circumscribed groups of disciplinary-specific readers — academic and intellectual monocultures — by carefully tailoring his written words to their intended audience. Venturing out into the realm of public science writing, where his readership was no longer predominately scientific or predominately literary, he soon realized that his usual strategy of taking refuge in "the brave use of seeming solid words," no matter how carefully crafted, would not in and of itself prevent confusion or protect their author from conflict (*Star* 278). Engaging more complex audiences would require the mastery and invention of ever more complex literary forms and strategies. Through his early life experiences and the critical reception of his public science writing, Eiseley would come to embody — and would personally live out — some of the most crucial consequences of his generation's two-cultures communication gap.

While the majority of literary critics and general reviewers responded favorably to his early efforts in writing science for general audiences, the negative reactions of others — his scientific colleagues, in particular — were surprisingly harsh, even vitriolic, in expressing their distaste and disapproval. For some professional science readers, Eiseley's broadly humanistic descriptions of the natural world and the discoveries and concepts of the natural sciences actually demoted him in their estimation from peer to mere "popularizer."[5] While the style of his popular essays seemed an only slightly worrisome violation of professional scientific decorum (*"we* don't talk like *that"*), their content represented a potentially more serious breach, relating adventitious and subjective narratives that, in their estimation, could mislead the public about the "true" nature of "the" scientific method and its discoveries. Others reacted most strongly against what they perceived to be the "mystical" (and therefore, by definition, antiscientific) elements of Eiseley's authorial voice, fearing that by including such insights, he had abandoned all scientific credibility and crossed irretrievably into the realm of "sentimental" and "inspirational" writing (e.g., Buettner-Janusch, qtd. in Angyal, *Loren* 33, 129n7). Eiseley took such reviews hard. Eventually working through his anger, shame, and the smoldering self-doubt that they reignited in him, he used such critiques to make his essays better.

Experiencing such a complex personal and professional history with both oral and written forms of language may well have heightened Eiseley's sensitivity to his complex audience's needs and played an essential part in his creative adaptation of the essay form to the problem of two-cultures communication between the humanities and sciences. Such struggles may also have had a strong shaping effect on the development of his unique voice and tone, as well as on his invention of effective rhetorical techniques and the organizational structure of his "concealed" essays (Pitts 68–108; Angyal, *Loren* 38–42).

Through his emotionally traumatic experiences with his mother, Eiseley seems to have learned that mutual understanding is partly a question of the mechanics of finding, and then effectively employing, a common language and symbolic system. Yet also through his difficult relationship with her he found that effective communication additionally depends on whether both parties share common perspectives, cultural reference points, and interpretative frameworks. Through his exchanges with his father, Eiseley became alive to the "music" of language and learned the important roles that aesthetic and poetic sensibility play in setting a shared emotional tone and preparing a communicative pathway along which a reader or listener can be drawn into a writer's or speaker's thoughts and feelings. Through the give-and-take of informal feedback from friends and the critical response of readers and colleagues on both sides of the two-cultures divide, Eiseley became adept at translating and transmitting thoughts and feelings between differing audiences and subgroups. He also gained a more nuanced appreciation for the multiplex issues he was facing in his attempts to achieve truly interdisciplinary communication: namely, the extent to which some of his scientific audience members were entrenched in their own professional mindsets and traditionally prescribed notions of scientific form and substance; the general public's growing need for nontechnical explanations of the "big picture" of scientific ideas and theories and their profound implications for the meaning of human life; and the universally insoluble problem of the ineffability of the human experience of the natural world locally and the cosmos at large.

Eiseley, of course, was far from alone in sensing the difficulties that would be involved in working toward any sort of resolution to this dilemma, but in some ways his timing could not have been worse. In the mid-1950s, he embarked on his "immense journey" toward interdisciplinarity in the midst of a perfect storm of cross-cultural ferment and fear. In the prime of his life, the powerful social and political forces of the postatomic era uneasily played themselves out within the rising complexities of the Cold War and Vietnam conflict and protests. Admiring and anxious public images of scientists were thrown against each other in stark contrast, even in the figure of a single man: Oppenheimer, the sophisticated intellectual whose coolly brilliant scientific direction of the Manhattan Project had saved so many lives by shortening the war, *versus* Oppenheimer, the humiliated martyr to McCarthyism whose inconsistent testimony and naming of names cast doubts on the trustworthiness of genius within national life. Oppenheimer also symbolized (as well as personally posed) some of the central questions then open for public debate: What is the meaning of human "civilization" and "progress" if in pursuit of them our technology creates the most destructive force in history? How can human societies peacefully and responsibly coexist in a world where some possess the power to annihilate others in an instant? Who should participate in the exploration of such problems and the formation of policies that will be ratified as a result of such queries? Politicians? Scientists? Humanists?

Such questions were far from academic. Yet both the queries themselves and their potential answers strongly polarized the groups most actively involved in considering their truth and consequences; many of their members comprised the teaching and research faculty on various college campuses. At Cambridge University, and elsewhere, professors of the humanities and sciences who had found ways to work cooperatively during the war effort now openly squared off against one another in postwar debates. To further complicate matters, the personal opinions and ideology of individuals within particular disciplines were by no means monolithic, and these differences further split their memberships. Within the scientific community, for example, some physicists who had worked diligently and devotedly for many years on weapons development projects found themselves profoundly changed by the experience and soon converted their significant talents and energies to life-promoting research in biology, chemistry, and medicine instead (Francis Crick, codiscoverer of the structure of DNA, being a notable case in point).

Although Eiseley scholars have tended to read his popular science essays against the background of the various layers of contention within the two-cultures debate, his commitment to interdisciplinary writing significantly predates C. P. Snow's famous Rede Lecture (first delivered in May 1959). Even more important, before Snow so influentially framed the relationship of the humanities and the sciences as a debate (following the lead of his fellow countrymen, T. H. Huxley and Matthew Arnold, in the previous century), many other significant figures had already long been engaged in work that emphasized their synthesis.

Perhaps best known among this group is Marjorie Hope Nicolson, whose studies of the historical interrelations of literature and science from the time of the Scientific Revolution through the eighteenth and nineteenth centuries are still often used today. One of the first literary scholars to so extensively employ a history of ideas approach, Nicolson provided an encyclopedic overview and analyses of hundreds of examples of primary works by poets, essayists, novelists, and other writers who capably learned, directly engaged, and creatively responded to the sciences of their day, from astronomy to zoology. Her earliest articles on literature and science began to appear in the mid-1930s, followed by numerous book-length studies and essay collections published over the next three decades.[6] By 1939 the field of Literature and Science studies had attracted enough inter-est among scholars with dual disciplinary interests (among them, Arthur Lovejoy, Richard F. Jones, Charles Monroe Coffin, Francis Johnson, I. A. Richards, Ivor Evans and Douglas Bush) that Nicolson was able to establish the subject as a subdivision within the Modern Language Association.

Eiseley knew Nicolson's work and cited it in his own, well aware that her approach to literature and science showcased the multifaceted ways that creative intellectuals across the centuries had combined and recombined their artistic, literary, historical, and philosophical interests with those of the natural sciences. He frequently referenced many of the same authors that Nicolson used as her primary examples of interdisciplinarity, includ-ing John Donne. By drawing on both literary studies and the history of science, Nicolson herself modeled one unique way (out of many other possibilities) to unite the science and humanities — and so did Eiseley. As he put it some years later, "I always had a joint interest in English literature and science so that the 'two culture problem' never concerned me and I was never conscious of it except to the degree that I have been castigated by nonliterary colleagues in science" (qtd. in Angyal, *Loren* 36).[7] Having explored and successfully participated in both literary and scientific creativity from a young age, Eiseley simply had not internalized the two modes of knowing and expression as inherently incompatible.

Strongly endorsing this view was Jacob Bronowski, who in the early spring of 1953 (six years before Snow's series) gave three timely lectures at MIT, which later formed the basis of the now classic *Science and Human Values*. In these lectures, published as journal articles in 1956 and as a book in 1958, Bronowski explored science, the arts, and the humanities as equally integral aspects of human culture. He explicated the shared nature of artistic and scientific creativity, their common quest for the discovery of unity in variety, and the similar deep joy and satisfaction experienced by both artists and scientists when they make such discoveries. Through careful analysis, Bronowski presented lucid and accessible explanations of the similarities in and subtle differences between the ways artists, writers, and scientists draw on sensory experience, reasoning, and experimentation in their work. Of most direct relevance to the postwar era was the compelling argument he made in the third lecture that the practice of the arts and sciences enables human beings to imagine and create essential values to live by that have the potential to ennoble and sustain us as individuals and societies.

While Bronowski expressed convictions that were later criticized for an overly idealistic reliance on the human nature and culture of scientists to evolve trustworthy and just professional practices and technological solutions to social problems, Eiseley's view of the historical and philosophical relationship between the humanities and sciences is in essential ways far closer to Bronowski's perspective than to Snow's. In a little more than a decade, in fact, Eiseley would collaborate with Bronowski, Detlev Bronk, and the literary scholar Howard Mumford Jones to produce *The Shape of Likelihood: Relevance and the University* (1971), a volume of published lectures addressing, among other issues, the implications of the two-cultures mentality for contemporary higher education. In the meantime, Eiseley refined his own views of the problem on both abstract and practical levels.

In 1957, just one year after Bronowski's lectures first appeared in print (and still two years before Snow's Rede talks), Eiseley wrote "The Enchanted

Glass." Ostensibly intended as an essay review critiquing a selection of new science books, he used the occasion to offer historical reflections on the origins of the rift between scientific and humanistic perspectives and the unintended — but not yet irreversible — consequences of that rift. The piece opens with a powerfully disturbing juxtaposition of two images of human observation: one, a description of a Cold War "radar scanner" that Eiseley can see on a nearby roof "endlessly sweeping the horizon" as "it waits for the coming of the Great Disaster for which it was built"; and two, an example of how the individual human mind is itself a "scanner," processing and making meaning out of random bits and pieces of stimuli received from its interactions with the natural world around it, as a specific case in point: his own observation of a small bird drinking upside down from an outdoor faucet. The two images encapsulate, for Eiseley, the extreme positions at either end of the spectrum of what has historically counted as natural scientific observation. The former represents the technological and military industrial consequences of what he describes as the Baconian tradition, an essentially violent approach to nature, "rack[ing] out of her, her secrets," "severely experimental, unaesthetic and empirical." The latter, by contrast, is the "literary, personal and contemplative" approach, employed and symbolized by "such parson naturalists as John Ray and Gilbert White." As Eiseley describes them, these "two streams of thought in Western culture . . . though sometimes partially commingling their courses . . . have come down these last three hundred years feeding different minds, serving different purposes, and mutually eschewed by the intolerant of both parties." Quickly noting that "it is not necessary to take sides" and that "good men . . . have always known the best that could be derived from either point of view," he nonetheless recognizes that essential differences in purposes and practices have become magnified over time and have resulted in increasingly mutually exclusive cultural mindsets (478).

Like Bronowski, Eiseley empathetically understands that the daily habits of professional practice within each style of natural investigation shape and change the practitioners and that each has its own inherent strengths and weaknesses. However well-intentioned the abstracting and reductive methods of the sciences and technology may be, and however valuable we may find their insights into underlying physical laws and their practical applications, the cumulative effects of such methods catch investigators unawares, gradually distancing them from the direct experience of nature and reducing its "emotional connotations," until for them "visible nature . . . has literally dissolved . . . away into fields of force, warps in space, or other abstractions." On the other hand, "the old-fashioned contemplative naturalist . . . is telling an essentially personal story," which, as anecdotal evidence, runs the risk of being easily dismissed and "scorned by some as trivial and unimportant." Yet, if not strictly reproducible, such "personal experiences" are, Eiseley insists, still "capable of being shared by every perceptive human being. They are part of that indefinable country which lies between the realm of natural objects and the human spirit which moves among them," and their practical applications include significant contributions to "the natural history of the human soul itself" (480).

Beyond the particular conventions of professional practice, Eiseley also places some of the blame for the persistence of the gap between these two approaches to knowing and describing nature on the "frenetic and excitement-loving" conditions of modern life itself and the demands of popular consumer culture, which do little to promote a thoughtful assessment or reconciliation of their differences. Despite the ubiquity of such pressures, he cites the appearance of Rachel Carson's 1951 bestseller, *The Sea around Us*, as a text that successfully melds scientifically accurate detail with literary and philosophical insight and effectively communicates with the general public — a hopeful sign that "the great tradition has never quite been broken" (480). Warning, however, of the typically fragile and transitory popularity of such texts within the fickle boom/bust cycle of public science writing and reading, he then notes the emergence of a number of new nature books in which the unique combination of the "factual" and "contemplative" also results in "a kind of partial transformation of data, a light from beyond the horizon that shines through the author's work even while he practices the scientific approach." For Eiseley, these texts, which include individual natural histories of waterfowl, rattlesnakes, monkeys, and puffins and Joseph Wood Krutch's *Great Chain of Being*, "reveal the futility of precise categories in literature and even in science" (482).

Again like Bronowski, who had framed his treatment of the creative fusion of science and human values in the context of his personal recollections of the postatomic devastation of Nagasaki, in this review Eiseley presents his consideration of the syncretic relationship between them as a matter of life and death. Humanity has a profound need to maintain a place for sympathy within scientific investigation. In Eiseley's view, mankind (*sic*) has already nearly become "his own neurotic rat caught in the maze of an experiment over which he has well nigh lost control, and which progresses at a furious pace to some unknown and increasingly fearful destination." Our very survival as a species may well depend on whether or not we can maintain "that supreme synthesis of [natural] knowledge and emotional insight," which, for him, is "typified" by an experience related by "the ill-fated John Keats: 'If a sparrow . . . comes before my Window I take part in its existence and pick about the Gravel.'" For Eiseley, it is imperative that a natural phenomenon "should be observed by those to whom it can be *doubly seen*" as a scientific event *and* as "a drama . . . understood in sympathy and full catharsis" (492; emphasis added).

From the perspective of readers in the early twenty-first century, Eiseley's argument for the vital role of those who can "doubly see" within modern scientific life may seem a barely veiled apologia for the kind of interdisciplinary science writer that he was already fashioning himself to be. Yet throughout the review, he works hard as both a natural scientist and a writer to maintain his dual professional stance, offering his perspective on the still potential synthesis of the two cultures. While the menacing shadows cast by his almost symbolist use of Cold War imagery across the opening and closing pages no doubt reflect Eiseley's own emotional response to the fallout from the fission of the two cultures, his central points are drawn primarily from historical considerations of the development of literature and science, not personal ones. Anyone with an interest or inclination to explore the interrelations of natural sciences and the humanities need not reinvent the wheel; anyone can follow the example of past writers of "literary" natural history, build on their models, and creatively adapt their techniques. Only the entire future of human nature depends on someone doing so. The stark truth of that realization haunted Eiseley through the coming years, serving him as significant motivation to continue to develop an interdisciplinary voice and the rhetorical and stylistic strategies necessary to communicate such profundity.

Seven years later, writing again for *The American Scholar*, Eiseley directly addressed Snow's hypothesis by describing his own views on the phenomenon that he pointedly called "The Illusion of the Two Cultures." In this piece, he did not so successfully conceal the extent to which the problem felt personal. Initially, Eiseley attempted to contextualize (and distance) then-current disciplinary contentions within the larger philosophical framework that Eric Ashby described as the "dialectic between orthodoxy and dissent" — a more recent variation on the theme of the Ancients and Moderns debate and the eternal tension between past tradition and new ideas (qtd. in Eiseley, "Illusion" 267). Eiseley's mid-1960s readership may have detected a faint allusion to the ways that the philosophical was professional, political, and personal for him, as just outside his office door American involvement in Vietnam was escalating, along with campus protests against it, and the author who so often identified himself as a youthful and rebellious rider of the rails was disconcerted to find himself on the wrong side of the generational tracks.[8] Moving quickly into a discussion of the historical precursors of Snow's "bipolar division," Eiseley's diction gathered emotional momentum, as he rapidly described the "caterwauling of poets" and the berating of professional scientists, the "animus . . . vented upon the literary naturalist," charges of "nature faking," and the generally "confused din" of the discursive fray. Amid this catalog of negatively charged rhetoric from both sides, he offered a conspicuously autobiographical aside: "I know of at least one scholar who, venturing to develop some personal ideas in an essay for the layman, was characterized by a reviewer in a leading professional journal as a worthless writer, although, as it chanced, the work under discussion had received several awards in literature, one of them international in scope" (268).

Almost immediately, however, Eiseley retreated behind another historical and philosophical overview, this time relating the ideas of George Santayana, J. R. R. Tolkein, Hans Christian Andersen, Jules Verne, and even the Egyptologist Flinders Petrie. Rhetorically pacing within this essay like a caged animal, moving back and forth across the contested territory, he seemed nervously trapped himself between the bars of disciplinary boundaries and his own fast-approaching publishing deadline. Feeling "humility and trepidation" over his commission to write about the relations of literature and science, Eiseley solicited the sympathy of other professional writers who may have felt similar pressures that "keyed all their senses and led them to glance wildly around in the hope that something might leap out at them from the most prosaic surroundings," and he recounted how, by chance, his "eye fell upon a stone in [his] office" (270). That stone inspired him to relate a parable about its making, a particularly human story in which practical need merges with "worthless" aesthetic embellishment.

For Eiseley, this artifact was emblematic of humanity's essential need to preserve and nurture its artistic and imaginative impulses, as well as its practical, realistic, knowledge-based sciences. Before such objects, "All talk of the two cultures is an illusion." In his view, the ongoing challenge we face as sentient beings on this planet is not to refine and improve our technological control over nature, but to better understand our own human nature. Offering a powerful reinforcement of Bronowski's vision of synthesis, Eiseley concluded, "Today we hold a stone, the heavy stone of power. We must perceive beyond it, however, by the aid of the artistic imagination, those humane insights and understandings which alone can lighten our burden and enable us to shape ourselves, rather than the stone, into the forms which great art has anticipated" (279).

In light of such poignant pleas for the creative fusion of the sciences and humanities, the history and sociology of science has yet to fully examine how and why, and in such a relatively short span, Snow's polarizing rhetoric came, instead, to so powerfully dominate interdisciplinary discourse across the United States and Europe. The process may well be similar to that seen in other large-scale manipulations of popular culture, in which marketing executives and political strategists deploy binary oppositions and false dichotomies that effectively simplify audiences' available options or set up dramatic controversies or "debates" that attract and hold their attention, for example, evolution versus intelligent design (aka ID).[9] There is no doubt that simple sells and metaphors matter (see Olson; Lakoff). Profundity, by contrast, is nuanced and complicated.

While Bronowski's subtle and elegant case for the synthesis of the sciences and humanities, beautifully reasoned and well written, has been read by thousands, is still frequently used as a college text, and remains in print today, the medium and message of Snow's two-cultures concept has effectively eclipsed Bronowski's view of their essential unity in the public mind. As a consequence, however accurate Eiseley's professional and personal assessment of the polarized nature of his diverse audience — scientist versus nonscientist, older generation versus new — even he may not have fully realized the extent to which, at a deeper level, his interdisciplinary project was also caught between two cultures *within* the "two cultures": those who saw the sciences and humanities as essentially incommensurable and ranked one or the other as superior and those who considered them inherently interrelated manifestations of a whole complex of human creative thought and activity.

As an increasingly unapologetic interdisciplinary writer, Eiseley's practical resolution of these interconnected abstractions seems largely to have evolved through trial and error. Initially, the wild range of reader responses generated by his popular essays brought him high hopes and intense distress. He ruminated over individual reviews as they came in, soaked up their praises or fretted silently and aloud over particular critical comments, by turns cautiously weighing and measuring their validity and then inveighing against their injustice or unnecessary cruelty. As a result, Eiseley further synthesized aspects of his poetic and scientific sensibility and his poetic and scientific writing styles, combining their content and form to fashion a new hybrid genre in which to explore and express his unified vision of the nature as he experienced it. Through ad hoc invention and experimentation, he developed a whole constellation of rhetorical and discursive strategies, all of which work well in various but partial ways to disarm aspects of two-cultures biases, fears, ignorance, and habits of thought and feeling.

In his personal experience, Eiseley's most successful attempts to communicate had typically been in conversations with friends and colleagues who shared with him significant commonalities of temperament and philosophical outlook. Much of Eiseley's repertoire of rhetorical and literary techniques works toward recreating those conditions, relating directly to those who were already kindred spirits yet simultaneously generating common feeling among those less like-minded. Among the approaches he most frequently employs are the eliciting of a sympathetic response from the reader for his narrator's "lost," "lonely," and abandoned self; the creation of a story-telling persona ("a guide by our side") who teaches by example, seeking common ground in human diversity and a hidden order in the apparent chaos of nature; and the development of themes that depend on the sheer assumption of commonality — if not universality — among human individuals across cultures. Disavowing the traditional stance of scientific authority, he utilizes a poetic-scientific voice that draws on the common sense of exploration, the basic human need to engage the natural world through thought and feeling and to find meaning in existence. Subtly acknowledging the importance of the author-audience relationship, and the phenomenological problem of individual perception, this voice is at once autobiographically intimate and set apart — someone who is at home with the sound of his own voice yet distantly aware that his thoughts will not sound the same to others "out there" and that they may not quite see what he thinks he sees. Eiseley's sophisticated and effective rhetoric of popular science continues to promote interdisciplinary understanding and "cross-cultural" communication between the sciences and the humanities, as the following brief case study suggests.

EISELEY'S RHETORIC OF PROFUNDITY
AND "TWO CULTURES" PEDAGOGY

More than thirty years after Eiseley's death, his readership does not carry the same burden of two-cultures contention. He would likely be dismayed to learn the reason. Despite continuous efforts by a growing number of individual scholars and academic organizations to foster interdisciplinary understanding, such work rarely reaches beyond the relatively esoteric confines of specific intellectual communities.[10] At the grassroots level, the existence of two distinct cultures — the sciences and technology on the one hand, and the arts and humanities on the other — is simply no longer contended. In the United States and much of Europe, the independent and mutually exclusive "nature" of the two is essentially accepted. On both continents, several generations of children have now been educated by a pedagogical system based on left brain/right brain models of cognitive function, in which our own gray matter is believed to physically and biologically segregate the arts on one side and the sciences on the other. Present-day learning environments and student attitudes display the unfortunate outcomes of "Gifted and Talented" programs that successfully taught students, their teachers, and parents to believe that they either have it (the natural ability to do math and science or art and writing), or they don't.

In today's university classroom, a professor is likely to find that a majority of her students have spent much of their K–12 education being "appropriately placed" or having "self-selected" into or out of the arts and humanities or mathematics and sciences. Fortunately, much of this sorting process has occurred in a cultural climate accepting of diversity, in which students' individual differences in educational and preprofessional choices are rarely subjected to the hierarchical value judgments or personal disparagement that Eiseley suffered. Having the opportunity to read his popular science essays in an academic setting largely free of the bicultural contention in which he originally wrote them, such students bring fresh eyes and open spirits to his work. Introducing his texts within such a different set of contexts, however, is not the same as teaching them without context. Our current students are not blank slates. In my own experience teaching Eiseley, I have tried to utilize my awareness of the too often oversimplified historical relations of the two cultures to help students become conscious of the stereotypical beliefs and attitudes about the sciences and the humanities that they have passively internalized, and actively learn to reevaluate them. Eiseley's popular science essays are remarkably effective for the many ways that they enable readers to recognize their own assumptions and transform them. In a very real sense, the rhetorical structure and organization of his writings help his readers work their way through complex ideas and problems with all the empathetic and pedagogical deftness of a master teacher.

At my current home institution, the University of Texas at Dallas (established by the founders of Texas Instruments), the vast majority of our science and engineering majors take few, if any, courses in the School of Arts and Humanities. Increasingly, over the past fifteen years, my development of new classes in the History of Science, Literature and Science, and interdisciplinary humanities has attracted far more science and technical students than usual (often more than 50 percent of the enrollment). The resultant two-cultures environment in these classrooms has serendipitously provided me with an interdisciplinary field laboratory of sorts.

In courses such as "Reading and Writing Texts: Natural Wonders" and "Reading and Writing Texts: Nature, Science, and Medicine," Eiseley's essay "The Judgment of the Birds" is the first text that my students and I read together. Once we have dispensed with the new semester's typical administrivia, I distribute a handout, asking them to take their time reading it.[11] In a brand new class, collective reading time may initially feel uncomfortable for some students, yet it also works to promote a sense of unity and social intimacy as nervous self-consciousness yields to a quiet awareness that they are sharing thoughtful space within the same text. When everyone has finished, I ask how the essay made them feel. Such a fundamental question usually catches both sides of the two cultures off-guard, as the humanities students have been trained to "find the thesis statement," and the science students have been conditioned to highlight topic sentences and key points of information. Eventually, their tentative responses include expressions of concern for the author's well-being and state of mind; confusion about "What kind of person is this anyway — a scientist or a poet? Is 'Loren' a man or a woman?" (perceived gender really seems to matter); empathetic "me too" remarks about emotionally touching descriptive details of the author's personal encounters with wildlife; and sober reflections on the overall "darkness" of the essay and its expression of mortality.

Asking the class to return to the first page, I pose another basic question of rhetorical analysis: *how* does the author *use words* to make us feel these things? In the deceptively simple and brilliant opening lines, Eiseley's rhetoric of profundity quickly takes shape. He promptly establishes a common framework for understanding spiritual insight that is easily recognizable to his readers regardless of their ethnic, cultural, or religious backgrounds. Acknowledging the complex experience of venturing out, alone, into the wilderness, he nonetheless asserts the universal value of the "visions or marvels" one can see there and the still current need for such "natural revelations" within the mad rush of modern life. In the third paragraph, Eiseley disavows, as narrator, any direct identification with the "mystical," while he simultaneously confesses that as a "man by himself," he has had, through no purposeful fault of his own, "certain experiences falling into" that classification (*Star* 27–28). Acknowledging that paradox, we then pause to observe how he also unites two dissimilarities by collapsing the usual distinction between New York City and the wilderness which, in turn, generates interest in the reader and builds a sense of intrigue about the narrator's unique way of seeing. Just as in nature, the exceptional specimen or atypical example of a particular phenomenon catches and holds the observer's eye, so here the narrator's self-identification as "atyp" encourages his readers to wonder, "If he is not quite what I expected, then, what is he?" In the space of a few brief paragraphs, Eiseley has already deftly made scientific investigators out of his readers and established an empathetic bond between them and his narrator.

At this point we pause to pay more careful attention to the essay's thesis statement: "I set mine down, therefore: a matter of pigeons, a flight of chemicals, and a judgment of birds, in the hope that they will come to the eye of those who have retained a true taste for the marvelous, and who are capable of discerning in the flow of ordinary events the point at which the mundane world gives way to quite another dimension" (28). Cautioning students that they probably ought not use such vague theses in their own expository writing (!), I ask them to ponder what they think it means. They usually admit to having no clue, which, I reassure them, is probably about as Eiseley would have wanted it. But why did he use such an apparently weak statement? Is there anything good about it? Here, someone will usually comment that the statement works to a certain extent because it is predictive, providing a road map, or checklist of the major examples and order of evidence that the writer will present in the body of the essay, even if the reader is not quite sure what he will say about them. As we look more closely at the way the thesis is introduced ("I set mine down, therefore"), one or two students may note that those words make them "see" a traveler returning from a journey and opening his pack. Unpacking this image usually opens up the meaning for the rest of the class, and they too then "see" that the three examples Eiseley lists are "like the three gifts of the magi" or "like the souvenirs that your grandparents bring you." We then discuss how other parts of the statement also function to create a connection between the "like-minded" narrator and his audience, as in it he compliments those readers he deems as having "true taste" and who are "capable of discerning," thus implying that if they accept membership in that category, they also identify themselves as readers capable of "getting" his text.

As we work our way through the essay's examples of the "marvelous," we notice how all of them occur in "border" spaces, on the margins betwixt and between different physical places and different ways of being. Perched precariously on a windowsill high above them, the narrator watches the pigeons of New York City "rise" into first light. From this position he occupies a space between up/down, in/out, night/day, and also, most students instantly feel, between "life and death." In such times/spaces, distinctions of all kinds are blurred, even those between human and bird. "See[ing] from an inverted angle," we gain a chance admission to a place where "borders may shift and interpenetrate," and we can encounter the "miraculous" (29). The same is true of the crow in the fog, the flying chemicals in the Badlands, the life-affirming song of the bereaved birds in the natural "cathedral," and the spider in the streetlamp. Each example evokes a profound gestalt shift in vision, thought, and feeling.

Such experiences, however, are difficult to share. At least some of these first-time student-readers empathize so strongly with the ineffability of such moments that they physically squirm when they reach Eiseley's description of his self-conscious mirror checking after the fog-bound crow's flyby. What kind of person would care what a crow thinks of his appearance and then write about it? And what kind of self-respecting scientist would allow himself to personify and anthropomorphize that crow? The inevitability of such reader responses is no doubt reflected in Eiseley's next example, where the lone observer, standing upon the surface of many millions of years' accumulation of fossilized remains, watches a hurtling flock of phosphorus, iron, carbon, and calcium rush over his head and feels transfixed between organic and inorganic chemistry, life above him and death beneath his feet. Returning to base camp, a fellow bone hunter asks, "What did you see?" and he replies, softly, "I think a miracle" . . . "but I said it to myself" (33).

Throughout this essay, Eiseley explores from different angles the notions that human expression has its limits, as do individual human perception and knowledge. As the hidden human observer at the verge of the clearing sees, the wisdom of nonhuman living things — "life is sweet and sunlight beautiful" — sometimes surpasses that of man, even one so fortunate as to have directly experienced such a miracle: "I knew I had seen a marvel and observed a judgment, but the mind which was my human endowment was sure to question it and to be at me day by day with its heresies until I grew to doubt the meaning of what I had seen. Eventually darkness and subtleties would ring me round once more" (34). Too much consciousness may be too much of a good thing. In the process of living and then relating this natural parable, the storyteller himself must face the uncertain facts of human sensory experience and meaning making. Here, science students and humanities majors alike appreciate Eiseley's profoundly humbling realization that no matter what our specialty or the depth of our expertise, we may never know — and never be able to know — what we so much need and want to know about ourselves or the universe at large.

Eiseley's final example of the spider reaffirms the same message and engages the same epistemological and existential dilemmas. As an emblem of the life force "caught" in the web of being, this spider is like the human mind, constantly and heroically weaving, no matter what the future may hold. Something of that truth "should be passed on" — but how? The narrator's mind first considers crafting a proverb: "In the days of the frost seek a minor sun," but he "hesitate[s]." Instead, he chooses to follow in the footsteps of past "emissaries returning from the wilderness" and decides to merely "record [the] marvel and not . . . define its meaning," making "a mental note: One specimen of Epeira observed building a web in a street light. Late autumn and cold for spiders. Cold for men too," as he "step[s] carefully over her shadow" and leaves (36).

As an aesthetically astute scientific observer, in this essay Eiseley takes his readers along on his wilderness trek, showing them nature's "Pictures at an Exhibition," reliving a series of emblematic experiences, whose collection and description gathers force and conviction. Although as both poetic proverb maker and scientific fact finder, this narrator strongly indicates that he has drawn specific meaning from these experiences, he abstains from limiting their profundity. Instead, his final rhetorical move is to leave "the lamp glowing . . . in [his] mind," show respect for another living being's "shadow," and walk away (36).

In general, we do not encourage students to come to inconclusive conclusions in their own thinking and writing. In this case, however, Eiseley's rhetorical maneuver carries a powerful and profound interdisciplinary message: sometimes the best teaching you can do, the most effective persuasive and pedagogical strategy you can employ, is *not* to tell others what you think, but to show them, instead, *how to make meaning for themselves.* As an essay, "The Judgment of the Birds" is the opposite of judgmental: it ends as it began, with an open-ended query and a wanderer on a quest. The traveler allows us a brief glimpse into his pack of provisional insights and tells us the story of how he found them, but he ultimately leaves the task of determining their "relevance" up to us. As he walks away, however, discerning readers will observe that he is *walking on* and *walking out toward* another experience and another opportunity for observation.

Beyond "The Judgment of the Birds," Eiseley employed this nonjudgmental interdisciplinary voice in many other essays, where he also walked a middle way between author and audience and between the sciences and the arts and humanities. His rhetoric of profundity drew deeply on a philosophy of life and a philosophy of nature that are equally dependent on his poetic and scientific sensibilities. As both a creative writer and a scientist, Eiseley developed a respectful awareness of the vagaries of individual perception and interpretation, as well as the "received wisdom" of traditional authority. He challenged the boundaries of disciplinary categories, deliberately seeking out relativistic perspectives and gestalt-shift-inducing experiences in borderlands and at the marginal interfaces of two worlds and different ways of being. Through a direct apprehension of the "life force" within him and around him and his abiding appreciation for the miracle of biological existence and human consciousness itself, he persisted in forging a life of active meaning making. For Eiseley it remained a profound and singular truth that as we journey through the wilderness of life alone, each of us must-need leave the ultimate meaning of human life and nature partial and provisional. That necessity contains its own beauty: in doing so we participate in and yet preserve the quest and the questions, accessible and amenable, to the *next* observer.

In the twenty-first-century two-cultures classroom, Eiseley's texts actively create an interdisciplinary readership. In composition, literature, history, and science education courses, his verse and essays can also serve variously as models for thinking, writing, teaching, and living on an ecologically fragile postmodern planet. They have lessons to teach within a wide variety of disciplinary frameworks and interdisciplinary contexts, such as nature and science writing, scientific biography and autobiography, genre studies in poetry and the expository essay, environmental studies and ecophilosophy, history and philosophy of science, the natural sciences, and science education.[12] As science majors and arts and humanities students read and discuss Eiseley's work, they develop their own bipartisan skills in "talking across the aisle" to each other, explaining their interpretations of and responses to such recurrent themes as the importance of appreciating transitory moments; the power of personal observation and meaning making; the complexity of the human-nature interface; the mysteries and scope of historical, geologic, and astronomical time; and the exquisite interconnectedness of living and nonliving things.

Eiseley's interdisciplinary life and work successfully model his synthesis of the humanities and sciences and provide students with a personal exemplum that offers compelling evidence against disciplinary biases still active across campuses and in business and professional communities. Such lessons empower students to generate their own creative fusion, personally and philosophically, as they venture out to explore — and fashion lives for themselves within — the challenging and complex social, political, and natural environments around them. Perhaps most significantly, through his rhetoric of profundity, Eiseley's words enable them to appreciate the necessary diversity of all natural things, including diverse ways of human expression and knowing.

NOTES

1. For the purposes of this essay, the term "culture" is used in the general anthropological and sociological sense to refer to any group or institution that shares conventions of symbolic communication and representation in the construction and expression of common social attitudes, values, and beliefs.

2. Christianson, *Fox* 18; Eiseley, *All* 25, 28, 30–32; *Notes* 23–25; *Unexpected* 85–86.

3. Recent research in cognitive science, neuroscience, and neuropsychology focuses on the primary role of the amygdala in the encoding and consolidation of memories, that is, emotional learning. The greater the emotional arousal associated with an event, the more one's memory of that event is enhanced and retained. Under circumstances where a particular memory or set of memories has been associated with fear conditioning, a persistent potential develops for that person's affected synapses to react more readily and strongly to similar stimuli in the future. For more detailed explanation of emotional memory, see Eichenbaum; Kandel; LeDoux, *Emotional, Synaptic*; Pinker; Rolls; and Thagard.

4. Some of the information included here was communicated to the author through a personal phone conversation with Mabel Langdon Eiseley.

5. My friends in physics tell me that this process of ranking the professional status of their peers in inverse proportion to their public science activity is alive and well today. Popular writing and other science education projects earn them "*negative* brownie points" (Hairston, Urquhart, and Earle).

6. Nicolson's most influential works include *Newton Demands the Muse* (1946), *Voyages to the Moon* (1948), *The Breaking of the Circle* (1950), *Science and Imagination* (1956), *Mountain Gloom and Mountain Glory* (1959), and separate interdisciplinary studies of the scientific interests and associations of Samuel Pepys, John Milton, Alexander Pope, and Anne Conway.

7. Eiseley to Dr. Edwin G. Boring, May 2, 1966.

8. Eiseley felt distinctly uneasy about being identified as part of the "Establishment" yet also wanted somehow to preserve some recognition for himself and his academic research and writing as "authoritative." For an example of this uneasiness, see the opening pages of his introduction and his account of being personally accosted by a student protester (Eiseley et al. 3–6 and 7–9).

9. As in the case of this chapter's thesis, for example, such a catchphrase might be "Eiseley is a synthesizer, not a polarizer."

10. Of particular note are the diverse groups of interdisciplinary scholars and practitioners in the Society for Literature, Science, and the Arts (SLSA, originally founded in 1985 as the Society for Literature and Science, or SLS); the Association for the Study of Literature and Environment (ASLE); the Popular Culture Association (PCA); and so on. In addition, the Modern Language Association and the History of Science Society continue to support the study of the relations of literature and science and the humanities and science.

11. "The Judgment of the Birds" was originally published in *The American Scholar* (1956) and as the third to last chapter in *The Immense Journey* (1957). It was later reprinted as the opening chapter in *The Star Thrower* (1978) in the version cited here. In class, with the permission of the editor, I distribute copies of the essay as it appeared, with useful explanatory material, footnotes, and glossary, in Fred D. White's highly recommended interdisciplinary anthology *Science and the Human Spirit*, now, regrettably, out of print.

12. Science education, the pedagogical theory and practical training of teachers of science, especially in the K–12 classroom, is an increasing vital interdisciplinary enterprise that has much to gain from the bicultural communication skills that Eiseley's works have to offer. See, for example, the innovative UTeach programs, founded within the University of Texas system (UTeach; UTeach Dallas).

8

Artifact and Idea

Loren Eiseley's Poetic
Undermining of C. P. Snow

MARY ELLEN PITTS

Loren Eiseley often scrawled questions and poems in the margins of texts that he read. Indeed, two years before the publication of Thomas S. Kuhn's *The Structure of Scientific Revolutions*, which footnotes *The Firmament of Time*, Eiseley wrote that "the intellectual climate of a given period may unconsciously retard or limit the theoretical ventures of an exploring scientist" (*Firmament* 61). Keenly aware of the limitations imposed by a worldview, Eiseley responded formally in "The Illusion of the Two Cultures" to C. P. Snow's pronouncement that scientific and literary cultures are so polarized that they fail utterly to communicate. Thus began an ongoing dialogue with Snow's argument.

Although Snow was purportedly reporting, rather than advocating, the bifurcation of the world of learning, he emerged as spokesperson for what Eiseley considered an oversimplified view, for Snow argued that literary intellectuals and scientists represent separate poles, each unable to understand the other. Famously, Snow declared that literary intellectuals could not explain the Second Law of Thermodynamics, a failure that Snow equates with a scientist's never having read anything by Shakespeare. This dichotomy Eiseley dismisses as an "illusion" born out of "a peculiar aberration of the human mind" that fails to recognize "the whole domain of value, which after all constitutes the very nature of man, as without significance" (*Star* 268–69).

Eiseley argues that the highest intellectual power is the human ability to stretch "an invisible web of gossamer . . . into the past as well as across [living] minds and . . . [to respond] to the vibrations transmitted through these tenuous lines of sympathy" (267). Perceiving science itself not as an end, but as a means to what Francis Bacon calls "the uses of life" — all life — Eiseley perceives that the greatest danger of Snow's dichotomizing lies in the human perception of self, for "the tool user grows convinced that he is himself only useful as a tool, that fertility except in the use of the scientific imagination is wasteful and without purpose" (269).

Eiseley's essay is a powerful argument, extended by an analysis of an arrowhead as a link between utility and beauty, between *techne* and *poiesis*. His writing is highly allusive and invokes Leonardo, Darwin, Einstein, and Newton, all of whom "show a deep humility and an emotional hunger which is the prerogative of the artist." Indeed, the essay is a tour de force for Eiseley, urging reexamination of both science and art as "constructs" of human beings, subject "to human pressures and inescapable distortions" (276, 277). But effective as this essay is, Eiseley's wily extension of his dialogue with Snow into his first collection of poems, *Notes of an Alchemist*, may be an even greater feat. Eiseley takes Snow's own exemplar, the Second Law of Thermodynamics, as the underlying concept in poetry and juxtaposes entropy — that tendency toward randomness, disorder, or mixing of molecules that characterizes all systems of energy — and the force that Eiseley (anticipating writers such as Ilya Prigogine and Isabel Stengers, who write about "self-organizing systems") calls "organization."[1] His poems undermine Snow's position through art created from scientific observation and knowledge.

Four poems in *Notes of an Alchemist* accomplish Eiseley's master stroke: "Notes of an Alchemist," "The Striders," "The Beaver," and "Arrowhead." In his guise as alchemist, Eiseley transmutes into poetic understanding not only entropy itself but its opposite — organization, or negentropy. Eiseley moves from the dialogue between the two in natural phenomena to the human quest for organization — a quest that is both physical and intellectual, the quest of "wise men" to "charm . . . / the cloudy crystal of the mind" (lines 60–61).

With an approach that is at once serious and playful, in these four poems Eiseley begins with chemistry — the formation of crystals through the action of a catalyst. He moves then to a simple principle of physics — the surface tension of water that provides a platform for a light-bodied insect, the water strider. He turns next to the dialogue of biological entropy and organization in the form of the beaver and its effects on the geography of a continent. The fourth poem draws together the forces that compose cultural entropy versus organization, in the setting of a cemetery where diggers have uncovered an ancient arrowhead.

Important in Eiseley's essays are figures of chance that often give images to the argument. The trickster from Native American legends is an image of accident or chance, perhaps represented by a tornado or the dancing rat that amused an audience while Eiseley unwittingly continued his lecture (*All* 11–12). The child playing his own game, rolling dice in an abandoned house, prefaces the theme of chance in *The Invisible Pyramid*. In *All the Strange Hours*, a complex metaphor of the Player leads the narrator into his final journey. These playful figures can both amuse and terrify, but there is another element of play in the poetic texts examined here. In an almost Derridean sense of the "play" of forces — as with the play of a rope or the play of natural forces that accidentally form substances and events such as a catalyst's action on inert substances or a beetle's breaking of the water's surface film or the beaver's preserving a continent or the human quest for space — Eiseley addresses the play of entropy, accident, and organization, echoing his own statement in *The Unexpected Universe*, "If there was order in us, it was the order of change" (103).

"Notes of an Alchemist" opens with the natural phenomenon of crystal formation and concludes with the poet's reflection "that out of order and disorder / perpetually clashing and reclashing / come the worlds" (*Notes*, lines 80–82). Crystals grow into organized forms through pressure, through fires or trickling waters. Like men they are "twisted" by their environments. Scars on the poet's hand are likened to the extraneous substances with which the crystal may be "marred" (18, 30). From his observation of the chemical process of crystal formation, Eiseley can "grasp," for the reader, two points: first, the role of the catalyst that can "transfigure" a clear substance into the vivid colors of sapphire and ruby; second, the necessity that the crystal must "lie / under the spell of its own fluid," isolated (37, 49–50). Although the catalyst triggers the transformation, it remains unexplained as one of the mysterious actions of the organizing tendency in nature.

The poem shifts then to the human attempt "to charm to similar translucence / the cloudy crystal of the mind" (60–61). In this analogizing of the formation of human thought and crystals, the poet asks us to comprehend "that order strives / against the unmitigated chaos lurking / along the convulsive backbone of the world" (63–65). The image is one that could have come from chaos studies, the clash of order and disorder or of negentropy and entropy. Referring to the "wild crystal," the poet stresses accident as crucial to emerging order (68). Positing his personal identification with the sapphire of night, he concludes that "out of order and disorder / perpetually clashing and reclashing / come the worlds" (80–82). Structurally, the poet himself, as T. S. Eliot suggested, is functioning as the catalyst, the "alchemist" who transmutes the clash of entropy and negentropy in chemicals and human minds. The poem is his "study" of earth's chemistry, of which mind is a part, of organization and entropy — a subtle suggestion of order in nature and the role of the poet or alchemist as catalyst in a poiesis transcending laws that, in their fixity, are incomplete.

"The Striders" takes the dialectic to a principle of physics and to a small life form, an insect that rows on the surface tension of water — a tension easily broken by a heavier, hard-shelled, awkward beetle. The delicate "film of water" and the fragile insect that can "row" on its tension constitute a physical example of organization, which is countered by the image of the beetle (*Notes*, line 1). The beetle's intrusion, however, is accidental, part of the principle of accident that, as Eiseley frequently emphasizes, Darwin reintroduced into nature. For the poet, "the molecule" seems almost "to think" (6–7), even as "uncanny things" seem to lurk in the water and even in the human erythrocyte (red blood cell), which will preferentially absorb carbon monoxide "while treacherously forgetting / the oxygen that it was born to serve" (8, 18–19). So precarious is the strider's rowing on organization that a slight movement, an uncanny thing in the water, can break the film, and so fragile is life itself that the red blood cell, given the chance, will absorb carbon monoxide rather than oxygen; entropy thus "hides" or "waits" (8, 20).

The poet images the human being as a "strider over light and air," while "darkness waits below" (21). So frail is organization that the universal "intricacies" suggest the inevitability of entropy. In contrast to such fragility, however, Eiseley perceives an "upward drive of things / that sets the strider rowing" (23, 28–29). If the water strider survives in its interaction with the water, humankind, the poet says, "glides magnificently / upon a web of music and of light" (33–34). Indeed, Eiseley envisions a conflict between "something below" and "the dark," a conflict whose outcome is never certain (36). But that upward force wins often enough that "music rises" and the notes of a mockingbird reproduce the notes of its ancestors (38–41). In a kind of Heideggerian "here and now" and in "little things" (33), Eiseley the poet again portrays the forces of entropy and organization as "players" in "a giant game" of light and darkness, and he notes that humans can and do play for both sides in this game (42, 46–47).

But the poet ends the stanza by returning to the mockingbird and its repertoire with a personal interjection parallel to the earlier "I think." The poet likes "the singing of the bird" and how it tends its nest (50). The bird's care for its young is part of that "upward force" of organization, preserving the life form and the code of song that it bears.

The last stanza opens with a third personal observation, which emerges from the first two, as the poet says, "I tread most gently in this season" (55). Identifying with the "tension" that the insect feels and aware of how precarious life can be, the poet concludes only, "I always watch the striders in the spring" (56–58). In the images of an insect "rowing" and a bird "bending" over its young, the poet — ever aware of the world's fragility — affirms negentropy.

In "The Beaver" Eiseley moves to a complex biological form of organization, one whose bones and "huge orange-colored incisors" remind the poet that this animal helped to preserve a continent, unwittingly, in its pursuit of survival (Notes, line 10). Recalling how he found the bones of the beaver's skeleton, scattered "like little pebbles" (5–6), he invokes the code of mechanism as he realizes that while he had all "the parts," nevertheless "the watch spring / eluded" him (15–16).

As if reiterating the stance of the evolutionist in the presence of these bones, the poet admits uncertainty, but hastens to qualify his statement — something he cannot do in the scientific literature, but can do as a poet (26). In the "puzzle" he has uncovered, he senses "intention," though it may be difficult to see (28, 30). This intention is adaptation. Through the image of the beaver's ear canals, which signify perfect adaptation to its environment, what the beaver knew was the sort of things that "nature whispers in thickets" although "scholars" cannot hear it (43, 45). What nature whispered was organization, the "upward drive" mentioned earlier, the force that, opposing entropy, makes possible new worlds of life.

The poet then muses in the first person, speculating that it was "the intricate chain of genes" that "taught" the beaver, and he recalls finding the beaver's bones amid the silence of a river (46). Here, Eiseley introduces one of his most complex images, as he recalls a visual and an auditory image amid the silence: "One leaf fell / and a one-dimensional bird / laughed from a tree" (53–55). The leaf is soundless beside the silent river, and the bird is one dimensional, existing for the poet only in the linear utterance of the sound. In recalling the moment, the poet confronts the very mystery of organization, but the scientist speaks through the mystery, admitting that teleology "is out of fashion" (56–57). Having ventured near Aristotle's entelechy, the poet is trumped by the scientist and left only to muse that the beaver preceded modern dam builders; he concludes that "old orange-tooth" and the "one-dimensional bird" are left, "summarizing confusion" (60–62). The beaver's bones are the relics of entropy, but in the beaver itself, order battled chaos for the destiny of a continent. The play of entropy and negentropy brings only a summary of the scientist/poet's confusion — the mystery not explained in rules; the text's echoed confusion; the chaos that, among any physicists and engineers, was already being perceived as the creation of information.[2] The paradoxical final words, then, mirror the work of chaos, the phase transition from which new order — organization, from the biological to the continental — arises. In the play of forces, as in the play of a rope, repeated motion creates its own inexplicable pattern, defying entropy and adding an ironic, positive trickster effect in preserving a continent.

Set in a human graveyard — entropy personalized — "Arrowhead" frames Eiseley's most explicit nod to Snow. The poet tells of finding an arrowhead, perceived at first as mere artifact, "just flint, rain-washed, glistening," but he knows that it was "designed to bring death on the snowy air (*Notes*, lines 2, 4). But the arrowhead, bearing its maker's craftsmanship, becomes a sign for the poet — a sign that the maker "had loved his instrument and so embellished it" that someone centuries later could feel it "lovingly" because of its beauty and be able to overlook its deadly purpose and admire instead the "glory of art" (13, 14, 15). For what had been meant to cause death had, through the craftperson's skill, become an object that would transcend time, as art does.

He says — ironically and metapoetically — that in the two-cultured world "the scientist is not the poet, / and the poet never clasps like a workman with his hands / true death from the air." Eiseley himself, the scientist as poet, does precisely what the two-cultured world would hold him incapable of doing: he has already felt the stone "lovingly"; he has briefly forgotten its brutal purpose "in the greater glory of art"; and in the next stanza, he reports that he has "made the crossing, realized the beauty" (16, 14, 15, 34). A similar sequence occurs in prose in "The Illusion of the Two Cultures" (270–72). Of course, the speaker *is* the scientist who is also the poet, a man who for most of his life has clasped, with hands rough from digging, the truth of death itself from the earth's ruins, but who has also clasped, intellectually, the organization that sometimes trumps entropy.

The poem's next stanza is personal — the poet, leaning on the gravestone of his own grandparents, tells us that he "made the crossing, realized the beauty" (line 34). As always, Eiseley's first-person pronoun signals a musing and a linking of the seemingly disparate. The "crossing" is that between science and art, between the Heideggerian techne and poiesis, the making that blends with techne. In Heidegger's words, "There was a time when it was not technology alone that bore the name *techne*. . . . The *poiesis* of the fine arts also was called *techne*" (34). In Eiseley's poem the carver decorated his flint out of love for the "instrument" (line 13). Feeling linked to the carver, the poet makes a "crossing" as the sharp edge draws blood, and the poet, on impulse, tastes the blood that links the life forms and feels that the voice of the arrowhead's maker also "entered" him and "sang of the arrow." But it also sang of the "straight divinatory lines of mathematics" that enable us and our tools to leap through space (27–31). Partaking of shared blood, the poet also partakes of the carver's "song," which images the "divinatory" lines of mathematics, the science that underlies the arrowhead's flight, later combining "art and science together" (31). All was shaped, the poet says, "in the mind of the first artist in flint," for this person contained "both the split worlds" (34–36). In the complex synecdoche of the carver's mind (38), Eiseley portrays the carver's perception of his techne's flight as a starting point for a dream: the dream of flight itself—the dream that is also poiesis. In grasping the dream of how a stone would be able to "pierce time / and be stopped nowhere," the carver's union of techne and poiesis speaks both *to* and *through* the poet, who sends it on its way, "hastening tomorrow" (47–49, 52). The arrowhead, which is a code of flight in its very shape, embodies, too, the fragile yet enduring fusion of art and science that leads to the future.

In these four poems, then, Eiseley is not only the alchemist transmuting scientific observation into poetry but the playful trickster, ever aware of the levels of meaning associated with words, who takes on C. P. Snow on his own turf, treating entropy through poetic images and juxtaposing entropy and negentropy through the mysterium tremendum of organization. The result is the sometimes playful (on multiple levels), often ironic, always deadly serious dialectic of entropy and organization. Science and art—each an order within disorder, a phase transition that contains the information of a time, a place, even a culture—are only richer for their interplay.

NOTES

1. Ilya Prigogine and Isabel Stengers explore the emergence of order from chaos in varied systems, from convection patterns to the growth of cities. In an unstable system, random fluctuations may be amplified by positive feedback and, under certain conditions, spontaneously produce new patterns. For a general reader's introduction to chaos studies, see James Gleick, *Chaos*.

2. Gleick notes that in the 1960s Benoit Mandelbrot at IBM, Hendrik Houthakker at Harvard, Gunter Ahlers at AT&T Bell Laboratories, and Conrad Lorenz at MIT were working in areas that would lead to the emergence of chaos studies (9–203).

9

The Spirit of Synecdoche

Order and Chaos Contend in the
Metaphors of Loren Eiseley

JACQUELINE CASON

It is a great thing, indeed, to make a proper use of
the poetical forms. . . . But the greatest thing by far
is to be a master of metaphor. It is the one thing
that cannot be learnt from others; and it is also a
sign of genius, since a good metaphor implies an
intuitive perception of the similarity in dissimilars.
ARISTOTLE, POETICS

It has ever been my lot, though formally myself a
teacher, to be taught surely by none.
LOREN EISELEY, "THE STAR THROWER"

The way we read the past shapes our present and future, and the genius of Loren Eiseley's evolutionary metaphors remains relevant to current cultural and ecological issues. William Zinsser describes the sixties as the "golden era of nonfiction" (56). Eiseley's books sold well after World War II, when the reading public developed an appetite for works that dealt directly with reality, preferring nonfiction to novels and short stories. W. H. Auden read everything of Eiseley's he could lay his hands on (15). Yet in spite of a loyal and diverse following, Eiseley has yet to receive critical attention commensurate with his poetic contribution.

The son of a traveling salesman during the Great Depression, Eiseley was sensitive to the extravagance of space flight amid poverty. Coming of age, he witnessed a fear of communism, followed by a revolt of the next generation, outraged by Vietnam. After World War II and the bombing of Japan, his fellow writers expressed a pervading sense of apocalyptic despair and a crisis of faith in aesthetic impulses. Katherine Anne Porter, writing in 1950, describes her own puzzlement with a neighbor who was "restoring a beautiful surface to put his books and papers on." Her neighbor's sense of faith, his "deep, right, instinctive, human belief that he and the table were going to be around together for a long time" leads her to contemplate human progress and destiny (194, 195).

Artists of Eiseley's era questioned the uses of technology and grew uneasy about the collaboration of scientists with the government-military-industrial complex. Porter's "The Future Is Now" sums the mood of a time when scientific progress collided with the possibility of nuclear annihilation as paradoxical. Eiseley addresses this paradox in "The Star Thrower": "Humanity was suddenly entranced by light and fancied it reflected light. Progress was its watchword, and for a time the shadows seemed to recede.

Only a few guessed that the retreat of darkness presaged the emergence of an entirely new and less tangible terror" (*Unexpected* 82). Nevertheless, Eiseley deliberately chose the path of Porter's neighbor — to labor in view of and in spite of the terror of nuclear annihilation. A writer committed to bringing coherence to his own handful of chaos, Eiseley began publishing in the decade of Porter's essay and continued during the Cold War, the Space Race, Vietnam, and the environmental movement. Reflecting on postwar science, both Porter and Eiseley were in an awkward position of questioning the progress and wisdom of science and technology during an age of medical miracles. And it wasn't only medicine. In 1957 the Soviet Union launched the satellite Sputnik, starting a race with the United States to claim and exploit the frontiers of space.

Amid public faith in scientific solutions, Eiseley questioned the wisdom of science and the moral responsibility of scientists: "To the student of human culture, the rise of science and its dominating role in our society presents a unique phenomenon"; he also observed that "the scientific worker has frequently denied personal responsibility for the way his discoveries are used" (*Firmament* 131, 135). It was not the institution of science, but scientists, he called to account, defending a tradition of disinterested observation while simultaneously prodding colleagues to recognize the moral implications of their work.

Though science was making great strides, Warren Weaver's 1947 essay, "Science and Complexity," already anticipated problems of organized complexity: statistics alone cannot address problems "dealing simultaneously with *a sizable number of factors which are interrelated into an organic whole*" (6; emphasis added). As interrelated parts in a larger system, "these problems . . . are just too complicated to yield to the old nineteenth-century techniques which were successful on two-, three-, or four-variable problems of simplicity." Although science has provided an intellectual tradition marked by global cooperation and a precisely defined language, it cannot "furnish a code of morals, or a basis for esthetics" (7, 12). Weaver posits that "our morals must catch up with our machinery" if we are to fill the gap between "our power and our capacity to use power wisely" (12–13).

Eiseley foresaw this horizon and was not only poised to address problems of organized complexity but ready to explore moral and aesthetic issues outside the strict boundaries of science, by concealing matters of beauty and virtue amid scientific concepts.[1] He is among the "generality of men" described by Matthew Arnold, seeking to reconcile evolution with ethics and aesthetics (465). Ironically, his regard for collective memory and history, and his belief in the regenerative role that evolutionary understanding could play, alienated him from the students who were similarly anxious about their futures. Eiseley sharply criticized college students who waged campus protests and challenged the authority of faculty and administrators, referring to them as "irrational activists whose rejection of history constitutes an equal . . . rejection of any humane . . . future" (*Unexpected* 5). Eiseley took campus protests personally, as reflected in a letter he addressed to President Richard Nixon, articulating his fear that the younger generation, with the help of the media, were losing critical awareness: "many people, particularly the young, are the more or less innocent dupes of unseen elements making use of the mass media for the purposes of propaganda" (Christianson, *Fox* 400). He was scheduled to deliver the commencement address at Kent State in the spring of 1970. After hearing the news of students being killed and injured by the National Guard, he remarked to a friend that "they got what they asked for" (401). Despite generational alienation, *The Invisible Pyramid* demonstrates that Eiseley had much in common with the students who challenged the increasing commercialism and militarism of society and who feared the possibility of a nuclear holocaust. But in his mind, the hippies were rejecting history altogether.

Joan Didion wrote more empathetically about a vertiginous decade when she was losing her own faith in narrative to interpret life's meaning. At the beginning of "The White Album," she muses, "We tell ourselves stories in order to live. . . . We look for the sermon in the suicide. . . . We live entirely, especially if we are writers, by the imposition of a narrative line upon disparate images, by the 'ideas' with which we have learned to freeze the shifting phantasmagoria which is our actual experience." Yet at the end of her narrative, Didion concludes that stories had not helped her to render the sixties meaningful after all (421, 446). In contrast, Eiseley's alienation from students and pensive anxiety about the future did not undermine his commitment to narrative coherence and myth making. Refusing to succumb to experiential fragmentation, he adopted what Victor Witter Turner describes as a debris theory in his search for coherence: "The culture of any society at any moment is more like the debris, or 'fall-out,' of past ideological systems, than it is itself a system, a coherent whole" (14). It is from the debris of personal and cultural memory that Eiseley creates metaphors and coherent myths.

For the most part, Eiseley ignored the contemporary scene, his writing more allegorical than topical. According to Peter Heidtmann, "Citizen Eiseley plays a remarkably minor role in his books. The focus instead is on his private, solitary experience — on the pilgrim side of his nature" (16). With his knowledge of evolutionary biology, the deep past became his looking glass into the present and future. It is perhaps best to defer analysis of citizen Eiseley and first investigate his poetic contribution, tracing the intellectual tradition in which he played a part as a means of discovering how his symbolic action might inform our own understandings and actions as citizens of the world.

Simply put, Eiseley's genius lies in his ability to create novel metaphors that help us to perceive the connections and resemblances among dissimilar things. For Eiseley, the universe is at heart a mystery, and the symbolic forms of language, a human tool, metaphorically express and give dynamic shape to that mystery:

> For many of us the Biblical bush still burns, and there is a deep mystery in the heart of a simple seed. If I seem for a time to be telling the story of how man came under the domain of law, how he reluctantly gave up his dreams and found his own footsteps wandering backward until on some far hillside they were transmuted into the footprints of a beast, it is only that we may assess more clearly that strange world into which we have been born — we, compounded of dust, and the light of a star. (*Firmament* 8)

Eiseley's power as a writer is his ability to create metaphors of an interdependent vision of human-nonhuman relationships that dissolve the hierarchy of human supremacy.

This chapter explores the role of metaphor and narrative in dramatizing a complex self-organizing universe. Eiseley participates in a philosophical and artistic tradition that disrupts reductionist explanations of the universe in favor of metaphors that help shift the paradigm toward compassion and complexity. His metaphorical trope of choice is synecdoche. Unlike metonymy, a zero-sum trope that fragments wholes into their constituent parts, synecdoche reinforces a gestalt understanding of the parts as organic components of a whole, whose totality remains greater than a sum of parts.[2]

To characterize Eiseley as a potential paradigm shifter who configures complex systems with his metaphors, we must understand how metaphors categorically redescribe the defining terms of our lives. As forms of symbolic action, metaphor and figuration operate at the level of word and sentence, but also at the level of story. Paul Ricoeur and Hayden White help to theorize a reading of Eiseley insofar as they extend Aristotle's lexical definition of metaphor to the broader level of narrative discourse. By virtue of its discursive nature, poetic metaphor is a form of mimesis, the narrative representation of human action (Ricoeur, "Between" 329, 334). A writer's poetic imagination configures symbolic resources to construct new plots and typologies. Such narratives enable human societies to become more than their material conditions alone would determine. This extension is why synecdoche is important — it allows for the figurative leap from word and sentence to plot.

To explore the roles of metaphor and narrative, I analyze "The Last Neanderthal" as a theory of natural and cultural creativity, a set of instructions for interpreting Eiseley's collected essays in *The Unexpected Universe*, which draws together the several plums and yields them in a gifting gesture to readers. I then turn to "The Star Thrower" as an essay within the collection that confronts a deterministic fatalism and dramatizes human choices as natural phenomena that can imaginatively shape the future. I conclude by exploring the relevance of metaphors of complex systems and the current approaches to addressing the challenges of our day.

ON METAPHOR

The poet is an artisan not only of words and sentences but also of plots.
RICOEUR, "RHETORIC — POETICS — HERMENEUTICS"

The power to change is both creative and destructive.
LOREN EISELEY, "THE STAR THROWER"

Metaphor is both destructive and creative. Mary Ellen Pitts describes
Eiseley's use of metaphor in cognitive terms (65). Pitts, following the
pragmatism of Richard Rorty, acknowledges the dependence of thought
on language. Language, far from being a mirror of nature, creatively shapes
human perceptions of natural phenomena and consequently shapes
human relationships and behavior (68).[3] Pitts explains that novel metaphors surprise us with new relationships and unravel our common-sense
assumptions about language as an objective mirror of the real (67). Most
notably for Pitts, Eiseley's poetic contribution effectively demythologizes
the dominant metaphorical concepts of the Cartesian-Newtonian-Lockean
paradigm and its impact on scientific thinking (93). Specifically, Eiseley
seeks to disrupt mechanical metaphors that suggest the human capacity
to subjugate nature is somehow inherent in human purpose and design
(74). As Eiseley displaces metaphors of industrial production and com-
petitive struggle, he supplants them with an indeterminate symbiosis of
coevolving species in which stability is illusory.

In addition to her emphasis on the relationship between metaphor
and cognition, Pitts is on the verge of identifying synecdoche as Eiseley's
dominant conceptual trope but stops short. Insightfully, Pitts writes that
"instead of seeing humankind as separate from and needing to 'control'
the environment, Eiseley explores an understanding based, not on parts
of the whole, but on the whole as an interactive system" (74–75). I offer
a subtle yet significant extension of her point by claiming that Eiseley's
figuration privileges neither parts nor wholes but maintains an intrinsic
identification between the part and the whole. According to Ernst Cassirer,
such synecdochic identification between part and whole is characteristic
of the mythic mind: "This mystic relationship which obtains between a

whole and its parts holds also between genus and species, and between the species and its several instances. Here, too, each form is entirely merged with the other; the genus or species is not only represented by an individual member of it, but lives and acts in it. . . . There is much more in metaphor than a bare 'substitution,' a mere rhetorical figure of speech; that what seems to our subsequent reflection as a sheer transcription is mythically conceived as *a genuine and direct identification*" (93–94; emphasis added).

The metonymic mode, by contrast, posits an extrinsic relationship among parts and wholes. Parts may be divided, substituted, and reconstituted without altering the quality of the whole. Take the concept of food, for example. From a metonymic perspective, food can be divided into its constituent nutrients, synthetic nutrients can be substituted for natural ones, and they can be reconstituted into new products. Food becomes a fungible aggregate of nutrients. We are what we eat. From a synecdochic perspective, however, food is not fungible but connected to the people and communities who grew it and the soil that nourished it. Extracting food from that larger system would alter its nature. The quality of food is inextricable from the food system. We are what we eat eats.

Once readers recognize that synecdoche carries the burden of interpretation, Eiseley's anecdotes of individual ethical action make more sense as qualitative representatives of complex interactive systems. The synecdochic mode, by prefiguring an inherent universalism, enables Eiseley to dramatize the individual as a microcosm who shares the spirit of the whole without sacrificing individual identity. Pitts describes the whole as an interactive system but does not fully acknowledge that the parts have an integrity of their own, distinct from yet consubstantial with the system. Synecdoche allows Eiseley to focus more exclusively on the freedom of the individual to choose a course of action rather than being determined by the material contingencies of the system.

While Pitts offers a thorough exploration of Eiseleyan metaphor in particular, Paul Ricoeur explains more generally how metaphor transgresses categorical boundaries to challenge and recreate the logical structures of language and thought. Specifically, Ricoeur furthers our understanding by explaining the relationship between poetics and rhetoric. Poetic language stirs up sedimented conventions, converts our imaginary store of common beliefs, and enters the world of rhetoric. By redescribing commonplace reality, poetics changes our perceptions of reality and provides rhetors new premises to which their audiences will tacitly agree, opening the path to innovative conclusions.

Hayden White's theory of emplotment, which he describes as an "essentially poetic act," complements Ricoeur's sense that narrative is a form of temporal allegory and that storytelling embodies the human quest for meaning in view of and in spite of the destructive power of time passing (*Metahistory* x). In this way, Eiseley's evolutionary narratives become allegories of temporality, poetic acts that endow an otherwise neutral evolutionary process with moral significance. The art of narrative, viewed as a ritual act, becomes an experiment in consequences. Moreover, Eiseley's metaphoric plots enact White's concept of metahistorical consciousness, which is an ironic awareness that frees the imagination to create life-serving myths in a full understanding of the fictive nature of narrative (xii), and in accord with aesthetic and moral preferences.

In Eiseley's case, the ironic trickster is an ever-present companion to synecdoche. The twisters and dust devils of the Plains manifest themselves in his mind, in "the dance of contingency, of the indeterminable": "There was a shadow I could not henceforth shake off, which I knew was posturing and would always posture behind me. That mocking shadow looms over me as I write. It scrawls with a derisive pen and an exaggerated flourish. I know instinctively it will be present to caricature the solemnities of my deathbed. In a quarter of a century it has never spoken" (*Star* 77–78). Yet because of his metahistorical awareness, the trickster does not stymie his will to celebrate the microcosm and to construct coherence and assign meaning to human action.

THE LAST NEANDERTHAL

> *Great poems and novels are like slow-burning fuses. As they enter into new, unpredictable situations, they begin to release new meanings that the author himself could not have foreseen, any more than Goethe could have foreseen commercial television.*
> TERRY EAGLETON, "WAKING THE DEAD"

What if I am, in some way, only a sophisticated fire that has acquired an ability to regulate its rate of combustion and to hoard its fuel in order to see and walk?
LOREN EISELEY, "THE LAST NEANDERTHAL"

We turn now to a representative example of Eiseley's metaphoric genius and his capacity to fashion a coherent narrative from the debris of memory, to an essay that aligns biological evolution with human creativity. Fire serves as the central metaphor in "The Last Neanderthal," a trope that reveals a resemblance between the radiation of heat from stones and the mind's creative ability to configure patterns, a resemblance between a wild plum thicket and the ancient library at Alexandria. Interestingly, "The Angry Winter" mentions that while our brains are hardwired for language, fire is of our own devising (*Unexpected* 115). Fire is synonymous with metabolism and oxidation, and it powers the organization and dispersion of energy through time. The metabolism of life, whether plant or animal or symbol, hoards energy and burns it with purpose to increase the level of complexity within the organism.

I claimed earlier that Pitts had not grasped the full significance of synecdoche in Eiseley's writing, and this becomes apparent in her interpretation of "The Last Neanderthal." She concludes that this final essay of *The Unexpected Universe* "undermines the expected unity of the conclusion" by ending with the "molecular dispersal of burning" (277). However, "The Last Neanderthal" is not exclusively about dispersion; it is equally about the character of order, the acceptance of mortality and the organized fruits of the imagination. In this concluding essay, Eiseley's figuration is not dispersive. To the contrary, his metaphors are tightly coordinated and structured to establish significant interrelationships between part and whole. Though the collection's title underscores the "unexpected," we might expect Eiseley to end with a dispersal of memories, organized plums bearing seeds to represent the several essays of the collection, beneficently strewn for readers to taste and to plant into new soil. This highly structured essay gathers together the seeds of the narrator's own imagination, producing a fruit that readers may carry forward through interpretation. By yoking the processes of evolution and creativity, the essay posits a set of instructions for reading the rest of the collection. Throughout, we hear echoes of the preceding essays, of an oracular message carrier who transmutes the trivial into an enchanted reality.

Taken as a whole, the three-part essay exhibits an inverted parallelism, in which the first and last parts mirror each other, revealing a synecdochic affinity. The first paragraph, a part of the essay, prefigures the structure of the whole; and the essay, a part of the collection, refigures the whole. The first and last parts each consist of fifteen paragraphs, and each explores the metabolic processes of memory and matter. The distinct metaphors of the first part — junkman and his cart, dead dog on the beach, lizards, apples, and plums — are metabolized and later reorganized into a meaningful pattern. The intervening middle section of the essay is roughly equal to the sum of the first and last sections and retells the narrator's encounter with a Neanderthal woman who represents a parallel and now extinct humanoid species. The narrator is reminded that our species could share a similar fate, and he contemplates by historical comparison the character and future of *Homo sapiens*. Eiseley does not frame Neanderthal extinction as a sign of progressive evolution but looks instead to evidence of compassion and to the cultural and symbolic differences that might explain their fate and our own.[4] The young woman embodies a persistent genetic memory, from which the narrator draws a lesson about homelessness and our evolutionary journey, a culmination of inquiry begun in the opening essay, "The Ghost Continent."

As with the structure of the whole, the highly structured five-sentence paragraph that begins the essay establishes the fire metaphor and resemblances among terms through the inverted parallelism of chiasmus. That is, the series of five sentences correspond to one another in mirror fashion — ABCBA.

It has long been the thought of science, particularly in evolutionary biology, that nature does not make extended leaps, that her creatures slip in slow disguise from one shape to another. A simple observation will reveal, however, that there are rocks in deserts that glow with heat for a time after sundown. Similar emanations may come from the writer or the scientist. The creative individual is someone upon whom mysterious rays have converged and are again reflected, not necessarily immediately, but in the course of years. That all of this wispy geometry of dreams and memories should be the product of a kind of slow-burning oxidation carried on in an equally diffuse and mediating web of nerve and sense cells is surprising enough, but that the emanations from the same particular organ, the brain, should be so strikingly different as to disobey the old truism of an unleaping nature is quite surprising, once one comes to contemplate the reality. (213)

The first and last sentences both focus on change and creativity and contrast slow rates of geologic change with flashes of imaginative creativity. While the first sentence describes evolutionary biology as a process of slow change (shape-shifting nature is the agent or grammatical subject slipping in slow disguise from one form to another), the last sentence inverts gradual change with cataclysmic leaps of the mind. Elsewhere, Eiseley has described imagination as a sudden illumination: "It is through the individual brain alone that there passes the momentary illumination in which a whole human countryside may be transmuted in an instant" (*Man* 102). The second and fourth sentences also mirror each other but this time focus on the absorption and radiation of energy. While the second sentence describes desert rocks that absorb solar rays during the day and continue glowing after sundown, the fourth sentence describes the mysterious rays that converge on the mind of the creative individual and continue to emanate for years to come. Absorption and dispersion occur in both stone and brain. The third, or middle, sentence of the paragraph is very short and functions as a bridge between writers and scientists, both of whom may absorb and disperse their creative energy, slowly and suddenly. In all three sections then, the fire metaphor connects dissimilar terms in a pattern of resemblance.

In this first section, we are witness to the nonlinear power of memory and metaphor. The essay appears as a random array of unrelated incidents, ending with dispersion, but is a deliberate act of poetic mimesis. As we learn early in the first part, the meaning of isolated incidents depends on interpretation. Seemingly random items include sounds of the ocean, the blaze of the sun, a manzanillo tree with poisoned apples, lizards darting through the sand. The poisoned apples, flashing back to the days of Columbus, help the narrator's mind to connect darting lizard patterns in the sand to an intentional memory of youth. At sixteen, the boy, now an old man, deliberately set the junkman and his cart to memory. The junkman and the contents of his cart represent history, the debris of the past, devoid of intrinsic meaning without interpretation. As the episode connects the beach sand to the junkman's cart, it reveals the mind's sudden capacity to connect dissimilar things. In his autobiography, Eiseley described this process of memory and history as "rat's country": "Make no mistake. Everything in the mind is in rat's country. It doesn't die. They are merely carried, these disparate memories, back and forth, in the desert of a billion neurons, set down, picked up, and dropped again by mental pack rats. ... Nothing is lost, but it can never be again as it was. You will only find the bits and cry out because they were yourself. ... That is all time is at the end when you are old — a splintered glass" (*All* 3–4). Much like rat's country, the first section ends with the persistence of memories, a power beyond the will of the individual to remember or forget. The fifteen paragraphs present a recursive pattern of images that sweep from the inanimate stone, to fruit, to animal life, to the entire galaxy. Each image underscores the capacity of life to hoard and organize energy and to disperse it creatively and destructively. Moreover, the brain's ability to transpose images leads to its insatiable thirst for more energy.

The longer middle section dwells on the parallels between a physical and a mental atavism, between persistent genetic traits and a metahistorical consciousness. The narrator is preoccupied with the way our narrative interpretation of the past shapes our future behavior and the course of history. The first and last paragraphs of the second part contrast the value of quantitative evidence with narratives of lived experience. While the numerical data once transcribed by the narrator has been lost, the experience has been configured as a tale and interpreted as a lesson about human homelessness and nostalgic longing.

As a physical atavism, the last Neanderthal embodies both the persistence of form and the probability of extinction and raises questions for the narrator. Were we the cause of her destruction? Would we be the cause of our own? To what end do we devour energy? Our climb up the energy ladder could mean triumph or doom, depending on whether we hoard energy beneficently or destructively. The penultimate paragraph of the middle section begins with a synecdoche for life — the cell — and telescopes out to the juggernaut of power growing beyond our control. At a more complex human scale, individual energy disperses at death, but that energy is coded symbolically and passed along to the next generation. While the cell controls and burns energy to a purpose, symbolic communication has caused "substance to vanish and earth to tremble," clearly a reference to the splitting of the atom's energy for the purpose of destruction. Language, carrier of cumulative knowledge and collective imagination, hoards energy through time. That juggernaut of power, once released, becomes more than our words can contain.

Like the darting lizard tracks of the first section, the blowing sands of the Wildcat escarpment in the middle section enable the creative mind to construct patterns — the mingling grains of time, past and present, mark the death or obsolescence of this girl. Literally, it is the death of rural life, of a young woman with few evolutionary choices in mating. Figuratively, it is the extinction of Neanderthals, a humanoid race exhibiting gentleness, who marked graves because they could see beyond the barriers of mortality. How would we procreate for the future? Would we germinate symbolic resources of an extinct species to invoke compassion, as Eiseley is doing here, or would we draw on the seeds of our own more immediate past to produce a bestial fighter similar to the one described in "The Inner Galaxy" (*Unexpected* 179)? Eiseley states the ambiguous proposition conditionally: "Perhaps in the end his last woman would stand unwanted before some fiercer, brighter version of himself" (224–25).

The essay's final section describes life as "a furnace of concealed flame," and fire or oxidation as the "essence of animal" (230, 231). While fire is the dominant metaphor in the first two sections, readers are invited to interpret the meaning of fire in relation to a metaphor of order and organization, the plums. To understand Eiseley's theory of meaning making, readers need to appreciate the full capacity of metabolic complexity, the power to destroy and the power to create, dissolution and integration. The allegorical quality of the plums and smoke, of an old man anticipating death and dissolution, allows the earlier essays to signify more than they would in isolation.

The third section of the essay offers a panoramic view of history as a way into the thickets of the future, turning to a complex human metabolism that hoards and burns, literally and figuratively: "Man, whose strange metabolism has passed beyond the search for food, to the naked ingestion of power, is scarcely aware that the energy whose limited planetary store lies at the root of the struggle for existence, has passed by way of his mind into another dimension" (230).

To dramatize the capacity of human metabolism to create and to hoard, the narrator juxtaposes two descriptions of plums, one from youth and one from old age. In both cases, the imagery of the plum thicket presents the interplay of randomness and order. Having met a woman whose features — cavernous eye sockets, low archaic skull vault, massive bones, head thrust forward — present a living phantom connected anatomically to the past, the narrator seeks to transform his memory of her, along with other memories, into a form of energy that will feed his readers' imaginations. First, the youthful memory of a wild-plum thicket:

> All the hoarded juices of summer had fallen with that lush untasted fruit upon the grass. The tiny engines of the plant had painstakingly gathered throughout the summer rich stores of sugar and syrup from the ground. Seed had been produced; birds had flown away with fruit that would give rise to plum trees miles away. The energy dispersion was so beneficent on that autumn afternoon that earth itself seemed anxious to promote the process against the downward guttering of the stars. Even I, tasting the fruit, was in my animal way scooping up some of it into thoughts and dreams. (230–31)

Second, from the perspective of an aging man who anticipates death, is the narrator's analogical extension, his transformation of smoke into plums, order out of chaos:

I remembered that star-filled night years ago on the escarpment and the heavy-headed dreaming girl drawing a circle in the dust. Perhaps it was time itself she drew, for my own head was growing heavy and the smoke from the autumn fields seemed to be penetrating my mind. I wanted to drop them at last, these carefully hoarded memories. I wanted to strew them like the blue plums in some gesture of love toward the universe all outward on a mat of leaves. Rich, rich and not to be hoarded, only to be laid down for someone, anyone, no longer to be carried and remembered in pain. . . . Perhaps all I was, really, was a pile of autumn leaves seeing smoke wraiths through the haze of my own burning. (232)

Both processes are continuous, hoarding and burning. Even as he formulates the plums of memory into a story, he senses the oxidation and dispersion that will lead to his own death. Memory, the human capacity to store energy through time, is a living concentration of energy that must be shared to shape the future.

THE TRICKSTER AND THE STAR THROWER

Man is himself, like the universe he inhabits . . . a tale of desolations. . . . But out of such desolation emerges the awesome freedom to choose — to choose beyond the narrowly circumscribed circle that delimits the animal being. In that widening ring of human choice, chaos and order renew their symbolic struggle — they contend for the destiny of the world.

LOREN EISELEY, "THE STAR THROWER"

Having examined "The Last Neanderthal" as a set of instructions for interpreting the interplay of order and chaos throughout *The Unexpected Universe*, I turn to "The Star Thrower" as a more explicit drama of human action on the evolutionary stage. For Eiseley, cooperation is more important than competition, on both micro and macro levels. Eiseley captures that idea in *Darwin's Century*, and in three sentences analogically characterizes both cellular survival and human survival as acts of compassion, acts of identification among parts and wholes, between oneself and a greater individuality: "Cells have joined to individual cells in the long ages of evolutionary advance, have even sacrificed themselves to build that vaster individuality of which they can have no knowledge. The cell itself is, in turn, a laboratory where chemical processes are being carried on in an amazingly co-ordinated fashion. One generation, as Bergson somewhere remarks, bends lovingly over the cradle of the next" (348–49). Eiseley's analogical leap from micro to macro levels, from cell to cradle, is similar to his depiction of the star thrower on both individual and planetary levels, as he sums up the cosmic significance of star throwing in the essay: "For a moment, we cast on an infinite beach together beside an unknown hurler of suns. It was, unsought, the destiny of my kind since the rituals of the ice age hunters, when life in the Northern Hemisphere had come close to vanishing. We had lost our way, I thought, but we had kept, some of us, the memory of the perfect circle of compassion from life to death and back again to life — the completion of the rainbow of existence" (*Unexpected* 90). Both extended metaphors affirm his dominant trope to be synecdoche. The conceptual moves that Eiseley makes with analogies, ranging from cell to cradle and from sea stars to planetary bodies, underscore a consubstantial identification between the part and the whole, an identification evoked by ritual acts of compassion.

Written nearly a decade before *The Unexpected Universe* and published as part of the final essay in *The Firmament of Time*, Eiseley's anecdote of snake and hen pheasant depicts a similar ritual. When the narrator comes across "two little whirlwinds of contending energy . . . beating each other to death" over whether the eggs would evolve into feather or scale, he decides to arbitrate the matter (174). He soon questions his own motive for intervening in an evolutionary process, drawing readers into contemplation: "And I, the apparition in that valley — for what had I contended? — I who contained the serpent and the bird and who read the past long written in their bodies" (175).

Readers themselves may wonder how a single instance of compassion, which on an evolutionary scale can only seem futile and insignificant, matters. But as a ritual act, it carries greater significance, and Eiseley's depiction in both essays is clearly ritualistic. The narrator is struggling to expand humanity's notion of self within an immense universe: "I had embraced them in my own substance and, in some insubstantial way, reconciled them, as I had sought reconciliation with the muskrat on the shore. I had transcended feather and scale and gone beyond them into another sphere of reality. I was trying to give birth to a different self" (178). Not only does the narrator of "How Natural Is 'Natural'?" characterize compassion through an act of ritual reconciliation, but he also describes the limitations of science with regard to the moral development of a species striving to relate its knowledge of biological descent to a sense within for conduct and beauty. That narrator's "cleansed and scoured mind" could be "an empiricist with the best of them. [He] would be deceived by no more music," if only his mind had not begun to converse during its descent "in a variety of voices, to debate, to argue, to push at stones" (161–62). The voices arguing with the stones teach him that we are composed of the "dust . . . [that] hears music and responds to it, weeps bitterly over time and loss, or is oppressed by the looming future that is . . . the veriest shadow of nothing" (172).

The narrator of "The Star Thrower" is similarly conscious of the futility of individual action in the presence of early morning shell collectors who boil the still living creatures in their shelling kettles, but he, too, "a little whirlwind of commingling molecules" (*Star* 87), confronts the universe and flings himself "as forfeit . . . into some unknown dimension of existence" "for the uses of life" (91). Those last five words are attributed to Francis Bacon, words that had been repeated as an incantation by Eiseley several times in *The Man Who Saw Through Time*, as he informs us that "five little words have shut us, with all our knowledge, from [the] shores [of the green continent] — five words uttered by a man in the dawn of science, and by us overlooked or forgotten" (65). In a similar manner, the final paragraph of "The Star Thrower" anaphorically repeats the words "I would walk" as a form of ritual incantation. The narrator would walk "with the knowledge of the discontinuities of the unexpected universe" and would honor in nature something above the role that humanity grants her. He attributes the qualities of love and compassion not to his own act but to a force of nature, a spirit in life itself. Compassion and consciousness are characterized as a gift of biological evolution that the limits of scientific thinking cannot comprehend or engage. The narrator comes to embody that natural compassion as he sees "the rainbow attempting to attach itself to earth" and joins the star thrower as "part of the rainbow — an unexplained projection into the natural" (*Star* 89). And so our narrator, a creature of the earth, mimics that spirit in life in his ritual reconciliation with death.

Hence, the limits of scientific thinking are dramatized similarly in the persona of an objective scientist who undergoes a transformation. In both essays, "How Natural Is 'Natural'?" and "The Star Thrower," each narrator consciously intervenes in the evolutionary struggle. In the latter, he describes himself as a dead "skull of emptiness" and an "endlessly revolving light without pity" that consumes ideas yet yields no meaning (68). The narrator is still a man of science in his first encounter with the star thrower, and the pitiless eye confirms that death is more fleeting than life and is the "only successful collector" on the beach (72). The ocular metaphor, moving in quick succession through different life forms, draws us to identify with each of those forms, to exchange our angle of vision and recognize our genetic ties to life's diverse forms. What adds to the particular beauty of this essay is that Eiseley incorporates into the planetary vision a strikingly intimate, autobiographical reconciliation with the legacy of pain and loneliness he had inherited from his deaf mother:

> Slowly that eye grew conscious of another eye that searched it with equal penetration from the shadows of the room. It may have been a projection from the mind within the skull, but the eye was, nevertheless, exteriorized and haunting. It began as something glaucous and blind beneath a web of clinging algae. It altered suddenly and became the sand-smeared eye of the dead cephalopod I had encountered upon the beach. The transformations became more rapid with the concentration of my attention, and they became more formidable.... Finally, there was an eye that seemed torn from a photograph.... I knew the eye and the circumstance and the question. It was my mother. (79–80)

It is a tale of reconciliation on a personal, professional, and planetary level. To reconcile the rift in the universe, to evoke sympathy for the vulnerable and lost, and to perform the ritual, he must renounce the single eye of science and meet the gaze of memory and history. In this process the narrator recognizes the familiar eye of other beings, including his mother, and the value of each within himself. Through the Freudian shadows, he pities her isolation and ascribes value to her own suffering as a child (85–87): "But I *do* love the world. I love the lost ones, the failures" (86). The rainbow associated with the star thrower adds to our earthiness a touch of something immaterial that cannot be explained by science. Eiseley narrates a sacred history in the fabled setting of Costabel, where the deeds of supernatural beings create a new reality, and he anchors his myth to the earthy process of evolution while simultaneously transcending Darwinian struggle. He perceives the differences among species no longer as a rift or a war for existence, but as "a joining: the expression of love projected beyond the species boundary by a creature born of Darwinian struggle, in the silent war under the tangled bank" (87).

Though the artist is aware of his own mimesis, Eiseley's metaphors contend in earnest to configure an order that honors human relationships with other forms of life. Renunciation of the single revolving eye and reconciliation with the past give him the resolve to mimic the star thrower. He could mock derisively, as could we, but he does not. His throwing, however futile on a large scale, performs a ritual of compassion, an allegorical reconciliation among species and loved ones.

MIMESIS, MEMES, AND BIOMIMCRY

> *When lofty thought*
> *Lifts a young heart above its mortal lair,*
> *And love and life contend in it, for what*
> *Shall be its earthly doom, the dead live there*
> *And move like winds of light on dark and stormy air.*
> PERCY BYSSHE SHELLEY, "ADONAIS"

We tell ourselves stories in order to live. They may be sermons about our own suicide, the tales of a species overpowered by its own fierce fitness. Or they may be tales of compassion, of biomimics who wish to accept rather than circumvent natural processes. Eiseley reminds us that the human drama takes place on a vast evolutionary stage, and from that stage we may learn the lessons of surviving, fitting in, coming home, though we are not likely to occupy center stage.

In his book *In the Spirit of the Earth*, Calvin Martin refers to the "siren song of history" as the "intoxicating belief that mankind is in truth a special creation, a superior being" (59). He calls for us to resist the siren song and to sing new melodies of our interrelationship with the planet. To that end, he quotes Emerson's description of history as a "shallow village tale," and Robin Fox's reference to history as a "brief episode in a temperate interglacial" (qtd. in Martin 122). He could easily have quoted Eiseley, who described the human drama as "a few trifling millennia" in earth history (*Man* 58), or as a single sentence at the end of a thousand pages (*Unexpected* 109). By adjusting our historical perspective, Martin sees human civilization standing "on the threshold of a major paradigm shift" that would integrate an evolutionary or ecological perspective. The center stage of historical consciousness would feature not humanity but a "great, brooding presence of earthy process" (120, 129).

Eiseley once claimed to have had no teachers, but his teachers are the same as those who still walk among us, our "mentors of the tangled bank" (Benyus, ded.). Within that brooding earthy process and the designs wrought by evolution, Eiseley discovered beauty and virtue, a "golden alphabet" full of meaningful messages to delight and instruct us (*Unexpected* 145–46). His semantic innovation is inspired by the innovation of natural processes that support conditions conducive to life. The future that will define Eiseley's metaphoric genius is the growing realization of ecological complexity, the knowledge that when we deconstruct organic systems and reduce them to industrial production values, we lose much that matters, relying on successive technological solutions to the problems we ourselves have created.

The "complexity paradigm," as publication dates suggest, is one of the latest configurations of general systems theory, which extends back to the fifties and perhaps earlier. Arthur Koestler reports that general systems theory was founded by Ludwig von Bertalanffy, author of *Problems of Life*, published in 1952. The early seeds of systems theory, characterized by opposition to atomism and reduction, may go back further. Koestler quotes from Joseph Needham's 1936 *Order and Life*: "The hierarchy of relations, from the molecular structure of carbon compounds to the equilibrium of species and ecological wholes, will perhaps be the leading idea of the future" (31). The key to general systems theory, suggests Koestler, is the dynamic interplay between a universal self-assertive tendency — epitomized by the slogans "survival of the fittest" and "instinct of self-preservation" — and a universal integrative tendency (67). The blue plums and smoke are metaphors representing these two tendencies, self-assertion and self-integration, part-whole. In a similar fashion, Erich Jantsch's synthesis of systems theory emphasizes creativity over adaptation and survival, openness over determinism, and self-transcendence over security. The paradigm of which Koestler and Jantsch write is neither holistic nor atomistic, but a recognition of integrated systems whose relationships adhere to a hierarchical organization. Synecdoche in this context prefigures neither reductionism nor vitalism but emphasizes the relations between levels of reality and terminology. In view of the work that has preceded and followed Eiseley's own writing, it makes perfect sense that he would prefigure his narratives with the trope of synecdoche.

Ironically, as Eiseley rejected early experimentation with artificial neural networks, he was perhaps unaware of how closely the sciences of complexity would echo his own integrative philosophy and would help readers of the twenty-first century better understand his figurative strategy for describing the natural world and its processes. *The Immense Journey*, written in the 1950s, dramatizes his belief in a greater whole and establishes his resistance to reductive science. In "The Judgment of the Birds," he describes himself standing "in the middle of a dead world at sunset," surrounded by the chemicals of a vanished age, where he witnesses the miracle of a flock of birds in flight, "a little close-knit body of black specks that danced and darted and closed again" (171). The flock consists of many individuals, but it also acts as one: "There went phosphorus, there went iron, there went carbon, there beat the calcium in those hurrying wings.

... It ran by some true compass over field and waste land. It cried its individual ecstasies into the air until the gullies rang. It swerved like a single body, it knew itself, and, lonely, it bunched close in the racing darkness, its individual entities feeling about them the rising night. And so, crying to each other their identity, they passed away out of my view" (172). Out of an aggregate of chemicals emerges a life form and a flock whose properties cannot be reduced, and this marks the difference between synecdoche and metonymy.

So how do Eiseley's semantic innovations shape our own understanding and behavior as citizens of the world? What does Eiseley contribute to the issues of our day, and what will become of his poetic contributions in an evolving discourse? Will the seeds of his plums find new soil in which to grow? We cannot say with certainty what Eiseley's legacy may be, but biomimicry is certainly one of his intellectual offspring, signs that Eiseley's metaphors offer adaptive memes. Janine M. Benyus has become the public persona of biomimicry, and she dedicates her book, *Biomimicry*, to "the mentors of the tangled bank." The subtitle of the book, *Innovation Inspired by Nature*, embraces the idea of nature as model, measure, and mentor for human behavior. Her book explores the proposition articulated by Arnold over a century ago: knowing what we know about our evolutionary descent, how will we live? Benyus pursues fundamental questions about "doing it nature's way" — about how to grow food, harness energy, make things, heal ourselves, store information, and conduct business. She reminds us that our prime directive as living beings is to seek to create conditions "for the uses of life."

Through symbolic figures like the last Neanderthal, the star thrower, a playful fox pup, a gray-backed gull, a spider's web, scarecrows, telephone booths in a cemetery, and many more, Eiseley contributes to the collective imaginary, and writers such as Benyus have the opportunity to draw from that store, for the tasks ahead will require both material and symbolic resources. She may be able to select metaphors and plots to persuade her audience to invest in the creation of a collaborative database shared by biologists and engineers who wish to solve design challenges about how we feed, fuel, heal, communicate, and trade.[5]

Benyus is more at home than Eiseley, more the citizen and policy proponent than he was, but she has clearly benefited from his poetics. Like him, she has an education in both the sciences and the humanities (forestry and literature) and recognizes the limits of a traditional scientific education. Her forestry curriculum, she explains, did not cover cooperative relationships, self-regulating feedback cycles, or dense interconnectedness. In reductionist fashion, they "studied each piece of the forest separately, rarely considering that a spruce-fir forest might add up to something more than a sum of its parts, or that wisdom might reside in the whole" (3).

Benyus is similarly concerned with the power of our own technology, which may be growing beyond our control. Eiseley warned in "The Last Neanderthal" that "a climbing juggernaut of power was leaping from triumph to triumph. It threatened to be more than man and all his words could master" (*Unexpected* 226–27). We can hear the echo as Benyus depicts humanity "strapped to our juggernaut of technology, [fancying] ourselves as gods, very far from home indeed." And she holds out hope that our actions today, "when we emerge from the fog," may turn the "juggernaut around, and instead of fleeing the Earth, we'll be homeward bound" (5–6). Eiseley hoped for the same.

Finally, Benyus is conscious of the need to tell stories in order to go on living. When she writes about the need for a change of heart, I am confident that Eiseley's metaphors are alive and reproducing fruit: "Perhaps in the end, it will not be a change in technology that will bring us to the biomimetic future, but a change of heart, a humbling that allows us to be attentive to nature's lessons. . . . If we are to use our tools in the service of fitting in on Earth, our basic relationship to nature — even the story we tell ourselves about who we are in the universe — has to change" (8). For Eiseley and for Benyus, it is in the heart where love and life contend for what will be our earthly doom. Eiseley's stories and the stories of numerous biomimics mirror nature, but that mirror is not a transparent replica. It is a mirror that is partly of our own design, our tool for interpreting the world "as if," for reflecting what we might become. To begin living more sustainably, we need to continue telling stories that assert the value of compassion to human character.

NOTES

1. Eiseley used the term "concealed essay" to describe the way that he merged personal anecdote with scientific observations. After an infection that caused temporary deafness, he had chosen to turn aside from the straitly defined scientific article and revive the art of the personal essay. *The Immense Journey* soon emerged from that experiment (*All* 177–78).

2. I rely on Kenneth Burke and Hayden White as the basis for my understanding of the four tropes. Based on traditional poetics and modern language theory, White identifies four basic tropes: metaphor, metonymy, synecdoche, and irony. He follows the fourfold conception of tropes utilized by Emile Benveniste, Giambattista Vico, and Kenneth Burke, because they collapse the distinction between poetic and prosaic language, allowing him to look at the degrees of integration and dispersion in language, and presenting a more continuous and less oppositional theory of human consciousness (*Metahistory* 31–33).

3. In fact, neuroscientists today working with phantom-limb patients are beginning to challenge the notion of perception as a result of sensory reception and are theorizing that perception relies primarily on inference and memory (Gawande 14).

4. While researchers once assumed *Homo sapiens* to be cognitively and technologically superior to Neanderthals, more recent research disputes that assumption and is looking more to cultural and symbolic differences (University).

5. The Biomimicry Institute promotes the study and imitation of biological designs, bringing together scientists, engineers, architects, and innovators who can use those models to create sustainable technologies. To that end, they are working to create a database of biological literature that can be accessed by architects and engineers facing design challenges.

10

In a Dark Wood

---

*Dante, Eiseley, and
the Ecology of Redemption*

ANTHONY LIOI

Nel mezzo del cammin di nostra vita
Mi ritrovai per una selva oscura,
Che la diritta via era smarrita.

In the middle of our life's road
I found myself in a dark wood,
The right way lost.

DANTE ALIGHIERI, *INFERNO*

The legend had come down and lingered that he
who gained the gratitude of animals gained help
in need from the dark wood.

LOREN EISELEY, "THE STAR THROWER"

On a midsummer night in 1985, I sit around a campfire with a dozen other high school students on the beach of Hardwood Island in the Bay of Maine, listening to professors from Case Western and the Yale School of Forestry read an essay: "The Star Thrower," by Loren Eiseley. Eiseley, we learn, was an anthropologist who moonlighted as one of the finest nature writers of the twentieth century. Natural history is important to us. For the last two weeks, we have been through ecology boot camp all over Maine. We have caught the stench of anaerobic decomposition in a freshwater bog; recorded reproduction statistics in a heron rookery; and climbed Mount Katahdin just for the hell of it. Now, after passing through a dark wood at the heart of the island, we sit under the stars to hear what it all means. It is clear that our teachers believe a thing they would never even whisper on campus: biology is not just an assemblage of facts and theories, but a worldview, a species of gnosis, a kind of revelation. Eiseley is a vector of that revelation, the scientist as shaman, the shaman as prophet. "The Star Thrower" is a sacred text. We have been ushered into a secret society, where the esoteric meaning of ecology can be uttered among illuminati. If it is possible to locate a moment when I became an ecocritic, this is it.

I suspect that many people have had this experience, whether or not they first encountered "The Star Thrower" around a campfire. Eiseley invites this kind of encounter; one of his acts as prophet and shaman was to declare himself prophet and shaman, after all. It is not the subtext of his writing, but the text, though he sometimes employs epithets, like "chresmologue," that would daunt a kabbalist (Carrithers, *Mumford* 247–71). This is one secret to his popularity among general readers, and, I suspect, the reason many critics avoid him. In some important sense, Eiseley — like his predecessor Dante Alighieri — transgressed against the cabal of criticism by defining his own lineage and specifying the principles for the interpretation of his work. He draws a hermeneutic circle around himself. As a result, readers feel a sureness of intimacy with the scribe from Nebraska, even as academics feel slightly superfluous. The strength of Eiseley's self-conception has almost guaranteed that several generations of critics would feel obliged to approach his work primarily through the charism of autobiography.[1]

It is no small thing to break this hammer hold with the power of a stronger poet acting as critic. In a review of *The Unexpected Universe* that would become the introduction to *The Star Thrower* anthology, W. H. Auden dares to trump Eiseley as arbiter of his literary lineage:

> Rather oddly, I first heard of Dr. Loren Eiseley not in this country but in Oxford, where a student gave me a copy of *The Immense Journey*, since which time I have eagerly read anything of his I could lay my hands on. His obvious ancestors, as both writers and thinkers, are Thoreau and Emerson, but he often reminds me of Ruskin, Richard Jefferies, W. H. Hudson, whom, I feel sure, he must have read, and of two writers, Novalis (a German) and Adalbert Stifter (an Austrian), whom perhaps he hasn't. But I wouldn't be sure. Some of the quotations in *The Unexpected Universe* surprised me. I would not have expected someone who is an American and a scientist to have read such little-known literary works as the *Voluspá*, James Thomson's *The City of Dreadful Night*, and Charles Williams's play *Cranmer*. (15)

Expectations of scientists and Americans aside, Auden began a process that Eiseley's critics have yet to address properly. He placed Eiseley in a transatlantic conversation about science, literature, and myth, of which Emerson and Thoreau, his "obvious ancestors," were more than aware. American critics — in compensation, perhaps, for the European opinion that there is no such thing as "American culture" — have insisted on the Nebraskan, middle-American, and contemporary provenance of his work. This insistence has prevented any approach that would allow the work to be framed as part of a cosmopolitan and intergenerational effort to grapple with the changes wrought by modernity on our sense of history, the structure of the psyche, and the fate of humankind in an unexpected universe. In this essay, I take up Auden's task in order to illuminate the narrative and theological connections between "The Star Thrower," perhaps Eiseley's signature essay, and Dante's *Comedy*. I believe that the *Comedy* is the ur-text of "The Star Thrower," and that attention to it reveals a descent, purgation, and transfiguration of Western metaphysics through psychoanalysis, Darwinian natural selection, and process philosophy.[2] Most importantly, "The Star Thrower" transforms the natural world, and other animals in particular, from the theater and supporting cast of human redemption to a communion of saints. Put another way, Eiseley remakes Dante's high-medieval humanism to recover the biblical sense of the New Earth for cosmocentric eschatology.

This is a strong claim, considering that Eiseley never mentions the *Comedy* by name. The *Comedy* is not the only text in European literature that could serve as a paradigm for a redemptive journey. In Eiseley's immediate Anglo-Protestant background, there is John Bunyan's *The Pilgrim's Progress*, and all of its Victorian successors. In transcendentalist literature, there is *Moby Dick*, a text to which "The Star Thrower" refers directly. There is the literature of shipwreck, beginning with Shakespeare's *The Tempest* and Defoe's *Robinson Crusoe*. All of these classics deserve attention as intertexts of "The Star Thrower." Moreover, the Bible itself provides the basic patterns of redemption narrative for the entire tradition. Why not defer to these sources, rather than pinpoint Dante as the crucial influence behind "The Star Thrower"? The answer lies in the narrative order of the essay and its epic precursor. The *Comedy* is structured as the journey of a single soul through damnation, purgation, and salvation. In terms of plot structure alone, there is no other text that provides this pattern, in part because the American, Calvinist literary tradition emphasizes the difference between the saved and the damned so strongly. The middle step of purgation is unavailable, in religious form, to the traditions of literature in English after the Reformation, because Protestantism rejected the doctrine of purgatory as a habitus after death. The Protestant paradigm that descends from *The Pilgrim's Progress* is so secularized that the grotesque images of damnation in "The Star Thrower," as well as the overt symbols of divine intervention, make far more sense as references to a medieval, rather than a modern, model. Lastly, the cosmological content of "The Star Thrower," the idea that redemption involves a journey from earth to the stars, parallels Platonic, Augustinian, and, finally, Dantean tropes more closely than anything in American literature. The only text that, by itself, provides the narrative, imagistic, and tropological precedents for "The Star Thrower" is the *Comedy*. Eiseley's adaptation of Dantean patterns of redemption allows him to recover their rhetorical power in the context of our own environmental crisis, renewing the medieval sense that the whole world, not just the individual, is in danger. The significance of this recovery should not be underestimated. As ecofeminist theologian Rosemary Radford Ruether observes, "Although [a] cosmological understanding of Christ as both creator and redeemer of the cosmos, and not just human beings separated from the cosmos, is central to much of New Testament thought, Western Christianity since the late medieval and Reformation periods has ignored this holistic vision" (229). Eiseley makes it possible for moderns to appropriate Dante's universal drama when it is no longer possible to take his universe at face value. As Joseph W. Meeker points out in *The Comedy of Survival*, Dante's universe is comedic not because it is funny, but because it enables the protagonist to overcome obstacles and continue his life (88–103). Eiseley, melancholic though he was, writes a comedy in this sense as well, and since he extends Dante's offer to animals, "The Star Thrower" provides not only a comedy of survival but an ecology of redemption.

Because so much depends on my phrase, "ecology of redemption," and the complex histories of its central terms, I take a moment to consider *ecology* and *redemption* and the relationship between them. Though Meeker asserts that "the view of life presented in the *Comedy* can be called ecological in the largest sense of the term," much has been said, in later ecocriticism, of the dangers of mishandling a scientific term (89). Dana Phillips and Michael P. Cohen, especially, have insisted that "ecology" cannot mean just anything a humanist wants it to mean (Phillips 2003; Cohen, "Blues" 2004). Therefore I affirm, with Glen A. Love, that ecology must mean "the study of the relationship between organisms and their living and nonliving environments" in a scientific sense before it can mean anything else (37). As the ecologist Sharon E. Kingsland points out, ecology as a science is defined by "the application of experimental and mathematical methods to the analysis of organism-environment relations," and Eiseley himself never lost sight of that basic meaning (1). It is the work of "The Star Thrower," however, to challenge the separation of the scientific from the existential and theological meanings of ecology. It is precisely not in a metaphorical, figurative sense that Eiseley's essay extends the sense of ecology; he does not confuse the data of field biology, the models and mathematics associated with biological communities, with metaphysical assertions of the unity of all things. Rather than using science as a proof-text for metaphysics, Eiseley asserts the cosmological consequences of scientific ecology, the influence of the biosphere on questions of personal and cultural transformation, the blowback of evolutionary theory on our model of God. To insist on the scientific meaning of ecology is also to recognize that its description of the physical world has become part of a postmodern worldview. If there is an ecology of redemption, it is founded on the relationship of humanity and other species to the physical environment understood as a divine milieu, as Pierre Teilhard de Chardin put it.

The second term of the phrase, "redemption," is understood here in its basic biblical sense, as rescue from captivity, particularly the ransom of slaves. Though Judaism and Christianity developed complex theories about the shape of history and its fulfillment, redemption first meant the deliverance of the Israelites from slavery in Egypt, and later the liberation of Christians from the tyranny of Rome as the demonic ruler of a fallen cosmos.[3] Redemption possesses a primary physical meaning that connotes a political and spiritual condition. It must be distinguished, in classical Christian theology, from the broader term "salvation," the process of being saved; redemption is seen as a particular kind or instance of salvation, often the first step in the work of returning to spiritual health (Latin *salus*, "health"). First one is redeemed from captivity, and then other steps in salvation can occur.

What do I mean, then, by the ecology of redemption in "The Star

Thrower"? First, the sense, which Eiseley shares with Dante, that redemption is a process whereby the self, aided by other creatures and the divine light, corrects its relationship to creation and its source. Redemption is, literally, finding a place and a practice of joy over the desire for death as a release from suffering. Dante — if he is the true author of the disputed "Epistle to Can Grande" — says as much of the *Comedy*: "we can say briefly that the purpose of the whole as well as the part is to remove those living in this life from the state of misery and to lead them to the state of bliss" (Alighieri). "The Star Thrower" translates this journey into post-Copernican, post-Darwinian, and post-Freudian terms, changing the shape of redemption inherent in it. For Dante, the physical creation is the setting for redemption of the individual soul, and then the church and the empire; interaction with the environments of hell, purgatory, and heaven is ineluctable. Dante is environed by redemption, but the environment itself is not a subject of redemption.[4] Because only humans (and angels) have an intellective soul, only they can sin. Animals, plants, and elements cannot sin, so they do not need to reconcile their will with their desire, as humans are taught to do in purgatory. Therefore, Eiseley's portrait of human redemption bound up in ecological communities constitutes a second sense of the ecology of redemption that Dante does not share. In "The Star Thrower," one joins a community of redemption that is not entirely human, a community that includes animals, oceans, and galactic space. One may become lost in a dark wood, but its animals point to the right road, and they *are* the right road. This is the significance of Eiseley's comedy, and it has important ramifications for contemporary readers coming to terms with human responsibility for the planetary biosphere.

The parallels between the *Comedy* and "The Star Thrower" begin with the dark wood itself, the place where Dante says he got lost in early middle age. It is worth pausing to remember what a dark wood would be like during the thirteenth century in Europe. It would not be a domesticated forest — the equivalent of an American state park — but a place with an independent life, where the rules of town and village faded. There would be no artificial lighting at night, no paved roads, and a great deal of wildlife, both human and otherwise. In this kind of wood Dante's progress toward a better life is blocked, famously, by three predators: a lion, a leopard, and a she-wolf.

Traditionally, critics have applied the technique of fourfold scriptural exegesis, in which a text is said to have a literal, a moral, an allegorical, and an anagogical meaning, to understand these predators as species of sin that hold the pilgrim back: fraud, malice, and so on. Given the association of animals with vices and virtues, found both in apocalyptic literature and the bestiary genre, it makes sense to read these predators as reifications of Dante's own flaws, as symbols, not moral patients. It is striking, then, that when the narrator of "The Star Thrower" begins by lamenting his existential misery, trapped on a desert island, he too associates the loss of the right road with a scene of predation. This time, however, animals are the victims, not the vectors, of violence. "The beaches of Costabel are littered with the debris of life," Eiseley says (*Star* 170). Mother sea spews out her most vulnerable children — hermit crabs, sponges, starfish — onto the shore, where human collectors wait to kill them for food and sport: "A kind of greedy madness sweeps over the competing collectors. After a storm one can see them hurrying along with bundles of gathered starfish, or toppling and overburdened, clutching bags of living shells whose hidden occupants will be slowly cooked and dissolved in the outdoor kettles provided by the resort hotels for the cleaning of specimens" (171). The scene is Dantean in the extreme, straight out of the *Inferno*, with its combination of environmental horror, human rapacity, and murderous despair. Its partnership between natural evil, as the Scholastic tradition would have it, and modern capitalistic consumption, is a familiar theme in *The Night Country* and *The Unexpected Universe*.

Though the existential dread is the same, the context is so different that it merits further attention. The system of Dante's Hell, as Amiri Baraka once called it, depends on what sinners have done to themselves. In his characteristic combination of Neoplatonic metaphysics and troubadour psychology, Dante assumes a God whose love individuals have chosen to reject, damning themselves to the center of the earth, the place farthest from God and devoid of the sunlight that stands for God in the vocabulary of mysticism. There are many people in purgatory and paradise whose earthly crimes equaled or exceeded the crimes of those in the inferno; the difference is that one group repented, turning back to the love of God, the motive power of the universe, while the other willfully refused this love, making themselves irredeemable. In Dante's system damnation is something one does to oneself; there is nothing God cannot forgive if sinners cling to love. For Dante, this love is embodied in the figure of Beatrice, the beloved of troubadour poetry transformed into a Christ figure, whose pity causes her to descend from heaven to rescue her lost love. In the system of Eiseley's hell, on the other hand, marine animals are cast onto the alien shores of Costabel through no fault of their own; one sees here the influence of Romanticism, of a Melvillean sort, in which innocent creatures can be trapped by elemental violence beyond their control. On this shore they are choked, burned, and boiled by corrupt humans overcome by the need to destroy in order to possess. In this scene there is a Beatrice, a human redeemer, too — the star thrower himself — but unlike Dante, whose recognition of danger leads him to accept help, Eiseley rejects the work of the star thrower, who throws living starfish back into the ocean. "'The stars,' he says, 'throw well. One can help them'" (172). Though Eiseley perceives that something numinous is going on — the thrower has "the posture of a god" — he rejects the invitation to throw because of the influence of the "cold world-shriveling eye" in his mind (171), which has already been associated with the scientific gaze (169). The outer struggle for existence is therefore matched by an inner force, the posture of absolute and rigid objectivity, that cuts off the viewer from compassion, and thus from redemption.

Though the first section of "The Star Thrower" is grim, one of the advantages of a Dantean reading is its capacity to reveal the hope already present in the scenes of infernal destruction. In the space of a few pages, Eiseley repeatedly associates the star thrower with a "gigantic rainbow of incredible perfection" that appears sometimes to engulf him and sometimes to stand just beyond him (171). In the biblical tradition, the rainbow is the sign from God after the Flood that the world will never again be destroyed by water: "This is the sign of the covenant which I establish between myself and you and every living creature with you, to endless generations:

My bow I set in the cloud
Sign of the covenant
Between myself and earth.
When I cloud the sky over the earth
The bow shall be seen in the cloud.
(*New English Bible*, Gen. 9:12–14)

Though popular culture today remembers the Flood story as kiddie lit, with the cute animals marching two by two, Jewish tradition took it far more seriously, as evidence that God made promises to all nations, not just to the Jews, and to all creatures, not just to humans. In light of the Noachian covenant, we might interpret the presence of the rainbow at this point in "The Star Thrower" as merely ironic: it appears that the promise has been revoked or that there was no God in the first place. However, an intertextual reading with the *Paradiso* reveals a promise, not an irony. When Dante ascends to the highest circle of paradise, he sees, not an old man with a beard, but a dazzling triple rainbow, whose center bow reveals the hint of a human face. Critics have read this, reasonably, as a vision of the Trinity with a glimpse of the Second Person in the second rainbow. This is as far as Dante gets; after a few moments, the light becomes too much and, as he says, his "high fantasy" fails him, and he collapses unconscious, to awaken in a redeemed life. Eiseley gives us the rainbow first, to underline the promise of redemption that the pilgrim cannot yet accept. The work of the journey will be to reconcile the promise of the rainbow and its thrower with the violence of Costabel and the alienation of the Darwinian gaze.

Before it is possible to appreciate how Eiseley revises Dante's process of purgation, it is necessary to review the nature of that process, because the Catholic idea of purgatory would not be known by all of Eiseley's readers. Though the doctrine of a place of purgation after death predates Dante, both heaven and hell received more artistic and theological attention. The idea that it is possible to die in a state of grace but not be ready for heaven itself belongs to a long debate about the fate of the soul after death and the possibility that punishment for sin does not last forever, that hell is not eternal (Newman 108–36). Dante chooses the orthodox version of purgation, which means that there are three possibilities for the soul after death: it can dwell in hell forever outside the light of God; it can be in a state of venial sin, which is not corrupt enough to sever the relationship with God but is not pure enough to dwell with God; or it can be freed from the bondage of sin completely and be ready for heaven. While the *Comedy* is full of exceptions to this rule, in general, the souls in hell stay in hell, the souls in heaven stay in heaven, and the souls in purgatory stay in purgatory until they are ready to go to heaven. John A. Scott explains, "An essential characteristic of purgatory is the fact that it is a temporal state, unlike hell and paradise. It will therefore cease at the Last Judgment, after which there will remain only the eternal states of separation from or union with God" (221). Purgatory is thus the only state of existence after death where change is possible; there is no such thing as unending purgation, because it is organized toward a redemptive end.[5]

The organization of purgation is the most original piece of Dante's vision, cosmologically speaking. According to Dante, purgatory formed when Satan fell to the center of the earth, displacing enough land above the surface of the Southern Hemisphere's ocean to form an island-mountain on the other side of the world, opposite Jerusalem. This mountain is divided into sections, each corresponding to one of the deadly sins: pride, greed, lust, and so on, where each sin is purged. Following the Scholastic system of Thomas Aquinas, Dante embraced an Aristotelian logic to describe how sinners recover from each kind of sin. Vice, according to Aristotle, is the result of bad habits fostered by ignorance of the good and can be corrected only through a process of rehabituation, in which the soul reshapes itself through the practice of virtue. Therefore, each level of purgatory is designed to reveal the true nature of sin and righteousness and to rehabituate sinners into the virtue that corresponds to the vice of that level. The bottom rung, pride, introduces sinners to humility through a number of strategies. There is the *contrapasso*, or poetically just punishment, which in hell afflicts sinners forever, but in purgatory teaches the nature of vice. In the circle of pride, sinners are forced to carry boulders on their backs to teach them to bow. They are also taught through sacred songs sung by the group in each circle and by stories carved into the stone of the mountain illustrating the virtues they must learn. This points to an aspect of purgatory completely absent from hell: the support of the community. No one suffers alone, and everyone is helped by others recovering from the same vice. Finally, the process of purgation is abetted by the grace of God, represented by the rays of the sun, which shines down on the mountain and empowers sinners to change.

Because "The Star Thrower" depicts a process of purgation in a post-Copernican, post-Darwinian, and post-Freudian world, it is impossible for the cosmological, biological, and psychological rules governing the *Comedy* to be transposed into Eiseley's essay. As Eric Auerbach points out, "The *Comedy* represented the physical, ethical, and political unity of the Scholastic Christian cosmos at a time when it was beginning to lose its ideological integrity" (175). Modern European literature began, in one sense, when it was no longer possible to take Dante literally. To compensate for this effect, Eiseley offers a process of double purgation, in which Dante's world is superseded by modernity, and modernity is superseded by postmodernity.[6] The geocentric universe of medieval Europe is displaced by the universe of galaxies, leaving the protagonist with Blaise Pascal's terror at the "eternal silence of these infinite spaces" (273). This terror is not taken for granted, but offered as a problem that needs to be overcome. Likewise, the biblical doctrine of the special creation of species and the Greek philosophical notion of changelessness as perfection are replaced by the Darwinian theory of evolution through natural selection. However, the use of natural selection as the ontological foundation of a hypercompetitive, capitalist materialism, the madness of the collectors at Costabel, is rejected as a kind of hell on earth. There is a strong existentialist undercurrent in "The Star Thrower," and this reflects the Dantean premise that sinners prefer the torment of self and other to the process of repentance. They could be redeemed, but they turn away from redemption willfully. Dante sides with Augustine, who taught that human free will is strong enough to eternally resist the love of God. Eiseley, in turn, sees the alienation of modernity as a kind of self-imposed exile from love but frames this rejection in both empirical and psychoanalytic terms. Humans are subject to an epistemological alienation due to the reign of the scientific method, which emphasizes distance, objectivity, and control rather than participation, empathy, and community. Eiseley sees modernity in Weberian terms, as the reign of disenchantment, though he does not agree that the iron cage is inescapable. This is due, in part, to his Freudian reading of modern alienation, which sees the normative male subject as reifying the loss of the mother into an anticosmos of warfare and rejection. The key to the redemption of modernity is the displacement of epistemological alienation through the resolution of emotional alienation in a reencounter with the power of the ocean as the power of the mother.

"The Star Thrower" represents his relationship with his mother as difficult because of her emotional instability — which he calls "the precipice of mental breakdown" — magnified through her deafness. Mrs. Eiseley is locked out of the world by her inability to hear it properly, which Eiseley suggests is also an inability to hear *him* properly. The story represents this primal wound in Christian terms as "glorified": like the wounds of Christ, it cannot be unmade, but it can become a vehicle of grace. The transformation begins in a bedroom in Costabel, as Eiseley tries to locate the center of his childhood trauma, the moment the alienation took hold. He thinks back to the last time he had visited his childhood home and remembers going into the attic and finding a satchel from childhood. It contains a note in his mother's hand: "This satchel belongs to my son, Loren Eiseley." Later, he calls this the "last message" from Dyersville — we hear the pun, *Diresville* — his mother's birthplace in Iowa (181). Though the experience itself is years past, the memory becomes meaningful in confrontation with the crisis that began with his mother's affliction. Remembering this simple act of love — *my son* — he is forced to recognize his own love of the world, which, he thinks, contradicts the Western heritage of science *and* religion:

> "Love not the world," the Biblical injunction runs, "neither the things that are in the world." The revolving beam in my mind had stopped, and the insect whisperings of intellect. There was, at last, an utter stillness, a waiting as though for a cosmic judgment. The eye, the torn eye, considered me.

"But I *do* love the world," I whispered to a waiting presence in the empty room. . . . It was like a renunciation of my scientific heritage. The torn eye surveyed me sadly and was gone. (182)

As a result of this epiphany, the alienation that characterizes the hell section of the essay is relieved. There is a sort of emotional cascade, from realizing that his mother had loved him to reconciling himself to his own love of the world, despite the disobedience against spiritual and scientific law as he understands it. It is the First Letter of John 2:15 that he quotes here, but the injunction also stands for Darwin's claim that any proven instance of altruism, of one species working for the good of another, would "annihilate" his theory (180). Neither the Darwinian nor the New Testament tradition is as pessimistic as these quotations imply.[7] The point is that, from the perspective of the alienated self, both traditions appear to say only one thing. Therefore, both must be lost, at least temporarily. One of the effects of Dante's purgatory is that shriven sins simply disappear from the body of the sinner, allowing the pilgrim to move to the next level, closer to the earthly paradise at the top of the mountain. This is happening to Eiseley, too. Therefore, the constraints of objective science and ascetic religion, in their alienating forms, fall away. The torn eye, sponsored by both traditions, disappears. But the end of vice is only the beginning of virtue, so the process of purgation is not complete until Eiseley accepts his losses, embraces his love of the world, and seeks out the star thrower.

If we read the transition from alienation to redemption as the shift between modernity and postmodernity, it becomes clear why the heaven section of "The Star Thrower" resembles its Dantean ancestor the least. In the system of Dante's *Paradiso*, redemption is represented as existence in the empyrean, the realm of pure spirit outside the created world, in which everyone dwells in the direct light of God. Like the other realms, paradise is organized into levels, according to the virtues of the dwellers: there is a circle of theologians, just rulers, and so on. The more capacious a soul became in life, the more bliss it can hold in the afterlife, and the closer it dwells to God, who is figured as absolute radiance. This system synthesizes an Aristotelian understanding of virtue, a Neoplatonic ascent of the soul, and a model of the self in which the intellective faculty fashions an airy body in the absence of the material body. This airy body is capable of sensation and intellection — or the punishments and pleasures of the realms would not be possible — but it does not breathe, eat, or sleep as a substantial body would. Though Dante recognizes that this state will be superseded by the resurrection of the dead at the Last Judgment, paradise is, nonetheless, imagined as a place where the elements and creatures of the created world are left behind. The state of bliss after death is not represented as life in a human city but as a sensory enjoyment of the noumenal realm itself. This solution to the problem of redemption before the Last Judgment is not possible for Eiseley, who shares neither the Ptolemaic cosmos nor the Scholastic metaphysics of the High Middle Ages. As a contemporary scientist dedicated to the model of the human as psychophysical unity, he must reject the medieval idea of redemption. But he must also reject the impossibility of redemption in the nature-red-in-tooth-and-claw tradition of social Darwinism. If the end of human life cannot be imagined as a disembodied existence outside the universe, neither can it be imagined as competition for its own sake. Modernity, understood as a project of scientific materialism and technological mastery, is no more acceptable than medievalism, because Eiseley perceives the universe revealed by science as powered by "the Love that moves the sun and the other stars," as Dante says in the final lines of the *Paradiso*. Therefore, a move beyond modernity into what might be called a reconstructive postmodernity is necessary.

This move is accomplished in the final section of "The Star Thrower," through a revision of the relationship between humans, the divine, and other creatures. At the beginning of the *Inferno*, Dante's way is blocked by three predators, and at the end of the *Purgatory*, Dante's last earthly experience at the top of the mountain involves a series of fantastic beasts, such as the griffin, who serve symbolic functions. Though there are visions of animals in the *Paradiso*, these animals are more ciphers than creatures, supporting semiotic rather than ecological transformations. Eiseley, on the other hand, spends almost all of his time in the final section dealing with animals and our relationship to them. Empowered by his revelation of mother love, Eiseley goes after the star thrower with a new faith in the ocean that, in the first section, had been coded as the bad mother, the mother as destroyer. Now the idea of throwing sea creatures back into the ocean seems less insane. When he finds the star thrower for the last time, he accepts a new spiritual vocation — "Call me another thrower," he says (184) — as rescuer of starfish. Because Eiseley envisions this role as solidarity with earthly stars rather than an ascent to the stars, his actions create a feedback loop in which the creatures he saves save him, updating the totemic relationship between hunter and hunted in Paleolithic cultures. Heaven is not abandoned, however, but enjoys a revolution through this new, and very old, practice of compassion. The vocation of star throwing turns into a model of God the Star Thrower, who saves galactic rather than earthly stars. The rainbow, whose promise is now fulfilled, connects the actions of the star thrower with the actions of the Star Thrower, restoring the Renaissance idea of correspondence between microcosm and macrocosm. The key to this restoration is love for the world expressed in ritual respect for animals:

> We had lost the way, I thought, but we had kept, some of us, the memory of the perfect circle of compassion from life to death and back again to life — the completion of the rainbow of existence. Even the hunters in the snow, making obeisance to the souls of the hunted, had known that cycle. The legend had come down and lingered that he who gained the gratitude of animals gained help in need from the dark wood.
>
> I cast again in an increasingly remembered sowing motion and went my lone way up the beaches. Somewhere, I felt, in a great atavistic surge of feeling, somewhere the Thrower knew. Perhaps he smiled and cast once more into the boundless pit of darkness. Perhaps he, too, was lonely, and the end toward which he labored remained hidden — even as with ourselves.
>
> I picked up a star whose tube feet ventured timidly among my fingers while, like a true star, it cried soundlessly for life. I saw it with an unaccustomed clarity and cast far out. With it, I flung myself in forfeit, for the first time, into some unknown dimension of existence. From Darwin's tangled bank of unceasing struggle, selfishness, and death had arisen, incomprehensibly, the thrower who loved not man, but life. (184–85)

Redemption is not a flight beyond the stars but a place among the stars of heaven and earth. Though the transfiguration of the struggle for survival — caring for life, not only for humans — appears to annihilate Darwin's theory, it is also accomplished *inside* the world, by means of evolutionary insight. The purgation of Western thought allows religion and science to change; even the idea of evolution evolves. As with other saviors, Eiseley has not come to abolish the law but to fulfill it, implying a community of redemption: "After us," he thinks, "there will be others" (184).

What is most remarkable about this passage is the way the economy of redemption becomes an ecology of redemption. The Dark Wood of Error that foils Dante's first attempt at salvation becomes the dark wood from which help arrives. Given the structure of the legend, help arrives when humans earn "the gratitude of animals." No longer just the theater or object of redemption, the wood and its creatures become subjects of salvation and saviors. Human suffering and purgation end through the loss of a human-centered model of redemption. The scene of exile is transformed into a community of healing, as stars and throwers join forces to resist senseless destruction. In the wake of the death of the God of classical theism, who is omnipotent, omniscient, and impassive, the ecology of redemption provides a new model of the divine as Thrower, who loves and saves without certainty of success, without the trappings of a sky god who conquers but cannot care. God must join creation as ecosystem, where the survival of the one depends on the survival of the community whose character evolves by choice in history. Though this model of the God-human-cosmos relationship bears little resemblance to the Hellenistic metaphysics adopted by Christian theology in late antiquity, it resembles the God of Hebrew and Christian scripture much more. The God who made the rainbow sign, who cares for the fall of sparrows and sends messengers into history, looks like the Star Thrower, not the Pantocrator, the strict Father of popular Christian culture. The Thrower is moved by Dante's "love that moves the sun and the other stars" in a post-Darwinian world.

To insist that we read Eiseley intertextually, with his most important sources in mind, is to insist that we read him contextually, in terms of the environmental crisis. If Dante helps us to see what is at stake in "The Star Thrower," we must then apply Eiseley's ecology of redemption, his new model of ecological spirituality, to contemporary efforts at ecotheology and, more generally, to the debates about religion and environmentalism. We must also connect him to other thinkers of his time who dealt with the transition to a postmodern cosmos in much the way he did, to identify his ideological cohorts and assess their potential as allies in the project of star throwing. To begin, I defer to Catherine Keller and Laurel Kearns's assessment in their introduction to *Ecospirit: Religions and Philosophies for the Earth*:

> Philosophy and theology have always been joined at the hip, for good and for ill. They are co-implicated in the disdain for the non-human. This volume invites that dispiriting complicity into an ecospirited complexity. Of course, much so-called postmodern theory has remained stubbornly modernist in its liberty from specific ecosocial contexts. It has tended to delegitimize any language in which we might witness to the reality or truth of climate crisis and to the ground — not to be confused with the foundation — that all terrestrials share. The indubitable interest of poststructuralist thought in justice and multiplicity has so far remained largely anthropomorphic and anthropocentric. (xii–xiv)

"The Star Thrower," in its engagement with millennia of cultural history, the meaning of modernity, the capacities of the postmodern, its love of the material world, an unwavering gaze at the disasters of the last century, and its commitment to radical hope for all creatures, even humans, seems ideally suited to the project of ecotheology. Given these facts, it remains a mystery why so many philosophers and theologians have ignored the ideational resources of literature in general, and Loren Eiseley in particular, in the face of a certain flexibility of thought, often absent in more systematic modes of writing, offered by the meditative essay as a genre.

In popular debates about the relationship between science and religion in the West, a simplistic opposition has reigned between orthodox Christian theism, founded, philosophically, in the Hellenistic metaphysics of late antiquity, and an agnostic scientism founded on the Enlightenment critique of religion, especially in the naturalist tradition, which fought the idea of a divine realm outside the sensible universe, ruled by an omnipotent superman. In this tedious, yet enduring, dualism, it is often supposed that classical theism is the only model of religion that counts, ignoring the many inroads made by liberal, feminist, and process approaches to God that are transforming theism. The literature on this topic is now vast, so I will concentrate on one of its fountainheads, the work of Alfred North Whitehead and his *Process and Reality*. For our purposes, the apposite argument of the book is that the reality of the universe is change, not stasis; the eternal essences and universal verities of Hellenistic Christianity are replaced by process, which Whitehead takes to be consonant with the Hebraic foundations of the Bible, as Greek metaphysics is not. In the aptly named *Omnipotence and Other Theological Mistakes*, one of Whitehead's heirs, Charles Hartshorne, summarizes the attributes of the classical model of God, world, and believer that are mistaken from a process perspective: divine immutability, omnipotence, omniscience, and apathy; immortality as a career after death; and revelation as infallible (2–6). In other words, God is not absolutely transcendent, unchangeable, unfeeling; capable of ending all suffering, but unwilling, mysteriously, to do so; or cognizant of what we are going to do before we do it. The reign of God is not about disembodied life with harps and clouds; the Bible is not free of all error, because inspired human writers are still human, and therefore limited by history and culture. A. C. Dixon's *The Fundamentals*, the twelve-volume compendium from 1915 that gave "fundamentalism" its name, is dedicated to all the ideas that process theology is trying to supplant. From the perspective of the Christian mainstream, process theology is heretical and probably tantamount to unbelief itself. This means, of course, that "The Star Thrower" is also a work of heresy, which tries to replace the God of orthodoxy with a God who is too weak and stupid to redeem anyone, not to speak of starfish.

Process philosophy is ready with an explanation of theology's obsession with strength, perfection, mastery, and dominion. Whitehead's attack on the orthodox perspective is devastating: "When the Western world accepted Christianity, Caesar conquered; and the received text of Western theology was edited by his lawyers. The code of Justinian and the theology of Justinian are two volumes expressing one movement of the human spirit. The brief Galilean vision of humility flickered through the ages, uncertainly . . . the deeper idolatry, of the fashioning of God in the image of the Egyptian, Persian, and Roman imperial rulers, was retained. The Church gave unto God the attributes which belonged exclusively to Caesar" (342). The key to the God of classical theism, the idea it embodies, which orthodox theology tries with all its might to protect, is the image of a cosmic emperor. This is why the metaphysics of stasis, knowledge, power, and apathy must be defended. This is why, as feminist process thinkers would later point out, the classical image of God is male (Keller). To this image he calls idolatrous, Whitehead compares the "Galilean" vision that "dwells upon the tender elements of the world, which slowly and in quietness operate by love. . . . Love neither rules, nor is it unmoved; also it is a little oblivious as to morals" (343). This is the content of Eiseley's epiphany as well. We can say, given Whitehead's perspective, that Eiseley's ecology of redemption embraces process; that the Star Thrower as a model of God redeems the "Galilean" side of the argument after a purgation of the imperial idol; and that star throwing is a model of redemption finally reconciled to evolution but no longer cathected to Caesar as implacable foe. To return to Auden's judgment that Eiseley has read many things one would not expect, it may be that *Process and Reality* is one of the texts we would find at the bedside of the pilgrim of Costabel.

The process perspective also changes the value of the cosmos, and all creatures in it, relative to the imperial paradigm. If God and humanity play out the drama of redemption *inside* rather than *beyond* the world, then redemption carries the world with it. Indeed, Whitehead defends what he calls the "consequent" nature of God, in which all of the joy and suffering of creatures is taken into God's being: "the actuality of God must be understood as a multiplicity of actual components in process of creation. This is God in his function of the kingdom of heaven. Each actuality of the temporal world has its reception into God's nature" (350). As generations of ecotheologians have noticed, the idea of God's consequent nature breaks with modern Christian eschatologies: liberal, radical, and evangelical.

The redeemed future is not just about humans but all "components" of creation-in-process — the lilies of the field, the sparrows, the ocean, the starfish, the stars. In process perspective, the kingdom of heaven is understood cosmocentrically, as the future of all beings in community, not as the destiny of humanity beyond the stars, out of the body, in a Rapture above the earth. Accordingly, when Eiseley parallels the human thrower and the divine Thrower, oceanic and galactic stars, we can see that a metaphor is at work, but not an empty metaphor. The Thrower who takes heart when Eiseley starts to throw stands for a divine agent whose concern is for the system of the world, not only for us; it would be better to say that this agent can be concerned for us only through a concern for the system. The ecology of redemption is Aldo Leopold's land ethic gone cosmic: redemption can be measured only in terms of the benefit to the cosmos as community. The Darwinian struggle for existence is taken up into the pathos of God: the "lost ones," the "failures of the world" that Eiseley comes to love, are not rescued or abandoned by an impassive overlord (182). Each creature has its own travail. The Thrower labors toward a hidden end, but the end is for the world as cosmos.

This reconfiguration of redemption as an evolutionary, cosmic process, is significant in the contemporary conflicts over New Atheism, which is led, significantly, by three Darwinian thinkers: Richard Dawkins, an evolutionary biologist; Sam Harris, a neuroscientist; and Daniel C. Dennett, a philosopher. Each of these thinkers opposes the God of classical theism, and therefore with the religions that promote this God.[8] They see Darwin as the thinker who demonstrates that the God of classical theism is unnecessary as the motive force of creation, and they do not hesitate to condemn as false consciousness all systems that promote this God. To process and ecotheologians, the New Atheists might say, why isn't the world enough? Why attempt to protect the world from ecological catastrophe using a fairy tale, a delusion, an imaginary tyrant whose time is long past?[9] Before I address Eiseley's relationship to these thinkers, I want to make my own position about their project clear. First, I believe that a criticism of classical theism, in Christian or any other form, is justified on intellectual, historical, and ethical grounds. Whitehead is as brutal a critic of this theology as any New Atheist. Furthermore, the critique of religion as a force for oppression, ignorance, and violence is unavoidable. On these counts, the New Atheists must be commended as defenders of justice in the tradition of the Enlightenment. However, I also agree with critiques of the New Atheists offered by Terry Eagleton's *Reason, Faith, and Revolution,* among others.[10] The New Atheists are afflicted with a literalist method of biblical interpretation as narrow as any fundamentalist's; they ignore the immanent critiques of religion from religionists themselves; they glibly dismiss the unethical behavior of other atheists; and they seem as incapable of self-critique, especially critique of scientific culture, as any ecclesial elite. Furthermore, as rationalists, they dismiss any form of knowledge that does not privilege reason absolutely, and as members of imperial cultures, they conflate "religion" with the Abrahamic monotheisms, despite the white flag waved halfheartedly at Buddhism. In this sense, they are as supersessionist as any pope or ayatollah; by virtue of a transitive property of supersession, their system of belief is superior to all the systems that Christianity and Islam claim to have superseded. Indigenous, nontheistic, and polytheistic worldviews are dismissed as unworthy of investigation, a stance that Eiseley, as anthropologist, did not share.

Though all of this is true, it is still worthwhile to see if Eiseley can be a useful interlocutor for them, and they for him. They share much in common. All are committed to rational inquiry in an established academic discipline. All are neo-Darwinists: they believe that speciation occurs through natural selection and that genes are the carriers of the information passed on by organisms to offspring, which are in turn acted upon by natural selection. As evolutionists, they are naturally process thinkers; stasis, as a pillar of ontology, is an illusion to all of them. Finally, institutional religion was anathema to Eiseley as much as to them; established churches have no memes of interest, especially because of Whitehead's critique, which they would all endorse, of the Church of Caesar. It is these similarities, however, that reveal the importance of their radical disagreement on the subject of redemption and its ecology. Their rationalism — the principle that reason is the sole or ruling faculty for obtaining reliable knowledge — makes

Eiseley's transcendentalist inheritance stand out in stark relief. As much as Eiseley loves reason, he sees mystery as inevitable, and emotion as a legitimate form of cognition, especially where reason itself fails in the face of the abyss. Standing behind him are Emerson, Thoreau, and Melville, who each found New England Calvinism and its daughter, Unitarianism, insufficient in the face of the world's tragedy and wonder. In response, they crafted an unchurched faith that affirmed reason but did not deny the aspects of existence that reason cannot grasp. Eiseley's existentialism and his respect for the autonomy of suffering descend from them, as does his trust in epiphany as a mode of revelation. The New Atheists are offended by human suffering and know who to blame for it, but it has no ontological status in their world system. It cannot be addressed by any process one might call redemption; they have no program to rescue humans or other creatures (unless it is the eradication of religion and the irrational as such). This points to a fundamental difference between them and Eiseley concerning the status of modernity and the proper reaction to it. For Eiseley, the Darwinian understanding of the struggle for existence is, by itself, an invitation to existential horror. It must be overcome through solidarity with other creatures, which I have called the ecology of redemption. Insofar as modernity rejects the remedies of traditional cultures, including religion, in the face of suffering, it is insufficient. There is no redemption without reason, but none with reason by itself either. In this sense the New Atheists favor the scientific path as an end to suffering because of its ability to end metaphysical delusion. Eiseley does not. Love is the force that allows the theory of evolution to evolve: love's knowledge is not a "rift, but a joining" of science to the life of the spirit; it conserves Darwinian reason but connects it to realms of being that cannot be grasped through reason alone (182). Modernity, as the aeon of mastery through instrumental reason, is also the object of the ecology of redemption.

These contending interpretations of reason and emotion, science and spirit, the sacred and the secular, cannot be resolved here. They point, however, to public conversations that "The Star Thrower" should join. In moving beyond biography to Dante as ancestor, Whitehead as companion, ecotheology as heir, and the New Atheism as foil, I seek to redeem "The

Star Thrower" from its status as last will and testament of a great, dead man. The bridge it began to build between biology and literature, theology and science, in the name of compassion for all creatures, is a project we must take up in an age of ecocide. We must make our way in the dark wood and earn the gratitude of animals. I know it from a man at the foot of a rainbow, a starfish thrower on the beaches of Costabel.

NOTES

My deepest thanks to the 1985 Hardwood Island crew and to everyone else who has helped me understand "The Star Thrower." The ideas in this essay were first presented to the Loren Eiseley Society in Lincoln, Nebraska, in 2000, and I thank the society for that opportunity.

1. A notable exception to the pattern is Mary Ellen Pitts's *Toward a Dialogue of Understandings*.

2. The best account of Dante's metaphysics and of the difference between a modern, materialist view of nature and a Dantean view of creation can be found in Christian Moevs's *The Metaphysics of Dante's Comedy*.

3. The complex history of early Christianity's idea of redemption relative to the Jewish and Hellenistic background of the time is explored in Ruether's "Gender and Redemption in the Patristic Era."

4. One of the clearest explanations of the way Dante symbolically figures the three realms of Creation using animal tropes, such as the heavenly hive, without including animals themselves as spiritual protagonists, appears in Cristopher Hollingsworth's *Poetics of the Hive* (76–114).

5. In his chapter on "Farinata and Cavalcante," Auerbach explores the paradox involved in the insertion of a living soul, still immersed in history, into an image of eternity (*Mimesis* 174–202).

6. For an account of an ecological postmodernism, see Arran E. Gare's *Postmodernism and the Environmental Crisis*.

7. On the potential for a Darwinian enchantment, see George Levine's *Darwin Loves You*.

8. My sketch of the New Atheism is based on a reading of Dawkins, *The God Delusion*; Dennett, *Breaking the Spell*; and Harris, *The End of Faith*. I regret that there is not more space in this chapter to engage their arguments in detail.

9. The best answer to these questions appears in Roger S. Gottlieb's "Introduction: Religion and Ecology."

10. Other critiques of the New Atheists are Haught, *New Atheism*; Weinberg, "Deadly Certitude"; and Harris and Sullivan, "Built on Lies."

11

Emerson and Eiseley

Two Religious Visions

JONATHAN WEIDENBAUM

Central to Emerson and the transcendentalists is a sense of sheer astonishment in the face of existence, a receptivity to nature as fresh and original as "Adam early in the morning" — to steal a phrase from Whitman (*Leaves* 95). The invitation to witness the universe "with new eyes" was not lost on Emerson's countless literary and philosophical progeny (*Essential* 39). Chief among these is Loren Eiseley, the anthropologist, author, and bone hunter who perceived his whole life to be a religious pilgrimage and who saw "deep mystery in the heart of a simple seed" (*All* 141; *Firmament* 8). The Emersonian amazement before being was so extensive in the writing of Eiseley that it served, in fact, to strain his reputation as a serious and committed scientist. "I have had the vague word 'mystic,' applied to me," he once complained, "because I have not been able to shut out wonder occasionally, when I have looked at the world" (*Night* 214).

For Emerson the quest to recapture a state of primal innocence is but one component of the spiritual life. Transcendentalism joins numerous contemplative traditions East and West in seeking to draw out the moral and metaphysical implications of its most cherished moods and feelings. In the *Varieties of Religious Experience*, William James includes the "noetic," or knowledge-bearing quality, as one of the four characteristics common to all mystical experiences (293), an analysis which fits Emerson's famous "transparent eyeball" epiphany at the very beginning of *Nature*. Here, "perfect exhilaration" and self-transcendence while traversing a field is understood as a state of unity with the divine, an interpretation alternatively lauded and derided by generations of critics (and even turned into a cartoon by Christopher Cranch, a contemporary of Emerson's [40–41]). "I am nothing; I see all," writes Emerson, "the currents of the Universal Being circulate through me; I am part or particle of God" (*Essential* 6).

The religious intuitions of Eiseley are not only knowledge bearing; they are the direct products of a sustained and ceaseless attempt to explore the natural world. As a scientist with a talent for poetry, Eiseley married the empirical with the personal in a fashion reminiscent of Thoreau, yet another of his strongest influences. Eiseley was well aware of this similarity, and identified with Thoreau's refusal to segregate science from literature and vice versa. Of Emerson's most famous disciple, Eiseley states, "He was a fox at the wood's edge, regarding human preoccupations with doubt" (*Star* 271). That Eiseley perceived himself in the same way is evident in his own self-description as "a fox at the wood's edge" (qtd. in Carlisle, *Loren* 186), a reference wisely chosen by Gale E. Christianson for the title of his biography.

It is when placed next to Emerson, however, that the uniqueness of Eiseley's religious thought is most vividly apparent. Though sharing classic Emersonian themes in some areas, the spirituality of Eiseley, a perpetual struggle with questions that exceed the limits of understanding, is often of an entirely different character. More specifically: while both authors acknowledge the reality of human finitude, it is the distinctive manner in which Eiseley approaches this central factor of our existence that provides for his richness as a contemplative thinker. Eiseley *spiritualizes* our finitude, and in a broad range of ways. He goes so far as to suggest, by way of love, the possibility of surmounting our physical and intellectual barriers and identifying with the rest of the cosmos. Hence, it is the mission of the pages that follow not only to detail some of the core similarities and differences between Emerson and Eiseley on topics of ultimate meaning and value, but to show by means of such a comparison the depth and relevance of Eiseley's spiritual vision.

Eiseley's own take on the Sage of Concord should put to rest any reservations concerning the historical distance between the two thinkers. Widely read in almost every period of Emerson's authorship, Eiseley repeatedly lauds "the great American essayist" for anticipating contemporary ideas: from the process metaphysics of Whitehead and his disciples, to the Darwinian indifference of nature to sentient life, human and otherwise (*Star* 221). Emerson's mature work, according to Eiseley, portrays the natural world as excessive, aloof, and vastly impersonal; a great "wastefulness of suns and systems" (216). That the religious philosophy of Emerson is no mere nature mysticism or wooly-headed idealism is attested to time and again in the writings of Eiseley.

It might be asked why I am justified in using the word "religious" in regard to Ralph Waldo Emerson and Loren Eiseley. The former left the faith of his upbringing to become the core figure in a predominately nondenominational movement, while the latter refrained from using the term "God" even when hinting toward the possibility of a divine reality. In defense, I draw on John Dewey's distinction between "religion" and "religious" from *A Common Faith*. "Religion," for Dewey, refers to the main dogmas and rituals of an organized faith (e.g., Islam), while "religious" denotes a certain quality found within our perceptual life — one that is heightened, intensified, and often ecstatic in character. Given this distinction, the second term is more than appropriate.

Eiseley once claimed to be unmoved by "the religious forms of the present" (*All* 139). Even if he were a professional theologian instead of a scientist, there would be nothing radical about this remark. Arguably, the most original American religious thought has been experiential and anti-institutional in character. If there is any larger purpose of this essay, it is to highlight Eiseley's genuine contribution to an authentically American spirituality.

TWO MEN WITHOUT A HANDLE

Before delving into the religious ideas of Emerson and Eiseley, it is worth taking note of the protean character of their thought. It is more than symbolic that Emerson began writing *Nature* on his return trip from Europe, a far older culture, for the author who reminds us that "the sun shines to-day" was a student of German idealism, the British Romantic poets, Emanuel Swedenborg, and the *Bhagavad Gita* (*Essential* 3). The essays and books of the celebrated transcendentalist are, after all, intended to awaken us to what is the most ancient of doctrines "cast into the mould of these new times" (81). Even "The American Scholar," what Oliver Wendell

Holmes called "our intellectual declaration of independence," was not so much a shoving off of all inherited human wisdom as a rediscovery of its veracity in the present (qtd. in Gura 12). To the demand in *Nature* that "we also enjoy an original relation to the universe" (*Essential* 3), Emerson's most popular recent biographer astutely directs our attention to the word "also" (Richardson 99). Part of Emerson's complexity as a thinker is this reverence for the past combined with a concern, more popularly associated with him, that his own civilization should achieve a vital and nonderivative connection to primordial truth.

Against this background we can appreciate Emerson's departure from his early career as a minister, for "corpse-cold" Unitarianism was the very epitome of a faith in which preaching came "out of the memory, and not out of the soul" (Miller 8; Emerson, *Selected* 117). Emerson rejected both the empty formalities of genteel religion and the dry reductionisms of Enlightenment philosophy (most particularly, the reliance on raw sense experience advocated by Locke and Hume). From then on, the work of Plotinus — the third-century Platonist who championed the blissful union between the soul and the One — became an integral part of Emerson's thinking (Geldard 74). And yet despite his Neoplatonism, Emerson possessed a lifelong passion for the sciences. It is also this conflux of the empirical with the spiritual that almost justifies his claim from the journals: "I need hardly say to any one acquainted with my thoughts that I have no System" (*Selected* 87).

In *The Firmament of Time*, Loren Eiseley recalls the words of a colleague who, after picking up a turtle, immediately returned it to the spot where he found it. "I have tampered enough with the universe," proclaimed the scientist, as he placed the reptile gently on the ground. After telling this story, Eiseley provides his own thoughts: "It was not a denial of science. It was a final recognition that science is not enough for man. It is not the road back to the waiting Garden, for that road lies through the heart of man" (148–49).

As many scholars have noted, the work of Eiseley also defies easy categorization. Reflections on the origins and future of our species, environmental issues, premonitions of mortality, and episodes recalled from his often morose and alienated upbringing are interwoven in his exquisitely crafted prose. Eiseley's writing is intensely personal, even when not overtly autobiographical; it is scholarly, even when not purely scientific. Much of Eiseley's most effecting and popular work is, after all, in the form of the "concealed essay," that presentation of scientific fact sandwiched by events weaned from his life at the beginning and philosophical reflection all throughout (*All* 177–78). Like Emerson, Eiseley denied possessing a consistent body of thought. "I doubt if I have a philosophy. I live more or less like the cardinals who come to my window day to day" (*Lost* 221). No less than the New England transcendentalist, the anthropologist from Nebraska could just as easily have been addressed by Henry James Sr. as a "man without a handle" (qtd. in Habegger 207).

THE PERENNIAL PHILOSOPHY AND THE AXIAL AGE

While both Emerson and Eiseley claimed to lack a steady and coherent scheme of ideas, there are themes that continually surface throughout their writing. One of these is a strong and abiding intuition that the world of the senses is not all there is.

Throughout his whole career, Emerson espoused a dualism between the fleeting objects of sense experience on the one hand, and the deeper source continually generating the material universe on the other. Emerson's Platonism is synthesized with a myriad of influences both Asian and occidental. In the minds of some, the result constitutes yet another chapter of a long-standing spiritual sensibility called the Perennial Philosophy. Popularized by Aldous Huxley, the Perennial Philosophy holds that the ground of the psyche and the ground of the cosmos are one and the same. Conversely, the sharp dualities that define our mundane lives — between "I" and the Other, self and world, ego and God — are ultimately illusions to be overcome. The most admired formulation of the Perennial Philosophy in the East is *Advaita Vedanta*, the nondual philosophy of Shankara. Based on the *Upanishads*, Shankara's school perceives that the soul (*atman*) is the very presence of the Absolute (Brahman) within the human being. A vivid example from medieval Europe is the Christian mystic Meister Eckhart, who, besides being listed in the index of Huxley's *Perennial Philosophy* more times than any other figure, claims that "the eye with which I see God is exactly the same eye with which God sees me" (179). Shankara and Eckhart would have delighted in the New Englander's own pithy summary from the journals: "Blessed is the day when the youth discovers that Within and Above are synonyms" (*Selected* 53).

But to simply label Emerson as a mystic, or as an American version of the Perennial Philosophy, is to overlook his most original contribution to the literature of the spirit. While much traditional mysticism encourages the complete nullification of the ego within the divine, Emerson extols its renewed vigor. When connecting to a deeper reality underlying and gestating the cosmos, the "I" discovers a new power and buoyancy (transparent eyeball notwithstanding). "A true man," proclaims Emerson, "belongs to no other time and place, but is the centre of things" (*Selected* 156). These words remind us of *Thus Spoke Zarathustra* for a reason, for evident in "Self-Reliance" is the proud amorality and joyful self-affirmation that, according to George J. Stack, would "serve as sparks to Nietzsche's philosophical flames" (60). "Do not tell me, as a good man did to-day, of my obligation to put all poor men in good situations. Are they *my* poor?" (Emerson, *Selected* 152).

For those who would like to see Loren Eiseley as a kind of contemporary transcendentalist, the case can readily be made. "Behind the ridiculous, wonderful tent-show of woodpeckers, giraffes, and hoptoads," explains Eiseley, there is "some kind of dark, brooding, but creative void out of which these things emerge" (*Night* 195). There is a dualism present within the human being as well, for the deeper layer of our psyche has its home within this dynamic ground. The origin of our authenticity and creativity is nothing less than the origin of all being: "The artist and the scientist bring out of the dark void, like the mysterious universe itself, the unique, the strange, the unexpected" (204). But this interior world also brings insight, and it is due to its neglect that Western culture, despite its material advances, has reached its current deracinated state. Throughout *The Immense Journey*, *The Firmament of Time*, and *The Night Country*, Eiseley argues that our frantic yearning to escape into the distant reaches of space or to build utopias out of technological advances alone has led to the vulgarity of consumer culture, the potential horrors of advanced warfare, and the despoiling of nature (*Night* 204). We are left with not a more developed humanity, but the "new asphalt animal"; not a more refined civilization, but the "world of artless, dehumanized man" (*Firmament* 128).

The future, however, is not set in stone. Eiseley joins the transcendentalists in drawing on inherited human wisdom as a correction to the shallowness of the present. Our most important legacy, according to Eiseley, is the period known as the Axial Age. Labeled by the German philosopher Karl Jaspers (and most recently articulated by Karen Armstrong) this was the auspicious era when seers such as the Buddha and Confucius spoke of compassion and how "the spaces within stretch as far as those without" (*Invisible* 147). With his use of figures such as John Donne, Kierkegaard, the anonymous author of *The Cloud of Unknowing*, and innumerable references to Jesus ("that lost receding figure on the dreadful hill of Calvary"), Eiseley had a particularly special place in his writing for the Christian spiritual tradition (*Star* 266). Indeed, the title character of one of his most emotionally potent essays, "The Star Thrower," is a thinly veiled symbol for Christ. Appearing under a rainbow along a lonely and desolate coast, a man tosses beached starfish back into the ocean. This character is a savior of the hurt and the lost, and the aesthetic power with which he is drawn almost vindicates the claim of Leslie E. Gerber and Margaret McFadden that Eiseley was a "reluctant Christian" (146).

Even when he is not borrowing from the world's spiritual traditions, Eiseley offers a sort of varieties of religious experience through his naturalism. He describes both Darwin's awe before the unity of life and our yearning for the "sunflower forest" from which humankind first arose (*Invisible* 1). A sense of oneness with the universe is expressed by Eiseley through a description of floating down a river: "I *was* water . . . that mother element which still, at this late point in time, shelters and brings into being nine tenths of everything alive" (*Immense* 20). From his extensive scholarship on the history of evolutionary theory to his account of how flowers have transformed the planet, Eiseley has contributed some of the most compelling and readable science writing in contemporary literature. And yet, one must appreciate that the author of *Darwin's Century* and a book on

Francis Bacon can state "that the venture into space is meaningless unless it coincides with a certain interior expansion, an ever growing universe within, to correspond with the far flight of the galaxies our telescopes follow from without" (*Star* 298).

DUALITY AND THE COSMIC PRISON

Accompanying the transcendentalism of both Eiseley and Emerson is a forceful meditation on the grittier and more concrete facets of the human predicament. These elements combine with the spiritual qualities of their writings in distinctive ways. Scholars typically note a change of tone between Emerson's earlier and later published works. In essays such as "Experience" and "Fate," there is a stronger pessimism, a concentration on the worldly and the finite. But the idealist and transcendentalist themes remain present, even if mostly eclipsed. In the wake of his beloved son's death for instance, Emerson ruminates over the elusiveness of experience, including his inability to grasp the meaning of grief. And yet in this very same essay we are instructed that "the consciousness in each man is a sliding scale, which identifies him now with the First Cause, and now with the flesh of his body" (*Selected* 240). In "Fate," Emerson lists the innumerable contingencies that plague human existence, from the cruelties of natural disaster to the circumstances of birth, and still writes of the way in which "the inward eye opens to the Unity in things" (390).

Though increasingly evident as Emerson's career progressed, the rift between his spiritual and earthly perspectives is not to be written off as a by-product of personal loss. As early as 1837, a mere year after publishing *Nature*, we find Emerson bemoaning his inability to infuse the transcendental self with his daily, day-to-day existence: "A believer in Unity, a seer of Unity, I yet behold two. . . . Cannot I conceive the Universe without Contradiction?" (*Selected* 68). It is Richard G. Geldard, a devoted student of transcendentalist spirituality, who most succinctly captures the purpose of Emerson's more realistic writings: while not disavowing the pantheism and idealism of *Nature* or "The Oversoul," his other works express "life lived in duality" (86).

Similar to Emerson, Eiseley makes human finitude a theme of his work. But Eiseley's treatment, besides being a constant motif of his whole authorship, is far more thorough and intense. It is also where Eiseley's religious vision begins to move in a novel direction from what is ordinarily taken as transcendentalist, at least in the Emersonian sense.

In "The Hidden Teacher," Eiseley recalls touching the rim of a spider's web with a pencil. The spider's reaction demonstrated that the pencil was an interference that it could in no way understand. Typical to form, Eiseley immediately draws conclusions from the encounter: "The spider was a symbol of man in miniature. The wheel of the web brought the analogy home clearly. Man, too, lies at the heart of a web, a web extending through the starry reaches of sidereal space, as well as backward into the dark realms of prehistory" (*Star* 119).

In *The Invisible Pyramid*, our relationship to the greater universe is likened to that of a blood cell residing within the human body: "We know only a little more extended reality than the hypothetical creature below us. Above us may lie realms it is beyond our power to grasp" (34). It is in this same book that Eiseley painstakingly outlines our "cosmic prison," the various temporal, spatial, and sensory cages in which we are enclosed. Unable to shove off our bodies and sense organs, nor to extend our life indefinitely, there is simply no god's eye perspective on the universe available to us.

"Certainly science has moved forward," Eiseley states in *The Firmament of Time*, "but when science progresses, it often opens vaster mysteries to our gaze" (5). To be a scientist is to stand on the cusp where all accumulated knowledge ends and new information first makes its appearance. Eiseley is fond of Newton's understanding of himself as a child toying with shells on a beach before a vast ocean. The ocean, of course, is the great undiscovered, and Eiseley refers more than once to a similar childlike wonder shared by Darwin and Einstein (*Star* 276). As a consummate writer, Eiseley is particularly adept at taking his readers to this very same experience. Whether brooding over the origins of life in *The Immense Journey* or the unfathomably cruel mechanisms of the Sphex wasp in *All the Strange Hours*, Eiseley allows us to see how scientific conundrums can easily become the stuff of religious contemplation. The encounter with the limits of our current knowledge, our cognitive finitude, becomes a form of spirituality. As Richard E. Wentz keenly observes, for Eiseley "the unknown is always encountered *in the midst* of the known. That is to say, the more one is aware of one's own involvement in a scientific enterprise, the more one understands it as a participation in a mystery, rather than as a conquest of exterior and objective territory" ("American").

This picture of the known, both fringed and permeated by the unknown, is most powerfully and artistically expressed in *The Night Country*. Generalized here beyond the matters of science, the unknown is a foreboding and nebulous place called the Night Country, while the known is a fragile bastion of security, a tiny island of light steadily overshadowed by the oncoming darkness. Apprehension before the Night Country is "the fear of the tide, the night tide, I call it, because that is the way you come to feel it — invisible, imperceptible almost, unless it is looked for — and yet, as you grow older you realize that it is always there, swirling like a vapor just beyond the edge of the lamp at evening and similarly out to the ends of the universe" (32).

It is not difficult to equate the Night Country simply with death. Mortality is a constant preoccupation of Eiseley, an author rightly labeled by Peter Heidtmann as an "artist of autumn" (124). But the Night Country also possesses qualities of the numinous.[1] At once alluring and terrifying, it is the transcendent reality that, teasing our experience from without, resists being subsumed without our rational and intellectual categories. Surrounding our daily existence like an "invisible wall," the Night Country's most common emissaries are the nonhuman members of the animal kingdom — particularly the nefarious rat (12). In perhaps the most unsettling scene in all of Eiseley's work, one makes an appearance at a friend's dinner party. Just as the friend smugly pronounces his faith in the limitless power of humanity over nature, the rodent, noticed only by Eiseley, sits directly under the host's chair. As those in the room clink glasses in agreement, Eiseley "felt for an uneasy moment that the creature might ironically applaud" (35).

If not through the glaring eyes of a sewer rat, what Eiseley calls a "natural revelation" occurs throughout his entire authorship. It could be an encounter with birds flying outside of a New York City window, a disheveled man at an airport, the hollow eyes of a skull jutting out from the wall of a deep crevice, a struggle between a serpent and a bird in the desert, a playful fox with a bone, a hawk soaring in victory toward its mate in the sky, or countless other examples.[2] In each scenario an awakening occurs, an old worldview is breached in a radical and sometimes painful, sometimes stirring fashion. Or, as Eiseley fancifully states, with each scenario "a terrible new sense has opened a crack in the Absolute" (*Firmament* 169). What is gained is, perhaps, a new form of seeing, an ability to step out of one's own being and peer through the eyes of another, a direct acquaintance with a formerly hidden and inaccessible aspect, or a return to one's natural self beneath the artificialities and trivialities of modern society. These moments can only be called a kind of grace — the depiction of which, as Ben Howard argues, might very well be Eiseley's most lasting contribution to contemporary writing (57).

A LOVE WITHOUT ISSUE

While spiritual grace is typically initiated from without, there is yet another trajectory of the spiritual life present in the work of Eiseley, one that has its origin at least partly from within. When the intellect, for all its hunger for answers, remains hemmed within the cosmic prison, there are situations where another force is permitted to awaken. In "The Inner Galaxy," Eiseley provides two particularly dramatic accounts of such an event: one, shortly after falling and gashing his head open on the sidewalk, and another while sitting on a discarded whiskey crate. In both cases Eiseley is confronted with life in abundance — living organisms that, for the most part, go unnoticed and overlooked. For the blood cells now "dying like beached fish on the hot pavement," and equally for the birds, wild dogs, and a hermit crab playing in front of his crate, a sense of compassion begins to well up from inside of Eiseley. Soon, this emotion intensifies and surges out of him, "a love without issue, tenuous, almost disembodied" (*Star* 310). In *The Invisible Pyramid*, Eiseley concludes that it is neither the breadth of our knowledge nor our supposed dominance over nature that, finally, can break down the walls of our cosmic prison. It is only love that can truly connect us to the rest of the universe in any meaningful way: "This is a crossing beside which light-years are meaningless. It is the solitary key to the prison that is man" (49).

In conceiving our passion for the well-being of others as a kind of transcendence, Eiseley can be said to have anticipated some recent trends in European philosophy. In the work of Emmanuel Levinas, for instance, the encounter with other human beings is not only laden with moral significance; it is an inherently spiritual event, an experience that both exceeds and resists all of our usual (if futile) attempts to close off a final perspective on the world. The essential difference between Levinas and Eiseley is that the latter broadened such a relationship to embrace all living things, thus lifting radical ethics out of a strict and parochial humanism.

As states of awareness arising from and addressing our finitude, both grace and love figure prominently in "The Star Thrower." Sprinkled through-out Eiseley's work are suggestions of an Absolute. "The Hidden Teacher," for instance, perhaps his most cryptic work, features a force abiding within and communicating through nature (116–28). There is also the endlessly mutating Life from "The Snout"; the Great Face behind from "The Secret of Life"; and the mystical zero from *All the Strange Hours* ("behind nothing, before nothing") (*Immense* 59, 210; *All* 264). Alternatively personal and impersonal, these intimations of a divine being never add up to a consistent theological position. Literary and philosophical conjectures on the part of Eiseley, they are designed to fit the thematic contexts in which they are found. They are also set off against other statements made by him at various stages of his career. In an early letter, a youthful Eiseley wrote, "I have no philosophy except the belief that the universe is indifferent and blind" (Christianson, *Fox* 80). *The Invisible Pyramid* also makes reference to the "indifference of the watching stars" (2).

It is in "The Star Thrower," however, that we find the most poignant expression of a deity. It is toward the very end of the essay that we are introduced to the celestial equivalent of the Christlike man under the rainbow. Eiseley is at first puzzled by the strange person who, laboring after the dejected and the forgotten, hurls the suffering starfish into the ocean. He returns to his room for the night. After a fitful and uneasy sleep, one troubled by images of his painful past (including the roving and manic eye of his psychologically disturbed mother), a harrowed Eiseley awakens to the healing and expansive power of love. Quickly returning to the beach, he is now the star thrower's disciple: "He is not alone any longer. After us there will be others" (184). It is here that Eiseley raises love to a cosmic but intelligent principle. Somewhere, a celestial Thrower hurls suns in the same manner that the star thrower tosses starfish. The Thrower is a being intuited by Eiseley outside of all evidence, a presence affirmed beyond the far boundaries of understanding.

THE AMERICAN RELIGION

The limitations of our knowledge also play an increasing role in the later works of Emerson. Eiseley recognized this fact, and approvingly quoted Emerson's "Method of Nature." Of the natural world, Emerson asks, "Who could ever analyze it? That rushing stream will not stop to be observed" (*Nature* 191). But even in Emerson's more earth-bound essays, it is the transcendental self that serves as the religious foundation for his thought. When this deeper self is overcome by more worldly concerns, the realm of everyday experience — though possessing an interesting dynamism of its own — is void of true spiritual meaning. This is arguably the reason for the somewhat more cynical feel of these writings.[3] Hence, if we now find ourselves in the midst of a staircase with steps both ascending and descending out of our sight, it is because we have drunken from the lethe (Emerson, *Selected* 229). We have forgotten our true place in the eternal, and must, in good Platonic fashion, remember our real and supernal home. As a mere shell covering the kernel of unity, the life of duality is both hard and bare.

Emerson's spirituality, the inauguration of that experiential faith labeled by Sydney E. Ahlstrom and Harold Bloom as the "American Religion," is very much a creed of interiority, one centered within the deep recesses of the psyche (Ahlstrom 605). As Bloom describes it, this is a spirituality of complete and self-contained solitude, the Gnostic belief that our essential being has existed with God since before the creation (*American* 22). There is not much of a place for Otherness in the face of such "egotheism" — as Elizabeth Peabody once labeled Emerson's brand of transcendentalism

(245). Eiseley graciously pays homage to a lovely and unique passage in Emerson's journals pronouncing love "as the bright stranger, the foreign self" (*Selected* 143). But the true apostle of transcendent love could never claim to "shun brother, sister, father, mother, lover, when my genius calls me" (152). To the rejoinder that no "mean egotism" exists when immersed in the Oversoul, one needs only to reexamine Emerson's proto-Nietzchean synthesis: the self is not dissolved but empowered — and literally so. In *The American Religion*, Bloom correctly points out that in Emerson, "ecstasy and power are intimately related" (176).

For Eiseley, however, the source of all true and abiding significance not only lies within the deep foundations of the psyche but encircles it from all directions. His religious vision is a haunted one, full of revelations and epiphanies, but with moments when love, overcoming the confines of the self, fuses one to the lives and destiny of others. That the intellect is faced by dimensions that exceed it is precisely what lends his work its otherworldly atmosphere. Even when Eiseley is not invoking explicitly religious themes, he seems to live, move, and have his being in a world of constant spiritual surprise. While reading him, page after page we come to feel as if our ordinary perception is a product, not of the way things truly are, but of seeing through a glass darkly.

Eiseley is also no stranger to "that strange inner light which has come from no man knows where, and which was not made by us" (*Firmament* 145). But other forms of religiousness are evident in his work besides the transcendental — even if through a mostly secularized and naturalistic form. In regard to matters of the spirit, it is Eiseley who offers the more complex and inclusive vision, a more than worthy addition to the American Religion.

NOTES

1. The term "numinous" was popularized by Rudolf Ottos's *Idea of the Holy*, and Eiseley appreciated both author and book. See Eiseley's "Science and the Sense of the Holy" (*Star*).

2. *Immense* 165–67; *Night* 176–78; *Immense* 5; *Star* 292–93; *Star* 63–64; *Immense* 191; *Star* 27.

3. See Donald L. Gelpi's chapter on Emerson, in *Varieties of Transcendental Experience*.

12

Epic Narratives of Evolution

John Burroughs and Loren Eiseley

STEPHEN MERCIER

In 1961 Loren Eiseley was awarded the prestigious John Burroughs Medal for *The Firmament of Time*, joining the ranks of distinguished authors of natural history such as Ernest Thompson Seton, Rachel Carson, Joseph Wood Krutch, and Roger Tory Peterson. Indeed, both Burroughs (1837–1921) and Eiseley (1907–77) belong to a long list of writers who imaginatively delve into environmental explorations, forging connections to ecological and evolutionary dynamics. Surely, their writings cannot escape influences from a long history of previous nature works, from Gilbert White's discursive firsthand observations on his beloved Selbourne, to Charles Darwin's profound theories of evolution, to Henry David Thoreau's paradigmatic *Walden*. In common with these predecessors they share close observation of phenomena, keen awareness of environmental processes, appreciation of species and their habitats, aesthetic engagement within the natural world, philosophical reflections, and a recognition of the deep kinship between humans and the biosphere. Adding their own unique refinements to the genre of literary natural history, Burroughs and Eiseley create novel rhetorical methods of transmitting aspects of evolution to the masses.

Burroughs was one of the first American nature writers to fold Darwinian ideas into his essays in a dramatic fashion for a widespread audience. Therefore, he helped chart new territory of literary narrative on deep time, on which Eiseley would later build. Eiseley inevitably follows Burroughs's path of influence and innovation, while further stretching the boundaries of literary naturalism. New discoveries in more specialized areas of science, such as anthropology, allowed Eiseley to provide more specific "evidence" for his evolutionary tale and relate it to his audience.

Burroughs's audience was from the late nineteenth and early twentieth centuries, while Eiseley's readership was of the Cold War period;

Burroughs lived through the Civil War and the Gilded Age, and Eiseley through World War II. The historical context during which these authors lived surely helped to shape their outlook on the tendency toward violence and the serious responsibility human beings have toward protecting each other and the natural world. Ultimately, they both felt the need to make the point that the fate of humanity and the planet is in our own hands.

Many readers may not be entirely familiar with John Burroughs, as he has only recently rejoined the canon of U.S. nature writers. Hailed as the most beloved author of the natural history essay, Burroughs sold more than one and a half million copies of his books. A prolific author, Burroughs penned 450 essays and twenty-seven books, which were published over a fifty-five-year period, from 1867–1922. Burroughs's perhaps most famous essays recount his rambles exploring native natural history in the Hudson River Valley and Catskills and life on the family farm. Burroughs celebrates rainwater, wildflowers, weeds, apples, strawberries, cows, chipmunks, squirrels, speckled trout, and tree toads, so often taken for granted in favor of more exotic species. Famously known as "John O'Birds," Burroughs is fascinated by the general behavior and habits of birds, considering not only how they migrate and build nests but also how parents raise their young and survive in the wild.

Burroughs remained an extremely popular figure throughout his lifetime. He dreaded the potential misuse of technology and felt that an obsession with materialism was deteriorating the nation. Therefore, he accentuated direct contact with the elements, the taste of wild berries, the enjoyment of taking morning and evening walks, the pleasure of viewing the stars, a bird's nest, or a wildflower. Enticing readers to see an array of natural beauty with childlike curiosity, Burroughs emphasized what they might recognize nearby in their own familiar surroundings. Miraculously, Burroughs could hitch familiar phenomena, such as a handful of soil or a leaf, with the huge tide of evolutionary processes. Certainly, he was far less known for his writings on evolution, a subject that greatly occupied his mind after reading Darwin. Surely, however, legions of dedicated Burroughs readers gobbled up his profound tracts on evolution and geologic time just as they had invested themselves in his observations of blue birds.

John Burroughs and Loren Eiseley developed epic narratives of evolution, and in doing so, they furthered the development of the natural history essay in essential ways.[1] They both creatively combine scientific hypotheses with a poetic sensibility. Both writers employ imaginative prose in the form of literary natural history to engage and aid readers' understanding and to foster a profound appreciation of evolution. Burroughs and Eiseley had the remarkable ability to conceptualize and transmit visions of evolutionary change that had occurred over aeons of geologic time. Significantly, they were able to imagine *one's very self* undergoing huge physiological and anatomical transformations.

One simply cannot separate the human story from the narrative of evolutionary history. Attending this imaginary journey are rhapsodic feelings and a supreme emotional reverence for the workings of various inorganic and organic forms, the very forces that aided the development of human beings. Burroughs and Eiseley enjoy the freedom of contemplating the wondrous nature of life forms, the true secret of which may never be solved by science. They allow the consideration of indestructible questions: How was life created? Why do life forms have a tendency to "reach out"? How is the human brain unique in the universe? Embracing mystery, their humble perspectives enable both authors to develop moral considerations regarding the future of the race.

In fact, John Burroughs's "The Long Road," published in *Time and Change*, and Loren Eiseley's *The Immense Journey* transmit epiphanies to readers by utilizing astonishingly similar tropes and rhetorical techniques. Most obviously, both writers employ the metaphor of the journey or road. For example, Burroughs begins, "The long road I have in mind is the long road of evolution, — the road you and I traveled in the guise of humbler organisms, from the first unicellular life in the old Cambrian seas to the complex and highly specialized creature that rules supreme in the animal kingdom to-day" (1). Eiseley explains that he is presenting a "bit" of his "personal universe, the universe traversed in a long and uncompleted journey" (9). Surely, both authors wish to carry their readers along with them on an evolutionary magic carpet ride through deep history. Miraculous sensibilities and an epiphanic tone accompany both evolutionary epics.

At the beginning of "The Long Road," Burroughs promises, "Our children and their children's children will be exhilarated by the journey." Science, offering a "revelation" and "startling disclosures" (2), directs "our attention to common near-at-hand facts for the key to remote and mysterious occurrences." Cultivating wonder, Burroughs profoundly appreciates the familiar: "It seems to me that evolution adds greatly to the wonder of life, because it takes it out of the realm of the arbitrary, the exceptional, and links it to the sequence of natural causation" (3). As one key strategy to persuade his readers, Burroughs grappled openly with the acceptance of Darwin and his texts; following his train of thought readers are brought through personal reflections of arguments, counterarguments, feelings, and doubts — all of which inevitably lead to an acceptance of evolution as the single most important doctrine science has ever revealed to humanity.

Sharing his difficulty in accepting natural causation with his readers is a way Burroughs attempts to persuade them to his point of view: "To believe that our remote ancestor, no matter how remote in time or space, was a lowly organized creature living in the primordial seas with no more brains than a shovel-nosed shark or a gar-pike, puts our scientific faith to severe test" (5–6). Scientific claims and poetic sentiment set the stage for a fantastic journey through deep history.[2]

Because the immense duration of geologic time "balks us," Burroughs devotes a great deal of his essay developing aids to the readers' understanding. In regard to geologic time, Burroughs confesses that "all the standards of measurement furnished us by experience are as inadequate as is a child's cup to measure the ocean" (8). His speaking in such down-to-earth terms, rather than obscure scientific terminology, allows readers to clearly follow Burroughs's train of thought. He must first prove what geologic forces are capable of doing to the earth; then, he can make the link to the organic: "See what the god of erosion, in the shape of water, has done in the river valleys and gorges — cut a mile deep in the Colorado canyon, and yet this canyon is but of yesterday in geologic time. Only give the evolutionary god time enough and all these miracles are surely wrought" (8–9). The prophetic tone is enhanced by Burroughs's posing of evolution as a "god," a sort of spiritual entity performing miracles.

Even as Burroughs again admits that, due to how "slowly, oh, so slowly," geologic changes have taken place, he humanizes elements of the natural world to construct a compelling story: "'Give us time,' say the dews and the rains and the snowflakes, 'and we will make you a garden out of those same stubborn rocks and frowning ledges.' 'Give us time,' says Life starting with her protozoans in the old Cambrian seas, 'and I will not stop till I have peopled the earth with myriad forms and crowned them all with man'" (10). This acts as an exercise for the imaginative leap from aspects of weather, to which most readers can relate, to geologic changes — the results of which we can all witness — to the penultimate claim of primordial life forms evolving into humankind. The passage illuminates complex interdependencies of species with organic and inorganic material over vast aeons of geologic time. Burroughs's presentation of evolutionary ideas in more common language, his use of personification, and his utilization of everyday touchstones for his readers mark his literary naturalism as particularly innovative. Moreover, his epiphanic perspective leads to supreme aesthetic appreciation and emotional reverie.

Following in Burroughs's footsteps, in *The Immense Journey* Eiseley also embeds within many passages the workings of geologic time — perhaps the most necessary component of realizing how one's own body has transformed. In what has perhaps been the most famous passage in *The Immense Journey*, in "The Flow of the River" Eiseley allows himself to imagine traversing through deep geologic time, as he literally floats on the waters of the Platte River in Nebraska: "Once in a lifetime, if one is lucky, one so merges with sunlight and air and running water that whole eons, the eons that mountains and deserts know, might pass in a single afternoon without discomfort" (16). Through an imaginative leap, Eiseley seems to actually experience vast epochs of geologic time. He addresses his readers directly, beckoning their identification: "You have probably never experienced in yourself the meandering roots of a whole watershed or felt your outstretched fingers touching, by some kind of clairvoyant extension, the brooks of snow-line glaciers at the same time that you were floating toward the Gulf over the eroded debris of worn-down mountains." The passage is very sensual and poetic as Eiseley shares with his reader his "extension of the senses" (16). Eiseley does not wish to represent a purely intellectual or abstract concept; sensual contact acts as a touchstone to the real earth. He wants the readers to imagine their own bodies as intimately and inseparably fused with the deep history of the environment.

Eiseley's fine crafting of the genre of literary natural history enables this perspective. He seems to create a new form of literary naturalism, what one may call an evolutionary autobiography, as his body appears fused in deep kinship to the earth. Early assessments of *The Immense Journey* recognized his talent: in a September 1957 review in *Christian Science Monitor*, the reviewer writes, "These highly personal reflections, queries, doubts, and affirmations make up a literary offering by a scientist thinking and feeling about the very fundamentals of life and being" (qtd. in Carlisle, *Loren* 155).

Eiseley offers a description of his environmental aesthetic experience of Nebraska's Platte River. The form of this personal anecdote provides a starting point for a journey in which the narrator experiences geologic time and a startling relationship with the geography of an entire continent:

> Then I lay back in the floating position that left my face to the sky, and shoved off. The sky wheeled over me. For an instant, as I bobbed into the main channel, I had the sensation of sliding down the vast tilted face of the continent. It was then that I felt the cold needles of the alpine springs at my fingertips, and the warmth of the Gulf pulling me southward. Moving within me, leaving the taste upon my mouth and spouting under me in dancing springs of sand, was the immense body of the continent itself, flowing like the river was flowing, grain by grain, mountain by mountain, down to the sea. I was streaming over ancient sea beds thrust aloft where giant reptiles had once sported; I was wearing down the face of time and trundling cloud-wreathed ranges into oblivion. I touched my margins with the delicacy of a cray-fish's antennae, and felt great fishes glide about their work. (*Immense* 19)

Eiseley's own first-person narrative, the repetitive "I was," creates a mantra of deep identification with evolutionary forces. The reader can adopt Eiseley's own "visionary" point of view toward the phenomena he so vividly encounters. This prioritization of somatic immersion is a participatory activity, with which readers may strongly identify. The act of fully engaging his senses — his entire body bobs and slides, he feels the cold and tastes the springs — catapults Eiseley across time and space; his very sensitivity appears to belong to a far-gone geologic era. Through immersing himself in the same womb of creation where "giant reptiles once sported," he himself nearly becomes an ancient creature. E. Fred Carlisle notes that "Without trying to explain it here, Eiseley indicates that all forms of animal life can be traced to common origins in water and living matter" (*Loren* 159). Imaginatively taking on characteristics of a crayfish, Eiseley implies that he shares fundamental features with creatures over deep time. Furthermore, he is able to intuitively grasp evolutionary activities and present them in a novel form for readers, not limited by the strictures of scientific discourse.[3]

Eiseley's consciousness remains centered on his deep identification with his surroundings: "I *was* water and the unspeakable alchemies that gestate and take shape in water, the slimy jellies that under the enormous magnification of the sun writhe and whip upward as great barbeled fish mouths, or sink indistinctly back into the murk out of which they arose" (*Immense* 19–20). Floating on his back and facing the sky, Eiseley conceives of his body in terms of primordial elements that helped to generate life. This striking passage uses vivid adjectives, such as "unspeakable," "slimy," "enormous," and the descriptive verbs "gestate" and "writhe and whip," all of which seem to signify a deeper era of origin, when life rose and fell from the waters.

Next, Eiseley makes a larger claim, linking together various life forms through the principle of water: "Turtle and fish and the pinpoint chirpings of individual frogs are all watery projections, concentrations — as man himself is a concentration — of that indescribable and liquid brew which is compounded in varying proportions of salt and sun and time" (20). Being "indescribable," the brew itself is a mysterious blend of elements tossed by powerful natural forces across history.

Forty-four years earlier, Burroughs made a similar observation:

Man seems to be the net result of it all, of all these vast cycles of Palaeo-zoic, Mesozoic, and Caenozoic life. He is the one drop finally distilled from the vast weltering sea of lower organic forms. It looks as if it all had to be before he could be — all the delay and waste and struggle and pain — all that long carnival of sea life, all that saturnalia of gigantic forms upon the land and in the air, all that rising and sinking of the continents, and all that shoveling to and fro and mixing of the soils, before the world was ready for him. (*Time* 25)

Preceding Eiseley, Burroughs looks across geologic epochs, with their geographic upheavals and biological transformations, and focuses on the primary importance of water. While Burroughs paints a vividly character-ized "carnival of sea life," it is Eiseley who imaginatively rides the stream through time, placing himself in the "actual" scene.

Marveling over a catfish's jump leads Eiseley to the evolutionary nar-rative: "A million ancestral years had gone into that jump, I thought as I looked at him, a million years of climbing through prairie sunflowers and twining in and out through the pillared legs of drinking mammoth" (*Immense* 24). The visual aids of the tale paint a detailed picture, an artist's sketch for the reader's imagination. Then, Eiseley realizes his deep con-nection to the catfish, what he calls their "watery brotherhood." Because both species share a common origin in water, Eiseley surmises, "We were both projections out of that timeless ferment and locked as well in some greater unity that lay incalculably beyond us. In many a fin and reptile foot I have seen myself passing by — some part of myself, that is, some part that lies unrealized in the momentary shape I inhabit" (24).

To see one's own body in terms of evolutionary processes and changes is to embrace the principles on which evolution stands. Earlier in his text, Eiseley claims, "The truth is that we are all potential fossils still carrying within our bodies the crudities of former existences, the marks of a world in which living creatures flow with little more consistency than clouds from age to age" (5–6).

Anticipating Eiseley, Burroughs develops explanations of human evo-lution by including experiential dimensions geared to amplify a sense of wonder. Burroughs begins "The Long Road" with the metaphor of a long journey, "stretching through immeasurable epochs of geologic time, and attended by vicissitudes of which we can form but feeble conceptions. The majority of readers, I fancy, are not yet ready to admit that they, or any of their forebears, have ever made such a journey" (*Time* 1). Appreciation for evolution is made possible through conceptualizing this process over aeons of geologic time and also imagining one's own body, one's very self, undergoing huge physiological transformations. A specific strategy initiated by Burroughs and later adapted by Eiseley is to imagine himself in the first person, evolving. The evolving "I" may be engaging to readers, as it seems to suggest there is something essential and unique in each of us that traversed through immense trials with great success.

In his essay "The Hazards of the Past," Burroughs relies on the same rhetorical tactic Eiseley would to help his readers imagine their own bodies transforming through various substances and forms over aeons of geologic time. This is certainly not an ordinary neighborhood bioregional ramble. He conceives of *himself* traversing through waters, rock formations, and atmospheric upheavals:

> When the rocks that formed my native Catskills were being laid down in the Devonian waters, I fancy that my aquatic embryo was swimming about somewhere and slowly waxing strong. Up and up I climbed across the sandstone steps, across the limestone, the conglomerate, the slate, up into Carboniferous times. The upper and nether millstones of the "millstone grit" did not crush me, neither did the floods and the convulsions of Carboniferous times that buried the vast vegetable growths that resulted in our coal measures engulf or destroy me. About that time probably, I emerged from the water and became an amphibian, and maybe got my five fingers and five toes on each side. (*Time* 227)

This is an intimate first-person portrayal of an evolutionary journey, in which organisms — and Burroughs's own body in particular — are fused to their environments in essential ways. The passage is remarkable in its blending of the personal. Through the figure of the evolving "I," Burroughs explains the incredible synthesis of geologic forces that led to his present biological form. It is hard to imagine a notion of kinship in more vivid concreteness. The visceral quality of the prose augments the physical forces at play during deep time. A poetic strata exudes the passage through the interplay of the active "I" with water, stones, floods, and amphibians. The passage concludes by emphasizing the ultimate significance of the emergence from water, a marvelous and essential occurrence toward the development of human beings in evolutionary history.

Burroughs and Eiseley also identify the principle of life as "reaching out" and "experimenting" as a key evolutionary factor; furthermore, both use the exact terms "blindly" and "persistently" to capture the nature of evolutionary forces. With the flavor of a Whitmanesque catalog, Burroughs expounds on this notion: "Experimenting and experimenting endlessly, taking a forward step only when compelled by necessity, — this is the way of Nature, — experimenting with eyes, ears, with teeth, with limbs, with feet, with toes, with wings, with bladders and lungs, with scales and armors, hitting upon the backbone only after long trials with other forms, hitting upon the moveable eye only after long ages of other eyes, hitting on the mammal . . ." (34). Such repetition of "hitting upon" forms a provocative cadence within these passages and artfully mirrors the messages the author wishes to convey. Physiological features shared by humans and other species are figured as the result of endless experimentation.

Unlike Burroughs's more general frame of reference, Eiseley would elaborate on one specific species, the squid, to demonstrate "its eternal dissatisfaction with what it is, its persistent habit of reaching out into new environments, and, by degrees, adapting itself to the most fantastic circumstances" (*Immense* 37). By repeating the phrase "reaching out," Eiseley hammers home the incredible significance of how life extends itself and adapts: "It was the reaching out that changed this pattern, the reaching out that forced the cells to bring the sea ashore with them, to elaborate in their own bodies the very miniature of that all-embracing sea from which they came. It was the reaching out, that magnificent and agelong groping that only life — blindly and persistently among stones and the indifference of the entire inanimate universe — can continue to endure and prolong" (43). Just as Burroughs had repeated "hitting upon" to capture this important aspect of evolution, Eiseley utilizes the repetition of his key phrase "reaching out" to emphasize his argument. Eiseley makes the critical point that this activity is still in play: "the reaching out that began a billion years ago is still in process" (44).

For his part, Burroughs credited a rather nebulous "creative energy" for being responsible for the reaching out: "The creative energy seems to have worked in geologic time and in the geologic field just as it works here and now, in yonder vineyard or in yonder marsh, — blindly, experimentally, but persistently and successfully" (*Time* 33). The vineyard and marsh act as "local" and contemporary touchstones for the reader's imagination.

For Burroughs, Darwin adequately described and accounted for the transformation of biological forms but did not answer the more complex question: why did these forms originate in the very first place? Unquenchable curiosity led Burroughs to seek out the answer to this age-old philosophical question. Life forms certainly adapted through natural selection. But why? Burroughs tells his readers to engage in an imaginative exercise: "Revert to the time when life was not, when the globe was a half-incandescent ball, or when it was a seething, weltering waste of heated water, before the land had yet emerged from the waves, and yet you and I were there in the latent potencies of the chemically and dynamically warring elements. We were there. . . . The creative cosmic chemistry in due time brought us forth, and started us on the long road that led from the amoeba up to man" (187–88). Burroughs's repeated contention that we "were there" in this chemical brew he describes helps to create human interest in the story of evolution as "our" story. Nonetheless, Burroughs had trouble believing that human existence was purely the result of an accident of physicochemical forces.[4] Life's progression to the full complexity of the human condition was too magnificent. In fact, Burroughs's account of the miraculous evolutionary epic generally places the crown of creation on humankind. Eiseley, though generally more biocentric, would later build a similar construct to Burroughs's extreme contrast between the "amoeba" and "man."

In "The Snout," Eiseley attempts to comfort readers with the proposition that humans have gone through incredible, even grotesque, transformations. This recognition leads to a greater appreciation of natural forces. Eiseley is heartened that "a Devonian fish managed to end as a two-legged character with a straw hat" (*Immense* 47–48). Carlisle describes the joining together of the Devonian fish and human being as a "radical juxtaposition" (*Loren* 173). Indeed, the passage travels back and forth in time and across species at what might be an alarming rate for readers.

To make his larger point about life emerging from the waters to land, Eiseley reminds his reader, "There are things down there still coming ashore. Never make the mistake of thinking life is now adjusted for eternity" (*Immense* 48). With poetic prose and alliteration, Eiseley expounds on the notion of "coming ashore," as he emphasizes the snout's need to breathe oxygen for survival. A mysterious tone pervades his description: "It began as such things always begin — in the ooze of unnoticed swamps, in the darkness of the eclipsed moons. It began with a strangled gasping for air. . . . The pond was a place of reek and corruption, of fetid smells and oxygen-starved fish breathing through laborious gills" (49). The vividness of the image he presents is so graphic, it becomes indelibly implanted in the reader's head, as the snout "breathed air for a few hours and hobbled slowly along on the stumps of heavy fins," all in his preparation to come ashore (51).

Contemporary paleontology supports Eiseley's contention. In *Your Inner Fish*, Neil Shubin recounts his team's discovery of the fossil of *Tiktaalik*, the "intermediate between fish and primitive land-living animal" (24). Furthermore, Shubin explains how "this fossil says something about my own body" due to its head being "completely free of the shoulder," like amphibians, reptiles, and humans (26). The fossil record, Eiseley knew, tells us a great deal about particular aspects of our own physiological development.

Eiseley constructs the essential transition between water and land as a bridge to his introduction of essential occurrences that would later separate humankind from the rest of creation. Human physiological development is entirely dependent on the natural occurrences that preceded it. Eiseley gives full credit to "the Snout and the ooze" for their role in the development of humanity, contemplating that "perhaps there also, among rotting fish heads and blue, night-burning bog lights, moved the eternal mystery, the careful finger of God. The increase was not much. It was two bubbles, two small thin-walled little balloons at the end of the Snout's small brain. The cerebral hemispheres had appeared" (*Immense* 52). The appearance of the first inklings of the human brain is framed as a key event in geologic history; it is such an important event, that Eiseley even evokes God into this juncture of his narrative to make the story of evolution a wondrous spiritual tale. Eiseley seems to be in complete agreement with Burroughs's proclamation four decades earlier that "you and I were there" in the "creative cosmic chemistry." Eiseley speaks of the "first" appearance of certain traits to highlight the remarkable accomplishments of evolution. By its own physiological adaptation, the Snout, or freshwater crossopterygian, helped humans into their present existence in an essential way.

Just as Eiseley gives a prominent role to "first" appearances, such as that of the cerebral hemisphere, so did Burroughs before him: "We have a stake in all the past life of the globe. It is no doubt a scientific fact that your existence and mine were involved in the first cell that appeared, that the first zoophyte furthered our fortunes, that the first worm gave us a lift. Great good came to us when the first pair of eyes were invented" (27). The repetition of the trope "first" creates an epiphanic tone. Burroughs also lists the "first pair of lungs," "first four-chambered heart," and "first warm-blooded animal," describing them as the "pioneers" and "dim remote forebears" who "conserved and augmented the fund of life and passed it along" (*Time* 28). Such fusion of anatomical and physiological features of the remote past with humanity represents the most powerful form of "kinship" one can imagine.

To see one's own body as a result of evolutionary adaptation enables the reader to conceive of the deep unity between oneself and previous organic life forms. I refer to the understanding that human physiological development is due to a complex array of natural forces, inorganic and organic forms, our "ecophysiology." Through an awareness of ecophysiology, we can realize the power of evolutionary forces in our own bodies. The theme of an inescapable, deep physiological kinship saturated Burroughs's and Eiseley's view of evolutionary forces, and they attempted to nurture this perspective in their readers. They hoped to instill a sensibility that would enable readers to view their everyday surroundings with wonder and awe, envision evolutionary forces constantly at work, and see themselves as forever an inseparable part of them.

Along with the development of the human brain and consciousness came the ability to form symbols and develop language. According to Eiseley, the arrival of human beings marks the beginning of a new epoch. Therefore, he labels the human species as a "dream animal," in part because of its ability to form and communicate with symbols and also because of the newfound awareness of good and evil (*Immense* 107). What other creature has knowledge of moral concepts? This remarkable turn of evolutionary events led to a dream animal with incredible capabilities *and* responsibilities.

Toward the end of *Time and Change*, Burroughs asks moral questions, reflecting on the future of humanity. Will technological advances "cut short his history upon this planet?" (239). Such contemplations are part and parcel of what makes Burroughs's and Eiseley's literary naturalism so striking. Readers are given the chance to think about how they themselves might answer such questions. Burroughs offers his own concluding principle: "But of course, man's fate is bound up with the fate of the planet and of the biological tree of which he is one of the shoots" (240).[5]

Surely, Burroughs's and Eiseley's epic narratives of evolution lead to important implications for environmental protection. The form of literary naturalism they developed allows for the reader to ponder broad hypothetical scenarios about the future of the human race. Burroughs makes the claim that there are "hazards incident to an exceptional being upon this earth — a being that takes his fate in his own hands in a sense that no other creature does" (239). Similar moral reflections abound, as Eiseley makes recommendations regarding our fate: "The need is not really for more brains, the need is now for a gentler, a more tolerant people than those who won for us against the ice, the tiger, and the bear. The hand that hefted the ax, out of some old blind allegiance to the past fondles the machine gun as lovingly. It is a habit man will have to break to survive, but the roots go very deep" (*Immense* 140). Both felt the need to make the point that the fate of humanity and its habitat are now in our own hands. If we understand evolution as a miraculous event, we may increase our respect for the natural world and its life-generating capacities.

Accordingly, if we believe, like Eiseley and Burroughs, that evolution is ongoing, we must seriously consider what contemporary human practices might be doing to divert sequences of evolution. How can flora and fauna adapt to abrupt disruptions wrought in the atmosphere, ocean, and soil? How can we begin to measure possible changes in the future course of evolution in light of human technological advance? Will humans eventually consider the impact of their actions on the physiological development of themselves and other species?

The incredible uniqueness of the story of life on our planet should fortify us with a supreme appreciation for our surroundings. Burroughs's and Eiseley's wider conceptions of evolution lead to a broader understanding of humans' place in the cosmos. Stimulating and inspiring, their accounts of vital and far-reaching relations are crafted to invoke wonder, awe, and humility.

NOTES

1. Phillip Marshall Hicks credits Burroughs as the key figure responsible for the development of the natural history essay. Hicks recognizes that Burroughs had the ability "to state the facts about nature truthfully, and to make those facts interesting by relating them to human experience. To write simply, truthfully and lovingly of a man's kinship with her creatures — this is the spirit of the natural history essayist" (82). Hicks sums up Burroughs's standard for literary naturalism, Burroughs's more precise term for the genre of nature writing: "first, the writer must tell the truth as to fact; second, he must make that fact interesting and significant by relating it to man's experience; third, he must write with simplicity, sincerity and clearness of his own love of nature" (143). Surely, Eiseley also abides by these major precepts.

In his biography, *Loren Eiseley*, Andrew J. Angyal explains that Eiseley himself termed his literary work the "concealed essay," which "starts with a vivid anecdote or reminiscence and gradually expands it in a scientific or contemplative direction. The subject matter of the essay, whatever it may be, is framed or 'concealed' by the personal approach, which serves as a rhetorical device to engage the reader's attention" (39). According to Angyal, Eiseley devised "a new mode of visionary natural history to convey his impression of the protean quality of life as viewed from a geologic perspective. In his imaginative synthesis of literature and science, he combines narrative and hypothesis, fact and feeling, metaphor and exposition. The result is a new style of scientific literature, a new literary genre, and expansion of the personal essay for scientific purposes" (42).

2. In helping to expand literary naturalism as a genre, Burroughs recognizes the central importance of combining scientific understanding with the spirit of poetry. This wondrous combination still constitutes the most important guideline for any definition of literary naturalism. In *Leaf and Tendril* Burroughs writes, "The man of science . . . is contented if he may understand the things that others may enjoy; this is his enjoyment. Contemplation and absorption for the one; investigation and classification for the other" (2). Burroughs identifies two types of "enjoyment": one that occurs through scientific knowledge; the other by sensory-emotive engagement. Ideally, people engage in both types: "We probably all have, in varying degrees, one or the other of these ways of enjoying Nature; either the sympathetic and emotional enjoyment of her which the young and the artistic and the poetic temperament have, or the enjoyment through our knowing faculties afforded by natural science, or, it may be the two combined" (2–3). Burroughs clearly argues for the assimilation of scientific and emotive engagement.

3. Angyal discusses aspects of Eiseley's "The Enchanted Glass" that reveal two mindsets: the factual and contemplative. Eiseley finds "the Baconian 'severely experimental, unaesthetic and empirical' and its opposite 'literary, personal and contemplative.' Then he shows how they differ in attitude and purpose: the scientific attempting to discover the 'underlying laws' that govern the natural world, and the contemplative seeking to record personal responses to that world." Eiseley recognizes "a more personalized scientific literature that reflects a labor of love, where fact and knowledge are balanced by affection" (*Loren* 34–35). Angyal asserts that Eiseley developed "a new prose idiom for science and for literature," just as biographer E. Fred Carlisle agrees that Eiseley established "a new genre — imaginative synthesis of literature and science" (39). Mary Ellen Pitts notes that in Eiseley's view "science and literature need not be separated" and that his "genre is a hybrid that participates in but also enriches the long-established tradition of 'natural history'" (50).

4. For the most part, Eiseley and Burroughs embrace an organic view of the world as a thriving web of relations rather than a strictly physicochemical phenomenon, in which the natural world runs as a clock or mechanism. It has proven difficult for philosophers to accord mechanistic entities with moral value or for us to feel an emotional connection with a natural world that is simply a machine. Importantly, Eiseley and Burroughs supply readers with a literary naturalism full of poetic fervor, even when they consider physical and chemical forces. They are able to harmonize the mechanistic and the organic view, for they find wondrous organic potential in matter itself and appreciate the physical forces for their roles in creating and sustaining life. In fact, they both sing paeans and praises to chemical compounds and to what Burroughs calls "the divine soil" (*Leaf* 215). In "The Judgment of the Birds," Eiseley's ecstatic experience of a handful of soil becomes a miraculous vision. Appreciation is actually heightened by understanding the potency of near-at-hand matter (*Immense*).

5. According to Julianne Lutz Warren, Burroughs's narratives teach us that "if people could understand themselves as part of a narrative of such intimacy with the 'earth as a whole,' it seemed less likely that they would use scientific knowledge to deface, exhaust, or poison it. If people could see themselves as humble voyagers and kin with all life, the rest of America's conservation story might unfold as one not merely about a civilization concerned with responsible resource use, but also with beauty, peace, and health" (258–59).

13

Eiseley and Jung

Structuralism's Invisible Pyramid

JOHN NIZALOWSKI

In his essay "Loren Eiseley's *Immense Journey*," Andrew J. Angyal celebrates the revered nature writer's unconventional public stance: "As Eiseley warns his readers repeatedly, he is not a spokesman for conventional science. Instead, he is a poet-shaman, a wizard-alchemist who adopts the disguise of a changeling" (70). The roots of this unorthodox self-definition are found in the depth psychology of Carl Jung. There are two central tenets of Jung's philosophical system that range throughout Eiseley's writing: the importance of the collective unconscious in shaping the structures of human intelligence and the essential dualism of human culture and experience.

Beginning with *The Immense Journey*, Eiseley establishes the Jungian features of his writing. In the "The Dream Animal" — his discussion of the human evolutionary achievement of larger brains, language, and a sociocultural drive — Eiseley argues for the essential importance of the unconscious dream realm with its archetypal mythological symbolism in determining human cognition and perception. At the same time, he notes the dualisms that our mental structures produced: "He was becoming something the world had never seen before — a dream animal — living at least partially within a secret universe of his own creation. . . . The unseen gods, the powers behind the world of phenomenal appearance, began to stalk through his dreams. . . . The Eden of the eternal present that the animal world had known for ages was shattered at last. Through the human mind, time and darkness, good and evil, would enter and possess the world" (120–21). Nearly the same concepts appear over a decade later in "The Star Thrower," though in a darker, more pessimistic aspect: "Two forces struggle perpetually in our bodies: Yam, the old sea dragon of the original Biblical darkness, and, arrayed against him, some wisp of dancing light that would have us linger, wistful, in our human form. 'Tarry thou, till I come again' — an old legend survives among us of the admonition given by Jesus to the Wandering Jew. The words are applicable to all of us. Deep-hidden in the human psyche there is a similar injunction . . . a plea to wait upon some transcendent lesson preparing in the mind itself" (*Unexpected* 76).

However, while Eiseley's Jungian content is pervasive, he rarely mentions Jung directly in his writings. He quotes Jung in "Walden: Thoreau's Unfinished Business," and there are other scattered references to Jung, most notably in *The Lost Notebooks*, but overall, Eiseley's references to Jung are sparse. Still, as the quotes from *The Immense Journey* and *The Unexpected Universe* indicate, there is a strong Jungian influence on Eiseley's work. So why the near silence about Jung in the essays?

While Eiseley probably knew about Jung as early as the 1930s, he may not have actually studied Jung's writings until the 1960s. For instance, the first journal entry in *The Lost Notebooks* that cites Jung is from 1969 (189), and the pieces that actually mention Jung or use Jungian terms, such as "Walden: Thoreau's Unfinished Business" and "Dance of the Frogs," were published in *The Star Thrower*, his final collection. But then why do Jungian concepts span Eiseley's oeuvre, starting with *The Immense Journey*? It is likely that Eiseley, through the influences of structural anthropology, developed parallel ideas to Jung's and then realized the Jungian connection in the 1960s. A similar situation holds between Eiseley and the transcendentalists. As noted by Angyal in *Loren Eiseley*: "With Emerson and Thoreau, the issue is not so much their influence as a coincidence of their thought with Eiseley's. Quite correctly, Eiseley insists in his autobiography upon the originality of his thought, pointing out that he did not return to literary studies until late in his life" (88–89).

I believe the same could be said for Jung. Eiseley's background as an anthropologist exposed him to writers who influenced Jung or whom Jung influenced. Sociologists and anthropologists such as Emile Durkheim and Lucien Lévy-Bruhl, writers whom Eiseley would have encountered as an academic anthropologist in the 1930s and 1940s, influenced Jung while he was developing the theory of the collective unconscious. Also, we know that Eiseley owned books by Claude Lévi-Strauss, the founder of structural anthropology, and cited him in *The Invisible Pyramid* (Carrithers, Mumford 249). As explained by John Raphael Staude in his essay "From Depth Psychology to Depth Sociology," the differences between Jung and Lévi-Strauss are minor: "Freud, Jung, and Lévi-Strauss were committed to the notion that there is a hidden order in the mental and cultural life of mankind, and they were convinced that this hidden order can be discovered by human reason. Behind the diversity of human cultures they believed they saw an underlying unity, and they explained this unity in terms of what they believed to be a universality of unconscious processes in the human mind" (333). So, whether Eiseley gained his Jungian ideas directly or indirectly through his readings of Lévi-Strauss and other structural thinkers, Jungian systems of thought consciously shape his essays.

In "The Concept of the Collective Unconscious," Jung defines his theory of a deep, structural unconscious, a theory that fundamentally shapes Eiseley's ideas on the formation of human cognition and social systems. Jung begins by differentiating what he calls the "personal unconscious" from the collective unconscious. For Jung, the personal unconscious consists of material we have experienced in our life that has either been repressed or consciously forgotten. However, as Jung explains, "the contents of the collective unconscious have never been in consciousness, and therefore have never been individually acquired, but owe their existence exclusively to heredity." While complexes emerge from the personal unconscious, the collective unconscious is the realm of the archetypes. "The concept of the archetype," Jung writes, "indicates the existence of definite forms in the psyche which seem to be present always and everywhere." Jung compares the term "archetype" to ethnographer Adolf Bastian's "elementary thoughts" and to the terms developed by Emile Durkheim's sociological circle: Lucien Lévy-Bruhl's "représentations collective" and Henri Hubert and Marcel Mauss's "categories of the imagination" (*Collected* 9.1:42–43).

For Jung, the collective unconscious is a "psychic system of a collective, universal, and impersonal nature which is identical in all individuals" (42–43). It and its archetypes are thus unbounded by time or space and go back to the dawn of human consciousness. Elsewhere, Jung states, "The unconscious, as the totality of all archetypes, is the deposit of all human experience right back to its remotest beginnings" (8:157). According to Jung, the collective unconscious, as the interaction of the deepest aspects of consciousness with the world, serves as a platform for all human culture and endeavor (9.1:33).

The deep-time roots of the collective unconsciousness and its archetypal patterns clearly appealed to Eiseley, who was obsessed by time and its relationship to human perception. "The Angry Winter" is one of Eiseley's finest portrayals of the immensity of time as found within the collective unconscious. In it, the author, working in his study past midnight, the time of the dream realm, absently places a ten-thousand-year-old leg bone of a bison on the floor. His dog, Wolf, grabs it and begins "mouthing it with a fierce intensity I had never seen exhibited by him before." Eiseley moves forward to retrieve the bone, but is met by snarling teeth — this from a dog that regards his master as "the most loved object in his universe." Eiseley realizes with a start that the dog has reverted to unconscious patterns from the last Ice Age: "A low, steady rumbling began to rise in his chest, something out of the long gone midnight. There was nothing in that bone to taste, but ancient shapes were moving in his mind and determining his utterance." With an even greater shock, Eiseley realizes that the ancient archetypal patterns had seized him too: "Had I not for a moment, in the grip of that savage utterance, been about to respond, to hurl myself upon him over an invisible haunch ten thousand years removed?" (*Unexpected* 94–95).

Eiseley's encounter with unconscious patterns formed during the Würmian Ice Age also occurs in "The Last Neanderthal." However, this time, it is a human intersection that sparks the racial memories. While at the site of a paleontological dig near Bridgeport, Nebraska, Eiseley finds himself face-to-face with a girl who is a throwback to a Neanderthal human (Christianson, *Fox* 118). The girl is there to deliver eggs from a nearby farm, and as Eiseley studies her, he realizes she is an atavistic throwback, with all the facial and bodily characteristics of a Neanderthal. "We are those who eliminated her long ago," Eiseley writes in reaction to her unease. "It is like an old scene endlessly re-enacted. Only the chipped stones and the dead game are lacking" (*Unexpected* 223).

As Robert G. Franke explains in "Blue Plums and Smoke," Eiseley in this scene has dropped the reader into Mircea Eliade's vision of sacred time, which rises above and beyond the historical and parallels Jung's ideas of timelessness in the collective unconscious. "In the elevation from linear to mythic time," Franke writes of Eiseley, "he offered a kind of religious or sacred experience" (147–48). In "The Time Effacers," Eiseley explains the timelessness of sacred time: "Sacred time is of another and higher dimension than secular time. It is, in reality, timeless; past and future are contained within it. All of primitive man's meaningful relationship to his world is thus not history, not causality in a scientific sense, but a mythical ordering of life which has not deviated and will not in future deviate from the traditions of eternity" (*Invisible* 112–13).

Of course, seizure by deep time and the collective unconscious is not always benign. In "The Relations between the Ego and the Unconscious," Jung warns against the power of archetypal energy to overcome the individual personality: "The forces that burst out of the collective psyche have a confusing and blinding effect. One result of the dissolution of the persona is a release of involuntary fantasy, which is apparently nothing else than the specific activity of the collective psyche. This activity throws up contents whose existence one had never suspected before. But as the influence of the collective unconscious increases, so the conscious mind loses its power of leadership. Imperceptibly it becomes the led, while an unconscious and impersonal process gradually takes control" (*Collected* 7:160–61). Jung could be describing the forces at work in Eiseley's short story, "The Dance of the Frogs."

Inspired by H. P. Lovecraft, Eiseley's tale begins with the unnamed narrator, presumably Eiseley himself, giving a lecture at the Explorers Club in Philadelphia about the shaking tent rite of the Naskapi of Labrador. Eiseley explains that the shaking tent rite has parallels with the medium's cabinet, where sleight-of-hand tricks and seemingly disembodied voices produce supposedly supernatural effects. But for the Naskapi, this is serious business, since the shaking tent rite is their mode of contact with the game lords, the outsize leaders of each species, whom the Naskapi must propitiate to have a successful hunt.

As Eiseley gives his lecture, a member of the Explorers Club, Albert Dreyer, begins to ask questions. Dreyer, we are told, was once a brilliant zoologist "famous for his remarkable experiments on amphibians." However, after his initial fame, he has become an eccentric hermit, who "kept to his solitary room, his solitary drink, and his accustomed spot by the fire" (*Star* 106). Dreyer's questions become increasingly more probing, and when he asks if the game lords are visible, Eiseley's answer evokes Jung's observations on the collective unconscious: "In a sense they remind one of the concept of the archetypes, the originals behind the petty show of our small, transitory existence. They are the immortal renewers of substance — the force behind and above animate nature" (107). But when Dreyer asks if Eiseley believes in the game lords, Eiseley's response is more prosaic and positivistic: "'My dear fellow,' — I shrugged and glanced at the smiling audience — 'I have seen many strange things, many puzzling things, but I am a scientist'" (108).

Later, Eiseley regrets his brusqueness toward the old gentleman, and he sits down with Dreyer and asks for his life story. As Dreyer begins his strange tale, Eiseley describes the pair sitting in a darkened room, a passage that evokes the solitary desk lamp in "The Angry Winter" and the "little circle of light" (*Unexpected* 93–94) that Eiseley leaves to fight Wolf for the ten-thousand-year-old bone: "There were just two men under a lamp, and around them a great waiting silence. Out to the ends of the universe, I thought fleetingly, that's the way with man and his lamps. One has to huddle in, there's so little light and so much space" (*Star* 109). With this imagery, Eiseley has plunged us into the vast, dark unknown of the collective unconscious. Dreyer's story explains why he can no longer work with frogs. One night, after his young wife died, he was taking a walk near his laboratory down a lonely roadway that ends at the Schuylkill River. It was spring, and thousands of frogs were out, skipping and hopping across the pavement. Dreyer began to skip with the frogs and soon became gay and frenzied in his movements. What he has done is to throw open the doors to his deep unconscious, and as Jung explains in the earlier quote, "the forces that burst out of the collective psyche . . . result [in] the dissolution of the persona [and] a release of involuntary fantasy." In this case, the involuntary fantasy manifested as the game lord of the frogs: "It was only as we passed under a street lamp," Dreyer explains, "that I noticed, beside my own bobbing shadow, another great, leaping grotesquerie that had an uncanny suggestion of the frog world about it" (113).

The unconscious material had taken control, and Dreyer could not stop skipping, his pace quickening. Finally, when the river came into sight, Dreyer saw a cross formed from the support struts of a streetlamp, and by calling out to God, he broke the spell. Eiseley then pulls the story back to the framework of the Explorers Club, where, under their solitary lamp, Dreyer proves his story by pulling off a glove and revealing a "webbed batrachian hand" (115).

From a Jungian standpoint, it does matter whether the fictional Dreyer "really" has an amphibian hand, the result of his encounter with the game lord of the frogs, or simply a hand burned from the various toxic chemicals that any zoologist involved with tissue transplants and specimen preservation would have around the lab (108). As Jung states, "Equally childish is the prejudice against the role which mythological assumptions play in the life of the psyche. Since they are not 'true,' it is argued, they have no place in a scientific explanation. But mythologems *exist*, even though their statements do not coincide with our incommensurable idea of 'truth'" (*Collected* 8:91). What is clear is that Dreyer, primed by grief for his deceased wife and inspired by the conditions of the moment, has entered the realm of the collective unconscious, where he encounters the powerful archetype of the game lord of the frogs.

Eiseley's fascination for frogs and toads as totem animals manifested itself thirty years earlier in an unfinished short story titled "The Toad." In this story an archaeologist uncovers a skull in a ceremonial cave near an Anasazi ruin somewhere in the American Southwest. Inside the skull, there is a frog. (In Eiseley's summary and unfinished text of the story, sometimes it is a frog that the archaeologist finds in the skull, at other times, a toad.) The frog jumps out, and over the days and weeks begins to grow, becoming the size of a dog. At the same time, the rains start up and begin to flood the Pueblo Indians' village and fields. The Indians warn the archaeologist that the skull must be returned to the ceremonial cave, or the disastrous rains will continue. The archaeologist does this, but the rains do not stop. At last, a medicine man visits the archaeologist, and "offers to 'lay' the ghost" of the frog. The shaman "makes fire under a blanket; rains intensify, trying to put out the fire. There is a sense of monstrous hopping 'elementals' outside the circle." Finally, after a pyrotechnic lightning storm, "a small frog, the original captor" hops out from the darkness and into the circle of firelight. With this arrival, the rains stop (*Lost* 53).

Many of the elements that appear in "The Dance of the Frogs" occur in "The Toad": a rational scientist having an irrational mythological experience, the efficacy of mystical action, outsize frog game lords, water as a manifestation of the unconscious, and the darkness beyond a small circle of light representing the unconscious material. Jung would say that the unnamed archaeologist and Dreyer have invited the archetypal energies of the unconscious into the open and have directly experienced their power. Scholar and archaeologist Marija Gimbutas, in writing about the ancient European association of frogs with pregnancy, notes that "in the Jungian psychology of dreams, this creature, not yet a human being, represents an unconscious impulse that has a definite tendency to become conscious" (251). This is clearly the case in both "The Dance of the Frogs" and "The Toad," both stories exploring the manifestation of inner archetypes in the outer universe.

Eiseley's fascination with the mythological imagery of the frog and its connection with the unconscious resulted in two short stories, which in itself is a demonstration of Jung's belief that creative material arises from the collective unconscious. In his essay "On the Relation of Analytical Psychology to Poetry," Jung explains, "I am assuming that the work of art we propose to analyze, as well as being symbolic, has its source not in the *personal unconscious* of the poet, but in the sphere of unconscious mythology whose primordial images are the common heritage of mankind. I have called this sphere the *collective unconscious*." Jung notes that even the scientific paradigm and its discoveries derive from the unconscious: "For it is out of himself and out of this peculiar constitution that man has produced his sciences. They are *symptoms* of his psyche" (*Collected* 15:80, 8:389).

Eiseley agreed with Jung that the unconscious is the source of creative thought, both artistic and scientific. In "Man against the Universe," Eiseley declares, "For out of the depths of unreason, the murkiness of the subconscious, have come also some of the most poignant works of great art and literature. Even scientists have, on occasion, acknowledged indebtedness to that subterranean river" (*Star* 210).

He takes this concept further in "The Hidden Teacher" by adding dreams as a direct source of creativity: "We of this modern time know other things of dreams, but we know also that they can be interior teachers and healers as well as the anticipators of disaster. It has been said that great art is the night thought of man. It may emerge without warning from the soundless depths of the unconscious, just as a supernovae may blaze up suddenly in the farther reaches of void space" (*Unexpected* 64). Examples abound of Eiseley's belief that dreams and visions are a major source of creative and scientific inspiration. In his biography of Loren Eiseley, *Fox at the Wood's Edge*, Gale E. Christianson relates Eiseley's intense disapproval when his friend, the writer Dorothy Thomas, burns her dream journal, thereby denying herself an important creative source (151). Later, Christianson quotes Eiseley's letter to Dr. Vernon Brooks, director of the C. G. Jung Foundation for Analytical Psychiatry: "It should be of interest to the society that some of these poems have arisen out of dreams so powerful that I have literally leaped out of bed, dashed to my study, and written them down in almost a frenzy before they departed." After Christianson notes that "Eiseley ascribed the process to the impulses and motivations of the subconscious," the biographer describes Eiseley's fascination with the Ouija board and other methods of communing with spirits (381–82). Leslie E. Gerber and Margaret McFadden identify this as Eiseley's "night-stalking side . . . a surreal world, a domain wherein the vivid illogic of nightmares and semiconscious musings reassembles things and connections (128). It's this "night-stalking side" that erupts in "The Innocent Fox," when Eiseley sees, running alongside his automobile in the depths of the midnight Pennsylvania woods, a shape-shifting form that keeps passing through a fantastic metamorphosis that includes wolf, dog, and the windigo, the Iroquois monster who eats humans (*Unexpected* 202).

Eiseley's essay "The Mind as Nature" also explores this ground. In it, he quotes psychiatrist Lawrence Kubie, who states that "the creative person . . . has retained his capacity to use his pre-conscious functions more freely than is true of others . . ." (*Night* 218). By quoting Kubie, Eiseley wishes to emphasize the uniqueness of the artistic vision, a vision that the artist often has to pursue in solitude. It is also a vision that can set the artist apart from the rest of humanity.

Jung concurs with this assessment:

> The man who takes to the back streets and alleys because he cannot endure the broad highway will be the first to discover the psychic elements that are waiting to play their part in the life of the collective. Here the artist's relative lack of adaptation turns out to be his advantage; it enables him to follow his own yearnings far from the beaten path, and to discover what it is that would meet the unconscious needs of his age. Thus, just as the one-sidedness of the individual's conscious attitude is corrected by reactions from the unconscious, so art represents a process of self-regulation in the life of nations and epochs. (*Collected* 15:83)

Jung's position that the creative mind ranges beyond the norm and thereby seizes the unconscious material that then reshapes the world finds a clear echo in "The Mind as Nature" by Loren Eiseley:

> It is frequently the tragedy of the great artist, as it is of the great scientist, that he frightens the ordinary man. If he is more than a popular storyteller it may take humanity a generation to absorb and grow accustomed to the new geography with which the scientist or artist presents us. . . . Subconsciously the genius is feared as an image breaker; frequently he does not accept the opinions of the mass, or man's opinion of himself. He has voiced through the ages, in one form or another, this very loneliness and detachment which Dewey saw so clearly at the outcome of our extending knowledge. . . . The artist is frequently a human mirror. If what we see there displeases us . . . we tend to revolt, not against ourselves, but in order to martyrize the unfortunate soul who forced us into self-examination. (*Night* 208–9)

Later in the essay, Eiseley applies this observation to Henry David Thoreau, his favorite example of the lone artist and philosopher. Eiseley's admiration for the author of *Walden* is well documented, and he included three essays on him in *The Star Thrower* (Angyal, *Loren* 88). One of these, "Walden: Thoreau's Unfinished Business," uses a passage by Jung on alchemy to depict Thoreau: "Medieval alchemy prepared the greatest attack on the divine order of the universe which mankind has ever dared. Alchemy is the dawn of the age of natural sciences which, through the *daemonium* of the scientific spirit, drove nature and her forces into the service of mankind to a hitherto unheard of degree. . . . Technics and science have indeed conquered the world, but whether the soul has gained thereby is another matter." Eiseley describes Thoreau with this quote for two reasons. The first is the quote's warning of science's limitations as a tool to understand nature and our deeper selves. Eiseley goes on to write, "Thoreau was indeed a spiritual wanderer through the deserts of the modern world. Almost by instinct he rejected that beginning wave of industrialism which was later to so entrance his century" (236). But second, as this quote implies, Jung viewed alchemists as spiritual adventurers who wandered in the soul's interior, and Eiseley viewed Thoreau as a wanderer who rejected both the city and the country, spending his short lifetime restlessly searching for transcendence and understanding.

Joseph Campbell, in his introduction to *The Portable Jung*, notes that, for Jung, alchemy acted as a bridge between the esoteric Christian tradition called Gnosticism and modern psychology, with its study of the unconscious (xxix). In this sense, Thoreau is an alchemist, acting as a bridge between the natural world and the human world, and between the Paleolithic world of the American Indian and the dawning industrial world of the European American (*Star* 237). Eiseley writes that the "alchemist's touchstone in Thoreau was to give him sight, not power" (238) and inspired Thoreau's concept of the "mindprint" — a term describing how an arrowhead implies the mind that made it. For Eiseley, the term "mindprint" indicates Thoreau's profound artistic vision, which can find the world's intimate connections and convert one substance into another, like the alchemists of old (241). Eiseley believes that Thoreau transforms his readers as well, and while most of us can never attain the purity of Thoreau's vision, we can at least share in his transcendent understanding of nature and our place in it: "Here and there alone the true alchemist of Jung's thought must come to exist in each of us. It is ours to transmute, not iron, not copper, not gold, but our tracks through nature, see them finally attended by self-knowledge, by the vision of the universal eye, that faculty possessed by the alchemist at Walden Pond" (243).

In "Walden: Thoreau's Unfinished Business," when Eiseley refers to "Walden's eye of ice and eye of summer," he is exploring another major Jungian theme — duality (238). Dualism and dualistic vision are significant motifs throughout Eiseley's writing and have their roots, like archetypes and the collective unconscious, in Jung's observations on psychological and social structures. Jung outlined a myriad of dualities involved in the human psyche, beginning with conscious/unconscious and continuing through extrovert/introvert, feeling/thinking, and sensation/intuition ("Approaching" 47–49). He also found dualities in archetypal imagery. So, for instance, the feminine aspect of a male, the *anima*, is balanced by the masculine aspect of the female, the *animus* (von Franz, "Process" 186, 198); and our self-aware personality is balanced by the aggregate of all our characteristics that we refuse to acknowledge — the archetype called the shadow (174). The goal of Jungian psychotherapy is to merge these opposites, both conscious and unconscious, into an integrated psyche in a process called individuation (169). The transcendent function, which is a synthesis of the opposite energies in the psyche, is the agent of this fusion (Jung, *Collected* 8:73).

Eiseley often evokes this Jungian concept of duality and the imagery of dual vision. For instance, in "The Innocent Fox," Eiseley writes, "Some men are daylight readers, who peruse the ambiguous wording of clouds or the individual letter shapes of wandering birds. Some, like myself, are librarians of the night, whose ephemeral documents consist of root-inscribed bones or whatever rustles in thickets upon solitary walks" (*Unexpected* 194–95). In "The Mind as Nature," Eiseley actually uses the Jungian terms of introverted and extroverted to describe his childhood worlds — one dark and interior, the other outward and active (*Night* 195). In *The Invis-*

ible Pyramid, Eiseley sets the "eye atop Palomar Mountain" against the eye of an electron microscope: "Both eyes are important. They are the eyes of understanding. They balance and steady each other" (88). Later, he describes a fish that possesses a split eye that devotes half its vision to the air, the other half to the water: "In this quality the fish resembles Blake, the English poet who asserted he saw with a double vision into a farther world than the natural" (119–20).

As does Jung, Eiseley believes that these dual systems need to merge to create an integrated vision, a unified totality. In "The Golden Alphabet," Eiseley argues that there are two pairs of "spectacles" that philosophers use to view the world: one looks to the past, the other to the future. He warns that "if we fail to use both pairs of spectacles equally, our view of ourselves and of the world is apt to be distorted, since we can never see completely without the use of both" (*Unexpected* 125). In "The Long Loneliness," Eiseley's essay on dolphin intelligence, he ends by proposing, "It is as though both man and porpoise were each part of some great eye which yearned to look both outward on eternity and inward to the sea's heart" (*Star* 43).

Even when Eiseley is not using the metaphor of dual vision, he favors the synthesis of opposites. "The Illusion of Two Cultures" portrays Eiseley's belief that a sense of aesthetics helped Cro-Magnon humans to survive, since they lingered over their tool making out a sense of beauty and craft. Eiseley goes on to argue that the modern split between utility and art, science and creativity, is artificial and dangerous, because to face the future successfully, we need to reconnect the aesthetic and utilitarian impulses found in Cro-Magnon humanity (275–78).

"Science and the Sense of the Holy" covers similar territory. While the essay's central tension between scientists who are reductionist and scientists who have a sense of wonder — personified by Sigmund Freud and Charles Darwin — is never resolved, Eiseley does merge science with a sense of mysticism in the figure of Ishmael, who alone survives the confrontation between Ahab and Moby Dick. Ishmael is the "wondering man . . . the acceptor of all races and their gods" (199).

The essay "The Star Thrower" also seeks to reconcile science with a transcendent sense of existence. In "Coasts Demanding Shipwreck," Anthony Lioi proposes that in "The Star Thrower," Eiseley "offers a new synthesis of love and analytic knowledge, a balance between self-protection through rational control and ecstatic solidarity with other creatures" (43).

In the essay, Eiseley is vacationing on the coast of a tourist island he identifies as Costabel. There, an abundance of sea life washes ashore, most of it dead and dying. What isn't dead is harvested by the natives and tourists. However, one day, Eiseley discovers a man who flings live starfish into the surf in the hope that they will survive both the human and tidal slaughter. At this point, Eiseley's response to this action is rather fatalistic. "I do not collect," he says to the star thrower. "Death is the only successful collector" (*Unexpected* 72).

However, the star thrower's actions send Eiseley into a crisis. He wonders if compassion has any place in a cold, mechanistic universe where death always triumphs. He pictures Costabel as a desert island, and "in the desert . . . the voices of God and the Devil are scarcely distinguishable" (73). Eiseley cannot find his way through the pair of opposites created by his encounter with the star thrower. Jung explains that before the process of individuation can proceed, a person needs to descend into a personal abyss, a process that, in the words of Jungian scholar Marie-Louise von Franz, "generally begins with a wounding of the personality and the suffering that accompanies it." During this time, everything may seem "meaningless and empty" ("Process" 169–70).

In "The Star Thrower," Eiseley plunges into a lengthy journey through his memories and in doing so develops more dualities. He ponders the difference between the Plains and the mountains, with the safety of the Plains representing the realm of nature, and the dangerous mountains corresponding to human intellect. This second path seems to have brought us great understanding and material success, but Eiseley warns that there is a trickster involved, a mythological version of Jung's shadow archetype, in the way that evolutionary science has blurred the dualities we thought operated as absolutes in the universe:

> A hidden dualism that has haunted man since antiquity runs across his religious conceptions as the conflict between good and evil. It persists in

the modern world of science under other guises. It becomes chaos versus form or antichaos. Form, since the rise of the evolutionary philosophy, has taken on an illusory quality. Our apparent shapes no longer have the stability of a single divine fiat. Instead, they waver and dissolve into the unexpected. . . . It is as if at our backs, masked and demonic, moved the trickster as I have seen his role performed among the remnant of a savage people long ago. (*Unexpected* 75–77)

For Eiseley, that trickster symbolizes the process by which logical positivism robbed humanity of love, compassion, and a sense of the mystical. His figures of this shadow realm are Freud, Einstein, Darwin, and Bacon — all men whom he deeply admires — yet their ideas have revealed a world wrapped in bitter survival, naked power, and cold equations. The way of post-Darwin humanity is to devour the starfish on the beaches of Costabel, not save them.

From a Jungian standpoint, Eiseley is seeking individuation, integration into the whole, and has descended into a mental labyrinth in which life's pairs of opposites are tearing him apart. Eiseley, a scientist, believes in the need to see the world as it really is, to view it with cool, rational eyes. But his heart says to pity the world, to feel compassion for all people and creatures who suffer. It is like a Zen koan — those Buddhist word puzzles that cannot be answered logically and batter the minds of the monks who attempt to solve them. This may explain why the essay begins with a quote from Seccho, a Zen patriarch: "Who is the man walking in the Way? / An eye glaring in the skull" (67).

Now is the time, according to Jung, for the transcendent function to appear and reconcile the irreconcilable: "The shuttling to and fro of arguments and affects represents the transcendent function of opposites. The confrontation of the two positions generates a tension charged with energy and creates a living, third thing — not a logical stillbirth in accordance with the principle *tertium non datur* but a movement out of the suspension between opposites, a living birth that leads to a new level of being, a new situation" (*Collected* 8:90). With the emotional memories of his deaf mother, who in this piece represents the Gnostic sacred feminine, sending him over the edge, Eiseley reaches Jung's crucible: "There was, at last, an utter stillness, a waiting as though for a cosmic judgment." And the judgment indeed arrives, as the transcendent function heals the rift: "But I *do* love the world. . . . I love its small ones, the things beaten in the strangling surf, the bird, singing, which flies and falls and is not seen again. . . . I love the lost ones, the failures of the world" (*Unexpected* 86).

Eiseley has passed through the gateless gate of the koan: he has attained individuation. When next he goes on the beach, he joins the star thrower in tossing living creatures back into the surf. As Anthony Lioi declares, "Eiseley is a seeker who achieved enlightenment through the intervention of a bodhisattva. The essay then becomes a kind of 'Star Sutra,' if you will, and Eiseley's throwing can be seen as the practice of the pledge, 'Sentient beings are numberless; I vow to save them'" (58).

Eiseley's Jungian dialectic reaches a climax in *The Invisible Pyramid*, since in this work, the crisis is planetary, not personal. As Mary Ellen Pitts states, "*The Invisible Pyramid* is Eiseley's strongest expression of his ecological ethic" (228). In it, Eiseley describes the collective unconscious as an invisible pyramid, "a spatial form embedded in the human conscious- ness" (Pitts 228), leading us toward space but also pushing us to destroy our home world, as if we are collectively Faust and "never at rest in the world" or, worse yet, some kind of slime mold sending out spores into space (*Invisible* 85, 89–90). The transcendent function of this collision of forces is to reconcile the two paths outlined in "The Star Thrower": the natural world of the Plains with the human intellectual world of the mountains.

In the book's final essay, "The Last Magician," Eiseley argues that the time has come for these two worlds to be brought together. He names them the first and second worlds, and the key to their connection is for humanity to apply the lessons of compassion from the axial religions — Christianity, Buddhism, and Taoism — to nature: "Today man's mounting numbers and his technological power to pollute his environment reveal a single demanding necessity: the necessity for him consciously to reenter and preserve, for his own safety, the old first world from which he originally emerged. His second world, drawn from his own brain, has brought him far, but it cannot take him out of nature, nor can he live by escaping in the second world alone. He must now incorporate from the wisdom of the axial thinkers an ethic not alone directed towards his fellows, but extended to the living world around him" (154–55).

Even though *The Invisible Pyramid* takes the path of individuation to a planetary level, Eiseley believes that the encounter with the collective unconscious and the journey for individuation are profoundly personal experiences. He examines this personal level most intimately in his poetry, especially in his first volume of verse, *Notes of an Alchemist*. In it Eiseley again uses the figure of the alchemist, the magician who transforms matter into spirit, as a Jungian metaphor for the enlightened psyche's power to link consciousness with the unconscious and the outer material world with the inner psychological realm. As Eiseley writes in the collection's preface, "The volume tells its own story, no doubt, of the eccentricities and diversities of my life — a kind of alchemy, in other words, by which a scientific man has transmuted for his personal pleasure the sharp images of his profession into something deeply subjective." Eiseley then explains how the alchemical process of writing these poems should, "if the psychologists are right," heal him by allowing him to "rest more easily hereafter" (11).

Of the Jungian images examined in Eiseley's poetry, one of the most notable is the stone as a symbol of transformation and of the ultimate, individuated Self. In "The Process of Individuation," von Franz explains the metaphor behind the alchemist's stone: "Medieval alchemists, who searched for the secret of matter in a prescientific way, hoping to find God in it, or at least the working of divine activity, believed that this secret was embodied in their famous 'philosophers' stone.' But some of the alchemists dimly perceived that their much-sought-after stone was a symbol of something that can be found only within the psyche of man" ("Process" 225).

A number of Eiseley's poems illuminate this alchemical meaning of stones and minerals. For instance, in the title poem to *Notes of an Alchemist*, Eiseley describes how crystals "grow / under fantastic pressures in the deep / crevices and confines of / the earth" (lines 1–4). He then describes himself metaphorically as a crystal that has gained wisdom through its metamorphic experiences. He has become, he writes, someone "who conceives therefore / that out of order and disorder / perpetually clashing and reclashing / come the worlds" (78–80).

Von Franz also notes that "it is relevant that a stone is itself something permanent." This permanence represents the unchanging nature of the true, individuated Self ("Process" 226). Eiseley illuminates this symbol in "The Hand Ax," an ode to the ancient stone ax described in "The Illusion of Two Cultures" and other essays: "this flint ax / will not alter / form like the old affectionate word for elf child, changeling, / transformed / slowly / to oaf / in a bleaker time. / The ax may have been out of fashion / a hundred millennia / but you can still / recognize its true purpose" (*Notes*, lines 48–58).

In "The Figure in the Stone" Eiseley evokes the Neolithic goddess, an image from mythology that Jung viewed as an anima guide to the unconscious (von Franz, "Process" 196–98). A man brings Eiseley what he believes is a pre-Columbian image of woman etched on a rock found in a newly dug subway tunnel. Eiseley determines that random glacial scratches cover the rock, and the image is in the worker's imagination. But when he explains this, the discoverer of the stone grows angry, for as with the alchemical stone of the Self, this etched rock represents the truth of an individual experience. Eiseley writes, "I saw it was an icon / and an object / such as men cherished in lost caves when only / the sacred mothers of the tribe / were real" (*Notes*, lines 50–54). Eiseley tells the man to treasure the stone, for "It is dark . . . down where / you've been working. / Maybe you've seen what can't be seen up here" (55–57).

Eiseley explores many other Jungian concepts in *Notes of an Alchemist*. For instance, as von Franz notes, "The Self is often symbolized as an animal, representing our instinctive nature and its connectedness with one's surroundings" ("Process" 220). Eiseley plays with this image in "The Changelings." In the poem, he identifies with canine predators, seeing their faces everywhere, and trying on "fox masks, wolf masks . . . / as if I were a savage" (lines 1–2). He evokes Jungian duality in "The Cardinals" when he describes God creating both good and evil, and the collective unconscious in "The Lost Plateau," with its deep, underground pool, "where all time has ceased," and its blind, prophetic "fish . . . tracing / upon those growing crystals runes so intricate" that only the ultimate Self, represented as "he who thundered in the torrents," could understand them (18–21). Indeed, an entire essay could be devoted to the Jungian materials found in Eiseley's poetry, particularly in collections published before his death: *Notes of an Alchemist* and *The Innocent Assassins*.

The Jungian motifs found in Eiseley's essays, stories, and poems provide one of their vital, timeless aspects. In 1972 von Franz proclaimed, "Because Jung's work encompasses so many varied fields of interest, his influence is still only in its beginnings. Today, interest in Jung is growing year by year" (*Jung* 3). In the decades following von Franz's prediction, Jung's ideas have indeed remained central to intellectual discourse. Post-Jungians, scholars from many disciplines who have updated and transformed Jung's concepts, have kept his writings relevant well into the twenty-first century. Naturalist Edward O. Wilson, in *Consilience*, his book on the "intrinsic unity of knowledge" (8), links Jungian archetypes to the possibility that "the brain is genetically predisposed to fabricate certain images and episodes more than others" and that Jung's theories "can perhaps be made more concrete and verifiable through neurobiology" (78). In a different, deconstructionist vein, Pellegrino D'Acierno and Karin Barnaby find a parallel between Jung's "polaristic structure of the psyche" and Jacques Derrida's "violent hierarchy" of philosophy and consciousness (xxiv–xxv). Edward S. Casey discusses a phenomenological link between Jung and the founders of deconstructionist systems of thought: "If Jung's suspicion of language vis-à-vis images is a suspicion of specifically metaphysical language, he is in league with Heidegger and Derrida in their assiduous efforts to deconstruct metaphysics" (320). And in the field of psychotherapy, as explained by Loura Griessel and Martina Kotzé, feminist post-Jungians are taking Jung's archetypal tropes and reformulating them for a new social condition: "The integration of this work with the model of individuation offers an understanding of the possible Feminine and Masculine archetypal images and modes of consciousness that are constellated in contemporary women, as well as the subtle tensions that they may have to endure as the Self emerges and comes into being. This understanding would not have been possible without the re-evaluation, re-formulation, and adaptation of Jung's seminal ideas. Through such re-thinking, a more extensive exploration and understanding of contemporary women's psychic processes becomes possible" (210).

Even the appearance of previously unpublished work by Jung continues to transform and revivify the study of his oeuvre, most notably with the 2009 appearance of *The Red Book*, the journal of Jung's exploration of his own psyche. As noted by its editor, Sonu Shamdasani, "This publication marks a caesura, and opens the possibility of a new era in the understanding of Jung's work" (221).

Loren Eiseley, through his personal and highly perceptive discussion of Jungian concepts, created a body of work that is vital to the ongoing examination of Jung's depth psychology, a process that Eiseley would certainly have encouraged. In his essay "The Inner Galaxy," Eiseley argues that "the venture into space is meaningless unless it coincides with a certain interior expansion, an ever growing universe within, to correspond with the far flight of the galaxies our telescopes follow from without" (*Unexpected* 174). Eiseley knew that Jung was one of the pioneers of that "growing universe within" and thus integrated Jung's ideas with his own literary attempts to understand both the inner and outer cosmos — to see the world with the "two-lensed eye" he describes in *The Invisible Pyramid* (119). Angyal is right to name Eiseley both alchemist and shaman, for like the alchemist he has united a knowledge of the material world with spiritual wisdom, and like the shaman he has journeyed far to bring back a message of great importance to his tribe, the human race. The books that resulted from Eiseley's alchemical and shamanic voyage will endure as classic guides to the evolution of human consciousness.

14

From the American Great
Plains to the Steppes of Russia

Loren Eiseley Transplanted

DIMITRI N. BRESCHINSKY

Please, never despise the translator. He is the mailman of human civilization.

ALEKSANDR PUSHKIN

Loren Eiseley was born in Lincoln, Nebraska, under the open skies of the Great Plains, and except for a brief business trip to England in 1951, never left the American mainland (see Christianson, *Fox* 298). Had he traveled to the steppes of southern Russia, he would probably not have felt out of place, recognizing in the gently rolling hills of the countryside the flat, treeless terrain of his childhood. The difference between the Plains and the steppes is to a large extent linguistic.

The reference to transplantation in the title of this essay is, of course, a metaphor for literary translation, which for centuries has served as a beneficent link between Russia and the West. Even after the Iron Curtain came down on Eastern Europe following World War II, the country was not totally isolated. A great deal of contemporary American literature was translated into Russian during the Cold War, which overlapped with Eiseley's most productive years. Thanks to a well-organized and highly professional translating industry that for years operated in the former Soviet Union, Russian readers were well acquainted with the works of such diverse writers as J. D. Salinger and John Steinbeck, Ernest Hemingway and Arthur Hailey (the latter's *Airport* was also a Russian best seller), but until recently Loren Eiseley was not among them.

Eiseley has been hailed as the Thoreau of the twentieth century, and his works have helped to inspire the environmental movement of our day. As was Thoreau, Eiseley was more interested in humanity's place in the universe than in partisan politics. Why then was he not translated into Russian, along with Salinger, Hailey, and others? Why did the Soviet literary establishment completely overlook him? It is an interesting question, and I shall return to it later. What concerns me more at this point is how that lacuna was ultimately filled.

INITIAL PUBLICATIONS IN
PERIODICALS AND THE FIRST BOOK

My report will of necessity be personal, because it traces my particular journey into Eiseley's universe and my fitful attempts at cross-cultural pollination. A bilingual who teaches Russian at Purdue University, I have for some time now been translating my favorite Eiseley pieces into my first language. It all began some twenty-five years ago, when I happened to come across *Time* magazine's 1962 special edition of Eiseley's first book, *The Immense Journey*. The essays it contains were so compelling that I resolved to search for other works by the author and soon had a virtually complete collection, including many first editions.

At about the same time, while discussing American nature writing with a Russian friend in Moscow who knew no English and had never heard of that literary mode, I got the urge to share with him an Eiseley essay and set about translating "The Flow of the River." Why did I choose Loren Eiseley and not, say, Peter Matthiessen, Annie Dillard, Barry Lopez, David Quammen, or any number of other outstanding American nature writers, not to mention Aldo Leopold and Rachel Carson? With the single exception of Leopold's *Sand County Almanac* (*Kalendar' peschanogo grafstva*), which appeared in the Soviet Union in 1980, thirty years after its publication in the United States, none of these authors' works had been translated into Russian either. But because Eiseley's literary sensibilities and perception of the natural world were in many ways congruent with mine, he had a particular appeal to me.

What started out as a desire to share the writer with a few Russian friends grew into an all-out effort, supported by several grants from Purdue, to introduce him to the Russian-speaking world. Between 1988 and 1993 nine works by Eiseley (transliterated Ayzli) in my translation appeared in such Russian periodicals as the Moscow literary journals *Smena* (The rising generation) and *Lepta* (Offerings), as well as in the weekly *Knizhnoye obozreniye* (Book review), the Russian equivalent of the homonymous *New York Times Book Review*. The fact that these translations originated abroad was not, in the era of glasnost and geopolitical disintegration, an impediment to their publication. The Russian writer Yury Nagibin, who had a developed a keen appreciation of Eiseley, was instrumental in getting the first ones published, providing a foreword or an afterword to several of them. I owe him a debt of gratitude that cannot be repaid (Nagibin died in 1994).

My ultimate goal, however, once I had established my translating credentials, was to publish in Russia a representative collection of Eiseley's essays and short stories. To facilitate the process, I applied for and received in 1991 a Purdue University Center for Artistic Endeavors Fellowship, which enabled me to actively pursue my translating activities for a semester. Here was my justification for the project: "The publication of Eiseley's works in the Soviet Union can only have a humanizing effect in a country emerging from a seventy-year experiment in utopia. Coupling science with poetry, Eiseley insists on the ascendancy of the human intellect — provided it is tempered by the equally human capacity for compassion. If there is a message in his works, that is it."

From the start, I envisioned the collection — never mind the language it was in — as an answer to Leslie E. Gerber and Margaret McFadden's considered call to produce a volume "of Eiseley's finest essays," excluding all that is scientifically "dated" and overly "sentimental" or "bombastic" and thus "allowing the full measure of his achievement . . . to be appreciated" (157–58). That volume, annotated and with a critical introduction, was brought out by Moscow University Press in 1994. Titled *Vzmakh kryla* (Wingbeat), it is divided into three sections, each containing four essays-cum–short stories — twelve works in all.[1] Four of the translations had not been previously published. The table of contents lays out the book's basic design:

I. MAN
The Gold Wheel (NC)
The Places Below (NC)
The Rat That Danced (ASH)
The Palmist (ASH)

II. LIFE

The Flow of the River (*IJ*)

The Bird and the Machine (*IJ*)

The Judgment of the Birds (*IJ*)

The Brown Wasps (*NC*)

III. EVOLUTION

[The Comet] (*IP*)

The Last Neanderthal (*UU*)

The Coming of the Giant Wasps (*ASH*)

The Star Thrower (*ASH*)[2]

The first item in the third section, "The Comet," is in brackets because the title is mine. It is actually the first, untitled, part of the essay "The Star Dragon" from Eiseley's book *The Invisible Pyramid* and stands on its own as a work of art.[3]

The first section ("Man") is largely autobiographical; the second ("Life") concerns, for the most part, the miracle of life; the third ("Evolution") — the most theoretical section of all — contains speculation as to the significance of biological evolution and humanity's place in the universe. There is a clear progression here from the simple to the complex and, within each section, from an optimistic view of life to a pessimistic one. The book does, however, end with the cautiously upbeat "Star Thrower," which has been called Eiseley's "seminal essay" (Cohen, "Leap" 206).

The selections reflect a wide range of Eiseley's writings: of his nine volumes of artful prose that do not repeat themselves, five are represented in *Wingbeat*.[4] With the exception of the recently published *Loren Eiseley Reader*, which has a similar tripartite structure, I know of no other such collection of the writer's selected works in any language.

The title, *Wingbeat*, is a reference both to Eiseley's frequent use of bird imagery and to the soaring quality of his prose (see Breschinsky, "Flights of Fancy"). The term actually occurs in the essay "The Bird and the Machine": "In the next second after that long minute [the sparrow hawk] was gone. Like a flicker of light, he vanished with my eyes full on him, but without actually seeing a premonitory *wing beat*" (*Immense* 191; emphasis added).

Here is another passage, this one from the essay "The Judgment of the Birds," that is, again, illustrative of the book's title: "I think of [those pigeons] sometimes in such a way that the wings, beginning far down in the black depths of the mind, begin to rise and whirl till all the mind is lit up by the spinning, and there is a sense of things passing away, but lightly, as a wing might veer over an obstacle" (*Immense* 167). These two quotations were to have served as epigraphs of the collection, shedding light as they do on its title, but unfortunately were deleted by the publisher for technical reasons. What these reasons were I will explain in due time.

As I have said, the collection is furnished with an introduction — "Loren Ayzli i iskusstvo èsse" (Loren Eiseley and the art of the essay) — and a set of annotations, which not only give the publication history of each translated piece but also offer detailed commentary on textual points that might otherwise elude the Russian reader. Concluding the volume is a bibliography, which though it focuses primarily on publications relevant to the works at hand, gives the interested reader the opportunity of accessing a much larger storehouse of information.

The book is imaginatively illustrated by Joyce Crocker, an Indiana artist and fellow Eiseley enthusiast. Her three illustrations, one for each part of the collection, incorporate motifs from all twelve works.

HOW I TRANSLATE

Translating Eiseley is not the same as translating the published results of recent research in, say, lipid oxidation. Nor is it anything like my former work as a freelance State Department conference interpreter. In a very real sense, the literary translator becomes a cocreator of the translated work, though admittedly a dependent one. That is to say, the process is not at all mechanical, recent advances in computer-translating technology notwithstanding. Some translators, who insist on the scholarliness of their work, assert that a translation is a kind of running commentary in another language on the original. While there is some truth in that, I prefer to think of artistic translation as a compromise between a genuine knowledge of both cultures involved — the performer of a musical composition or choreographed ballet does not share that intellectual burden — and the fortissimos and pirouettes of the performing artist, for a translator is that, too, his score being the written text.

All my translations go through three distinct stages. First, I do a quick literal transposition from one language into the other, indicating along the way as many variants of a particular word or expression as come to mind. Here there is almost a one-to-one correspondence between text and meaning, and consequently the translation sounds very much like, well, a translation: it is flat and lifeless. Then I surround myself with reference works and begin the laborious and time-consuming task of finding the best variant to fit the given context. To provide an annotation to the occasional obscure technical term I sometimes, when all else fails, consult a specialist in the field. At this point, the translation begins to take on body and shape.

Finally, then, I put all the reference works back on the shelf, set the original aside, and *listen* to what I have produced from the standpoint of a critical reader. This is where the fortissimos and the pirouettes come in. The objective in this final stage is to make the work sound as though Eiseley's native tongue were Russian. Not only is meaning important here but also the sound of the words, the cadence of the lines, the particular associations that are peculiarly Russian. Slowly, painfully, joyously Eiseley, who was born in Nebraska of pioneer German stock, *becomes* Russian. And in that metamorphosis, it is my firm belief, he loses nothing.

HOW RUSSIAN REFORMS CHANGED LOREN EISELEY

Nothing, that is, unless the censor intervenes. Of course, the day of the censor is over in Russia, and *Wingbeat* was untouched by the censor's pen. However, journal versions of the text were subject to editorial revision over which I had no control, including one case of outright censorship.

It occurred in 1988 at the height of perestroika, during Mikhail Gorbachev's misguided anti-alcohol campaign. While it lasted, the war against alcohol was pervasive, spilling over even into the literary realm, where I had been taking my first tentative steps as a translator of Loren Eiseley.

My first two published translations, of "The Flow of the River" ("Techeniye reki") and "The Palmist" ("Khiromantka"), appeared together that year with no overall heading in the above-mentioned glossy magazine *Smena*, a Moscow bimonthly geared to the younger set. Except for an unfortunate editorial error in the former essay that radically altered the sense of a passage — as a result of a proofreader's ignorance of biological terminology, a single letter was added to a word, and *osmos* ("osmosis") became *kosmos* ("the cosmos") (Ayzli, "Techeniye reki" 8) — the essay remained virtually unchanged.[5] It is to the latter essay that the watchdogs of Soviet political correctness directed their baleful and sober gaze.

In "The Palmist," which was published in Eiseley's collection *All the Strange Hours*, the hero is on a Caribbean island attending a professional conference. He has an encounter with fate that had been predicted years earlier by a fortuneteller, is obsessed with dire memories of a troubled past, recalls playing dice with the universe as a child, and at the very end of the story goes to a bar to have a drink. The final paragraph reads, "In the all-night bar at the corner I asked for a shot glass of bourbon. When the barkeeper had turned, I made a faint gesture to the face before me in the mirror. 'To whatever I won with the dice in childhood,' I murmured. 'And to the last cast.' As I sipped, the old expected tremor in my hands was stilled. The palmist was gone" (218). This is where the censor's pen begins to quiver.

Bourbon in Russian is a cognate, *burbon*, and a shot glass is *stopka*; my translation was faithful to the original. However, these words do not appear in the published version. The censor had deleted them, replacing the definitive clause "I asked for a shot glass of bourbon" (*"ya zakazal stopku burbona"*) with the noncommittal "I placed an order" (*"sdelal ya zakaz"*) (Ayzli, "Khiromantka" 11). As far as the young readers of *Smena* were concerned, the narrator could well have been sipping Coca-Cola or perhaps mineral water, but certainly not Wild Turkey bourbon whiskey, which Eiseley in fact preferred (see Christianson, *Fox* 374).

Thus, it might be said, Russian reforms changed Loren Eiseley — textually, that is. However, with the appearance of *Wingbeat* in 1994, the original text was fully restored, and the narrator of "The Palmist," Eiseley's alter ego, got to have his drink after all.

SUBSEQUENT PUBLICATIONS IN PERIODICALS
AND THE SECOND BOOK

Even while preparing my first Eiseley collection for publication, I had unwittingly begun work on a companion volume. By the late 1990s my translations had begun to appear in the prestigious St. Petersburg literary journal *Zvezda* (The star). For the intellectual readership of that periodical, Loren Eiseley, I suspect, provided an exotic diversion from the usual Russian-oriented sociopolitical and literary fare.

Periodicals may reach a wider audience than books, but they are an ephemeral repository of literary art. This is why I decided, when the opportunity presented itself, to bring out a second volume consisting of just three pieces — the very first ones to have come out in *Zvezda*:

I. One Night's Dying (*NC*)
II. The Secret of Life (*IJ*)
III. The Time of Man (*DMX*)

In style and content they correspond closely to the three thematic sections of the first volume: "Man," "Life," and "Evolution." Thus, for example, the final work, "The Time of Man," concerns the latest developments in research on human evolution circa 1962, when it was first published, and is a true essay (as opposed to a short story), with no plot to speak of and relatively few first-person intrusions by the author.

Accepted by St. Petersburg University Press, the second volume, which after the central essay I called *Tayna zhizni* (The secret of life), came out in 1999. Besides an introductory article, it contains a plethora of otherwise inaccessible material on Eiseley in Russian: annotations to the texts, a complete bibliography of current Russian publications of and about Eiseley (now dated), and a chronology of the writer's life and works. There are also illustrations — this time I chose traditional Japanese heraldic motifs, which in their stark simplicity underscore Eiseley's basic themes (a dried out empty seedpod, for example, does *not* reveal the secret of life) — and an epigraph. Taken from the title essay, the epigraph is ironic in intent: "Every so often one encounters articles in leading magazines with titles such as 'The Spark of Life,' 'The Secret of Life,' 'New Hormone Key to Life,' or other similar optimistic proclamations" (*Immense* 205). Fortunately, this time around the epigraph did not get lost in the shuffle.

Since then I have completed six more translations, four of which have appeared in various issues of *Zvezda*: "Tri ètyuda: Razmyshleniye o cheloveke, prirode i Boge" (Three vignettes: Meditations on man, nature, and God [*Lost*]), "Priroda, chelovek i chudo" ("Nature, Man, and Miracle" [*Firmament*]), "Shchel'" ("The Slit" [*Immense*]), and "Samy chudesny den' na svete" ("The Most Perfect Day in the World" [*All*]).[6] The other two translations — of Eiseley's essay "The Innocent Fox" (*Unexpected*) and his only science fiction short story, the surrealistic "Dance of the Frogs" (*Star*) — are still awaiting publication. In recent years, the Novgorod miscellany *Chelo* (Forefront) brought out anew two of my previously published translations, "Burye osy" ("The Brown Wasps") and "Zolotoye koleso" ("The Gold Wheel"), both taken from *Wingbeat*. After agreeing to publish the first of them, the editor said, "It took my breath away."

All told, I have made accessible to the Russian reader some twenty essays and short stories — the best of Eiseley, so to speak. The majority of these works appeared in periodicals, mostly literary journals such as *Zvezda*, which to date has published seven of them. A few were published in more than one periodical, and fifteen were collected, as discussed earlier, in my two books of translations.[7]

As I look over my extensive collection of Eiseley's works in search of new pieces to translate, it becomes increasingly apparent that, for me at least, it would be a repeat performance — variations on themes already played out. Not only is the subject matter all too familiar, so also are the settings and the situations, the imagery and the figures of speech.[8] That is why I propose to leave what remains to be done to my successors, who might find innovative ways, perhaps in the digital realm, to fill in some of the missing details.

WHAT REMAINS TO BE DONE AND COPYRIGHT PROBLEMS

Should such successors come forward, they might wish to translate, as the next step in an ongoing process, not individual essays but whole books.

Eiseley's most widely translated book, without question, is his first one, *The Immense Journey* (I have published in translation five of its thirteen essays and short stories). It should be the first one to be rendered completely into Russian, with *The Unexpected Universe* and *All the Strange Hours* following in close succession. This will give the Russian reader a solid foundation on which to build a true appreciation of the writer, whom my efforts did little more than introduce.

As experience has shown, there will be a copyright issue with *All the Strange Hours*. The autobiography was published in 1975, two years after the Soviet Union became a signatory of the International Copyright Agreement, which means that permission must be obtained to reproduce the book or "any part thereof," even in translation. Simon & Schuster, which currently holds the copyright, will grant that permission, but not without a lot of hassle and a stiff fee in hard currency, which most Russian publishers, given the disarray in the post-Soviet publishing market and the current global economic downturn, will probably be unable or unwilling to pay (in my case, the necessary funds were provided by my home institution). Happily, most of Eiseley's works are not covered by the provisions of the copyright agreement and remain in the public domain.

I can now explain why the epigraphs of *Wingbeat*, which were to shed light on the collection, were deleted by the publisher. Copyright negotiations with Simon & Schuster were concluded after a camera-ready copy of the text had been forwarded to Moscow University Press. And because the copyright release statement needed to be belatedly included in the publication, my epigraphs were replaced by a last-minute expression of gratitude to Simon & Schuster. Oblivious of the fact that I had referred to the epigraphs in my introduction to the volume, Moscow University Press excised them, thus compromising, however slightly, the integrity of the text. It is virtually the only part of the publication process over which I had no control.

THE CRITICAL RESPONSE

Perhaps because the two Eiseley volumes were published by university presses, which like their American counterparts have a small readership base and limited resources for promotion, they were overlooked by the mainstream media, including, significantly, periodicals specifically devoted to literature. It is also possible that the mainstream media simply ignored an area that has been traditionally alien to it: American nature writing. In any case, what response there was to Eiseley was itself limited to a few obscure and/or specialized publications with a narrow range of distribution.

To my knowledge, only four discussions of the collections appeared in print, three of them (authored by A. I. Subetto, M. V. Rumyantseva, and S. I. Malyshev) concerning the first volume and one (authored by Andrey Astvatsaturov) treating both volumes. I refer to them collectively as "discussions," because only two (the Malyshev and the Astvatsaturov articles) can be classified as reviews, the other two being explorations of wide-ranging philosophical interests (Subetto) or elaborations of narrow scholarly concerns (Rumyantseva) evoked by the Eiseley translations. Let me consider the latter group first.

As the title of his lengthy treatise "Bessoznatel'noye zhizni i èvolyutsion-naya pamyat': V dialoge s Lorenom Ayzli . . ." (The collective unconscious and evolutionary memory: In dialogue with Loren Eiseley . . .) would suggest, Subetto, a specialist in sociology and the philosophy of science, attributes Eiseley's profound sense of the earth's evolutionary past not to the writer's professional insight augmented by years of reflection, but rather, as the scholar's theory of the unconscious predicts, to a kind of sublimated Jungian "memory" residing in the protoplasm. According to Subetto, this ancient memory is brought to light and distilled into vivid images (reflecting the scholar's elaborate, not to say fantastic, mental constructs) in "trans-like states" (70), such as the one Eiseley describes in his essay "The Flow of the River." The treatise is a part of Subetto's book on these and related matters called *Bessoznatel'noye. Arkhaika. Vera* (The unconscious. Antiquity. Faith).

No less esoteric, though perhaps a bit more firmly grounded in reality, is Rumyantseva's brief study, "Tipy èmpatiynykh vyskazyvaniy (na materiale èsse L. Ayzli 'Kometa' v perevode D. N. Breschinskogo)" (Types of empathic utterances [based on L. Eiseley's essay "The Comet" in D. N. Breschinsky's translation]). Originally presented at the Thirty-Fourth

International Conference on Philology in Saint Petersburg, it was published in the conference proceedings (2005). As the latter part of the title
suggests, the study treats only one Eiseley piece — the shortest one of all
in *Wingbeat*. An empathic construction, as I learned, is one in which a
sense of empathy or emotional involvement on the part of the speaker/
narrator is conveyed through various lexical or syntactical means, such as
simple substitution: "I think *you* will live to see it," the father whispers in
his three-year-old son's ear as they watch Halley's comet, which will return
in three-quarters of a century, streak by in the night sky, "*for me*" (italics in
the original). "In this example," Rumyantseva, a Russian-language specialist
at Saint Petersburg University, writes, "one can clearly see the substitution
of one subject by another" (49). She calls this, logically enough, the "sub-
stitutional type" of empathic utterance (ten other types are identified and
illustrated), averring that the study of such constructions can significantly
enhance the teaching of Russian as a second language. I truly hope it does.

What these nonreviews point to — without making it explicit — is, on
the one hand, the breadth of Eiseley's compass, which is much wider than
that of most other American nature writers, including as it does a vast evolutionary dimension (Stephen Jay Gould, a fellow scientist, is an obvious
exception); and on the other hand, his insistent emphasis on compassion
(Rumyantseva's strictly grammatical term "empathy" has considerable
philosophical ramifications) as a way for *Homo sapiens* to escape "Darwin's
tangled bank of unceasing struggle, selfishness, and death" — a strategy
that is so powerfully presented in "The Star Thrower" (*Unexpected* 185).

True reviews are necessarily more revealing because, by their very nature,
they deal with what the writer was actually trying to say. Malyshev published
a one-page appreciation, "'Shkatulka nablyudeniy' Lorena Ayzli" (Loren
Eiseley's "trove of observations"), in the reviews section of a "scholarly-
practical" journal with the unlikely name *Upravlencheskoye konsul'tirovaniye*
(Management consulting). In his review, he makes an astute observation
regarding Eiseley's approach to nature writing: "Alongside real events,
which are presented as the author's reminiscences and convey his awe of
Life [*sic*], one sees the workings of the imagination, which, though it does
not arise in a vacuum, represents a reality of a different order. The tight

interweaving of these two modalities creates the finely wrought images and allows for the compositional perfection of the stories" (46). At the same time the reviewer claims that, lacking the requisite background information pertaining to American culture, history, and geography, he found himself ill-equipped to fully appreciate "certain aspects of the text." (How many Eiseley aficionados, one wonders, have actually seen the Nebraska Badlands or experienced firsthand the Great Depression, which frequently appear as backdrops for his essays?) But then Malyshev, as if catching the inconsistency, says that "given the universal nature of the problems the author addresses, this is only a minor 'limitation' . . . compensated for in part by the translator's annotations" (46).

Much more perceptive is Astvatsaturov's review, "Priroda i tsivilizatsiya v èsseistike Lorena Ayzli" (Nature and civilization in Loren Eiseley's essays). Published in the first ever issue of *Collegium*, a journal of the Smolny Institute of Liberal Arts and Sciences, it is the only commentary that treats both Eiseley volumes.[9] I know of no other query in any language that sets forth so succinctly yet incisively *what* Eiseley writes about: the eternal struggle between the two worlds inhabited by humans — the natural one from which they came (the original "Garden of Eden") and the artificial one (the world of culture and civilization), which with the discovery of language and science, they drew from their own mind and indiscriminately spread across the planet. Unfortunately, what is missing from Astvatsaturov's argument is the *how* — the resources of language and literary device that Eiseley uses to convey his vision and that I sought to reproduce in my translation. It is, of course, that magical union of the "what" and the "how" that assures Eiseley a permanent place among the giants of American nature writing.

THE INTERNET CONNECTION

Despite the promise that the critical response to my translations holds (occasionally off base and sometimes recondite, the remarks, as we have seen, were positive), its influence, given the size of the potential audience, was negligible. As if to compensate for that shortcoming, one enthusiastic reader of *Wingbeat,* V. V. Chekletsov, who I doubt had seen any of the commentary, came up with a unique solution: he digitally scanned most of the book, and though it can still be purchased through dealers, he made it available online. First published in 2007 on Webblog.ru, the electronic version soon appeared on two other sites, Litsovet.ru and the popular Lib.ru (*Vzmakh kryla*).

This same enthusiast, who sometimes goes by the user name of Aion when dealing with Eiseley, also posted an article on the writer, lifted virtually verbatim from the first, biographical, part of my introductory essay to the collection, on the Russian Wikipedia.[10] Not only did he break the text up into titled sections of his own design, but he also added a photograph or two and cross-referenced the whole to his electronic version of *Wingbeat.* Subsequently, the Wikipedia article ("Ayzli, Loren") appeared on several other Russian online user-generated reference sources, including the *Bol'shaya sovetskaya entsiklopediya* (The great Soviet encyclopedia), whose scope is broad, and *Lyudi* (People), which specializes in personalities and biographies.

In all of this feverish publishing activity Chekletsov took care to delete all references to the primary source of his material — the hardcover 1994 Moscow University Press edition of *Wingbeat.* That is why he did not scan the book's title page, the last page of the signed introduction, and parts of the addenda. He also excluded the subtitle, *Rasskazy i èsse* (Short stories and essays), severing even this superficial link to the original. Although the entire enterprise, due to copyright restrictions if not ethical considerations, would seem to have been ill-advised (I hold the copyright to the original edition), it was actually the single most productive "critical response" that my efforts have thus far elicited.

With the collection now in the "virtual" mode, Chekletsov proceeded to mount a veritable publicity campaign — the creation of an Eiseley entry in Wikipedia and other online reference sources was only the first step in this process. He has repeatedly tried to engage potential readers by posting on various websites a promotional blurb consisting of my annotation to *Wingbeat* (the descriptive note that comes after the ISBN number in Russian books) and his suggestion that the reader start with "The Flow of the River," followed by a provocative quotation from that essay — the swimmer's sobering reflection upon emerging from the river: "As for men, those myriad little detached ponds with their own swarming corpuscular life, what were they but a way that water has of going about beyond the reach of rivers? I, too, was a microcosm of pouring rivulets and floating driftwood gnawed by the mysterious animalcules of my own creation" (*Immense* 20). The network address for downloading the entire collection is helpfully provided (see Chekletsov, "Loren Ayzli").

Web blogs are, of course, a way to reflect on art, and Chekletsov, always eager to promote his favorite writer, initiated on one of his blogs a discussion of Eiseley's *Wingbeat* by offering his opinion that "the short story 'The Flow of the River' . . . is one of the most beautiful works I've ever read" ("Kommentarii," msg. 1). One of the respondents, Blondi, calls the story "powerful" and "a great read, slow and meditative" (5). "Eiseley is one of us" (6), Chekletsov confidently replies.

On another site, Vadim, a participant in the online forum "Knizhki, kotorye stoit prochitat'" (Books worth reading), cited *Wingbeat* as his choice. Linking it to the Internet version, he wrote, "Incredibly beautiful poetic-philosophical essays . . . sadly virtually unknown in Russia." He goes on to recommend that the reader start with "The Flow of the River." It is not hard to deduce that the respondent is none other than Vadim Viktorovich Chekletsov himself, making yet another attempt to spread the word.

When all is said and done, I am grateful to this thirty-year-old computer buff and would-be litterateur for making Eiseley accessible on the Internet and promoting him so energetically among Russian readers but hold him accountable for appropriating the writer's works as his own. Amazingly, he has not only taken out a copyright for the electronic version of *Wingbeat* but also routinely lists the book among his literary achievements.[11] Even for Russia, where intellectual property rights are commonly ignored, such egregious conduct is beyond the pale.

But the range of Russian-language references to Eiseley on the World Wide Web is broader and more varied now than this. Completely unknown in Russia before my translations were published, the writer has recently become, among other things, a source of corporate wisdom and, oddly, of ideological confrontation with the West — something that I would never have predicted.

Although it may be unrelated to my translation, there is, for example, a curious "mission statement" posted by sт Management Consulting (not to be confused with the journal of the same name in which S. I. Malyshev published his review of *Wingbeat*). The consulting firm for business managers — an economic service unimaginable in Soviet times — states its mission metaphorically, by presenting a succinct synopsis of Eiseley's quasi-metaphysical essay "The Star Thrower." Once the principal character (referred to as "the philosopher") joins the original star thrower (referred to as "the young man") on the beach to save stranded starfish, the optimistic promotional line takes over. I quote the English version of the text: "We have all been gifted with the ability to make a difference. And if we can, like that young man, become aware of that gift, we gain through the strength of our vision the power to shape the future." Just below the title, a wide-angle view of sea shells strewn on the shore, with water palpably lapping in the background, intensifies the story's emotional appeal. An accompanying burst of starfish in the upper left-hand corner of the web page serves as a kind of company logo. At the bottom there is an attribution: "Adapted from *The Star Thrower* by Loren Eiseley" ("Mission"). The initial "sт" in the agency's English-only designation, an acronym that is nowhere deciphered, clearly stands for "Star Thrower." Eiseley's motif — understood as redemption not through compassion but rather through willful self-affirmation — has been used by motivational speakers in the United States since the early nineties ("Star Thrower"). It was picked up by the emergent Russian business community, probably via the Internet, and put to use for purely practical purposes — to inspire sound business practices designed to shape Russia's imminent capitalist future.

That future is far from certain. Though he remains within the economic paradigm, a different tack is taken by A. I. Subetto, whose interest in Eiseley seems not to have waned since his initial critical response. In "Kapitalokratiya" (Capitalocracy), a series of diatribes against American capitalism posted on the Internet, he invokes the writer as his ideological comrade-in-arms.[12] "In his essays," Subetto writes, "Loren Eiseley captures the emptiness of monetary space where the God of Capital reigns and no 'air' is left for a human being to 'breathe.' . . . *So worship it, the zero*" (5; emphasis added). In the essay that Subetto cites, "The Rat That Danced," the italicized words of the quoted passage appear three times (*All* 8, 12, 14). A quick check of the context confirms that what Eiseley is referring to is not "monetary space" at all — or, for that matter, any other aspect of economic theory — but rather the metaphysical emptiness that death, whether of the individual animal or of an entire species, leaves in its wake (a recurrent theme in Eiseley's work). I have no explanation of this gross misinterpretation by Subetto.

Many Internet references to Eiseley simply mention or list him in contexts where he had never appeared before. He has become one of the few American nature writers now known in Russia.[13] As a writer regularly published in *Zvezda*, he is held in high regard by intellectuals.[14] And Russian-language searches on the web uncover him as a writer at large.[15] Even this dubious recognition of Eiseley's works in a country undergoing momentous social upheaval is encouraging.

But perhaps the most gratifying Internet find of all is that of a budding Russian writer from Kaliningrad, who claims his literary legitimacy from having read in his youth a Russian "glossy magazine" that contained Eiseley's essay "The Flow of the River." The year was 1988 and the magazine was *Smena*, which also contained "The Palmist" — my first two translations. The writer, Pavel Nastin, also known as Trishna, was fifteen years old at the time, and he relates his reading experience in a lyrical essay called "Vremya Lorena Ayzli: 'Techeniye reki'" (The time of Loren Eiseley: "The Flow of the River"). Composed ten years after the fact and modeled on the American nature writer's uniquely intimate style, it deals with the narrator's childhood, a frequent theme in Eiseley. As a college student, Nastin, like Eiseley, majored in the natural sciences and soon began to put his philosophical musings into poetic form. Among the writers that inspired him, including Vladimir Nabokov, Samuel Beckett, and G. K. Chesterton, he lists Loren Eiseley first on his home page. And in a blogosphere exchange, he writes, "Who would have thought that I would be so smitten by Loren — by his 'Flow of the River.' It was probably the single most powerful 'literary' impression that I have had in my life" (Online discussion). One is reminded of Chekletsov's transformational encounter with the story.

Clearly, my efforts to introduce Loren Eiseley to the Russian reader have not gone unnoticed. But that does not mean that the seedling, transplanted from the American Great Plains to the steppes of Russia, has taken root. Though the terrain is similar, the climate is different, the soil incompatible, and there have been storms.

DOES EISELEY HAVE A FUTURE IN RUSSIA?

The question lingers: why was Eiseley not translated into Russian earlier? After all, his first book was rendered virtually into all the major European languages, including Greek and Portuguese, as well as into a large number of non-European tongues, such as Arabic, Korean, Hindi, and Urdu. Why not Russian?

Part of the answer is that nature writing as practiced in the United States never materialized in Russia. There is not even a special term for it in the language, so I coined one — *naturografiya*, with its derivative *naturograf*, or "nature writer." At first glance this may seem odd. Given Russia's bountiful natural resources, most of which, especially east of the Urals, are untapped and unspoiled, and such distinguished writers as Aksakov, Turgenev, Prishvin, and Paustovsky, whose works span the past two centuries and reveal a deep appreciation of the natural world, one would think that the country would have a school of nature writing to rival the one that blossomed in twentieth-century America.[16] Unfortunately, nineteenth-century Russia lacked transcendentalist thinkers such as Ralph Waldo Emerson and Henry David Thoreau to set the stage. The intelligentsia of the time was preoccupied with the country's social ills (serfdom was abolished only in 1861). Nor was there a true parallel in Russian history to the conquest of the American Wild West, which enabled the early settlers to experience the wilderness firsthand and witness its grandeurs. On the contrary, Siberia, because of its sheer vastness and more northerly location, has remained largely untouched by civilization.

Consequently, what writing there was in Russia with nature as its subject can hardly be said to represent a "school." The writers involved were too few in number and never saw themselves as part of a common cause. Moreover, they were perfectly content to observe nature, not interpret it; to describe the "beauty" of its individual manifestations, not speculate on the universal significance of the whole. Looking at nature from the "outside," as it were, they did not seek to find their place as humans in it. In contradistinction to their American counterparts, Russian writers dealing with the natural world lack the philosophical underpinnings that transcendentalism provides. What is more, the ecological concerns that inform the modern American nature-writing ethic would strike many of them as utilitarian and vulgar.

The problem is compounded by the fact that the genre of the personal or, as Eiseley calls it, the "concealed essay," into which most observation and contemplation of the natural world is distilled, has itself never secured a foothold in Russia (*All* 177). A possible reason for this is suggested by Phillip Lopate in the introduction to his 1994 anthology of personal essays (Eiseley's are not among his selections). Without referring specifically to Russia, Lopate writes,

> In many countries and cultures, the "I" [that is at the heart of the personal essay] has been downplayed, either because of communal factors (Native Americans have viewed the tribe, not the self, as the key unit of identity) or ideological forces (in communist regimes, individualism is considered a reactionary, bourgeois concept) or spiritual traditions. . . .
>
> Particularly in religions with mystical traditions, in both East and West, where the surrender of the ego is seen as paramount, spiritual striving and the enterprise of the personal essay seem somewhat at cross-purposes. (lii)

All the factors Lopate cites are in evidence in Russia, with its tradition of communalism (the peasant *mir*), its recently failed experiment in communism, and its millennium of Eastern Orthodoxy, which has always emphasized mass ritual over individual introspection. However, it seems obvious that, despite it all, the best of modern Russian letters, from Aleksandr Pushkin to Aleksandr Solzhenitsyn, has been untrammeled by such sociocultural constraints. In particular, the "I" of Russian lyric poetry, which has its roots in the Romantic movement, today is very much on display. So the question as to why the personal essay with its much less pronounced "egocentric tendencies" never took hold in that country is a moot one.

Although he may be unfamiliar with the personal essay in general and nature writing in particular, the Russian reader has, at least until recently, delighted in literature endowed with politics and plot, precisely the features that are in short supply in Eiseley's works. The writer usually pursues no overt political agenda and does not concern himself with the vicissitudes of everyday life to which the average reader is accustomed, focusing instead on the natural world at large and humanity's place in it. No wonder that, with few exceptions (the writer Yury Nagibin comes to mind), most Russians whom, through oral reading or written text, I personally introduced to Eiseley had no idea where he was "coming from." They did not understand his abiding love of nature, especially nature in the abstract — the timeless Pleistocene altiplano of the writer's imagination. The nature that most Russians know seldom extends beyond the mushroom hunt in the nearby woodland or the picnic in the park.

What is worse, modern Russians do not really understand Darwin, whose evolutionary thinking informs much of Eiseley's oeuvre. It is symptomatic that the Russian intelligentsia, which produced such writers as Tolstoy and Dostoevsky in the nineteenth century, turned largely mystical before it was swept away in the October Revolution. Darwin, with his unrelenting positivism and materialism, was never a part of the Russian intellectual landscape, which was dominated by the likes of the theosophist Madame Blavatsky and the followers of German anthroposophist Rudolf Steiner, purveyors of the occult. The hardheaded Marxists who succeeded them also had little use for Darwin: with a huge and mostly illiterate peasant population to manipulate and control, "survival of the fittest" was not a slogan they could readily exploit to their political advantage, especially when the fittest — the kulaks — were among the first "enemies of the state" to be eliminated. Today, in the mainstream media, Darwinism is likened to Marxism as an outdated nineteenth-century philosophy that has no basis in fact ("missing links," long since established, are invariably cited as evidence).[17] Creationism has captured the popular imagination, and the Russian Orthodox Church is actively seeking to introduce the principles of orthodoxy (Zakon Bozhiy) as a grade school subject.

Worst of all, after the disintegration of the Soviet Union, one of the most literate societies in the world lost its readers.[18] Overnight, they were sucked into the black hole of the Internet, and to hold them in their fold publishers began churning out books on alternative medicine, gardening and shed building, black and white magic, astrology, and even pornography. Great literature, if it existed at all, dissolved into the background. It does not bode well for Eiseley in the steppes of Russia, at least not for the short term.

So the question put to me by one worthy critic, a personal friend and connoisseur of traditional Russian literature with whom I had shared some of my first translations, did not surprise me in the least. "Your translations are beautiful," he remarked. "But why do you waste your time on Eiseley?"

I do not believe I have been wasting my time. On the contrary, I have been building a bridge, one of many that will be needed if Russia is ever to fully embrace the best of Western civilization. And Russia's acceptance of Loren Eiseley may well be a measure of how far it is willing to go in that precarious endeavor.

NOTES

This chapter includes interpolated passages from my previous publication on the subject, "Loren Eiseley in Russia."

1. Further references to this title will use the English translation. Unless otherwise indicated, all translations from the Russian here and elsewhere are mine.

2. Loren Eiseley's original collections are indicated here by their acronyms, as listed below in chronological order:

IJ   *The Immense Journey* (1957)

UU   *The Unexpected Universe* (1969)

IP   *The Invisible Pyramid* (1970)

NC   *The Night Country* (1971)

ASH   *All the Strange Hours* (1975)

DMX   *Darwin and the Mysterious Mr. X* (1979)

The Star Thrower (1978), *Darwin and the Mysterious Mr. X* (1979), and *The Lost Notebooks of Loren Eiseley* (1987) were published posthumously, though Eiseley himself made the selections for *The Star Thrower*, his "last literary project" (Angyal, *Loren Eiseley* 85).

3. *Audubon* magazine published the text in its November 1985 issue, treating it as an independent work and giving it the title "But Once in a Lifetime."

4. I am not counting *The Mind as Nature*, which is a single essay in book form, and *The Brown Wasps: A Collection of Three Essays in Autobiography*. The contents of both books were reproduced in later collections.

5. As Vladimir Nabokov has remarked in another context, the difference between the "comic" and the "cosmic" "depends upon one sibilant" (142).

6. The first of these, the "vignettes," are poetic meditations that Eiseley set down at different times in his so-called *Lost Notebooks*, presumably for future use. Though the pieces are untitled in the original, I give them brief headings that reflect their content. The overall title is, of course, also mine.

The second piece, "Nature, Man, and Miracle," is the original title of the essay Eiseley published in the magazine Horizon (1960). When he later incorporated the work into his collection *The Firmament of Time*, Eiseley changed the title to "How Natural Is 'Natural'?" to make it conform to other interrogative titles in the volume. I based my translation on the latter text (the two differ slightly) but retained the original title because it gives a better sense of the work's essence.

7. Regarding the matter of republication, it should be said that most Russian journals do not accept previously published work. An exception to this rule, besides *Chelo*, is the Moscow literary journal *Lepta*, which brought out a set of six of my Eiseley translations, two of which had appeared earlier in other periodicals (see Ayzli, "Rasskazy i èsse"). I included all of them in the *Wingbeat* volume, thus further expanding their reach.

8. In his laudatory review of *All the Strange Hours*, literary scholar James Olney observes that Eiseley "has written this same book, under various disguises and titles, more than half a dozen times before" (31). This is not meant as a put-down but simply as an observation of fact based on, as Olney sees it, the autobiographical nature of Eiseley's writings.

9. Astvatsaturov's review has been incorporated into his critically acclaimed study of English and American literature, *Fenomenologiya teksta* (The phenomenology of the text).

10. Chekletsov's occasional use of the name "Aion" deserves an explanation. It is his infelicitous transcription of the Russian word of Latin origin èon ("eon"). Rare in Russia to the point of being excluded from standard dictionaries, it is common enough in English and was frequently used by Eiseley — and hence also occurs in my translations — as a measure of the geologic time spans the writer so often invoked (see Breschinsky, "Reaching"). Chekletsov seems to have been so enamored of the term that he adopted it as a mystifying nickname, but got the transcription wrong.

11. In regard to the misappropriation issue, see, for example, the main page of *Vzmakh kryla* on the Lib.ru website, where a copyright in Chekletsov's name appears above my unattributed annotation to the collection.

Chekletsov, to be sure, is a writer in his own right. But on his author page (*stranitsa avtora*) he routinely lists *Vzmakh kryla* among his own online works without any indication that *Loren Eiseley Wingbeat* (as he renders the title) is in fact a translation from the English of works *by* Loren Eiseley, thus blurring the line between fact and fiction.

12. "Capitalocracy" is one of Subetto's many coinages, some of which are superfluous, such as this one (cf. "plutocracy," a term that also exists in Russian).

13. Unfortunately, Eiseley is still virtually unknown among Russian ecologists, though his name did appear in the Russian online weekly newspaper *Ekoklub* (Ecoclub), where he is listed among a dozen or so American nature writers to whom environmentalists in the United States "turn for guidance" (Skars).

14. See, for example, the interview given by Andrey Ar'ev, coeditor of *Zvezda*, regarding the journal's publication plans for 2008. Among other works projected for that year, he mentions Loren Eiseley's "The Most Wonderful Day in the World," calling the author "one of the most . . . interesting nature philosophers in the world" (Ar'ev).

15. If one searches the Internet for references to Eiseley in Russian-language sources, one eventually comes across a list of names titled "Pisateli po alfavitu" (Writers in alphabetical order); Eiseley will be found under the letter "A" (Ayzli). If one looks a little closer, one will see that the list is based on entries in the Russian Wikipedia. Chalk one up for Chekletsov.

16. According to a recent issue of the English-language magazine *Russian Life*, "Some 70% of Russia is forested and 22% of the world's forests are in Russia. As such, Russia — which has been called the 'lungs of Europe' — is second only to the Amazon in the amount of carbon dioxide it absorbs" ("One Hundred Things" 31).

17. The last decade has seen an upsurge in Russian newspaper and magazine articles alleging that Darwinism is a false philosophy. Even their titles, which I give here in translation, sputter righteous indignation: "Materialists on the March" (Lebedeva); "Darwin, Go Home! The Struggle for Nonexistence" (Ponomaryov and Gamalov); "Where Darwin Went Wrong: Why Don't Monkeys Become Men?" (Pisarenko). One suggested answer to that last question is that Darwin had it wrong: humans did not evolve from monkeys; rather, monkeys are *devolved* humans. Lamentably, periodicals that publish such "revelations" are often geared to the better-educated elements of society (it is to the prerevolutionary Russian elite that Madame Blavatsky appealed).

18. Universal literacy was a major achievement of the Soviet regime, but its primary purpose was the political indoctrination of the masses.

Works Cited

Aberbach, David. "Mystical Union and Grief: The Báal Shem Tov and Krishnamurti." *Harvard Theological Review* 86.3 (1993): 309–21. Print.

Ahlstrom, Sydney E. *A Religious History of the American People*. 2nd ed. New Haven: Yale University Press, 2004. Print.

Aiken, Conrad. "Vachel Lindsay." *Profile of Vachel Lindsay: Charles E. Merrill Profiles*. Ed. John T. Flanigan. Columbus OH: Merrill, 1970. 3–5. Print.

Alighieri, Dante. "Epistle to Can Grande." Trans. James Marchand. *Epistle to Can Grande: Text and Translation*. 26 June 1996. Web. 13 Jan. 2010.

———. *The Inferno of Dante: A New Verse Translation*. Trans. Robert Pinsky. New York: Farrar, Straus, and Giroux, 1997. Print.

———. *The Paradiso*. Trans. John Ciardi. New York: Signet Classics, 2001. Print.

———. *Purgatory*. Trans. Anthony Esolen. New York: Modern Library, 2004. Print.

Anderson, Nels. *The Hobo: The Sociology of the Homeless Man*. 1923. Chicago: University of Chicago Press, 1961. Print.

Angyal, Andrew J. *Loren Eiseley*. Boston: Twayne, 1983. Print.

———. "Loren Eiseley's *Immense Journey*: The Making of a Literary Naturalist." *The Literature of Science: Perspectives on Popular Scientific Writing*. Ed. Murdo William McRae. Athens: University of Georgia Press, 1993. 54–72. Print.

Ar'ev, Andrey. Interview. "Zabota o vechnom: Plany peterburgskikh izdateley na novy god" [Concern for the eternal: Plans of Saint Petersburg publishers for the new year]. By Tat'yana Vol'tskaya. *Rossiya v kraskakh*. 8 Jan. 2008. Web. 20 Aug. 2009.

Armstrong, Karen. *The Great Transformation: The Beginning of Our Religious Traditions*. New York: Anchor Books, 2007. Print.

Arnold, Matthew. "Literature and Science." 1882. *Matthew Arnold*. Ed. Miriam Allott and Robert H. Super. Oxford: Oxford University Press, 1986. 456–71. Print.

Arvich, Paul. *The Haymarket Tragedy*. Princeton: Princeton University Press, 1984. Print.

Ashby, Eric. "Investment in Man." Presidential address delivered to the British Association for the Advancement of Science. Aberdeen, Scotland. 28 Aug. 1963. *Advancement of Science* 20.85 (1964): n.p. Print.

Asquith, Pamela. "Why Anthropomorphism Is *Not* Metaphor: Crossing Concepts and Cultures in Animal Behavior Studies." *Anthropomorphism, Anecdotes, and Animals.* Ed. Robert W. Mitchell, Nicholas S. Thompson, and H. Lyn Miles. Albany: SUNY Press, 1997. 22–34. Print.

Astvatsaturov, Andrey. *Fenomenologiya teksta: Igra i repressiya* [The phenomenology of the text: Play and repression]. Moscow: Novoye literaturnoye obozreniye, 2007. Print.

———. "Priroda i tsivilizatsiya v èsseistike Lorena Ayzli" [Nature and civilization in Loren Eiseley's essays]. Rev. of *Vzmakh kryla* and *Tayna zhizni*, by Loren Eiseley. *Collegium* 1–2 (2004): 51–56. Print.

Auden, W. H. "Concerning the Unpredictable." *The Star Thrower.* By Loren Eiseley. New York: Times Books, 1978. 15–24. Print.

Auerbach, Eric. *Dante: Poet of the Secular World.* Trans. Ralph Manheim. New York: New York Review Books, 2001. Print.

———. *Mimesis: The Representation of Reality in Western Literature.* Trans. William R. Trask. Princeton: Princeton University Press, 1953. Print.

Ayzli [Eiseley], Loren. "Burye osy" ["The Brown Wasps"]. Trans. Dimitri N. Breschinsky. *Chelo* 33 (2005): 91–94. Print.

———. "Khiromantka" ["The Palmist"]. Trans. Dimitri N. Breschinsky. *Smena* Feb. 1988: 10–11. Print.

———. "Priroda, chelovek i chudo" ["Nature, Man, and Miracle"]. Trans. Dimitri N. Breschinsky. *Zvezda* Feb. 2005: 206–19. Print.

———. "Rasskazy i èsse" [Short stories and essays]. Trans. Dimitri N. Breschinsky. *Lepta* Feb. 1992: 105–43. Print.

———. "Samy chudesny den' na svete" ["The Most Perfect Day in the World"]. Trans. Dimitri N. Breschinsky. *Zvezda* Jan. 2008: 91–97. Print.

———. "Shchel'" ["The Slit"]. Trans. Dimitri N. Breschinsky. *Zvezda* Sept. 2006: 65–70. Print.

———. *Tayna zhizni: Liriko-filosofskiy triptikh* [The secret of life: A lyrico-philosophical triptych]. Comp. and trans. Dimitri N. Breschinsky. St. Petersburg: St. Petersburg University Press, 1999. Print.

———. "Techeniye reki" ["The Flow of the River"]. Trans. Dimitri N. Breschinsky. *Smena* Feb. 1988: 8–10. Print.

———. "Tri ètyuda: Razmyshleniya o cheloveke, prirode i Boge" [Three vignettes: Meditations on man, nature, and God]. Comp. and trans. Dimitri N. Breschinsky. *Zvezda* May 2002: 120–25. Print.

———. *Vzmakh kryla* [Wingbeat]. *Lib.ru.* 27 June 2007. Web. 23 Feb. 2010.

———. *Vzmakh kryla* [Wingbeat]. *Litsovet.ru.* 13 Apr. 2007. Web. 16 Feb. 2009.

———. *Vzmakh kryla* [Wingbeat]. *Webblog.ru.* 13 Apr. 2007. Web. 15 Feb. 2009.

———. *Vzmakh kryla: Rasskazy i èsse* [Wingbeat: Short stories and essays]. Comp. and trans. Dimitri N. Breschinsky. Moscow: Moscow University Press, 1994. Print.

———. "Zolotoye koleso" ["The Gold Wheel"]. Trans. Dimitri N. Breschinsky. *Chelo* 36 (2006): 87–90. Print.

"Ayzli [Eiseley], Loren." *Bol'shaya Sovetskaya Entsiklopediya.* Encyclomedia Foundation. N.d. Web. 15 Feb. 2010.

———. *Lyudi.* 11 Nov. 2009. Web. 14 Feb. 2010.

———. *Wikipedia.* Wikimedia Foundation. 2 Mar. 2009. Web. 16 Apr. 2009.

Bachelard, Gaston. *The Poetics of Space: The Classic Look at How We Experience Intimate Places.* Trans. Maria Jolas. Boston: Beacon, 1994. Print.

Bacon, Francis. "The New Atlantis." 1626. *The Major Works.* Ed. Brian Vickers. Oxford World's Classics. New York: Oxford University Press, 2008. 457–89. Print.

Baltimore Ecosystem Study. Home page. 2009. Web. 3 Jan. 2010.

Baraka, Imamu Amiri. *The System of Dante's Hell.* New York: Grove, 1965. Print.

Bekoff, Marc. *The Emotional Lives of Animal: A Leading Scientist Explores Animal Joy, Sorrow, and Empathy — and Why They Matter.* Novato CA: New World Library, 2007. Print.

———, and Jessica Pierce. *Wild Justice: The Moral Lives of Animals.* Chicago: University of Chicago Press, 2009. Print.

Bennett, Michael. "From Wide Open Spaces to Metropolitan Places: The Urban Challenge to Ecocriticism." *ISLE: Interdisciplinary Studies in the Literature and Environment* 8.1 (2001): 31–52. Print.

Benston, Kimberly W. "Experimenting at the Threshold: Sacrifice, Anthropomorphism, and the Aims of (Critical) Animal Studies." *PMLA* 124.2 (2009): 548–55. Print.

Benyus, Janine M. *Biomimicry: Innovation Inspired by Nature.* New York: Harper Perennial, 2002. Print.

Berkove, Lawrence I. "Refuge in the Valley of Dry Bones: Loren Eiseley's Accommodations to Death." *CEA Critic* 54.1 (1991): 87–97. Print.

Bertalanffy, Ludwig von. *Problems of Life.* New York: Wiley and Sons, 1952. Print.

Biomimicry Institute. Home page. *AskNature.org.* 2008–11. Web. 21 June 2011.

Bloom, Harold. *The American Religion: The Emergence of the Post-Christian Nation.* New York: Simon & Schuster, 1992. Print.

———. "The Sage of Concord." *Guardian.* 24 May 2003. Web. 27 Feb. 2011.

Boardman, Kathleen. "Loren Eiseley." *Dictionary of Literary Biography.* Vol. 275. Farmington Hills MI: Gale, 2003. Print.

———. "Loren Eiseley: *The Immense Journey* (1957)." *Literature and the Environment.* Ed. George Hart and Scott Slovic. Westport CT: Greenwood, 2004. 25–37. Print.

Breschinsky, Dimitri N. "Flights of Fancy: Birds in the Works of Loren Eiseley." *ISLE: Interdisciplinary Studies in Literature and Environment* 15.1 (2008): 39–73. Print.

———. "Loren Ayzli i iskusstvo èsse" [Loren Eiseley and the art of the essay]. Introduction. *Vzmakh kryla.* By Loren Eiseley. Moscow: Moscow University Press, 1994. 5–22. Print.

———. "Loren Eiseley in Russia: An Update." ISLE: *Interdisciplinary Studies in Literature and Environment* 4.1 (1997): 71–78. Print.

———. "Reaching beyond the Bridge: Time's Arrow in the Works of Loren Eiseley." ISLE: *Interdisciplinary Studies in Literature and Environment* 9.2 (2002): 75–99. Print.

Bruns, Roger. *Knights of the Road: A Hobo History.* New York: Methuen, 1980. Print.

Bryson, J. Scott. Introduction. *Ecopoetry: A Critical Introduction.* Ed. J. Scott Bryson. Salt Lake City: University of Utah Press, 2002. 1–13. Print.

Bryson, Michael A. "Nature, Narrative, and the Scientist-Writer: Rachel Carson's and Loren Eiseley's Critique of Science." *Technical Communication Quarterly.* Ed. Richard Johnson and Paul Bogard. Spec. issue of *Science and Nature Writing II* 12.4 (2003): 369–87. Print.

Buber, Martin. *Daniel: Dialogues of Realization.* New York: Holt, Rinehart, and Winston, 1964. *Google Book Search.* N.d. Web. 10 Apr. 2010.

Buettner-Janusch, John. Rev. of *The Firmament of Time,* by Loren Eiseley. *American Anthropologist* 65 (1963): 693–94. JSTOR. N.d. Web. 6 Nov. 2009.

Burke, Kenneth. "The Four Master Tropes." *A Grammar of Motives.* New York: Prentice Hall, 1945. 503–17. Rpt. Berkeley: University of California Press, 1969. Print.

Burroughs, John. *Leaf and Tendril.* Boston: Houghton Mifflin, 1908. Print.

———. *Time and Change.* Boston: Houghton Mifflin, 1912. Print.

Bushnell, Jack. "Loren Eiseley and the Dancing Rat: Science as Autobiography." *a/b: Auto/Biography Studies* 13.2 (1998): 257–70. Print.

Campbell, Joseph. Introduction. *The Portable Jung.* Ed. Joseph Campbell. Trans. R. F. C. Hull. New York: Penguin, 1971. vii–xxxii. Print.

Carlisle, E. Fred. "The Literary Achievement of Loren Eiseley." Raz 38–45.

———. *Loren Eiseley: The Development of a Writer.* Chicago: University of Chicago Press, 1983. Print.

Carman, Bliss. "The Vagabonds." *Poems.* New York: Dodd and Mead, 1931. 338–39. Print.

Carrithers, Gale H., Jr. "Loren Eiseley and the Self as Search." *Arizona Quarterly* 50.1 (1994): 75–85. Print.

———. *Mumford, Tate, Eiseley: Watchers in the Night.* Baton Rouge: Louisiana State University Press, 1991. Print.

Casey, Edward S. "Jung and the Postmodern Condition." *C. G. Jung and the Humanities: Towards a Hermeneutics of Culture.* Ed. Karin Barnaby and Pellegrino D'Acierno. Princeton: Princeton University Press, 1990. 319–24. Print.

Cassidy, David C. *Uncertainty: The Life and Science of Werner Heisenberg.* New York: Freeman, 1992. Print.

Cassirer, Ernst. *Language and Myth.* Trans. Suzanne K. Langer. New York: Dover, 1946. Print.

Chekletsov, V. V. "Kommentarii k *Vzmakh kryla*" [Commentary on *Wingbeat*]. *Samizdat.* 10 Apr. 2007. Web. 18 Aug. 2009.

——. "Loren Ayzli" [Loren Eiseley]. *LiveJournal.* 13 Mar. 2007. Web. 18 Aug. 2009.

——. Stranitsa avtora [Author page]. *Litsovet.ru.* 13 Apr. 2007. Web. 13 Oct. 2009.

Chen, Bing. Message to Tom Lynch. 28 Sept. 2009. E-mail.

Christianson, Gale E. *Fox at the Wood's Edge.* 1990. Lincoln: University of Nebraska Press, 2000. Print.

——. Introduction. *The Night Country.* By Loren Eiseley. Lincoln: University of Nebraska Press, 1971. vii–xiii. Print.

Cohen, Michael P. "Blues in the Green: Ecocriticism under Critique." *Environmental History* 9.1 (2004): 9–36. Print.

——. "The Leap: Loren Eiseley's Uses of Life." *North Dakota Quarterly* 59.2 (1991): 198–210. Print.

Comprone, Joseph J. "Narrative Topic and the Contemporary Science Essay: A Lesson from Loren Eiseley's Notebooks." *Journal of Advanced Composition* 9.1 (1989): 112–23. Print.

Cranch, Christopher. *The Life and Letters of Christopher Pearse Cranch.* Ed. Leonora Cranch Scott. New York: Houghton Mifflin, 1917. Print.

Crist, Eileen. *Images of Animals: Anthropomorphism and Animal Mind.* Philadelphia: Temple University Press, 1999. Print.

Cronon, William. *Nature's Metropolis: Chicago and the Great West.* New York: Norton, 1991. Print.

——. "The Trouble with Wilderness; or, Getting Back to the Wrong Nature." *Uncommon Ground: Rethinking the Human Place in Nature.* Ed. William Cronon. New York: Norton, 1996. 69–90. Print.

D'Acierno, Pellegrino, and Karin Barnaby. Preface. *C. G. Jung and the Humanities: Towards a Hermeneutics of Culture.* Ed. Karin Barnaby and Pellegrino D'Acierno. Princeton: Princeton University Press, 1990. xv–xxix. Print.

Daston, Lorraine, and Gregg Mitman. "The How and Why of Thinking with Animals." *Thinking with Animals: New Perspectives on Anthropomorphism.* Ed. Lorraine Daston and Gregg Mitman. New York: Columbia University Press, 2005. 1–14. Print.

Dawkins, Richard. *The God Delusion.* Boston: Houghton Mifflin, 2008. Print.

Dennett, Daniel C. *Breaking the Spell: Religion as a Natural Phenomenon.* New York: Penguin, 2006. Print.

DePastino, Todd. Introduction. *The Road.* By Jack London. 1907. Subterranean Lives: Chronicles of Alternative America. New Brunswick NJ: Rutgers University Press, 2006. i–xxxiii. Print.

De Waal, Frans B. M. Foreword. *Anthropomorphism, Anecdotes, and Animals.* Ed. Robert W. Mitchell, Nicholas S. Thompson, and H. Lyn Miles. Albany: SUNY Press, 1997. xiii–xvii. Print.

Dewey, John. *A Common Faith.* New Haven: Yale University Press, 1934. Print.

Didion, Joan. "The White Album." 1979. *The Best American Essays of the Century.* Ed. Joyce Carol Oates and Robert Atwan. Boston: Houghton Mifflin, 2000. 421–46. Print.

Dixon, Terrell, ed. *City Wilds: Essays and Stories about Urban Nature.* Athens: University of Georgia Press, 2002. Print.

Dubkin, Leonard. *The Murmur of Wings.* New York: McGraw-Hill, 1944. Print.

———. *My Secret Places: One Man's Love Affair with Nature in the City.* New York: McKay, 1972. Print.

Eagleton, Terry. *Reason, Faith, and Revolution: Reflections on the God Debate.* New Haven: Yale University Press, 2009. Print.

———. "Waking the Dead." *New Statesman.* 12 Nov. 2009. Web. 15 Nov. 2009.

Eckhart, Meister. *Selected Writings.* Trans. Oliver Davies. New York: Penguin, 1994. Print.

Eichenbaum, Howard. *The Cognitive Neuroscience of Memory: An Introduction.* New York: Oxford University Press, 2002. Print.

Eiseley, Loren. *All the Strange Hours: The Excavation of a Life.* New York: Scribner, 1975. Print.

———. *Another Kind of Autumn.* New York: Scribner, 1977. Print.

———. *The Brown Wasps: A Collection of Three Essays in Autobiography.* Mount Horeb WI: Perishable Press, 1969. Print.

———. "But Once in a Lifetime." *Audubon* Nov. 1985: 54–57. Print.

———. *Darwin and the Mysterious Mr. X: New Light on the Evolutionists.* New York: Dutton, 1979. Print.

———. *Darwin's Century: Evolution and the Men Who Discovered It.* New York: Doubleday, 1958. Print.

———. "The Enchanted Glass." *American Scholar* 26 (1957): 478–92. Print.

———. "Epilogue: Jack London, Evolutionist." 1962. *Before Adam.* By Jack London. Ed. Dennis McKiernan. Lincoln: University of Nebraska Press, 2000. 243–51. Print.

———. *The Firmament of Time.* 1960. New York: Atheneum, 1980. Print.

———. *Francis Bacon and the Modern Dilemma.* Lincoln: University of Nebraska Press, 1962. Print.

———. "The Illusion of the Two Cultures." *American Scholar* 33.3 (1964): n.p. Rpt. in *The Star Thrower.* New York: Harvest-HBJ, 1978. 267–79. Print.

———. *The Immense Journey*. New York: Random House, 1957. Print.

———. *The Innocent Assassins*. New York: Scribner, 1973. Print.

———. *The Invisible Pyramid*. New York: Scribner, 1970. Print.

———. Letter to Leonard Dubkin. 12 Feb. 1972. Personal Papers. Pauline Dubkin Yearwood, Chicago. Print.

———. *The Loren Eiseley Reader*. Lincoln: Abbatia, 2009. Print.

———. *The Lost Notebooks of Loren Eiseley*. Ed. Kenneth Heuer. 1987. Lincoln: University of Nebraska Press, 2002. Print.

———. *The Man Who Saw Through Time*. New York: Scribner, 1961. Print.

———. *The Mind as Nature*. New York: Harper, 1962. Print.

———. "Nature, Man, and Miracle." *Horizon* 11.6 (1960): 25–32. Print.

———. *The Night Country*. 1971. Lincoln: University of Nebraska Press, 1997. Print.

———. *Notes of an Alchemist*. New York: Scribner, 1972. Print.

———. "Reading Nature." *Harpers*. Sept. 1987. Web. 7 Nov. 2009.

———. "Rock Redondo: Science and Literature in the Galápagos." *Galápagos, the Flow of Wildness: Photographs by Eliot Porter*. Ed. Kenneth Brower. San Francisco: Sierra Club, 1970. 22–38. Print.

———. *The Star Thrower*. Ed. Kenneth Heuer. New York: Times Books, 1978. Print.

———. *The Unexpected Universe*. New York: Harcourt Brace, 1969. Print.

———. "Walden: Thoreau's Unfinished Business." *The Star Thrower*. New York: Random House, 1978. 235–50. Print.

———, et al. Introduction. *The Shape of Likelihood: Relevance and the University*. Franklin Lectures in the Sciences and Humanities, Auburn University, Ser. 2. Birmingham: University of Alabama Press, 1971. Print.

Emerson, Ralph Waldo. *The Essential Writings of Ralph Waldo Emerson*. Ed. Brooks Atkinson. New York: Modern Library, 2000. Print.

———. *Nature*. Emerson, *Essential* 5–39.

———. *Nature, Addresses, and Lectures*. Boston: Munroe, 1849. Print.

———. *Selected Essays, Lectures, and Poems*. Ed. Robert D. Richardson. New York: Bantam, 1990. Print.

———. *Selected Writings of Ralph Waldo Emerson*. Ed. William H. Gilman. New York: New American Library, 1965. Print.

Evans, Terry. "Revealing Chicago: An Aerial Portrait." *Openlands Project and Chicago Metropolis 2020*. 27 Sept. 2005. Web. 9 Oct. 2005.

Finch, Robert. "A Pessimist in the Cosmos." *New York Times*. 20 Sept. 1987. Web. 21 Nov. 2009.

Franke, Robert G. "Blue Plums and Smoke: Loren Eiseley's Perception of Time." *Western American Literature* 24.2 (1989): 147–50. Print.

Friedman, Maurice. *Martin Buber's Life and Work: The Middle Years, 1923–1945.*

Detroit: Wayne State University Press, 1988. *Google Book Search.* N.d. Web. 10 Apr. 2010.

Gamble, David E. "Loren Eiseley: Wilderness and Moral Transcendence." *Midwest Quarterly* 33.1 (1991): 108–23. Print.

Gare, Arran E. *Postmodernism and the Environmental Crisis.* New York: Routledge, 1995. Print.

Gawande, Atul. "The Itch." *The Best American Science Writing 2009.* Ed. Natalie Angier and Jesse Cohen. New York: HarperCollins, 2009. 1–21. Print.

Geldard, Richard G. *The Spiritual Teachings of Ralph Waldo Emerson.* New York: Lindisfarne, 2001. Print.

Gelpi, Donald L. *Varieties of Transcendental Experience: A Study in Constructive Postmodernism.* Collegeville MN: Liturgical Press, 2000. Print.

Gerber, Leslie E., and Margaret McFadden. *Loren Eiseley.* New York: Ungar, 1983. Print.

Gifford, Terry. *Green Voices: Understanding Contemporary Nature Poetry.* Manchester: Manchester University Press, 1995. Print.

Gilcrest, David W. *Greening the Lyre: Environmental Poetics and Ethics.* Reno: University of Nevada Press, 2002. Print.

Gimbutas, Marija. *The Language of the Goddess.* San Francisco: HarperCollins, 1991. Print.

Glass, Gene V. "Searching for Loren Eiseley: An Attempt at Reconstruction from a Few Fragments." *American Buddha Online Library.* 20 Oct. 1998. Web. 21 Nov. 2009.

Gleick, James. *Chaos: Making a New Science.* New York: Viking Penguin, 1987. Print.

Gordon, Sarah H. *Passage to Union: How the Railroads Transformed American Life, 1829–1929.* Chicago: Dee, 1997. Print.

Gottlieb, Roger S. "Introduction: Religion and Ecology — What Is the Connection and Why Does It Matter?" *The Oxford Handbook of Religion and Ecology.* Ed. Roger S. Gottlieb. New York: Oxford University Press, 2006. 3–24. Print.

Griessel, Loura, and Martina Kotzé. "The Feminine and the Masculine Development of the Self in Women." *Women's Studies* Mar. 2009: 183–212. Print.

Griffin, Donald R. *Animal Minds: From Cognition to Consciousness.* Chicago: University of Chicago Press, 2001. Print.

Grimm, Nancy, et al. "Global Change and the Ecology of Cities." *Science* 319 (2008): 756–60. Print.

Gura, Philip F. *American Transcendentalism: A History.* New York: Hill and Wang, 2007. Print.

Habegger, Alfred. *The Father: A Life of Henry James, Sr.* New York: Farrar, Straus, and Giroux, 1994. Print.

Hairston, Marc, Mary Urquhart, and Greg Earle. Personal communications with Pamela Gossin. 1998–2010.

Haraway, Donna. *When Species Meet.* Minneapolis: University of Minnesota Press, 2008. Print.

Harris, Sam. *The End of Faith: Religion, Terror, and the Future of Reason.* New York: Norton, 2004. Print.

———, and Andrew Sullivan. "Is Religion 'Built on Lies'?" *Beliefnet.com.* 7 Jan. 2007. Web. 20 July 2011.

Hartshorne, Charles. *Omnipotence and Other Theological Mistakes.* Albany: SUNY Press, 1984. Print.

Haught, John F. *God and the New Atheism: A Critical Response to Dawkins, Harris and Hitchens.* Louisville: Westminster John Knox Press, 2008. Print.

Heidegger, Martin. "The Question Concerning Technology." *The Question Concerning Technology and Other Essays.* Trans. William Lovitt. New York: Colophon-Harper, 1977. 3–35. Print.

Heidtmann, Peter. *Loren Eiseley: A Modern Ishmael.* Hamden CT: Archon Books, 1991. Print.

Hicks, Phillip Marshall. "The Development of the Natural History Essay in American Literature." Diss. University of Pennsylvania, 1924. Print.

Hollingsworth, Cristopher. *Poetics of the Hive: The Insect Metaphor in Literature.* Iowa City: University of Iowa Press, 2001. Print.

Holmes, Oliver Wendell. *Ralph Waldo Emerson.* Boston: Houghton, Mifflin, 1885. Print.

Howard, Ben. "Loren Eiseley and the State of Grace." Raz 57–59.

Huxley, Aldous. *The Perennial Philosophy.* New York: Perennial Classics, 2004. Print.

James, William. *The Varieties of Religious Experience.* New York: Penguin, 1958. Print.

Jantsch, Erich, ed. *The Evolutionary Vision: Toward a Unifying Paradigm of Physical, Biological, and Sociocultural Evolution.* Boulder CO: Westview, 1981. Print.

Jaspers, Karl. *The Origin and Goal of History.* Trans. Michael Bullock. New Haven: Yale University Press, 1953. Print.

Johnston, William, ed. *The Cloud of Unknowing and the Book of Privy Counseling.* New York: Doubleday, 1973. Print.

Jung, Carl. "Approaching the Unconscious." *Man and His Symbols.* Ed. Carl Jung. New York: Dell, 1964. 1–94. Print.

———. *The Collected Works of C. G. Jung.* 20 vols. Ed. Herbert Read et al. Princeton: Princeton University Press, 1953–79. Print.

Kandel, Eric R. *In Search of Memory: The Emergence of a New Science of Mind.* New York: Norton, 2007. Print.

Keller, Catherine. *Face of the Deep: A Theology of Becoming.* New York: Routledge, 2003. Print.

———, and Laurel Kearns. "Introduction: Grounding Theory — Earth in Religion and

Philosophy." *Ecospirit: Religions and Philosophies for the Earth.* Ed. Laurel Kearns and Catherine Keller. New York: Fordham University Press, 2007. xi–xiv. Print.

Kennedy, John S. *The New Anthropomorphism.* Cambridge: Cambridge University Press, 1992. Print.

Kingsland, Sharon E. "Defining Ecology as a Discipline." *Foundations of Ecology: Classic Papers with Commentaries.* Ed. Leslie A. Real and James H. Brown. Chicago: University of Chicago Press, 1991. 1–13. Print.

Koestler, Arthur. *Janus: A Summing Up.* New York: Random House, 1978. Print.

Kuhn, Thomas S. *The Structure of Scientific Revolutions.* Chicago: University of Chicago Press, 1969. Print.

Kwan, Virginia S. Y., and Susan T. Fiske. "Missing Links in Social Cognition: The Continuum from Nonhuman Agents to Dehumanized Humans." *Social Cognition* 26.2 (2008): 125–28. Print.

Lakoff, George. *Political Mind: Why You Can't Understand 21st-Century American Politics with an 18th-Century Brain.* New York: Viking, 2008. Print.

Lambert, Bruce. "John Buettner-Janusch, 67, Dies; N.Y.U. Professor Poisoned Candy." *New York Times.* 4 July 1992. Web. 9 Nov. 2009.

Langdon Eiseley, Mabel. Telephone conversation. Spring 1982.

Least Heat-Moon, William. *PrairyErth.* New York: Houghton Mifflin, 1991. Print.

Lebedeva, Natal'ya. "Marsh materialistov" [Materialists on the march]. *Persona* 10 (1999): 87–91. Print.

LeDoux, Joseph. *The Emotional Brain: The Mysterious Underpinnings of Emotional Life.* New York: Simon and Schuster, 1998. Print.

———. *Synaptic Self: How Our Brains Become Who We Are.* New York: Penguin, 2003. Print.

Leopold, Aldo. *A Sand County Almanac: With Essays on Conservation from Round River.* New York: Ballantine Books, 1990. Print.

Leopol'd, Oldo [Leopold, Aldo]. *Kalendar' peschanogo grafstva* [*Sand County Almanac*]. Trans. I. G. Gurova. Moscow: Mir, 1980. Print.

Levinas, Emmanuel. *Totality and Infinity.* Trans. Alphonso Lingis. Pittsburgh: Duquesne University Press, 1969. Print.

Levine, George. *Darwin Loves You: Natural Selections and the Re-Enchantment of the World.* Princeton: Princeton University Press, 2008. Print.

Lindsay, Vachel. *Collected Poems of Vachel Lindsay.* Charleston SC: BiblioLife, 2009. Print.

———. "The Congo." Lindsay, *Collected* 103–10.

———. "General William Booth Enters into Heaven." Lindsay, *Collected* 207–9.

———. "On the Road to Nowhere." 1912. *The Poetry of Vachel Lindsay, Complete and with Lindsay's Drawings.* Ed. Dennis Camp. Vol. 1. Peoria IL: Spoon River Poetry Press, 1984. 142–43. Print.

Lioi, Anthony. "Coasts Demanding Shipwreck: Love and the Philosophy of Science in Loren Eiseley's 'The Star Thrower.'" *ISLE: Interdisciplinary Studies in Literature and Environment* 6.2 (1999): 41–61. Print.

London, Jack. *The Road*. Ed. Todd DePastino. 1907. Subterranean Lives: Chronicles of Alternative America. New Brunswick NJ: Rutgers University Press, 2006. Print.

Lopate, Phillip. Introduction. *The Art of the Personal Essay: An Anthology from the Classical Era to the Present*. Comp. and ed. Phillip Lopate. New York: Anchor, 1994. xxiii–liv. Print.

Louv, Richard. *Last Child in the Woods: Saving our Children from Nature-Deficit Disorder*. Chapel Hill NC: Algonquin, 2005. Print.

Love, Glen A. *Practical Ecocriticism: Literature, Biology, and the Environment*. Charlottesville: University of Virginia Press, 2003. Print.

Luebke, Frederick C. *Nebraska: An Illustrated History*. 2nd ed. Lincoln: University of Nebraska Press, 2005. Print.

Lynn, Kenneth S. *Charlie Chaplin and His Times*. New York: Simon & Schuster, 1997. Print.

Maharidge, Dale, and Michael Williamson. *The Last Great American Hobo*. Rocklin CA: Prima, 1993. Print.

Malyshev, S. I. "'Shkatulka nablyudeniy' Lorena Ayzli" [Loren Eiseley's "trove of observations"]. Rev. of *Vzmakh kryla*, by Loren Eiseley. *Upravlencheskoye konsul'tirovaniye* 1 (1998): 46. Print. Severo-zapadnaya Akademiya gosudarstvennoy sluzhby. 2 Apr. 2009. Web. 3 Feb. 2010.

Martin, Calvin. *In the Spirit of the Earth: Rethinking History and Time*. Baltimore: Johns Hopkins University Press, 1992. Print.

McNeill, John R. *Something New under the Sun: An Environmental History of the Twentieth-Century World*. New York: Norton, 2000. Print.

Meeker, Joseph W. *The Comedy of Survival: Literary Ecology and a Play Ethic*. 3rd ed. Tucson: University of Arizona Press, 1997. Print.

Merton, Thomas. *The Collected Poems of Thomas Merton*. New York: New Directions, 1977. Print.

Miller, Perry. Introduction. *The Transcendentalists: An Anthology*. Ed. Miller. Cambridge: Harvard University Press, 1950. Print.

"Mission." ST Management Consulting. N.d. Web. 5 Oct. 2009.

Mitchell, Sandra D. "Anthropomorphism and Cross-Species Modeling." *Thinking with Animals: New Perspectives on Anthropomorphism*. Ed. Lorraine Daston and Gregg Mitman. New York: Columbia University Press, 2005. 100–117. Print.

Moevs, Christian. *The Metaphysics of Dante's Comedy*. Oxford: Oxford University Press, 2005. Print.

Nabokov, Vladimir. *Nikolai Gogol*. New York: New Directions, 1944. Print.

Nastin, Pavel. Home page. *Staratel'*. Oct. 2002. Web. 18 Aug. 2009.

———. Online discussion. *LiveJournal*. 21 Oct. 2004. Web. 18 Aug. 2009.

Needham, Joseph. *Order and Life*. New Haven: Yale University Press, 1936. Print.

The New English Bible: With the Apocrypha. Ed. Samuel Sandmel et al. Oxford study ed. New York: Oxford University Press, 1976. Print.

New Haven Railroad Historical and Technical Association. Home page. 1 July 2011. Web. 20 July 2011.

Newman, Barbara. *From Virile Woman to WomanChrist: Studies in Medieval Religion and Literature*. Philadelphia: University of Pennsylvania Press, 1995. Print.

Nietzsche, Friedrich. *Thus Spoke Zarathrustra*. Trans. R. J. Hollingdale. New York: Penguin Books, 2003. Print.

Olney, James. Rev. of *All the Strange Hours*, by Loren Eiseley. *New Republic* 1 Nov. 1975: 30–34. Print.

Olson, Randy. *Flock of Dodos: The Evolution-Intelligent Design Circus*. Dir. Randy Olson. Docuramafilms, 2006. Film.

"One Hundred Things Everyone Should Know about Russia." *Russian Life* May–June 2009: 29–44. Print.

Otto, Rudolf. *The Idea of the Holy*. Trans. John Harvey. New York: Oxford University Press, 1958. Print.

Pascal, Blaise. *Pensées and Other Writings*. Ed. Anthony Levi. New York: Oxford University Press, 2008. Print.

Peabody, Elizabeth. "Egotheism, the Atheism of To-Day." *Last Evening with Allston, and Other Papers*. Boston: Lothrop, 1886. 240–52. Print.

Phillips, Dana. *The Truth of Ecology: Nature, Culture, and Literature in America*. New York: Oxford University Press, 2003. Print.

Pinker, Steven. *How the Mind Works*. New York: Norton, 1997. Print.

Pisarenko, Dmitriy. "Gde Darvin dal makhu: Pochemu obez'yana ne stanovitsya chelovekom?" [Where Darwin went wrong: Why don't monkeys become men?]. *Argumenty i fakty* 11 Feb. 2009: 28. Print.

"Pisateli po alfavitu" [Writers in alphabetical order]. *Wikipedia*. Wikimedia Foundation. 1 Feb. 2010. Web. 1 Mar. 2010.

Pitts, Mary Ellen. *Toward a Dialogue of Understandings: Loren Eiseley and the Critique of Science*. Bethlehem: Lehigh University Press, 1995. Print.

Platt, H. Rutherford, ed. *The Humane Metropolis: People and Nature in the 21st-Century City*. Cambridge: MIT Press, 2006. Print.

Ponomaryov, Vladimir, and Andrey Gamalov. "Darvin, gou houm! Bor'ba za nesushchestvovaniye" [Darwin, go home! The struggle for nonexistence]. *Ogonyok* 33 (2000): 26–28. Print.

Porter, Katherine Anne. "The Future Is Now." 1950. *The Best American Essays of the*

Century. Ed. Joyce Carol Oates and Robert Atwan. Boston: Houghton Mifflin, 2000. 193–98. Print.

Prigogine, Ilya, and Isabel Stengers. *Order Out of Chaos*. London: Heinemann, 1984. Print.

Raz, Hilda, ed. *Loren Eiseley: Commentary, Biography, and Remembrance*. Lincoln: University of Nebraska Press, 2008. Rpt. of spec. issue of *Prairie Schooner* 61.3 (1987): n.p. Print.

Richardson, Robert D. *Emerson: The Mind on Fire*. Berkeley: University of California Press, 1995. Print.

Ricoeur, Paul. "Between Rhetoric and Poetics." *Essays on Aristotle's Rhetoric*. Ed. Amélie Oksenberg Rorty. Berkeley: University of California Press, 1996. 324–84. Print.

———. "Rhetoric—Poetics—Hermeneutics." *Rhetoric and Hermeneutics in Our Time*. Ed. Walter Jost and Michael J. Hyde. New Haven: Yale University Press, 1997. 60–72. Print.

Rivas, Jesús, and Gordon M. Burghardt. "Crotalomorphism." *The Cognitive Animal: Empirical and Theoretical Perspectives on Animal Cognition*. Ed. Marc Bekoff, Colin Allen, and Gordon M. Burghardt. Cambridge: MIT Press, 2002. 9–17. Print.

Rolls, Edmund T. *The Brain and Emotion*. Oxford: Oxford University Press, 2000. Print.

Roorda, Randall. "Deep Maps in Ecoliterature." *Michigan Quarterly Review* 40.1 (2001): 257–72. Print.

Rorty, Richard. *Philosophy and the Mirror of Nature*. Princeton: Princeton University Press, 1979. Print.

Rotella, Carlo. *October Cities: The Redevelopment of Urban Literature*. Berkeley: University of California Press, 1998. Print.

Ruether, Rosemary Radford. *Gaia and God: An Ecofeminist Theology of Earth-Healing*. San Francisco: HarperSanFrancisco, 1992. Print.

———. "Gender and Redemption in the Patristic Era: Conflicting Perspectives." *Women and Redemption: A Theological History*. Minneapolis: Fortress, 1998. 45–78. Print.

Rumyantseva, M. V. "Tipy èmpatiynykh vyskazyvaniy (na materiale èsse L. Ayzli 'Kometa' v perevode D. N. Breschinskogo)" [Types of empathic utterances (based on L. Eiseley's essay "The Comet" in D. N. Breschinsky's translation)]. *34 mezhdunarodnaya filologicheskaya konferentsiya, 14–19 Mar. 2005: Russkiy yazyk kak inostrannyi i metodika yego prepodavaniya 17*. St. Petersburg: St. Petersburg University Press, 2005. 47–51. Print.

Ryden, Kent C. *Mapping the Invisible Landscape: Folklore, Writing, and the Sense of Place*. Iowa City: University of Iowa Press, 1993. Print.

Sandburg, Carl, comp. *The American Songbag*. New York: Harcourt, 1927. Print.

Schmidt, Jacqueline. [Gypsy Moon]. *Done and Been: Steel Rail Chronicles of American Hobos*. Bloomington: Indiana University Press, 1996. Print.

Schultz, C. Bertrand, and Loren Eiseley. "Paleontological Evidence for the Antiquity of the Scottsbluff Bison Quarry and Its Associated Artifacts." *American Anthropologist* 37.2 (1935): 306–19. JSTOR. Web. 9 Apr. 2010.

Scigaj, Leonard M. *Sustainable Poetry: Four American Ecopoets*. Lexington: University Press of Kentucky, 1999. Print.

Scott, John A. *Understanding Dante*. Notre Dame IN: University of Notre Dame Press, 2004. Print.

"Scottsboro Boys." *Wikipedia*. Wikimedia Foundation. 2003. Web. 1 Nov. 2009.

Serpell, James. "People in Disguise: Anthropomorphism and the Human-Pet Relationship." *Thinking with Animals: New Perspectives on Anthropomorphism*. Ed. Lorraine Daston and Gregg Mitman. New York: Columbia University Press, 2005. 121–36. Print.

Service, Robert W. "The Tramps." 1907. *The Spell of the Yukon, and Other Verses*. New York: Dodd, Mead, 1944. 123–24. Print.

Shamdasani, Sonu. Introduction. *The Red Book*. By C. G. Jung. Ed. Sonu Shamdasani. New York: Norton, 2009. 193–221. Print.

Short, John Rennie. *Imagined Country: Environment, Culture, and Society*. New York: Routledge, 1991. Print.

Shubin, Neil. *Your Inner Fish: A Journey into the 3.5 Billion-Year History of the Human Body*. New York: Pantheon, 2008. Print.

Skars, Rik. "Ekovoiny: Radikal'noye dvizheniye v zashchitu prirody" [Eco-warriors: The radical movement in defense of nature]. *Ekoklub*. Mezhdunarodny sotsial'no-èkologicheskiy soyuz. 9 June 2003. Web. 20 Aug. 2009.

Snow, C. P. *The Two Cultures: And a Second Look*. Cambridge: Cambridge University Press, 1964. Print.

Stack, George J. *Nietzsche and Emerson: An Elective Affinity*. Athens: Ohio University Press, 1992. Print.

"The Star Thrower." *Wikipedia*. Wikimedia Foundation. 22 Feb. 2010. Web. 26 Feb. 2010.

Staude, John Raphael. "From Depth Psychology to Depth Sociology: Freud, Jung, and Lévi-Strauss." *Theory and Society* 3.3 (1976): 303–38. Print.

Subetto, A. I. "Bessoznatel'noye zhizni i èvolyutsionnaya pamyat': V dialoge s Lorenom Ayzli, 1907–77, izvestnym amerikanskim antropologom i èsseistom" [The collective unconscious and evolutionary memory: In dialogue with Loren Eiseley, 1907–77, a well-known American anthropologist and essayist]. *Bessoznatel'noye. Arkhaika. Vera. Izbrannoye: Fragmenty neklassicheskogo chelovekovedeniya*. St.

Petersburg: Issledovatel'skiy tsentr problem kachestva podgotovki spetsialistov, 1997. 59–96. Print.

———. "Kapitalokratiya (filosofsko-èkonomicheskiye ocherki). Ocherk 10. Kapitalokratiya protiv kul'tury. Kapitalisticheskaya gibel' kul'tury" [Capitalocracy (philosophico-economic studies). Study 10. Capitalocracy versus culture. The capitalist destruction of culture]. *Academiya Trinitarizma.* 9 Mar. 2004. Web. 18 Aug. 2009.

Tallmadge, John. *The Cincinnati Arch: Learning from Nature in the City.* Athens: University of Georgia Press, 2004. Print.

Teilhard de Chardin, Pierre. *The Divine Milieu.* New York: Harper Perennial, 2001. Print.

Thagard, Paul. *Mind: Introduction to Cognitive Science.* 2nd ed. Baltimore: MIT Press, 2005. Print.

Torrey, R. A., and A. C. Dixon. *The Fundamentals: A Testimony to the Truth.* Grand Rapids MI: Revell, 1994. Print.

Trishna [Pavel Nastin]. "Vremya Lorena Ayzli: 'Techeniye reki'" [The time of Loren Eiseley: "The Flow of the River"]. *Russkiy literaturny klub.* 11 Apr. 2002. Web. 18 Aug. 2009.

Turner, Victor Witter. *Dramas, Fields, and Metaphors: Symbolic Action in Human Society.* Ithaca: Cornell University Press, 1974. Print.

University of Exeter. "New Evidence Debunks 'Stupid' Neanderthal Myth." *ScienceDaily.* 26 Aug. 2008. Web. 29 Oct. 2009.

UTeach. Home page. School of Natural Science, University of Texas at Austin. N.d. Web. 6 July 2011.

UTeach Dallas. Home page. School of Natural Sciences and Mathematics, University of Texas, Dallas. N.d. Web. 6 July 2011.

Vadim [V. V. Chekletsov]. "Knizhki, kotorye stoit prochitat'" [Books worth reading]. Online posting. 23 Oct. 2007. Web. 18 Aug. 2009.

Vedanta, Advaita. *The Essentials of Indian Philosophy.* Delhi: Motilal Banarsidass, 1995. Print.

von Franz, Marie-Louise. *C. G. Jung, His Myth in Our Time.* New York: Putnam, 1975. Print.

———. "The Process of Individuation." *Man and His Symbols.* Ed. Carl Jung. New York: Dell, 1964. 157–254. Print.

Wagner, Jeffrey. "Free Riding on Eiseley's Star Thrower, Thoreau's Huckleberry Patch, and Havel's Streetcar in the Local and Global Commons." *ISLE: Interdisciplinary Studies in Literature and Environment* 11.1 (2004): 101–19. Print.

Warren, Julianne Lutz. "Alienation or Intimacy? The Roles of Science in the Conservation Narratives of Gifford Pinchot and John Burroughs." *ATQ: 19th C. Literature and Culture* 21.4 (2007): 249–59. Print.

Weaver, Warren. "Science and Complexity." *The Scientists Speak*. Ed. Warren Weaver. New York: Boni and Gaer, 1947. 1–13. Print.

Weinberg, Steven. "A Deadly Certitude." *London Times Online*. Richard Dawkins Foundation for Research and Science. 17 Jan. 2007. Web. 20 July 2011.

Wentz, Richard E. "The American Spirituality of Loren Eiseley." *Christian Century* 14 (1984): 430–32. *Religion Online*. Web. 15 May 2010.

———. "Loren Eiseley." *The Encyclopedia of Religion and Nature*. Ed. Bron Taylor. New York: Continuum, 2005. 582–84. Web. 21 Nov. 2009.

Wheeler, Stephen M., and Timothy Beatley, eds. *The Sustainable Urban Development Reader*. 2nd ed. New York: Routledge, 2009. Print.

White, Fred D. *Science and the Human Spirit: Contexts for Writing and Learning*. Belmont CA: Wadsworth, 1988. Print.

White, Hayden. *Metahistory: The Historical Imagination in Nineteenth-Century Europe*. Baltimore: Johns Hopkins University Press, 1973. Print.

Whitehead, Alfred North. *Process and Reality: Corrected Edition*. Ed. David Ray Griffin and Donald W. Sherburne. New York: Free Press, 1978. Print.

Whitman, Walt. *Leaves of Grass*. 150th anniversary ed. New York: Signet, 2005. Print.

———. "Song of the Open Road." *Leaves of Grass*. Philadelphia: McKay, 1884. 120–29. Print.

Wilson, E. O. *Consilience: The Unity of Knowledge*. New York: Knopf, 1998. Print.

Wisner, William H. "The Perilous Self: Loren Eiseley and the Reticence of Autobiography." *Sewanee Review* 113.1 (2005): 84–95. Print.

Woodward, Kathleen. "The Uncanny and the Running Man: Aging and Loren Eiseley's *All the Strange Hours*." *Southern Humanities Review* 16.1 (1982): 47–60. Print.

Wright, John K. "*Terrae Incognitae*: The Place of the Imagination in Geography." *Annals of the Association of American Geographers* 37.1 (1947): 1–15. Print.

Wydeven, Joseph J. "'Turned on the Same Lathe': Wright Morris's Loren Eiseley." *South Dakota Review* 33.1 (1995): 66–83. Print.

Wynne, Clive D. L. *Do Animals Think?* Princeton: Princeton University Press, 2004. Print.

Yearwood, Pauline Dubkin. Personal interview by Michael A. Bryson. 15 Mar. and 18 Apr. 2007.

Zinsser, William. "Nonfiction as Literature." *On Writing Well: An Informal Guide to Writing Nonfiction*. 4th ed. New York: HarperCollins, 1990. 53–58. Print.

Contributors

KATHLEEN BOARDMAN is a professor and associate dean at the University of Nevada, Reno. She specializes in Western autobiography and memoir, including the work of Loren Eiseley, and has coedited a collection of essays titled *On Western Subjects: Autobiographical Writing in the North American West*, published in 2004 by University of Utah Press.

DIMITRI N. BRESCHINSKY is an associate professor of Russian at Purdue University. He has published numerous articles on Russian literature and on Loren Eiseley. As his essay in this collection illustrates, he is the foremost translator of Loren Eiseley's writing into Russian.

MICHAEL A. BRYSON is an associate professor of humanities and sustainability studies at the College of Professional Studies, Roosevelt University, Chicago. He specializes in American science and nature writing and has published widely in the field. His book *Visions of the Land* was published in 2002 by University of Virginia Press. He is at work on an ecocritical study of the literature of Chicago titled *Mapping the Urban Wilderness*.

JACQUELINE CASON is an assistant professor in the English department at the University of Alaska, Anchorage. Her dissertation examines the science essays of Loren Eiseley. She has taught courses in the evolution of the essay genre, nonfiction prose, public science writing, and technical and scientific writing. Her research interests include the rhetoric of science in professional and public contexts, landscape writing, Canadian nonfiction writing, multimedia forms of the essay, and digital literacies in first-year composition.

M. CATHERINE DOWNS is an associate professor of English at Texas A&M University, Kingsville. Her specialty is twentieth-century American literature, especially the works of the realists and modernists. Her volume *Willa Cather's Modernism*, published in 1990 by Fairleigh Dickinson University Press, describes how Cather's profession of journalism shaped her later works as a writer of fiction. Her current work concerns how Charles Darwin's new science shaped the writings of women realists and modernists.

PAMELA GOSSIN is a professor of the history of science and literary studies and the director of medical and scientific humanities at the University of Texas, Dallas. She studies the interdisciplinary interrelations of literature, history, and science — especially astronomy and cosmology — from the ancient world through the Scientific Revolution to the present. Her most recent book, *Thomas Hardy's Novel Universe: Astronomy, Cosmology and Gender in the Post-Darwinian World*, was published in 2007 by Ashgate. It was nominated for the inaugural British Society for Literature and Science book prize and the Michelle Kendrick Memorial book prize for 2007, sponsored by the Society for Literature, Science and the Arts. As director of The Neihardt Projects, she is currently developing a digital archive and interpretive website concerning the life and works of John G. Neihardt.

SUSAN HANSON is a senior lecturer in English at Texas State University, San Marcos, and a widely published journalist and nature writer. Her first collection of essays, *Icons of Loss and Grace: Moments from the Natural World*, was published in 2004 by Texas Tech University Press. She also coedited *What Wildness Is This: Women Write about the Southwest*, published in 2007 by University of Texas Press.

ANTHONY LIOI is an assistant professor of humanities at the Juilliard School in New York. He is a specialist in contemporary American literature, environmental literary criticism, and writing studies. His research interests include gender studies, popular culture, and digital media, and he is the founding editor of *Planetary: Teaching Writing, Rhetoric, and*

Literature for the Environment, an international blog. He is the author of numerous scholarly articles on the writers Loren Eiseley, Alice Walker, Susan Griffin, Rachel Carson, Gloria Anzaldúa, and Robert Sullivan, as well as an article on the place of the swamp in literary criticism and another on the kabbalistic background of Tony Kushner's *Angels in America.* His current project is a monograph on the response in American nonfiction to the global environmental crisis.

TOM LYNCH is an associate professor in the English department at the University of Nebraska, Lincoln, where he specializes in ecocriticism and place-conscious approaches to literature. He is the author of *Xerophilia: Ecocritical Explorations in Southwestern Literature,* published in 2008 by Texas Tech University Press. He is currently at work on a comparative study of literature of the American West and the Australian Outback from ecocritical and postcolonial perspectives and is also coediting a collection of essays titled *The Bioregional Imagination.* He serves on the board of directors of the Loren Eiseley Society.

SUSAN N. MAHER is dean of the College of Liberal Arts at the University of Minnesota, Duluth. Prior to that appointment, she was a Peter Kiewit Distinguished Professor and chair of the Department of English at the University of Nebraska, Omaha. She has published widely on the literature of the American and Canadian West, with particular emphasis on contemporary fiction and creative nonfiction. She coedited *Coming into McPhee Country: John McPhee and the Art of Literary Nonfiction,* published in 2003 by University of Utah Press, and is currently completing a book-length study of Plains nonfiction writers, titled "Deep Map Country: A Literary Cartography of the Great Plains." She also serves on the executive boards of the Willa Cather Foundation (as vice president), the Mari Sandoz High Plains Heritage Society, and the Loren Eiseley Society. In 2001 she was president of the Western Literature Association.

STEPHEN MERCIER is a teaching associate in the School of Liberal Arts at Marist College, Poughkeepsie, New York. A specialist in the writing of

John Burroughs, he has produced numerous articles and papers. He has edited a double special issue on Burroughs for *American Transcendental Quarterly*, as well as a special issue of the *Hudson River Valley Review*. His dissertation is titled "Revaluing the Literary Naturalist: John Burroughs's Emotive Environmental Aesthetics." A regular contributor to *Wake-Robin: Newsletter of the John Burroughs Association* at the American Museum of Natural History, he has also been interviewed for pieces about Burroughs that appeared in the *New York Times* and on National Public Radio.

JOHN NIZALOWSKI is a freelance writer and journalist whose work has appeared in a variety of venues, including *New Mexico Magazine, Puerto del Sol, Southwest Profile, Telluride Magazine, Bloomsbury Review, Albany Review, Blueline, Harp*, and *The Listening Eye*. He teaches creative writing and composition at Mesa State College in Grand Junction, Colorado, and is at work on a biography of Frank Waters.

MARY ELLEN PITTS is an adjunct professor of English at Dowling College in Oakdale, New York. She previously served as a professor at Memphis State University, Western Kentucky University, and Rhodes College, Memphis. Her specialties include interdisciplinary writing and innovations in using technology in teaching. She is the author of *Toward a Dialogue of Understandings: Loren Eiseley and the Critique of Science*, which was published in 1995 by Lehigh University Press.

JONATHAN WEIDENBAUM is a professor of liberal arts and sciences at Berkeley College, New York, where he teaches world religions, ethics, and philosophy. He has published a variety of essays on his areas of specialty, including the philosophy of religion, American philosophy and process thought, phenomenology and existentialism, and theoretical and applied ethics.

Index

CPSIA information can be obtained at www.ICGtesting.com
Printed in the USA
BVOW010849060212

282148BV00004B/3/P